Intellectual Development
Birth to Adulthood

DEVELOPMENTAL PSYCHOLOGY SERIES

SERIES EDITOR
Harry Beilin

Developmental Psychology Program
City University of New York Graduate School
New York, New York

The list of titles in this series continues on the last page of this volume.

Intellectual Development

Birth to Adulthood

Robbie Case

Centre for Applied Cognitive Science
The Ontario Institute for Studies in Education
Toronto, Ontario, Canada

1985

ACADEMIC PRESS, INC.

Harcourt Brace Jovanovich, Publishers

Orlando   San Diego   New York
Austin   Boston   London   Sydney
Tokyo   Toronto

For the Dunbar Clan,
and those who married into it

ACADEMIC PRESS, INC.
Orlando, Florida 32887

United Kingdom Edition published by
ACADEMIC PRESS INC. (LONDON) LTD.
24–28 Oval Road, London NW1 7DX

Library of Congress Cataloging in Publication Data

Case, Robbie.
  Intellectual development.

  (Developmental psychology series)
  Includes bibliographical references and index.
  1. Cognition in children. 2. Piaget, Jean, 1886-
I. Title. II. Series.
BF723.C5C37 1985   155.4'13   84-12440
ISBN 0-12-162880-9 (alk. paper)

PRINTED IN THE UNITED STATES OF AMERICA

87 88   9 8 7 6 5 4 3 2

When I was a child, I spoke as a child, I understood as a child, I thought as a child: but when I became a man, I put away childish things.
I Corinthians, 13:11

Development is a process of involution as well as evolution, and the elements come to be hidden under the forms of complexity which they build up.
J. M. Baldwin, 1895

Contents

PART II   INTELLECTUAL FUNCTIONING AT DIFFERENT STAGES OF DEVELOPMENT

Preface

The seeds of the present volume were sown in the late 1970s. At that time, the field of intellectual development was in a state of transition. On the one hand, the weaknesses of Piaget's theory were well known. On the other, no new theory had been proposed that appeared capable of matching all its strengths. The challenge that the field faced, therefore, was a serious one. It was to construct a new theory of development, one that would preserve as many of the strengths of Piaget's theory as possible, while eliminating as many of its weaknesses as possible. A number of psychologists responded to this challenge, myself among them. The theory I proposed was a restructured version of a theory that had been proposed earlier by Juan Pascual-Leone, whose theory had in turn been a restructured version of Piaget's.

When Harry Beilin invited me to write a volume in the Developmental Psychology series, it was my intention to summarize the theory I had developed, and to present the empirical data I had gathered in its support. The volume I actually ended up writing, however, was considerably different from the one I originally intended.

First of all, my goals changed considerably in the course of writing. As I reviewed the recent developmental literature, I realized that there had been a virtual explosion in the data base to which the field now had access. Within the

Piagetian tradition, a large number of studies had been conducted on the intellectual competencies of infants and preschoolers. Within other traditions, an even larger number of studies had been conducted. Some of these were relatively atheoretical, such as those done in standardizing new IQ tests (e.g., the WPPSI and the Griffeths). Some of these had been stimulated by theories in other areas, such as Chomsky's theory of language, or Newell and Simon's theory of problem solving. Still others had been motivated by social concerns, such as the desire to understand the cognitive prerequisites of formal schooling, or early patterns of mother–infant interaction. Taken together, however, the new studies provided a truly massive corpus of data on topics as varied as perceptual and motor development in infancy, linguistic and conceptual development in early childhood, and social cognition from birth to adolescence.

In reflecting on the various experiments that had been conducted, it occurred to me that the real test of any new developmental theory would probably not be its ability to account for the two or three classes of data that had proved problematic for Piaget's theory: for example, data on early logical competencies, or on logical learning. While this would certainly be important, the real test would probably be the theory's ability to integrate the full range of data that were now available, regardless of the particular context in which the data had originally been gathered or the particular issue that had motivated their collection. I therefore decided to attempt this task.

As my focus changed, so did my theory. I began by simplifying the type of task analysis I presented for each intellectual domain to what I considered its barest structural essentials. My initial reason for doing so was to achieve a greater economy of exposition. I soon found, however, that the structural form of analysis also generated new insights. Then, as I explored the ramifications of these insights, I found that I had to introduce further modifications, not just in the complexity of the analyses, but in their form as well. Finally, as I introduced these further modifications, I found that new theoretical hypotheses were suggested, particularly with regard to the importance of intentionality in the developmental process, the relationship between structure and process in children's thought, and the mechanisms of stage transition. In effect, then, my theory of intellectual development itself underwent a considerable process of development, as a result of my attempt to use it in an integrative fashion.

As the general structure of my theory developed, so did my experimental interests and techniques. During the 6 years it took to complete the present volume, my students and I conducted some 40 new studies, each of which was aimed at testing or clarifying some new aspect of the theory, and each of which employed some new experimental technique. Needless to say, I felt obliged to include some account of these studies in the book. Thus, the third change that took place was in the data that the book was designed to summarize.

A final change that took place was in my plan for introducing the book. As I reviewed previous theories of development, I began to get a clearer picture of the way in which these theories had changed from generation to generation. Certain notions had been present from the start, and had become progressively refined. Others had been discarded, only to be reintroduced. Still others had been imported from work in related fields. As my sense of these changes began to take shape, I decided that the most fitting form of introduction would be historical. I would introduce the theory of development I had evolved in a fashion that would itself be developmental.

The present volume, therefore, has four main objectives. The first is to provide an account of the general theory I have developed over the past 6 or 7 years. The second is to use this theory as a basis for interpreting and integrating the empirical findings from a variety of other research groups, and from a variety of other theoretical traditions. The third is to present the new data we have gathered in our own research group, in order to test and refine the theory. Finally, the fourth is to place the theory in historical perspective, by specifying its relationship to other theories in the field, both previous and contemporary.

Throughout the writing process, I have tried to keep three different audiences in mind. The first audience is my colleagues in developmental and educational psychology. The second audience is psychologists who study adult language and cognition. The third audience is clinicians or educators, whose work brings them into daily contact with young children. Keeping three different audiences in mind has often resulted in a certain tension of objectives, which the reader will no doubt find reflected in the book itself. Nevertheless, I have found this tension to be a productive one, and hope my readers will excuse those passages that they feel are either ahead of, or behind, the growing edge of their thought.

The writing of this book has been a difficult yet rewarding process for me. It has been difficult in that I have been forced to come to grips with many of the details of children's intellectual functioning that are easy to gloss over in shorter presentations. As a consequence, I have had to rework many of the original notions with which I set out, and to rewrite a number of chapters virtually from scratch. It has been rewarding in that, as I have grappled with these details and done the necessary rethinking and rewriting, I have found myself acquiring a deepening respect for the underlying order and coherence of the developmental process.

My hope for the readers is that they will experience few of the difficulties I have encountered, and most of the rewards.

Acknowledgments

Psychology is a community affair. Although it is practiced by individuals, these individuals are in constant contact with each other. Directly or indirectly, the influence that they exert on each other's work is profound. I have been particularly fortunate in that many of the individuals who have had the greatest impact on my work have also been my closest personal friends.

I would first like to acknowledge the contribution of my colleagues in Toronto. Carl Bereiter has had a great influence on my intellectual development from my earliest days as a graduate student. However, his contribution has been particularly important during the past few years. He encouraged me in my attempts to formulate a theory of my own, provided valuable criticism at a number of key points in the theory's development, and assisted my students and me in developing empirical studies to test the theory's central postulates. He also read the first draft of the present book in its entirety and pointed out a number of fundamental problems with it. Andrew Biemiller is another Toronto colleague whose help I have greatly appreciated. Andy met with me on a weekly basis when I began work on the present volume, and discussed the progress of each chapter in detail. He also devoted hours of his time to helping the members of my research group. Without his criticism and encouragement, and without our weekly baklava and coffee, the book would not have been nearly as exciting a project to undertake as it was. Two other Toronto colleagues whose help I have greatly appreciated are Marlene Scardamalia and David Olson. Like Carl and Andy, Marlene and Dave have commented on large sections of the manuscript. They have also welcomed me into their homes, and combined tough-minded scholarship with the warmest of fellowship. Finally, a special word of thanks is reserved for Juan Pascual-Leone. Juan received my initial interest in his work with enthusiasm, and my decision to develop a theory of my own with grace. Although we have had little contact over the past 7 years, the interactions we had during the previous 7 years were of great value to me and had a lasting impact on my thought.

The second group whose assistance I would like to acknowledge are my graduate students. Their contribution to my research programme has been immense. In fact, I suspect it has been far greater than they themselves may realize. I would particularly like to acknowledge the assistance of Meredyth Daneman, Sonja Dennis, Thomas Fiati, Jill Goldberg, Sonia Hayward, Frances Khanna, Midian Kurland, Peter Liu, Zopito Marini, Ann McKeough, Susan Rich, Tsilia Romm, Bob Sandieson, Debra Sandlos, Jim Wagner, Rita Watson, and Frank Wyatt at the Ontario Institute for Studies in Education. Each of these individuals has made a unique contribution to my current research programme, which readers will, I hope, come to appreciate more fully as they read the various studies on which we have collaborated. I would also like to acknowledge the contributions of my students at Berkeley to the research programme out of which was born the programme reported here. Of particular help were Bart Bödy, Sue DeMerssman, Frank Dempster, Veronica Fabian, Tamar Globerson, Alan Gold, Meg Korpi, Wendy Portnuff, Ron Serlin, Irene Subleman-Furman, and Libby Wyatt.

A third group whose assistance I would like to acknowledge are my colleagues at other universities. In recent years, I have found my conversations with Mike Cole, Bob Siegler, Liz Bates, Miki Chi, Dave Klahr, and Kurt Fischer to be particularly helpful. In the years I spent at Berkeley, I profited greatly from my discussions with Paul Ammon, Bill Rohwer, and Elliot Turiel. Finally, I have appreciated the comments I have received on specific chapters from Jacques Vonèche (Chapter 2), Sandra Trehub (Chapter 7), Miki Chi (Chapter 16), Frank Dempster (Chapter 16), and Bob Siegler (Chapters 1–9).

Psychological theory cannot simply be honed in the quiet of one's study, or in discussion with one's colleagues and students. It depends on empirical experimentation, which in turn requires financial support. I would like to acknowledge the assistance of the National Institute of Education, the National Institute of Mental Health and Child Development, and the Van Leer Foundation, which were the first agencies to support my research program at Berkeley. I would also like to acknowledge the assistance of the Canada Council and the Social Sciences and Humanities Research Council, which continued this support when I returned to Canada. At a number of points in my career, I have found myself "between grants." Each time this has happened, the Spencer Foundation has rallied gallantly to my assistance. Finally, and most recently, I am indebted to the John Simon Guggenheim Memorial Foundation, which provided a fellowship that enabled me to take a year's sabbatical leave and devote myself fulltime to the present project.

A book is, of course, more than the record of one's thought and work. It is also an entity in its own right. I would like to thank Cheryl Williams for her assistance in typing (and retyping!) the present manuscript; Gwen Egar for her help in preparing the illustrations; and Harry Beilin for inviting me to publish the book in his series, and for acting as my editor.

My final acknowledgment is to my family. It was my daughter Rebecca who provided me with my first intimate view of the mental life of early childhood, and who served as the inspiration for many of the tasks that are described in Chapters 8 and 14. Rebecca also kept me in touch with the fun and mischief in life during the 6 years it took to write the present volume, particularly on days when the world threatened to become one giant "task analysis." My son Jonathan was born just as I was starting the section on stage transition, and soon made a contribution of his own. Not only did he serve as a source of valuable insights, but he added a new dimension to our family life and brought his own unique brand of sunshine to our home. Needless to say, Rebecca and Jonathan were not my only sources of inspiration. It was my wife Nancy who first suggested that I undertake a volume of the present sort, and who helped me extricate myself from the many impasses I created in the course of doing so. It was also Nancy who went over every chapter with me in detail, with a view to improving its conceptual clarity. Finally, it was Nancy who shared my inner life during the years in which the book was being written, as well as those that led up to it. In a sense that only she will understand, this book is hers as well as mine.

PART I

The Present Theoretical Approach
and its Historical Foundation

CHAPTER 1

The Phenomena and Questions of Intellectual Development

INTRODUCTION

During the first few weeks of its life, the human infant demonstrates a number of remarkable capabilities. If given the opportunity, it can make a wide variety of complex sensory discriminations. Some of these involve inanimate objects, such as the visual patterns made by parallel lines in different orientations (Maurer & Martello, 1980), or the sound made by different mechanical devices (Siqueland & Lipsett, 1966). Others involve other human beings, such as the visual patterns made by different facial expressions (Meltzoff, 1981) or the sounds made by different consonant–vowel blends (e.g., "puh" versus "buh"—Eimas et al., 1971). In addition to these complex sensory capabilities, the human infant demonstrates a number of remarkable motor capabilities as well—or at least remarkable given the overall awkwardness of its movements. For example, the infant can reach out toward small objects, or turn its head to localize the position of interesting sounds (Bower, 1974; Chap. 6). Both of these responses require the coordination of information from different sensory modalities, and the generation of a complex sequence of motor movements.

In addition to these complex sensory and motor capabilities, the human infant comes equipped with another vital capability as well, the capability for adapting to *new* sensory situations, and generating *novel* motor patterns. For example, the infant can learn to turn its head one way to attain a sweet-tasting solution in the presence of a buzzer, and another way in the presence of a tone (Siqueland & Lipsett, 1966). It can also *un*learn such responses, and replace them with new ones when the contingencies in its environment are altered (Papousek, 1969). Perhaps more importantly, the infant can adapt to novel social situations and environments as well. By the age of a few weeks, for example, it normally shows signs of recognizing certain of the most common social behaviours of its primary caretakers, and of actively adapting its own social behavior to them (Condon, 1975; Sander, 1969; Schaffer, 1977; Trevarthan, 1977, 1980).

In spite of these remarkable capabilities, however, the newborn human infant also has a number of clear and pronounced limitations, ones which are often hard for us as adults to understand. As an illustration, suppose that you were placed in an entirely novel environment. Suppose further that you saw an interesting object move across the horizon from left to right, and then disappear. Suppose finally that the same object reappeared on the left hand side of the horizon a few seconds later, only to move across it again from left to right. After a very few repetitions of this sequence, you would no doubt find yourself anticipating the re-arrival of the interesting object on the left side of the horizon, as soon as it disappeared on the right. Your eyes would flick over to the left and hover there, waiting for the object to re-appear. This eye-flicking response would not have to be conditioned. It would appear as soon as you had grasped the connection between the object's disappearance on the right and its re-appearance on the left. Moreover, the response would remain for as long as you continued to be interested in the object. Much the same sort of response, under the same sort of voluntary control, might appear in a dog or a chimpanzee. In the newborn human infant, however, it would not (Uzgiris & Hunt, 1975).

On the surface, newborn infants appear to have all the elementary capacities and dispositions that are required, in order to exhibit this sort of anticipatory response. If a small object is moved across their field of vision from left to right, they will track it until it disappears. If the object re-appears on the left side of their field of vision, they will shift their eyes to the left and begin to track it again. Finally, if several trials are presented in succession, they will remain interested, and continue to track the object during each trial. In short, newborn human infants appear to possess all the perceptual capacities, motor skills, and motivational dispositions that this task requires. One would therefore expect that they would behave in much the same fashion as adults, and quickly learn to anticipate the object's re-arrival.

Yet the fact remains that they do not. Indeed, even if the task is repeated a large number of times, and even if they track the object with obvious attention on every trial, they still do not come to anticipate its re-arrival (Uzgiris & Hunt, 1975). Nor is their behavior on this task by any means anomalous. In a wide variety of situations, where they are exposed to some particular sequence of events and where they show every indication of attending to each element in the event-sequence, they fail to grasp almost all of the temporal and spatial relations that exist *among* the elements.

The central paradox of human intellectual development, then, is this: While the mind of the newborn is remarkably sophisticated in many ways, in many other ways it is also remarkably limited. And the central problem in the study of intellectual development is to explain the transformation that takes place, as time passes and these limitations slowly disappear.

The intellectual transformation that takes place with time is by no means a rapid one. The aforementioned anticipatory eye flick appears by the age of about 4 months. However, it is not until the age of 4 or 5 years that children reach a level of functioning that is clearly superior to that of all lower species (Premack, 1983), and at least another 10 years are required before they attain a level of functioning that could be described as fully adult.

There are, it is generally recognized, certain extremely important achievements that take place prior to full maturity. The attainment of the ability to speak at around the age of 2 years is one such achievement. It permits children to communicate with the members of their family at an entirely new level, and signals the beginning of a period in which they master basic family roles and expectations. The attainment of the ability to read and to do simple mathematics at the age of 5 or 6 years is another important intellectual achievement. It signals the beginning of a period in which children become capable of mastering the basic intellectual tools of their culture, tools which in our own culture include such skills as reading, writing, and arithmetic.

A third important achievement is the ability to reason at an abstract level, which appears in its first preliminary form at around the age of 11 or 12 years. The onset of abstract reasoning marks the beginning of a period in which the transition to adult forms of thought nears completion. In advanced technological cultures, this is the period when instruction is initiated in abstract theories and procedures, particularly in mathematics and science. In less-technological cultures, this is the period when children are expected to grasp the underlying system or mythology on which the basic social rules of their society are based. By the age of 15 to 18 years, then, although children may not know as much about the world as their elders, they are capable of thinking about it in much the same fashion.

All of these attainments—the ability to speak, the ability to read and compute, and the ability to reason abstractly—mark great changes in children's intellectual functioning. Moreover, all these attainments provide the growing child with important new tools for learning about the world. Given that the process of intellectual development is such a slow one, and that it is marked by the emergence of such qualitatively different forms of intellectual activity, the general question with which the study of intellectual development is concerned is normally broken down into two subquestions. First, what is the best way to characterize children's intellectual functioning at various key points in their growth? Second, what is the best way to characterize the process by which they progress from one of these points to the next? A third question is often addressed as well: how can the developmental process be optimized? That is, how can parents and teachers ensure that each individual child will realize his or her full intellectual potential?

THE ORIGIN OF COGNITIVE-DEVELOPMENTAL THEORY

Scientific interest in children's intellectual development dates back to the late nineteenth century. Although human beings have been concerned from time immemorial with the education of their offspring, it was not until Darwin proposed his theory of evolution that the task of explaining human intellectual development was recognized as an important scientific question. Prior to that time, a human adult who looked at a human infant might well have seen much what you or I would see if we looked at a baby pigeon or a baby turtle: an organism that was smaller than the adult of the species, and that behaved in a less-sophisticated fashion, yet whose capacities were quite different from those of any other species.

Once Darwin proposed his theory of evolution, however, it became possible to view the functioning of different species as sharing important biological properties in common, both with each other and with human beings themselves. Moreover, it became possible to view each form of life as having evolved out of a previous form of life, and to look at the development of individuals as recapitulating the development of their species.

It was this basic viewpoint that gave rise to the first theory of intellectual development. In 1859, Darwin published *The Origin of Species*, in which he set forth the basic postulates of his evolutionary theory. In 1871, he published *The Descent of Man*, in which he explicitly placed man at the top of the evolutionary tree. In 1872, he published *The Expression of Emotion in Animals and Man*, in which he suggested that the principles of evolution apply to behaviour as well as to biological structure. Finally, at about the same time, Haekel suggested that the development of the individual goes through the same stages as that of the species (Haekel, 1866). This notion was made popular in North America by G. Stanley Hall (1883, 1908), who articulated the dictum that "ontogeny recapitulates phylogeny."

It was this sequence of ideas that paved the way for the first theory of intellectual development. The notion that human development unfolds through the same series of stages as that of the species was a provocative one, which posed a clear challenge for the psychologists of the day. The challenge was to describe these stages, and to explicate the process by which the infant passed from one of them to the next. From the start it was also hoped that, once these two basic challenges were addressed, scientific guidance could be provided for those whose concern was optimizing the developmental process.

OBJECTIVES OF THE PRESENT BOOK

The present volume is an attempt to provide a new answer to the preceding three questions. That is, it is an attempt to provide a new description of how children's minds function at various points in their development, of the factors that control the transition from one of these points to the next, and of the steps that can be taken to optimise the developmental process. Such an attempt seems desirable for a number of reasons.

1. As has already been hinted, there has been a substantial increase in our understanding of early cognition during the last 10 to 15 years. Whereas it is still acknowledged that great differences separate the thinking of younger age groups from the thinking of older age groups, it is now recognized that the thinking of young infants has a fascinating degree of sophistication and complexity in its own right. As yet, no theory has been proposed that can adequately capture this complexity while at the same time differentiating it from later functioning.

2. Since the early 1970s, there has also been a substantial increase in our understanding of children's linguistic and social development. What were once thought to be relatively autonomous strands of development are now recognized as sharing important properties in common, both with each other, and with other forms of development (Bates, 1976; Beilin, 1975; Gopnik, 1982; Slobin, 1973). As yet, no theory has been proposed that does full justice to this general factor in development while allowing for domain-specific differences as well.

3. Since the mid-1960s, there has been a dramatic increase in the sophistication with which young children's intellectual functioning can be modelled, as a result of developments in the fields of cognitive psychology and computer science. As yet, however, there have been relatively few attempts to integrate the new data that have been acquired concerning the details of children's cognitive functioning, or to combine these data with the data that were gathered earlier, concerning the global pattern of children's thought. As a result, the general picture that we have of children's development remains unnecessarily fragmented and incomplete.

4. Finally, since the mid-1970s, the implications of a number of our current general theories of development—both *functional* and *structural*—have been tested. While many of the predictions have been confirmed, many others have not. As yet, no satisfactory explanation has been offered for these anomalies.

For all of the preceding reasons, therefore, a fresh answer to the classic questions of development seems necessary. In short, it seems necessary to propose a new general theory of intellectual development.

In the present volume, one such theory is presented. While the theory that is presented is new, however, it is not radical. It has not been developed by rejecting the core postulates of previous theories, and replacing them with new ones. Rather, it has been developed by preserving and refining as many of these previous postulates as possible, and replacing only those that seem most strongly in need of revision. Because the theory has been developed in this fashion, the best way to introduce it is historical. Once one understands the postulates of previous theories, and the problems to which they have given rise, the reasons for the present theory's structure becomes apparent.

It is with this objective in mind, therefore, that I turn to a description of the tradition out of which the present theory of development has arisen, and to which it hopefully will contribute.

CHAPTER 2

Traditional Theories of Intellectual Development

The first theory that attempted to explicate the process of intellectual development appeared in 1894, only a few years after G. Stanley Hall had articulated the dictum that ontogeny recapitulates phylogeny. The author of the theory was an American psychologist, James Mark Baldwin.

BALDWIN'S THEORY OF INTELLECTUAL DEVELOPMENT

Baldwin was a student of Hall's and, like him, a neo-Darwinian. He believed that children's intellectual functioning at birth is similar to that of invertebrates, and that it gradually moves through a series of higher stages or *epochs*. During these epochs, children's functioning first assumes the properties of lower vertebrates (4–8 months), then higher vertebrates (8–12 months), and finally human beings (2 + years). To account for this sequence of intellectual development Baldwin postulated two processes, *habit formation*, and *accommodation*.

Baldwin described the process of habit formation in considerable detail. The infant's first habits, he believed, are formed by means of *circular reactions*. These reactions are adaptive responses that human infants exhibit to the stimulation provided by people and objects. At a general level, they are somewhat analogous to the adaptive responses observed in lower organisms, such as plants, in response to the stimulation provided by light and chemical nutrients. According to Baldwin, the infant's first circular reactions proceed as follows. First, the perceptual system detects some change in the environment, such as the arrival of a face, the sound of a voice, or the chance movement of a small object nearby. In response to this stimulation, the motor system energizes itself. With the increased energization, there is a spontaneous activation of a global set of movements aimed at orienting toward the stimulation and maximizing its intensity. To the extent that certain of these movements actually do produce a slight orientation, the intensity of the stimulation increases because it is now more directly in the center of the perceptual field. The result is that another burst of energization is triggered, in a cyclic or *circular* fashion. Finally, the source of the stimulation ends up in the middle of the perceptual field, and the infant achieves a state of maximum energization.

As circular reactions are repeated many times, in response to different types of stimulation, the movements that prove successful in producing an orientation toward any given stimulus gradually become habitual. Conversely, those that do not prove successful are gradually eliminated. Internally, the result is the development of a blueprint for orienting toward a particular stimulus. This blueprint represents both the nature of the stimulus itself, and the nature of the orienting response. Baldwin called this blueprint a *schema*. He assumed that the more firmly established a schema becomes, the more automatic becomes a child's response. Eventually, when an extremely familiar stimulus is presented, the appropriate schema is activated completely automatically, and a smooth, well-coordinated response is observed. Baldwin called the process of schema activation *assimilation*. For him, well-established schemata assimilate stimuli as naturally as organic structures assimilate food.

The concepts of schema and assimilation seemed sufficient to Baldwin to explain the process of habit formation. However, the process of habit formation did not seem sufficient to explain the process of development. Precisely because schema consolidation and assimilation do work so automatically, both in infants and in lower species, Baldwin felt it necessary to postulate a process that can break up old habits, and which can lead to higher levels of adaptation. He called this process *accommodation*.

According to Baldwin, the process of accommodation takes place as follows. First, the infant assimilates a new situation to an already existing schema. Second, it discovers that this assimilation is not successful. At this point it experiences conflict, and activates whatever other schemas or components of schemas seem of possible relevance. Finally, these schemas are coordinated into a higher order schema. The new schema is then applied, and the process of habit formation begins again.

The underlying mechanism that was responsible for activating and coordinating schemas according to Baldwin's theory was attention. Like William James, Baldwin believed that the reason humans have the capability for higher-order accommodations than other species is that they have a greater power of attention. In turn, he believed that the reason humans have this great power of attention is that they have attained a greater degree of cortical coordination. Under this term Baldwin included a variety of neurological factors, such as the development of brain cells, the development of fibres connecting different parts of the brain, and the myelinization of interconnecting nerve fibres.

For Baldwin, the reason humans are the most sophisticated and adaptive of species is that their brain has attained the greatest degree of cortical coordination and is capable, via attention, of effecting the most complex accommodations. The reason the human infant is *not* capable of such complex accommodations is that its brain has not yet attained this degree of cortical coordination.

If intellectual development is produced by the coordination of schemata, and if the complexity of children's coordinations is determined by the maturation of their cortex, it would seem reasonable to expect that a universal sequence of developmental stages might be observed, with each stage corresponding to a different level of *schematic coordination*. Baldwin believed that there are, in fact, such universal stages. It was these stages to which he assigned the name *epochs* and which he believed recapitulate the development of the species. Baldwin traced the development of his own children through three such epochs in the course of their first year of life.

Baldwin suggested that infants pass through a developmental stage from birth until about 4 months, which he labeled the epoch of *sensorimotor suggestion*. During this epoch, the stimulation afforded by a person or an object induces (*suggests*, was the term of the day) a diffuse orienting response, and the first circular reactions are observed. Although the infant's schemas become more differentiated during this period, as yet they cannot be kept active in the absence of some direct perceptual stimulation. That is, they cannot be retained in immediate memory. As a consequence, two schemas that are not triggered by the same perceptual input cannot be coordinated with each other.

An important consequence of this inability to coordinate schemas is that the infant cannot know external objects in the way that adults do. Baldwin gave the example of one of his own infants, who appeared to recognize her bottle when it was presented nipple first, but not when it was presented in any other orientation. He suggested that this was because she had not yet constructed an overall schema or *copy* of the object, by coordinating the schemas representing its various possible perceptual manifestations. Prior to Baldwin's theorizing, it had often been assumed that the perception of objects as solid bodies as well as the perception of certain other basic properties of the external world such as time and space, were innate. This was the view proposed by Kant in his *Critique of Pure Reason* (1781/1966). As a result of his work with infants, Baldwin challenged Kant's view. He suggested that all the basic categories of human knowledge actually have to be constructed, and that this is one of the major intellectual tasks of infancy.

Baldwin saw the infant as entering a second stage at about the age of 4 months, which he labeled the epoch of *ideomotor suggestion*. During this stage, the memory function emerges. The infant is now able to preserve a copy of interesting patterns or responses in immediate memory. As a consequence, motor movements may be induced by such copies rather than by direct stimulation. One example of ideomotor suggestion is to be found in the child's imitation. Baldwin believed that children do not engage in true imitation prior to the age of 4 months. After this age, a copy of interesting movements remains active in their memory, and they then produce similar movements in order to prolong the activation of this copy. Baldwin suggested that, although this imitation represents behaviour of a higher sort than the first orienting response, it still constitutes a circular reaction. The infants are still attempting to preserve positive stimulation. The only difference is that they now do so by preserving a *copy* of the stimulation, rather than the stimulation itself.

At the stage of ideomotor suggestion, Baldwin believed that the memory function is *monoideistic*: although infants can preserve a copy of some previous stimulation, they can only preserve one such copy. As a consequence, their abilities remain rather limited. For example, they cannot compare two patterns that are no longer present. At about the age of 8 months, however, infants' memory becomes *polyideistic*. This means that they now become capable of true volition. For Baldwin, true volition depended on being able (1) to imagine a goal, (2) to note how far one had progressed toward it, and (3) to compare one's current point with one's original objective. It was this sort of capability that Baldwin believed distinguishes higher from lower vertebrates. The ability requires the comparison of two copies or memory images, and it is the achievement of the third epoch of development. One illustration of its emergence is that persistent imitation now appears for the first time. Infants now imitate something, appear dissatisfied with their imitation, and work at improving it until they are satisfied. Another illustration is that infants begin to use flexible methods for achieving their goals. Baldwin gave the example of one of his own infants, who at this stage was able to retrieve a set of keys by pulling the blanket on which they had been placed.

Finally, at an age which Baldwin left unspecified, the child enters a stage that he called simply the stage of *thought*. It is at this stage, according to Baldwin, that the child's thinking begins to operate at a higher level than that attained by even the highest of other vertebrates. Even then, however, the child's development is not fully complete. Baldwin distinguished four different forms of intellectual activity or *logic* that follow the prelogical thinking of infancy. These were (1) the stage of *quasilogical* thought, in which play is a primary mode of intellectual activity, (2) the stage of *logical thought* in which judgment and reasoning become possible, and (3 + 4) the stages of *hyperlogical* and *extralogical thought*, in which advanced moral and aesthetic judgment become possible. At each of these stages, because the form of children's mental activity is different, Baldwin assumed that the type of knowledge they are capable of acquiring from the external world is also different. He labeled this study—the study of the manner in which a subject comes to attain objective knowledge of the world—*genetic epistemology.*

Baldwin's theory provided a broad view of intellectual development, and one which was compatible with the best available data and theories of the time (see James, 1918/1950). By all rights, therefore, one would have expected the theory to spawn a generation of further theoretical speculation and research. In North America, however, this did not occur. One of the major reasons was that behaviorism became the dominant school of academic psychology. Behaviorists were more interested in external behavior than in internal processes. Also, to the extent that they were interested in internal processes, they were interested in simple processes such as habit formation and association. They had little interest in processes such as schematic accommodation or coordination. Finally, because the simple processes in which they were interested were clearly evident in lower species and in children, behaviorists had little interest in notions such as *developmental recapitulation, universal stages,* or *child logic.*

In France, however, behaviorism never gained the influence that it did in Germany and America. Moreover, Baldwin lived for a number of years in France. His work was translated into French, and he developed close ties with a number of French psychologists, particularly Pierre Janet and Alfred Binet. The responsibility for carrying on Baldwin's work thus ultimately passed to a young man who came to Paris from Switzerland in order to study with Janet. The young man's name, of course, was Jean Piaget.[1]

PIAGET'S THEORY OF INTELLECTUAL DEVELOPMENT

Piaget de-emphasized two concepts that had played an important role in Baldwin's theory, namely, attentional power and cortical coordination. However, he preserved virtually all of Baldwin's other concepts, and he set about to explore the two areas that Baldwin had outlined at a general level, but left largely uncharted. These were (1) the universal changes in the psychological mode of functioning that take place as the child moves from infancy to adulthood, and (2) the relationship between these changes and changes in the child's knowledge of the objective world. Piaget was particularly interested in those categories of knowledge that Kant had held to be a priori, but which

---

[1] It is an interesting footnote to history that Piaget's original field was biology, and that Baldwin, in one of his prefaces, suggested that the appropriate persons to carry on his work, and to develop the field of genetic epistemology, would be biologists.

Baldwin had presumed must be constructed. By the mid-1950s, Piaget had completed a detailed empirical investigation of children's thinking in most of these areas of knowledge, and had extended and revised Baldwin's theory (Piaget, 1950, 1951, 1952, 1954; Piaget & Szeminska, 1952). Piaget divided the child's intellectual development intò three broad periods or stages.

The Sensorimotor Stage

Piaget distinguished a substage during the first year of life that Baldwin had not mentioned, namely the first month after birth. During this month, according to Piaget, the child's mode of functioning was a purely reflexive one. Thus, even elementary circular reactions were not possible. In his description of infancy, Piaget also included the second year of life with the first, and he distinguished two further substages in it. He was thus left with a total of six substages rather than three. Piaget's real contribution to the study of infancy, however, was not his expansion of the number of substages that could be identified. Rather, it was his explication of the relationship between the child's level of schematic coordination and the understanding of which he or she is capable.

For each of the six substages that he isolated, Piaget devised a task that revealed children's level of schematic coordination. He then invented a series of other tasks to assess their level of understanding in each of the categories of knowledge listed by Kant. What he found was that, for each increase in the level of schematic coordination, there was a corresponding increase in the child's level of understanding. As an example, consider two tasks that Piaget devised for probing the transition from the substage of isolated circular reactions (1–4 months), to the substage of coordinated or secondary circular reactions (4–8 months).

The task designed to reveal the level of schematic coordination was simple yet ingenious. A ribbon was tied around an infant's hand, and then attached to a mobile that was hung over its crib. The question of interest was whether the infant would use its hand as means to prolonging the interesting movement of the mobile; that is, whether the infant would be capable of a circular reaction, in which one schema was used as a means to prolonging the activation of a second. What Piaget found was that, as Baldwin had suggested, this did not occur before the age of about 4 months. Prior to that time, infants would appear interested in a mobile when their hands happened to move it. However, they would not repeat their hand movement in order to prolong the movement of the mobile (Piaget, 1952, p. 161).

Consider next a task that was designed to assess the infant's understanding of a very basic concept: that objects have an existence independent of our own perception, and are capable of independent movement. In order to assess this understanding, Piaget devised the task that was mentioned in the introductory

chapter: he repeatedly moved an interesting object out of the infants' field of vision on one side, brought it around behind their heads, and reintroduced it on
the other side. He discovered that at the age of 2 months the infants repeatedly
searched for the object at its point of disappearance. By the age of 4–8 months,
they could overcome this habit, and switch the direction of their search to the
point of re-appearance. For Piaget, this change in behavior was evidence that
the children were constructing a notion of object movement that was independent of their own perception. In effect, the children were constructing a notion
of invisible movement.

What is the connection between the concept of independent or invisible
movement, and the secondary circular reaction? For Piaget, as for Baldwin, the
connection was that the understanding of invisible movement, because it cannot
be perceived, must be *constructed*. And the mechanism of this construction was
the coordination of schemes. Thus, for Piaget, the ability to coordinate two
primary circular reactions was a necessary prerequisite for the construction of
the concept of invisible movement. Piaget did not try to specify exactly which
two schemes would have to be coordinated in order to attain this concept.
However, to presage the analyses of later chapters, one could speculate that they
would be (1) a scheme for tracking an object and noting its disappearance, and
(2) a scheme for noting an object's reappearance and tracking it from that point.
Only if those two schemes were clearly differentiated from each other and coordinated, could a regularity in the object's invisible movement be detected.

At each of the six substages of infant development Piaget constructed a similar
pair of tasks, and demonstrated a similar relationship between them. He
therefore concluded (1) that children's ability to differentiate and coordinate
schemes increases in complexity during each substage, and (2) that there is a corresponding increase in their understanding of the laws relating to the movement
of vanished objects. In and of itself, this would have been an important suggestion. However, Piaget also discovered that there is a parallel development at
each substage in children's understanding of all the other categories of
knowledge specified by Kant. In each case, his suggestion was the same:
knowledge of the world must be constructed. Thus, the increase in knowledge
that is observed comes about as a direct result of the increase in children's constructive capability. This in turn is a function of the increased differentiation
and coordination of their repertoire of schemes.

Given the parallel development in understanding across so many domains,
and the inferred role of schematic coordination in producing this development,
Piaget felt it important to characterize the nature of the underlying schematic
coordination in greater detail. Drawing on contemporaneous developments in
mathematics and symbolic logic, he did so in the following manner. First, he
described a number of general characteristics of the infant's schematic repertoire. Then, he represented these properties by means of symbolic logic. For ex-

ample, Piaget noted that one of the properties of children's schematic repertoire in the second year of life is that the effect of any one scheme (e.g., pushing) can be reversed by activating some other scheme (e.g., pulling). He labeled this property *reversibility*, and symbolized it as follows:

$$AB + BA = 0$$

where A and B are spatial points, and the zero indicates that the net result of movement from A to B and back is no change.

Another important property of children's repertoire during the second year of life is that the effect of any two given schemes (e.g. extending the arm and moving it laterally), can be achieved by activating a third scheme (e.g. swiping). Piaget labeled this property *combinativity* and symbolized it as follows:

$$AB + BC = AC$$

where A, B, and C once again represent spatial points. Finally, Piaget noted that the total set of these characteristics, when symbolized in this fashion, could be represented as a mathematical structure. That is, it could be represented as a set of elements and transformations. This mathematical structure could then be used as a model for representing the organizational characteristics or *structure* of infants' sensorimotor repertoires. Piaget's general assertion, therefore, was that children attain the variety of insights that they do at the age of 2 years, because the insights all share the same requirement. The requirement is not for any particular set of schemes, but for a particular type of schematic organization or *operational structure*. Only when children have acquired this operational structure, are they capable of constructing representations of objects that are completely invariant in the face of temporal and spatial displacement. These invariant representations of the external world are important because they serve as the building blocks for the next major stage of development.

The Representational Stage

Piaget labeled the next stage of development the *representational stage*, and he divided it into two major substages that he labeled the stages of *preoperational* and *concrete operational* thought.

Preoperational Thought

During the period of preoperational thought, children go through a similar sequence with regard to their representational schemes as they did earlier with regard to their sensorimotor schemes. To begin with, their schemes are relatively undifferentiated and uncoordinated. Gradually, and in a step-by-step fashion, the schemes become more differentiated and coordinated. With each progressive increase in coordination, the children's understanding of the regularities in their world becomes greater. Just as the world of objects took on an increasing coherence and stability during the first stage of their lives, so the world that depends on symbolic representation—the world of socially shared meaning, categories, and relations—begins to take on a greater coherence and stability during the second stage of their lives. This increasing stability and coherence is evidenced in a variety of activities. It is evidenced in children's symbolic play, symbolic gestures, and social interactions. Perhaps the clearest domain in which it appears, however, is in their first verbal concepts.

At the age of $1-1\frac{1}{2}$ years, children do not yet differentiate their verbal concepts from their own activity of producing them. Piaget gives the example of his daughter, Jacqueline, who used the sound "choo-choo" to indicate a train passing by her window. At first glance, the use of this sound appeared to be merely a childlike phonological representation of an adult verbal concept, namely, *train*. Jacqueline went on to use the same sound, however, to indicate any other vehicle, any other sound that came from the window, or anything that appeared as suddenly as a train (Piaget, 1951, p. 206).

By the age of $1\frac{1}{2}-2$ years, Piaget noted that Jacqueline began to use words in a fashion that indicated she did make a differentiation between her own actions and external concepts. At the same time, she began to use words for reporting or *re-presenting* events that had taken place in the past, rather than events that were taking place in the present. In spite of this obvious advance, however, it was a long time before she could completely detach the central meaning of verbal categories from their perceptual appearance. This difficulty was illustrated in a later study by DeVries (1969). What DeVries found was that children who see a mask of a cat placed on a dog will think that the animal is a cat. In fact, prior to the age of 4 years, they will insist that it is a cat, in spite of explanations to the contrary. From a Piagetian perspective, one could say that the attainment of the insight that the animal is still a dog depends on the availability of a complex system of intercoordinated symbols and meanings. Only once this system has attained the property of *reversibility* is the child able to abstract the critical properties of the class that this symbol represents, and which remain invariant in the face of such transformations.

As will no doubt be apparent, there is a direct parallel in Piaget's system between the course of children's intellectual development during the sensorimotor and the representational stages. At the beginning of each stage children do not differentiate the object to which their activity is applied from the activity itself. As each period progresses, they not only make this differentiation, they realize that certain properties remain invariant in spite of substantial perceptual transformations. Finally, throughout each period these two types of changes are closely linked. There is a close link between the differentiation and coordination of sensorimotor schemes during the first stage, and the construction of physical invariants. And there is a close relation between the differentiation and coordination of symbolic schemes during the second stage and the construction of symbolic invariants. In effect, children's development during the second stage of development *recapitulates* their development during the first stage, but at a higher epistemic level. Piaget labeled this recapitulation *vertical dècalage.*

In the chapters that follow, this sort of dècalage will be examined in greater detail, and a number of additional ways in which sensorimotor and representational development are similar will be pointed out. Before this can be done, however, it is necessary to consider the further developments that take place, as the child moves into the second half of the representational stage.

Transition to Concrete Operations

Between the age of about 4 and 10 years the child goes through another important sequence of intellectual steps. This sequence of steps may be illustrated by reference to the apparatus shown in Figure 2.1.

At about the age of 4 years, children's quantitative schemes are relatively isolated. Thus, although they can accurately report that the spring becomes longer when a weight is added to the pan, they do not realize that the magnitude of the weight increase and the magnitude of the spring increase are necessarily linked. By the age of $4\frac{1}{2}$ to 5 years, they do realize this, and a variety of other direct or inverse relationships as well. Piaget refers to these relations as one-way mappings or *functions*, and symbolizes them as follows:

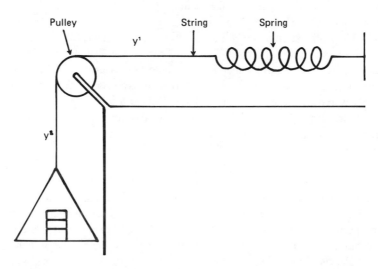

Fig. 2.1. Apparatus for demonstrating children's functional logic at 5–6 years of age. (From Piaget *et al.*, 1977.)

$$x = f(y)$$

where x and y are any two variables, and f indicates that they are connected in some one-to-one fashion (Piaget *et al.*, 1977).

By the age of 7 or 8 years, children become capable of effecting coordinations that are more complex still. They can now focus simultaneously on two functional relations, for example, the relationship between the weight and spring, and the relationship between the vertical and horizontal segment of the string. Finally, by the age of 9 or 10 years, the child's quantitative schemes become assembled into a fully coordinated system. Once again, one of the basic properties of this system is reversibility. Children can realize, for example, that the effect of adding a number of weights can be reversed by subtracting the same number of weights. This understanding may be represented as follows:

$$w - w = 0$$

Another property of the system is combinativity. Thus, children can now realize that the two segments of the string can be combined into one overall length. This may be symbolized as follows:

$$y_1 + y_2 = y$$

where y_1 = the horizontal segment, y_2 = the vertical segment, and y = the total length.

Once again, the set of such properties can be represented by a mathematical structure (called a *grouping*), which can then serve as a model of children's underlying psychological structure. When, and only when, children's symbolic schemes have been coordinated into quantitative structures of this form does Piaget refer to them as having attained the status of logical *operations*.

Once the children have acquired a set of intercoordinated logical operations having this structure, they become capable of extracting higher concepts or *quantitative invariants*. For example, prior to the age of 7 years, most children think that adding a weight to the pan increases the quantity or length of the string. It is not until their internal operations become more coordinated that they realize it remains constant. In effect, it is not until they can coordinate the increase in the length of segment y^2, with the reverse effect that is caused in the segment y^1 by the same operation, that this higher-order invariant becomes apparent to them.

By the time children reach the end of this period, they understand that quantities obey laws that are independent of any specific perceptual state. Once they have attained this understanding, they are ready to combine these laws into theoretical systems in a fashion that is at a higher level of understanding still. In Piaget's terminology, they are ready for the transition to abstract or *formal* operations.

The Formal Stage

The nature of the change that occurs as children make the transition to the formal stage may be illustrated by means of the apparatus shown in Figure 2.2. Children in the period of concrete operations, who are told that 3 grams have just been placed on the left side of the balance, can imagine reversing this effect by removing the same amount of weight. They can also imagine reversing this effect by putting the same amount of weight at the same point on the other side. Finally, they can coordinate these relations with each other. However, if they are given the opportunity to discover the similar set of operations that can be conducted with regard to distance from the fulcrum, they cannot then coordinate this set of operations with the first set. For example, they cannot say what precise change in the distance from the fulcrum on the right side will reverse the effect of a 3-gram addition on the left side. As the reader may verify, to determine this value requires an understanding of the operation of a balance beam which is quite abstract, together with a set of calculations that are quite complex and formal as well.

During the formal-operational period, children's repertoire of schemes becomes sufficiently differentiated and coordinated that such higher-order operations, or operations on operations become possible. As a consequence, another qualitative change takes place in their intellectual functioning. They now begin to show an aptitude for, and an interest in, systems for relating variables, that is, abstract theories. With this interest comes the capacity for operating in a hypotheticodeductive fashion: for seeing specific events as examples of general principles, and for arranging events such that these principles can be identified. Finally, with the ability to conceptualize systems of interacting variables and to operate in a hypotheticodeductive fashion comes the ability to

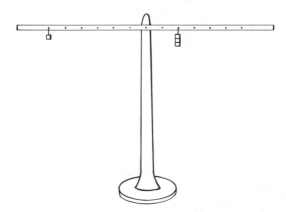

Fig. 2.2. Apparatus for distinguishing concrete from formal operations.

isolate one variable, while controlling other variables. In general, the adolescent's thought comes to take on a far more abstract, systematic, and scientific quality during the teenage years.

As with the earlier stages, the change in children's intellectual activity as they enter the formal period does not occur rapidly. Rather, it occurs gradually and in a sequence of steps. There is a substage in children's understanding of a balance beam, for example, in which they have a sound qualitative appreciation of the relationship between weight and distance from the fulcrum, but cannot yet express this quantitatively. And, as in the earlier stages, the culmination of this step-by-step coordination is an overall structure with certain specificable formal characteristics. What can now be reversed or combined are not just elements such as functions, but relations between functions themselves. Finally, with the acquisition of a set of abstract intercoordinated schemes comes an increase in the understanding of the laws regulating the behavior of objects in the external world, and the construction of invariants of a higher order still. One of these invariants is the notion of *ratio*, which is a relationship that remains constant in spite of quantitative variation in each of its parts.

Factors Affecting Progression through the Stages

Piaget listed several factors that affect the rate at which children progress through the four stages of intellectual development.

1. The first factor is *maturation*. While Piaget acknowledged the importance of this factor, unlike Baldwin, he did not assign it a major role. Moreover, he stated that whatever role it does play is largely confined to the first few years of life.

2. The second factor is *physical experience*. The necessity for postulating experiential effects in development is no doubt clear. If infants never had any experience with the physical world, they could not abstract the invariances or laws that govern its operation. Because the sort of physical experience that is prerequisite for intellectual development is apt to be universal, however, Piaget assigned a relatively small role to it. In effect, he believed that most forms of physical experience have equal potential with regard to their effect on intellectual growth.

3. The third factor is *social experience*. Social experience was assigned a slightly greater role than physical experience. It was assumed to be necessary, for example, for the development of socially agreed-upon symbols. It was also presumed capable of playing a role in alerting children that their current structures are inadequate, and in providing a forum for them to experiment with more comprehensive ones. By far the most important factor, however, was the fourth one.

4. The fourth factor was the child's own internal coordinating activity.

Piaget believed that this activity is dominated by the child's concern to achieve *equilibrium*, that is, to achieve a cognitive state in which the greatest number of external events can be explained with the most parimonious and least contradictory set of internal structures. If cognitive structures were relatively specific entities, or if their construction were dependent on external events only, then the process of equilibration might proceed relatively rapidly. However, because cognitive structures have great generality, and because they must be abstracted from patterns in children's own operations on the world (i.e., reflexively) rather than by direct apprehension of the world itself (i.e., "empirically"), Piaget saw the pace of development as being necessarily a slow one.

As will no doubt be apparent, Piaget charted the relationship between the form of children's internal activity and their apprehension of the external world in much greater empirical detail than Baldwin had. However, in explaining the new data that he had gathered, he preserved and explicated many of Baldwin's concepts, most notably: (1) the notion of a schema, (2) the notion of a circular reaction, (3) the notions of assimilation and accommodation, (4) the notion of a developmental stage, and (5) the notion of qualitatively distinct types of logic. In addition, Piaget introduced a number of new concepts, including, (1) the notion of a logical structure, (2) the notion of an invariant whose construction is permitted by that structure, (3) the notion of cyclic reconstruction of structures at higher levels (vertical décalage), (4) the notion of equilibration, and (5) the notion of reflective (as opposed to empirical) abstraction. At the same time, he de-emphasized two of Baldwin's concepts, namely, (1) attentional power and (2) cortical coordination. The net result of these changes was that the overall picture of the young child that emerged from his theory was considerably different from the one that had emerged from Baldwin's. Baldwin's predominant image of the young child had been as a biological organism, whose development recapitulated that of its species. While Piaget preserved the biological metaphor, his predominant image of the child was that of a young scientist building successively more sophisticated models of the world, by the application of successively more sophisticated logical structures.

STRENGTHS OF PIAGET'S THEORY

The strength of Piaget's theory lay both in the breadth of the data it was able to explain, and in the elegant manner in which it did so. Consider first the data for which the theory provided an explanation.

1. The fact that formally similar understandings tend to be acquired at about the same age across a wide variety of domains was explained by suggesting that these understandings all require the application of the same underlying logical structure.

2. The fact that certain sequences of intellectual development are universal was explained by suggesting that higher-order structures are assembled out of lower-order structures, thus following them in a logical sequence.

3. The fact that children do not appear to acquire certain types of understanding—understanding that seems so obvious to adults—until such a late age was explained by suggesting that these understandings can only be achieved once a particular level of logical structure has been constructed, and that the construction of such a structure takes a great deal of time.

4. The fact that parallels exist in the earliest motor learning of infants and in the more complex forms of learning that take place later in life. Piaget explained by suggesting that although the type of structure underlying the learning changes, the fundamental process—the differentiation and coordination of schemes in response to cognitive disequilibrium—remains functionally invariant.

5. Finally, the fact that children must have achieved a certain degree of readiness before they can profit from certain types of experience was explained by suggesting that until children have acquired the appropriate logical structure, they cannot possibly profit from certain kinds of experience, because they have no internal mechanism for assimilating it.

To say that Piaget's theory could account for the above-mentioned empirical phenomena is to tell only part of the story. Prior to Piaget's work, very little was known about children's development of logical concepts, let alone the parallels that exist across a wide variety of domains. Similarly, prior to Piaget's work, it was not known that the sequence of development is invariant, that the rate of development is so slow, or that training is so difficult. Whereas the fully articulated theory was developed to explain these phenomena, it was the core assumptions of the theory that led to their discovery in the first place. Thus, it is fair to say that Piaget's research program not only had impressive *explanatory* power, but impressive *heuristic* power as well (see Lakatos, 1970).

If these had been the only advantages of the theory, they would have been impressive in their own right. However, the strength of the theory did not derive exclusively from its ability to discover and to explain a wide variety of empirical phenomena, but from the compelling fashion in which it integrated these discoveries and explanations. Although a number of factors no doubt contributed to this quality, four of the most important, it seems to me, were as follows:

1. The theory was extremely broad in scope. Not only did it account for all the major phenomena of children's intellectual development, it offered a reasonable framework within which to view the development of scientific knowledge, as well as certain types of biological development.

2. The theory was parsimonious. Given the great diversity of the phenoma for which it accounted, it utilized remarkably few constructs and postulates.

3. The theory was not reductionist; that is, it did not achieve its parsimony by ignoring essential differences, either between higher and lower organisms, or between higher and lower levels of intellectual functioning in the human organism.
4. The theory was highly systematic. That is, its basic constructs and postulates formed a sophisticated, coherent, and tightly interrelated system.

Finally, Piaget's theory suggested a number of important educational applications. The most important of these were

1. That the instruction to which children are exposed should be geared to the type of intellectual functioning of which they are capable.
2. That the general approach that is taken should be one that fosters the *auto-regulative* or *constructive* process.

In a very real sense, therefore, Piaget played the same role for intellectual development as Darwin had played for the development of the species. He gathered a vast fund of empirical data on the intellectual behavior of the human organism at different points in time. He developed and integrated a number of previously existing notions within a framework that not only explained the existing data, but led to the discovery of a wide variety of new data. Finally, he provided a view of mankind the significance of which transcended the particular discipline and data from which it was derived, and which was of great social significance.

No matter what its strengths, of course, no theory lasts forever. Each generation that re-experiences the strengths of a theory also becomes more aware of its limitations. This awareness is heightened if a new set of data is discovered, or a new type of conceptional tool is developed. Such an occurrence took place in biology at the turn of the century, when Darwin's theory of evolution came into contact with Mendel's theory of genetics. The confrontation revealed certain weaknesses in Darwin's theory that subsequent generations of evolutionary theorists were forced to redress.

A similar occurrence took place in developmental psychology, when Piaget's theory became popular in North America, and came into contact with learning theory. The confrontation between the two theories served to highlight the strengths of Piaget's theory. However, it also served to reveal a number of important weaknesses, which subsequent generations of developmental theorists have attempted to redress, with the new conceptual tools that have since become available. The nature of these weaknesses, and the modifications of Piaget's theory that have been proposed as a consequence, are the subjects of the next two chapters.

CHAPTER 3

Critical Responses to Traditional Developmental Theory

INTRODUCTION

As was mentioned in the previous chapter, Piaget's theory was developed in relative isolation from work in North America. Between 1920 and 1955—the years in which Piaget developed the major elements of his theory—the dominant school of psychology in North America was behaviorism. Behaviorists had a different view of human development from Piaget. They also had a different view of knowledge, and of psychology. As long as the behaviourist view predominated, there was little interest in Piaget's work.

In the late 1950s, however, the intellectual climate in North America began to change. Work on human attention, language, and problem solving all began to point in the same direction: toward the influence of complex internal structures (Bruner, Goodnow, & Austin, 1956; Chomsky, 1957; Miller, 1956; Newell, Shaw & Simon, 1958). As a consequence, the influence of behaviorism began to wane. There was an increased receptivity to theories that attempted to specify the nature of humans' mental structures, and the processes by which they develop.

In 1961, J. McVicker Hunt published a book entitled *Intelligence and Experience*. In it, he described Piaget's view of development, and contrasted this view with maturationist and environmentalist views. In 1963, John Flavell published a book entitled *The Developmental Psychology of Jean Piaget*. In it, he provided a detailed summary of Piaget's work for English-speaking readers, and a brief evaluation. These two books had an important influence on the field, and stimulated a great deal of interest in Piaget's work. The stage was therefore set for a confrontation between Piaget's view of knowledge and its development, and the view held by behaviorists.

The first issue over which the confrontation took place was a basic one: the role of experience in determining the course of intellectual growth.

According to Piaget's theory, children's learning is severely limited by their general stage of development. Until they have developed the appropriate logical structures, there are certain types of experience from which they cannot profit. According to behaviorist theory, children's learning is determined only by their previous experience. If they cannot profit from one experience, it is because they have not had sufficient exposure to some other experience, which is a necessary prerequisite (Gagné, 1968).

Between 1964 and 1974, over 200 studies were conducted in an attempt to clarify and/or resolve the disagreement between the two theoretical positions. Most of the studies focused on children's understanding of conservation: the notion that the quantity of an object remains invariant in spite of perceptual transformations. In order to explore the effects of experience on the development of this concept, a variety of training procedures were developed. Nonconservers were then exposed to these training procedures, and their understanding of conservation was assessed. The first studies that were conducted showed very little effect (Flavell, 1963). Even direct didactic instruction seemed to have little impact. Later, however, a number of dramatic successes were reported (e.g., Gelman, 1969). Unfortunately, the interpretation of these successes was by no means unequivocal. Behaviorists regarded them as showing the sufficiency of their concepts for explaining the process of development. Piagetians regarded them as revealing inadequate assessment techniques, based on a lack of understanding of Piaget's theory.

At the time, the results of the confrontation appeared to be a standoff. Each school attracted its own devotees, and the rhetoric that was exchanged between them was inconclusive. In retrospect, however, the confrontation may be seen to have considerably clarified the strengths and weaknesses of each position.

DIFFICULTIES WITH PIAGET'S THEORY

The two postulates of Piaget's that provided the greatest difficulty were the assertion that children's development is controlled by the emergence of general logical structures, and the assertion that transition from one stage of development to the next is produced by a process of equilibration.

Difficulties with the Notion of a Logical Structure

From a purely rational point of view, two major criticisms were made concerning the notion of a logical structure. The first was that the concept was rather abstract, and hence difficult to operationalize (Brainerd, 1976; Flavell, 1963). The second was that the particular logical models that were proposed by Piaget contained mathematical or logical errors (Ennis, 1975).

From an empirical point of view, the problems that emerged were more serious. Two sets of data were particularly problematic.

1. Certain tasks, which appeared to share the same logical structure, were found to be passed at widely different ages. For example, conservation of number was passed at 5 or 6, conservation of liquid volume at 7 or 8, and conservation of weight not until 9 or 10. This phenomenon was difficult to explain within the context of Piaget's theory because—according to his theory—the only mental requirement for passing such tasks was the availability of a general logical structure. Why there should be a delay of several years between the application of a structure to one task and to another was not apparent. Piaget referred to this problem as the problem of *horizontal décalages*.

2. The second problematic finding was that the correlations among developmental tasks were often low or insignificant (Pinard & Laurendeau, 1969). This was true even for tasks that were passed at about the same age, such as conservation, classification, and seriation: the child who was the first in his or her age group to pass one was rarely the first to pass all the others as well. This phenomenon posed a difficulty for Piaget's theory for the same reason as the first. The theory assumed that the primary determinant of children's success on developmental tasks was whether or not they possessed the appropriate logical structure. If this were really the case, it is difficult to see why children who had the highest scores on one task of a given logical type should not also have the highest scores on the others as well (see Beilin, 1971a). And, if they did, one would expect a high degree of consistency in their rank order from one task to the next, and a high rank-order correlation as a result.

Finally, as a consequence of these rational and empirical problems, there were practical problems with the notion of a logical structure as well. Whereas the suggestion that instruction should be matched to a child's level of logical development was a promising one, it proved difficult to translate into practice. Matching instruction to a child's available logical structure depends on being able to specify what logical structure is of relevance to the subject area in question. It also depends on being able to assess the presence or absence of this structure in the student population. Neither of these objectives, however, was easily realized. The first objective was difficult to realize due to the abstractness of the theory. The second was difficult to realize due to the existence of décalage and low intertask correlations (Case, 1978b).

Difficulties with the Notion of Equilibration

The notion of equilibration was beset by a similar set of problems. From a purely rational point of view, the difficulty was that the term was not defined with much precision, at least in early versions of the theory. The result was that readers were left with only a vague idea of what the concept entailed, and hence of the process by which children progressed from one stage of development to the next.

From an empirical point of view there were problems as well. The major problem was how to explain the results of the training studies, particularly those concerned with the concept of conservation. As was mentioned in the opening paragraphs, the first conservation training studies did not show effects of significant magnitude. Subsequent studies, however, showed large and consistent effects. Moreover, as the years progressed, it became clear that these results were not simply obtained by investigators who did not understand what the conservation concept entailed. They were also obtained by investigators in the Genevan tradition, who understood the construct very well (e.g., Lefebvre & Pinard, 1972). These investigators showed that instruction could bring children who were not even on the verge of acquiring conservation to complete mastery. In keeping with Piaget's assessment criteria they also showed (a) that the insight would transfer to a wide variety of tasks, (b) that it would be retained over long periods of time, and (c) that it would resist countersuggestion as successfully as a naturally acquired concept.

If it could have been shown that successful instruction depended on inducing cognitive disequilibrium, then the results of these training studies could actually have been taken as a confirmation of Piaget's notions regarding stage transition. This claim was advanced to begin with (Lefebvre & Pinard, 1972; Strauss, 1972). However, it seemed difficult to maintain as further studies were conducted (Beilin, 1971; Case, 1977a). Thus, to a growing number of investigators from both camps it appeared that the training findings presented difficulties, both for the notion that development must invariability proceed at a slow pace, and for the notion that development can only occur by means of equilibrium.

Once again, in the face of the above rational and empirical problems, there were practical problems as well. To encourage equilibration and reflective abstraction in the classroom, one must have a good idea of what the processes entail. In the absence of such specification, all that educators can do is to utilize some of Piaget's testing materials as curriculum materials (see Kamii & Radin, 1967), or to base their curricula on traditional progressive principles. Neither of these approaches is a direct or satisfactory application of Piaget's theory (Case, 1978b; Groen, 1978).

In summary, it may be said that, as the 1960s wore on, an increasing number of difficulties became apparent with Piaget's theory, both to those who shared his fundamental epistemological assumptions, and to those who did not. The presence of such difficulties was of course to be expected. Any theory goes through its own growth cycle, in which its difficulties become progressively more apparent (Lakatos, 1970). What the difficulties did indicate, however, was the need for some sort of further theoretical development. Either a new theory would have to be proposed, or the existing theory would have to be revitalized in some fashion.

One of the first persons to respond to this challenge was Juan Pascual-Leone, a student of Piaget's whose original training had been in medicine and psychiatry. And the path which he chose to follow was the one of revitalization.

PASCUAL-LEONE'S THEORY OF INTELLECTUAL DEVELOPMENT

Pascual-Leone did his doctoral work in Geneva during the years in which the confrontation between Piagetian theory and learning theory was at its height. In response to this conflict, Pascual-Leone proposed a reformulation of Piaget's theory. He presented this theory in his doctoral dissertation, which he completed in 1969.

As Piaget had done with Baldwin's theory, Pascual-Leone preserved and explicated many of the elements of Piaget's theory. He also de-emphasized other elements, and introduced several new ones. The elements of Piaget's theory that Pascual-Leone preserved were as follows.

1. *The notion of a schema or scheme.* Pascual-Leone defined a scheme as a psychological unit consisting of two components: a releasing response (s) and an effecting response (r). The releasing component was hypothesized to consist of a finite set of distinctive features, which corresponds to an invariant pattern in the world. The effecting component was hypothesized to consist of an organized set of responses, whose activation is triggered by the releasing component.

2. *The notion of assimilation.* In keeping with Piaget's theory, Pascual-Leone defined assimilation as the transfer of an old scheme to a new context.

3. *The notion of differentiation.* Pascual-Leone defined differentiation as the modification in a scheme which takes place as a result of repeated application. He hypothesized that this modification involves the addition of new elements to the releasing or effecting component of the original scheme.

4. *The notion of accommodation.* Pascual-Leone defined accommodation as the change which takes place when a subject's attempt to assimilate a new situation to an old scheme proves unsuccessful. The simplest type of accommodation is the inhibition of the response associated with the original scheme. This process is available to most lower organisms, and accounts for extinction in the absence of reinforcement. Another type of accommodation is the application of a second scheme instead of the original one. This process is also available to lower organisms, and accounts for the sort of operant learning that is observed when a

reinforcement contingency is altered. Finally, more complex types of accommodation also exist, and are observed in higher organisms. The most important of these is the process by which structural invariants are formed.

5.   *The notion of a structural invariant.* Pascual-Leone defined a structural invariant as a superordinate scheme representing the relationship between two or more lower order schemes. He symbolized it as follows:

where s and r stand for the releasing and effecting components of two schemes, and where the bidirectional arrows stand for the association or relationship which is formed between them. Note that the existence of such structures implies a different sort of learning from simple differentiation. Baldwin had referred to this sort of learning as *coordination*. Piaget had distinguished several different types of coordination, including *reflective abstraction* and *reciprocal assimilation*. Pascual-Leone used the term *logical learning* to refer to any coordination of this sort. By the use of this term, he intended to emphasize that the underlying type of learning was the sort that led to Piaget's logical structures: what was learned was not some direct property of the external world, but some property inherent in the functioning (or logic) of the schemes that the child used to represent the world. For Pascual-Leone, as for Piaget, the child's higher order learning was not a direct product of external experience in the way that differentiation was. Rather, it was a product of the child's internal, logicomathematical experience, that is, the experience of schematic intercoordination and reflective abstraction.

In defining the above concepts in this fashion, Pascual-Leone was clearly attempting to come to grips with the problem of theoretical precision, and to adopt a notation that would be understood by, and permit more meaningful dialogue with, behaviorists. In addition to explicating these elements of Piaget's theory, Pascual-Leone suggested a number of additions to the theory, which produced a change in its overall structure.

1.   *Schematic activation weight.* Pascual-Leone hypothesized that, when any scheme is activated, it is activated with a certain strength or weight. He suggested that this weight is a function of several different factors.

a.   The number of cues that are present in the subject's psychological field, and which function as releasers for the scheme. The greater the number of these releasing cues, the greater the strength of the scheme's activation.

b.   The salience and organization of the cues in the perceptual field. The greater the salience of a set of cues, the greater the activation weight of the scheme that they release. Similarly, the greater the structural simplicity or *gestalt* of these cues, the greater the activation weight of the scheme that they release.

    c.   The number of cues releasing structurally related schemes. Once a scheme has been incorporated into a higher-order structure, activation of the other components of the structure will tend to activate the scheme itself, even in the absence of its own releasing cues. Thus, the greater the number of structurally related components that are activated, and the greater the degree of structural learning, the greater the activation strength of any structurally related scheme.

    d.   The degree of the subject's attention. The greater the subject's attention to a set of cues, the greater the weight of the scheme that they release.

    Pascual-Leone symbolized these four sources of activation weight or *schematic boosting* as follows:

> C (for the scheme's own cues)
> F (for the field effects)
> L (for the structurally related, or logical cues)
> M (for mental power, or attention)

He also pointed out that children's cognitive behaviour was always "overdetermined"; that is, that it was the product of all four of these energy sources applying together, and boosting an entire set of schemes, not just one scheme.

    To understand how these four factors might interact, it is useful to consider a concrete example. If one looks at the sentence in Figure 3.1, one will discover that it stands out quite sharply from the rest of the page. This is because the cues on the page are arranged in a particularly compelling fashion. The letters are larger and clearer. The words are surrounded by a large field of white. And the entire set of words is set off from the rest of the page by a dark black line. These particular aspects of the display constitute what gestalt psychologists termed *field effects*. In Pascual-Leone's system one would say that these cues give the words in question a high *field-weight*.

    Now if one directs one's attention to the actual words themselves, one will notice that the fifth word is not as easy to identify as any of the others. The specific bits of ink are just as dark. Moreover, they are organized in a pattern that is just as coherent. Thus, the problem is not due to a low field weight.

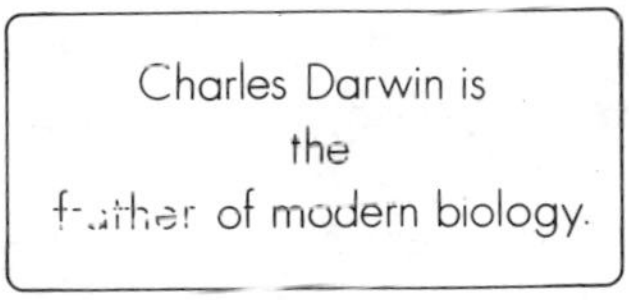

> Charles Darwin is
> the
> further of modern biology.

Fig. 3.1. Perceptual array illustrating functioning of Pascual-Leone's boosters.

Rather, it is due to the fact that one of the letters is not completely represented. The individual letters of a word constitute its releasing cues. Thus, one could say that the fifth word receives a lower *cue weight* than the others.

Although some of the cues for the word in question are missing, one will notice that one has no trouble in divining what it must be. The reason is clear. The other words in the sentence constrain the meaning of this word, so that the only logical possibility is *father*. In the context of Pascual-Leone's system, one would say that the low cue weight is compensated for by a high logical weight. The word *father*, in the context of Darwin and biology, has a higher logical association than any other possibility (e.g., *feather*).

The final thing to note is that one has no trouble in focusing on any one individual word by itself, even though it is part of a higher-order unit, and even though its full activation weight is identical to that for every other word. In everyday parlance, one would say this is because one has the power of selective attention. In Pascual-Leone's system, attention is seen as a reserve of mental energy, which is at the disposal of one's conscious processes. Thus, one would say that the total activation weight of any individual scheme may be increased by the application of M *power*.

2. *Misleading task structure.* A second element that Pascual-Leone added to Piaget's theory was the formal definition of a misleading task structure. When Baldwin first presented his theory of development, he illustrated the necessity for postulating a developmental change in the child's power of accommodation by putting two of his own children in a situation where a well-learned habit was elicited by a salient visual cue. He then pitted this habit against the demands of learning a complex new response. Whereas his older child had little trouble in accommodating to the new situation, his younger child kept being misled every time she saw the salient visual cue (Baldwin, 1894, p. 364). When Piaget designed his developmental tasks, he often adopted a similar procedure. For example, to determine whether infants truly understood the principle of object permanence, he first established the habit of looking for an object under one handkerchief and then—setting this same handkerchief plainly in view—placed the object under a different handkerchief. Children over the age of 10 months could overcome the original habit, and accommodate to the new situation. Children younger than that could not.

Pascual-Leone formalized the intuition of these two earlier theorists. He suggested that developmental tasks often have the following misleading structure:

a. The problem situation as set up by the experimenter requires that a particular set of schemes (x) be applied, if a successful solution is to be reached.

b. The perceptual field, often in conjunction with the child's previous learning, suggests that a different set of schemes (y) be applied. The application of these schemes leads to an incorrect solution.

The problem is therefore not solvable unless the child actively attends to the first set of schemes. This will boost their activation weight, and makes it higher than that of the misleading set. Pascual-Leone symbolized this sort of task structure as follows:

$$M_x \underline{v} \, (FvL)_y$$

This notation was intended to indicate that children could *either* apply those schemes (x) that would lead to success, and that were boosted by active attention (M), *or* they could apply those schemes (y) that would lead to failure, and that were boosted in the field (F) and/or previous learning (L). In effect, children experience a cognitive conflict, which must be resolved in favor of one set of schemes or another.

3. *Quantitative increase in* M. A third addition to Piaget's theory was the specification of a new rule for stage transition. The rule was that children progress from nonsolution to solution on a developmental task when their attentional power (M) increases to the point where it can activate all the task-relevant schemes. In formulating this rule, Pascual-Leone was of course returning to a notion that had originally been suggested by Baldwin, and which Piaget had deemphasized. However, he went beyond Baldwin's suggestion in providing an explicit definition of attentional power. Attentional power was defined as the maximum number of independent schemes that can be brought to full activation simultaneously. Pascual-Leone also went beyond Baldwin's suggestion in a second way, by specifying a set of quantum values for attentional power. The values he suggested are shown in Table 3.1. In this table, the symbol a stands for the attention required for attending to the task instructions and the perceptual display. The numeral represents the number of additional (task-relevant) schemes that can be centrated [1]

4. *Cognitive style.* A fourth element that Pascual-Leone added to Piaget's theory was the introduction of an *individual difference* factor. He suggested that subjects differ in their characteristic style of resolving the internal conflict that is elicited by tasks with the $M_x \underline{v} \, (FvL)_y$ structure. Moreover, he equated these differences with differences in the cognitive style that Witkin had discovered and labeled field dependence–independence (see Witkin *et al.*, 1962).

5. *Types of learning.* A final element that Pascual-Leone added to Piaget's theory was a formal specification of the process by which schematic differentiation (or *cue learning*) and schematic coordination (or *logical learning*) take place. Logical learning was assumed to take place quite rapidly, whenever schemes with a high (and equal) degree of activation weight were repeatedly coactivated.

[1] The same underlying hypothesis, but with different absolute values, was suggested independently by McLaughlin (1963) and has been developed by Halford (1980).

TABLE 3.1

Values of M Proposed by Pascual-Leone in 1969 and 1970

Piagetian stage	Age	M-Value[a]
Early preoperational	3–4	$a + 1$
Late preoperational–early concrete operational	5–6	$a + 2$
Middle concrete operations	7–8	$a + 3$
Late concrete operations	9–10	$a + 4$
Early formal operations	11–12	$a + 5$
Middle formal operations	13–14	$a + 6$
Late formal operations	15–16	$a + 7$

[a] This symbol represents the M-power required for storing task instructions, and directing a scan of the perceptual array.

Cue learning was assumed to take place a good deal more slowly, under conditions where only one member of a set of schemes had a high activation weight and the other schemes (the cues) all had low activation weights.

In addition to the features that he added or explicated, Pascual-Leone also de-emphasised two features of Piaget's theory; the role of logical structures in development, and the role of major qualitative shifts in cognitive functioning. Neither feature was eliminated. Logical structures were seen as playing a vital role in determining a child's thought. However, they were seen as the *product* of this development rather than the mechanism that produced it. Qualitative shifts were also acknowledged (in fact demanded) by the theory. However, no explicit distinction was made between the kind of qualitative shift that takes place within a general stage, and the kind that takes place across stages.[2] The four major stages thus played a relatively minor role in Pascual-Leone's theory, with the major role being assumed by the $a + 7$ M-levels.

COMPARISON OF PASCUAL-LEONE'S
AND PIAGET'S THEORIES

The object of Pascual-Leone's theory, it will be remembered, was to eliminate the weaknesses of Piaget's theory, while preserving its strengths. Before proceeding, it is worthwhile to examine how successfully this objective was achieved.

Consider first the basic phenomena of development for which Piaget's theory

[2] The only exception to this was the stage of infancy, which was treated as a distinct stage in some of Pascual-Leone's verbal presentations.

already provided an explanation. Pascual-Leone's theory was also capable of explaining these phenomena. The exact nature of the explanation, however, was somewhat different.

1. Piaget's explanation for the delayed acquisition of apparently simple concepts such as conservation had been that these concepts can only be attained by constructing a general logical structure, and that the construction of such structures is an inherently slow process. Pascual-Leone's explanation was that the tests of these concepts have a misleading task structure, and that the correct solution can therefore not be attained until a certain M-power has been achieved. In Pascual-Leone's system, then, it was the growth of M, not the rate of structural development per se, which was the inherently slow process.

2. Piaget explained the cross-task similarities in performance at different age levels by postulating cross-task similarities in the logical structure of the tasks, and a stage-related "structure of the whole" in the subject. Pascual-Leone explained these same similarities by postulating a common demand for coordinating schemes across tasks, and a stage-related size of M-power in the subject. Cross-task parallels in logical structure were of course not precluded by Pascual-Leone's explanation. Nor was the existence of very general structures in the subject. However, such very general structures were no longer seen as *necessary* for producing cross-task similarities in performance.

3. Piaget had explained developmental differences in readiness for learning by postulating differences in the structures that were available to different age groups. Pascual-Leone explained these same differences by postulating differences in available M-power. Developmental differences in logical structures were again not precluded by this explanation. In fact, their existence was virtually demanded. However, such structural differences were not seen as playing a necessary role. Within the context of Pascual-Leone's system, developmental differences in learning readiness were to be expected due to differences in the power of M, even if the internal structures of two different age groups were equated.

4. Piaget had explained universal sequences in development within a given domain by postulating a logically related sequence of underlying structures. Pascual-Leone's explanation was essentially identical. However, such structural sequences were again not seen as absolutely *necessary* for producing invariant behavioural sequences. Two tasks in structurally unrelated domains (e.g., walking and seriating cups) might be expected to show universal sequences if they differed in the number of schemes whose coordination they required (i.e., their M-demand).

Because the explanation Pascual-Leone offered for the basic phenomena of development was somewhat different from Piaget's, he was also able to explain most of the phenomena that had *not* been explicable within the Piagetian framework.

1. The phenomenon of horizontal décalage, which had been so troublesome

for Piaget's theory, was explained in a very straightforward fashion. It was suggested that tasks that share the same logical structures often make different demands on the subject's attentional resources. That is, they often require the coordination of a different number of more primitive schemes. Accordingly, such tasks are passed at different ages. Pascual-Leone analyzed a number of the more common types of décalage. He also generated a new set of tasks, and predicted the pattern of décalage that would occur on them (Pascual-Leone & Smith, 1969). A similar pattern of results, embedded in a more elaborate experimental design, was also found by Scardamalia (1974, 1977).

2.   The phenomenon of low-intertask correlation, which had proved equally troublesome for traditional Piagetian theory, was easily explained within the context of Pascual-Leone's system as well. Pascual-Leone pointed out that not all developmental tasks have a misleading task structure. Some merely require the coordination of a large number of schemes. Because a subject's degree of field independence influences his or her performance on the former sort of task but not the latter, one would expect that high-intertask correlations would be found only within a particular task type. In his doctoral dissertation, Pascual-Leone actually predicted the pattern of correlations for some 40 Piagetian and psychometric tasks (Pascual-Leone, 1969). The results confirmed his expectations. A similar set of high within-class correlations was predicted and demonstrated in a subsequent study by Toussaint (1974).

3.   The success of training studies was explained by suggesting that training could produce *chunking* between schemes which had formerly been independent, and thus lower the demands on the subject's attentional power (Pascual-Leone & Smith, 1969). Again, this suggestion was subjected to several empirical tests, and was confirmed in each case. It proved possible, by careful control of the M-demand of an instructional sequence, to predict the lowest age group for which it would be effective (e.g., Case, 1972b).

Because Pascual-Leone's theory preserved the empirical strengths of Piaget's theory, while eliminating its weaknesses, it had increased empirical power. The theory also had increased theoretical power. Most of the theoretical strengths of Piaget's theory were preserved: Pascual-Leone's theory was equally broad in scope, equally parsimonious, equally free of reductionism, and equally systematic. At the same time, the theoretical weaknesses were considerably reduced. The new definitions increased the theoretical precision of the theory. The specification of a stage transition rule and a rule for structural learning increased its completeness.

In addition to its increased empirical and theoretical power, the theory provided increased heuristic power. It suggested a number of new predictions concerning the relationship between task complexity and age of developmental acquisition, and between measured M-power and learning potential. Once again, most of these were confirmed (see Case, 1970, 1972a, 1972b, 1974; Pulos, 1979; Scardamalia, 1977).

Finally, the theory provided a framework in which the basic instructional implications of Piaget's theory could more easily be translated into practice. The reason was that instruction did not have to be geared to some general logical structure, but to the specific prerequisite structures of relevance to the domain in question, together with the level of M-power of the age group. Although a technology for accomplishing this objective was already in the process of being developed (see Case, 1968), Pascual-Leone's theory provided an excellent theoretical framework for interpreting the effectiveness of this technology, and for distinguishing its essential from its nonessential attributes (Case, 1978b). In effect, Pascual-Leone's work also increased the *practical* power of developmental theory.

In addition to these specific ways in which Pascual-Leone's theory differed from Piaget's there was one very general way in which it differed as well. This was in the overriding image of the young child that it presented. For Piaget, it will be remembered, the growing child was seen primarily as a young scientist: constructing ever more powerful models of the world, with a series of ever more powerful logical tools. While Pascual-Leone accepted this view as valid, it was not the primary one that he himself adopted. In his theoretical system, the young child was seen as an organism that was endowed with multiple sources of energy (M, F, L, etc.), and which encountered certain natural and recurrent conflicts as a result. Individual children were presumed to have their own distinctive styles of dealing with these conflicts. Regardless of their individual style, however, they were all presumed to develop intellectually because one of their energy sources (M) increased in magnitude, and acquired the power to override the others. Thus the predominant image of the child in Pascual-Leone's system was a dynamic one, which was closely allied with the image that is used in Freudian theory.[3]

To summarize, the particular form that Pascual-Leone's theory took was a direct and logical outgrowth of the confrontation between learning theory and developmental theory that took place in the 1960s. Pascual-Leone preserved and explicated most of the core constructs and postulates of developmental theory, in a fashion which made them more precise and more easy to operationalize. He also de-emphasized the two aspects of the theory that had been most prob-

---

[3]Readers of Pascual-Leone's more recent work may find this suggestion somewhat surprising because the image of the child as a *processor of information* is also present. In the early work, however, it was the Freudian or dynamic image that was the primary one. In fact, although this may be a moot point, I would argue that this dynamic image remains the central one today, and accounts for much of the theory's distinctive nature and power.

lematic: the assertions concerning the role of general logical structures and the role of equilibration. Finally, he re-introduced certain constructs that Piaget had eliminated, and added several new ones as well, ones that were shaped by his own intuitions about the mental life of the developing child, and his prior work within the psychoanalytic framework.

The results of these changes was a theoretical structure that was more precise and more easily operationalized on the one hand, and more dynamic on the other. In addition, it explained considerably more data. Not only did the theory explain the basic phenomena with which the field had traditionally been concerned, but also the more newly discovered phenomena that had appeared anomolous up to that point. The theory also led to a number of new predictions, many of which were confirmed; that is, it revitalized the heuristic power of the constructivist approach. Finally, the theory provided a firmer bridge between developmental theory and educational practice than had previously been possible. In large measure, then, Pascual-Leone attained the goal that was his original intent. He increased the theoretical, empirical, heuristic, and practical power of existing developmental theory, by addressing himself to its problematic aspects, and constructing a revised and expanded system in which they were eliminated.

CHAPTER 4

The Current Dilemma

INTRODUCTION

At the same time that Pascual-Leone was developing a revised theory of children's development in Geneva, an important change was taking place in North America. This was the replacement of behaviourist theory by information-processing theory, as the dominant framework in academic psychology. As was mentioned in the previous chapter, the studies that signaled the end of the behaviourist hegemony in North America were initiated in the mid 1950's. It was at that time that Newell and Simon, Chomsky, Miller, and Bruner all began their pioneering work. Although the penetration of their ideas into mainstream psychology was relatively slow, it was steady, and by the beginning of the 1960s there was a renewed receptivity to theories that attempted to model the complex internal processes which human intellectual functioning entails. It was during this period that Hunt (1961), and Flavell (1963) introduced North American readers to Piaget's work, and it was also during this period that Bruner introduced them to the work of Vygotsky (1962). Shortly thereafter, a distinctively North American brand of cognitive developmental psychology began to emerge, one that combined Piaget's and Vygotsky's insights with those of the new information-processing theory.

In the present chapter, no attempt will be made to summarize all of the changes that took place in North America between 1962 and the present time. Three major developments will be described, however, which had an important impact on the field, and which have influenced the approach that will be taken in the present volume.

BRUNER'S THEORY OF COGNITIVE DEVELOPMENT

The first of these developments was the emergence of Bruner's theory, as a counterpoint to Piaget's. As had Piaget, Bruner accepted Baldwin's notion that man's intellectual development is shaped by his evolutionary past, and that the thinking of the young child cannot be understood unless it is viewed in its proper phylogenetic perspective. He also accepted Baldwin's notion that intellectual development proceeds by a series of accommodations, in which lower-level schemes or skills are integrated to form higher-order ones. Finally, Bruner accepted many of Piaget's basic ideas, including the notions (1) that general structures play an important role in the developmental process, and (2) that it is important to have some formal means of representing these structures (Bruner, 1966). What Bruner could not accept, however, were the notions (1) that the process of structural acquisition is exclusively or even primarily an autoregulative one, and (2) that formal logic is an adequate device for representing the internal functioning of children's cognitive structures. To replace these notions Bruner proposed that (1) children's culture and language should be seen as playing a vital role in their intellectual development, and (2) children's intellectual functioning should be modelled using the formalisms provided by contemporary information science. The particular theory that Bruner constructed around these central notions was as follows.

1. Of the various biological capacities that emerge during the first 2 years of a child's life, three of the most important are the capacities for enactive, ikonic, and symbolic encoding. These three capacities emerge in their order of phylogenetic appearance, at approximately 6, 12, and 18 months of age, respectively (Bruner et al., 1966, Chaps. 1 and 2).

2. In and of themselves, these biological capacities are relatively insignificant. They gain their significance from the fact that they permit young children to develop elaborate representational systems; i.e., systems for encoding and transforming the information to which they are exposed, and on which they must act (Bruner, 1964, 1966).

3. Children do not invent such representational systems on their own. Rather, they re-invent them, in response to the active efforts of their culture on one hand, and their own biological disposition to attend to these efforts on the other. Development is therefore a process that takes place as much from the outside in as from the inside out (Bruner, 1964).

4. Of the various representational systems to which young children are exposed, none is more important than language. It is the mastery of the structure

of their native tongue that permits children to go beyond the sort of cognitive strategies that ikonic representation permits, and to develop the logical strategies that are characteristics of Piaget's concrete and formal periods (Bruner, 1964, 1966).

5. Although mastery of language is in certain respects complete by the age of 5 years, this sort of mastery is not sufficient to produce the qualitative shift in thought that takes place in the concrete period. In addition, children must learn to coordinate their *use* of language with their use of other forms of representation. In effect, they must learn to impose the structure of their language on that of their perceptual world (Bruner, 1964).

6. Different cultures provide a different amount of support for this process. Transition to the sort of abstract logical competence that Piaget described requires a type of cultural support that is provided only by formal schooling. Formal schooling separates symbolic from ikonic functioning, by putting children in a situation where words are systematically and continually present without their referents (Greenfield & Bruner, 1966, p. 389).

Of the various postulates that Bruner advanced, some of course attracted more attention than others and were subjected to closer empirical scrutiny. Two of the postulates that were evaluated most carefully were the ones dealing with the importance of cultural influences in general (Postulate 3) and formal schooling in particular (Postulate 6). Here it was found that (1) progress through the Piagetian stages varies much more widely than previously had been assumed, as a function of the culture in which a child is raised (e.g., Bruner *et al.*, 1966, Dasen, 1972) and (2) success on Piaget's tests of formal operations, as well as success on tests of certain other types of decontextualized functioning, appears to be strongly dependent on formal schooling (Cole *et al.*, 1971; Olson, 1977; Scribner & Cole, 1973, 1980; Sharp, Cole, & Lave, 1979).

Two further postulates that attracted a great deal of interest were the fourth and fifth ones; that is, the ones that dealt with language and its importance in the developmental process. Here, the pattern of results was somewhat more complex. On one hand, it was found that (1) certain broad structural parallels did exist between linguistic development and development in other domains (e.g., Greenfield *et al.*, 1976; Beilin, 1971), (2) children who had no verbal language at all—that is, the profoundly deaf—were also profoundly retarded on many Piagetian measures (Furth, 1966), and (3) verbally based instruction was capable of helping certain children acquire certain Piagetian concepts, at a younger age than they would have acquired them spontaneously (Beilin, 1971).

On the other hand, however, it was also found that (1) children who were deaf lagged only slightly behind their peers on Piagetian measures where they had received the appropriate background experience, and where the goal of the task could be communicated to them clearly (Furth, 1966), (2) there were many other measures of nonverbal development on which the deaf showed a perfectly normal developmental progression (Furth, 1966; Ray, 1974), and (3) training nonconservers to use the language of conservers appropriately had no impact on their conservation performance (Sinclair, 1969). While it was clear that verbal interaction could facilitate children's conceptual development, then, it seemed equally clear that such interaction was not absolutely necessary for development, and that such effects as were present did not stem simply from the appropriate use of language in a particular context.

A final pair of postulates that attracted considerable attention were those dealing with children's preferred modality of representation, and the impact of this mode on the cognitive strategies they employed. Olson was one of the first to undertake a study in which children's cognitive strategies were examined, and what he showed was that the pattern-verification strategies of 3-, 5-, and 7-year-olds were quite different (Olson, 1966). A similar result was found by Mosher and Hornsby, who found a qualitative shift in children's strategies for approaching the game of "20 questions" (Mosher & Hornsby, 1966). Both of these studies were conducted at the Center for Cognitive Studies at Harvard, and both were interpreted within the framework of Bruner's theory: that is both were interpreted as resulting from a change in children's preferred mode of representation.

At about the same time, however, Inhelder and her colleagues in Geneva also began an investigation of children's cognitive strategies, and they interpreted their findings within the more classic Piagetian framework: that is, they interpreted the shift in strategies as a consequence of a more general shift in children's logico-mathematical structures (Cellerier, 1972; Vonèche, October, 1979, personal communication). Finally, during the same general period Flavell (Flavell et al., 1963), Belmont and Butterfield (1971), and Brown (1974) began investigations of children's strategies on traditional tests of short-term memory. They, too, found a clear age-shift in children's strategies—a shift that accounted for a great deal of the improvement in children's performance during middle childhood and adolescence. However, they treated this shift as a datum to be explained by developmental theory, not as something that supported one theory or another. And, in fact, while subsequent research tended to support the hypothesis of a close connection between the *form* of children's representations and strategies used, it did not, by and large, support the notion that it is the *mode* of representation that is most important (Pascual-Leone & Smith, 1969; Strauss & Langer, 1972; Chi, 1981; Goldin, 1982).

In summary, it may be said that Bruner's theory led to three distinct lines of research, each of which bore considerable fruit. However, although the research on the role of cultural factors provided substantial support for Bruner's claims, the research on language and cognition provided only partial support, and the research on mode of representation provided little support at all. Rather, what it suggested was that it is the form of children's representation, not its mode, that is most significant.

At first glance, the foregoing results might appear to be rather disappointing. It might appear that the main value of Bruner's theory lay in its heuristic power, not its predictive power. To draw such a conclusion, however, would be unfair. For it must be remembered that the postulate of Bruner's theory that was not supported was a relatively peripheral one, while the postulates that were supported were those that were more central. At the heart of Bruner's theory lay the image of the child as the inheritor of cultural tools, one of the most important of which was language. And this image was in no way tarnished by the research that the theory generated. On the contrary, it was supported.

As the preceding lines of research were pursued, then, what happened was that Bruner de-emphasized or reworked those peripheral aspects of his theory that were not supported, and buttressed those more central aspects that were. Thus, by the mid-1970s, he had abandoned his claim that the major periods in children's lives could be defined by the mode of representation they used, and he had softened his claim about language, such that what he emphasized was its importance for providing children with easy access to the other intellectual tools developed by their culture, and which they would have to master themselves if their full intellectual potential was to be realized (see Bruner, 1980). Finally, Bruner had elaborated his claim about cultural transmission, stressing the importance of understanding the structure of the social context in which this transmission takes place, in order to understand the nature of the mental structures that result (Bruner, 1980a).

Between 1975 and the present, then, it has been this revised theoretical position on which Bruner and his colleagues have focussed. As a consequence, one of the major objectives of their research has been to elucidate the precise nature of children's early social experience, and the connections between this experience and their later development—both linguistic and nonlinguistic (Bruner, & Sherwood, 1976; Ninio & Bruner, 1978; Scaife & Bruner, 1975; Bruner, 1979). The data to which this research has given rise will be considered later, both in the present chapter and in the chapters which follow. First, however, it is necessary to consider several other events that took place in North America, at the same time as Bruner's theory was being developed.

INFORMATION-PROCESSING THEORIES OF COGNITIVE DEVELOPMENT

Newell and Simon's Theory and Its Implications

At about the same time Bruner began applying decision theory to the analysis of concept acquisition (Bruner et al., 1956), Newell, Shaw, and Simon began applying the same theory to the analysis of problem-solving in the domain of symbolic logic (Newell et al., 1958). The technique that these investigators adopted for testing their ideas, however, was quite different. Rather than simply describing subjects' performance as a sequence of decisions or operations, they programmed a digital computer to execute these operations, and fed it a sequence of problems in elementary logic. They then examined the fit between the performance of the computer and the performance of human subjects who were given the same problems, with regard to such variables as which problems could be solved and which could not, how long different sorts of problems took to solve, and what sorts of blind alleys were entered on difficult problems. To the amazement of almost everyone (and the horror of many!), the fit was remarkably good. In effect, the computer was behaving "intelligently" and providing a reasonable simulation of high-level human functioning.

From the time when they first presented their results, Simon and his colleagues pointed out that their work had important implications for theories of cognitive functioning, and theories of cognitive change. And, as early as 1962, Simon proposed a way in which his work could be integrated with Piaget's (Simon, 1962). His suggestion was that Piagetian stage-shifts could be viewed as the result of applying more sophisticated heuristic strategies to the sorts of logical problems that Piaget had invented, and that were solved at different characteristic ages.

In making this suggestion, Simon was pursuing a line of thought that was similar to that being pursued by Bruner during the same time period. It is important to realize, however, that there were important differences as well. Rather than viewing strategy changes and changes in logical insight as two related consequences of an underlying change in mode of representation, Simon was proposing that strategy changes might actually produce changes in logical insight, independently of any shift in mode of representation, or in the use of language. In effect, Simon's proposal was much more closely allied with Inhelder and Piaget's. For Simon, as for Inhelder and Piaget, changes in logical understanding flowed from changes in the set of organized cognitive operations that children had at their disposal. The only bone of contention concerned the most profitable formalism for representing such operations, and the ability of this formalism to capture the flow of cognitive events through time; i.e., to capture cognitive process as well as cognitive structure.

Evolution of Pascual-Leone's Position

A stringent test of Simon's hypothesis in the form of a running computer programme was not attempted until the early 1970s. During the interim, however, Pascual-Leone's theory underwent a substantial process of development, in response to the changing climate of the times. One of the first developments that took place was in the way in which children's cognitive structures were modeled.

As was mentioned in Chapter 3, these structures were first modeled as sets of schemes having the form

and a common logical complexity or M-demand (Pascual-Leone, 1969).

Given the power of the notion of a cognitive strategy, however, it was soon suggested that it might be profitable to reconceptualize such structures as sets of *strategies* or *executive procedures* (Case, 1970). It was also suggested that the primary role of children's culture might be to shape their executive repertoire, while the primary role of maturation might be to determine the rate at which their M-space grew (Case, 1970). Finally, it was suggested that developmental training might profitably be reconceptualized as an attempt to change the type of strategy children employed, and consequently its M-demand, rather than as an attempt to produce chunking (Case, 1970).

During the early 1970s, Pascual-Leone's theory underwent a process of differentiation and expansion, as these and other notions were tested, refined, and eventually integrated within its body power. In 1972, Pascual-Leone formally incorporated the notion of an executive scheme into his theoretical system, and relabelled his M-estimates accordingly.[1] He also began to model the step-by-step process through which such schemes were constructed and applied. Finally, he described the general flow of information that his theory implied. The result of this work was a further increase in the theoretical and predictive power of his system.

Klahr and Wallace's Theory

During the early 1970s, a number of other investigators were influenced by the change in the psychological *Zeitgeist* that was taking place. Consequently, a number of other information-processing models of cognitive development began to appear. The first models were those proposed by Klahr and Wallace to account for children's performance on tests of conservation and classification. Klahr and Wallace built their models in a fashion that could be simulated on a computer, which meant that the processes had to be modeled in microscopic detail, as programs composed of organized *program statements* or *production*

---

[1]Instead of describing a subject's M-space as consisting of two components, labelled *a* and *x*, it was now described as consisting of two components labelled *e* and *x*, where *e* was intended to stand for the space required for activating an appropriate executive scheme.

systems. After developing and testing a number of these computer models, Klahr and Wallace described the general systemic architecture that a young child would have to have, in order to develop in the fashion that their models described.

By and large, the assumptions they made about the hardware of the child's information-processing system were similar to those being made by other information-processing theorists at the time. The assumptions they made about the software of the child's system, however, were both original and important.

Consider first the software with which the human infant was presumed to come equipped at birth. According to Klahr and Wallace, three qualitatively distinct and hierarchically organized types of production systems were present. The first type was responsible for processing perceptual patterns and for directing the flow of attention from one pattern to the next (Tier 1). The second type was responsible for setting goals, and controlling the general flow of goal-directed activity (Tier 2). Finally, the third type was responsible for modifying existing production systems of either of the first two types, and for establishing new production systems (Tier 3). Thus, within the context of Klahr & Wallace's theory it was the third type of production system that regulated the organism's development, by the way it modified the production systems at the first two tiers.

Klahr and Wallace advanced a number of general hypotheses concerning the operation of their Tier 3 production systems, the most important of which were as follows:

1. During times when the organism is not engaged in processing much external information—such as those times every day when it is asleep—the third type of production system directs a *review* or *re-play* of its previous mental activity.

2. The object of this replay is to detect sequences in the organism's previous activity that are *consistent.* Thus, special production systems are available which monitor the record of previous events during the review period, segment this record into potentially consistent segments, and determine the degree of consistency from segment to segment.

3. Once such a consistent sequence is noticed, (i.e., once the similarity among segments reaches some critical value) another special production system is called into play, one which sets up a new production system to represent the consistency that has been detected.

4. Once several local consistencies have been detected, the group of new production systems is also scanned, in order to detect consistencies of a more general nature (i.e., patterns that remain invariant across a broader variety of situations).

5. Once such *common consistent sequences* are detected, new production systems are again established, in order to represent the more general invariants that these commonalities have revealed. These final production systems correspond to the logical structures that were described by Piaget. Thus, the process

that leads to their formation may be considered as Klahr and Wallace's explication—within the context of their information processing or computational metaphor—of the process that Piaget referred to as *reflective abstraction.*

Comparison of Pascual-Leone's Theory with Klahr and Wallace's Theory

At a general level, the approach taken by Klahr and Wallace was quite compatible with the approach taken by Pascual-Leone. Both theorists made similar assumptions about the overall structure of the child's cognitive system, and the flow of information within it. Both theorists also made similar assumptions about the basic units that represent this information, and the way in which they should be classified.[2] Finally, both theorists made similar assumptions about the way in which new structures are formed. Although Pascual-Leone did not propose a third type of scheme that was responsible for generating new schemes, his proposal for M-based logical learning was similar in many respects to Klahr and Wallace's proposals concerning Tier 3 production systems (see Pascual-Leone, 1972).

Although there were important similarities between Klahr and Wallace's theory and the expanded version of Pascual-Leone's theory, there were important differences as well. The first of these concerned the assumption that was made about general stages. For Pascual-Leone, Piaget's assumption concerning the existence of system-wide changes in development was accepted, and the notion of M-growth was invoked to explain them. For Klahr and Wallace, the notion of system-wide changes was not accepted. As they put it, "individual variations in the nature of the subsystems and in the developmental order of their appearance are regarded as being the rule rather than the exception" in children's development (Klahr & Wallace, 1976, p. 195).

The second difference between the two theories was related to the first. To explain the process of stage transition, Pascual-Leone postulated a growth in the size of the child's M-space, an entity that corresponded approximately to Klahr and Wallace's semantic short-term memory. Because Klahr and Wallace did not postulate the existence of any system-wide changes, however, they did not postulate any growth in the size of semantic short-term memory. And, although they did not suggest how the measured changes on short-term memory measures might be explained, their colleagues and students at Carnegie Mellon did (see Cavanagh, 1972 personal communication; Chi, 1976; Simon, 1972). The suggestion was that the measured changes in short-term span could be explained by

---

[2] Note the similarity between the definition of a scheme (an ordered pair, *s-r*) and a production system (a condition-action pair). Note, too, the similarity between strategic and nonstrategic production systems, and executive versus nonexecutive schemes.

the same sort of changes in the repertoire of production systems as had been postulated to explain the process of intellectual development itself. That is, the apparent development of short-term memory could be explained by the acquisition of sophisticated production systems: either production systems for representing and chunking the information to which the children were exposed (Tier 1), or production systems for dealing with the strategic demands that any cognitive task imposes (Tier 2).

Subsequent Empirical Investigations and Criticisms

The differences between Pascual-Leone's theory and Klahr and Wallace's theory were not nearly as central as those between Piaget's theory and behaviorist theory, or even between Piaget's theory and Bruner's theory. Nevertheless, they did prompt a number of interesting studies, which highlighted the advantages and disadvantages of each position. Two findings were quite easily handled by Pascual-Leone's theory, but were problematic for Klahr and Wallace's theory.

1. A number of studies revealed that the same rate of M-growth took place across tasks with very different formats, very different content, and very different operational requirements (e.g., Case, 1972b; Case & Kurland, 1978; DeAvila, 1974; Pulos, 1978, Parkinson, 1976). A similar parallel in the rate of development was noted across problem-solving tasks that involved different content (Siegler, 1976, 1978), different task formats, and different operations (Toussaint, 1974). While the absence of developmental synchronies was easily explained by Klahr and Wallace's theory, the presence of such synchronies was problematic. Because the model was one that ascribed the process of development to the detection of local consistencies, and to their gradual generalization within a particular domain, it was by no means clear how cross-domain parallels could be explained. In fact, they appeared to directly contradict Klahr & Wallace's statement that variation in the rate and order of subsystem emergence was the rule and not the exception in cognitive development.

2. Another set of studies revealed that, when children had a certain level of M-space, they tended to profit from instruction quite easily; however, when they did not have this critical level of M-space, they tended to progress very slowly, if at all (see Case, 1972, 1974, 1977b). Whereas the presence of learning could be accounted for quite easily by Klahr and Wallace's model, the absence was not nearly so easily explained, especially a highly regular absence that was predicted by the absolute level of a subject's M-space.

As is normally the case when one theory is compared with another, the data that were gathered were by no means one-sided. The findings that were easy for Klahr and Wallace's theory to explain, but which were problematic for Pascual-Leone's theory, were as follows:

1. Studies of basic operations such as pattern identification, visual scanning,

and counting showed large changes in speed and efficiency with development, even when a great deal of practice or *overlearning* had taken place (Day, 1974; Klahr & Chi, 1976). These findings challenged a basic assumption of Pascual-Leone's theory, which was that all schemes require the same amount of attention or M-power to activate, once overlearning has taken place. And this in turn raised the possibility that adults' and children's M-power might be equivalent, if the speed or efficiency of these basic processes was controlled (Case, 1978a; Chi, 1975, 1976; Dempster, 1977, 1978).

2. A second problematic finding concerned the performance of preschool children on tests of short-term span. For some time, it had been known that the performance of 4-year-olds on tests of word span was not 1 but 4 units. This had been explained by pointing out that no higher transformation of the stimuli (i.e., no cognitive *work*) was required. As new tests were designed for this age group, however, results began to appear that were not easily explained in this fashion. One of these came from my own research group on a test of short-term memory for familiar gestures. What we found, first, was that 4-year-olds received scores that were considerably better than 1 on this test. In addition, we found that adults received scores that fell several units short of Pascual-Leone's $e + 7$ units, even after they had been trained in gestural encoding and reproduction for several hours (Case, 1976; Furman, 1976). These findings suggested that the growth of span might be somewhat more complex than had originally been postulated, and that its relationship to the emergence of general stages should be re-examined.

In addition to the above empirical problems, a theoretical problem was raised with regard to each theory as well.

1. In the case of Pascual-Leone's theory, this problem concerned the grain at which tasks were analyzed, and the resulting difficulties in computing M-demand. Values of $e + 1, 2$, and 3 were quite reasonable estimates of the load of concrete operational tasks if one adopted a global level of analysis. However, it was pointed out that values much higher than this would be obtained if one adopted a finer grain of analysis (Klahr, personal communication, October, 1981). At a global level of analysis, for example, it is reasonable to assume that the 6-year-old strategy for determining which side of a balance beam will go down requires an M-space of $e + 2$ because what the children do is to compute and compare two quantities, namely, the number of weights on each side of the beam (Siegler, 1976). If one adapts a finer grain of analysis, however, it becomes clear that the act of quantification itself requires that a significant number of schemes be activated, both symbolic schemes in the counting string, and motor schemes for touching the weights and ensuring that they are considered in a sequential fashion. When viewed at this grain of analysis, one could say that the task involves an M-demand that is a good deal higher, for example, $e + 10$ or $e + 12$.

The point Klahr made was not that Pascual-Leone's theory was wrong, but that it needed some method for determining the grain of analysis that would be appropriate for any particular task if it was to be adequately tested. Without such a method one could not determine whether a failure to confirm one's hypothesis about the passing of a test was due to some fault of the general theory or to the fact that one had adopted an inappropriate grain of analysis, and hence computed the quantitative load incorrectly.

2. Ironically, the theoretical problem that Klahr and Wallace's theory encountered concerned the same difficulty, namely that of specifying the appropriate grain of analysis at which a cognitive task should be analyzed. This difficulty was first pointed out by Chi and Rees (1983). What Chi and Rees suggested was that, although Klahr and Wallace acknowledged that children's grain of analysis changed with development, they continued to model most of children's performance at an extremely fine-grained level, that of individual production systems. Because they did so, it was often difficult to perceive any general pattern in the developmental sequences which were modeled, including patterns that were quite apparent when children's higher-level production systems, or rules (Siegler, 1976), were considered.

Preliminary Evaluation
of the Information-Processing Contribution

Although early information theories ran into problems, they made at least two important contributions to the study of children's intellectual development. The first of these was the provision of a new set of conceptual tools for analyzing children's mental representations and procedures in a more precise fashion. The second was the realization that data on children's basic sensory and memorial capacities and data on their logical understanding should be unified. The debate concerning the mechanism of short-term memory growth not withstanding, investigators came to an implicit agreement that any theory of development must ultimately provide a unified account of the changes that are revealed by tests of children's higher cognitive processes and by tests of their more basic processes and capacities.

NEW DATA ON CHILDREN'S EARLY
COGNITIVE DEVELOPMENT

At the same time that information-processing models and theories of children's development were beginning to appear, important empirical discoveries were being made about children's intellectual competencies prior to the age of 5 years. Three major categories of discovery were of particular relevance to the work which will be reported in the present volume, because they posed a further difficulty for each one of the post-Piagetian theories that has been considered so far.

Studies of Early Language Development

The same revolution that led to a change in theories of human cognition also led to a change in theories of human language. The linguistic revolution was initiated by Chomsky, who proposed a structural theory of human grammar (Chomsky, 1957, 1965). As Chomsky's work became known to researchers in cognitive development, it began to influence the way in which they viewed the child's initial acquisition of language, as well as the way in which they investigated it. Rather than focusing on the child's acquisition of isolated words, they focused on the child's attempts to abstract the rules by which these words were generated. Although different investigators used different concepts and terminology, they by and large generated similar results, and arrived at similar conclusions. One important conclusion was that children's first two-word utterances already possessed a distinct structure or grammar of their own, one which was different from that of adult speech (Braine, 1963; Brown & Bellugi, 1964; Brown & Frase, 1963; Miller & Ervin-Tripp, 1964). Another important conclusion was that children went through a distinct series of stages from 2 to 5 years of age, en route to acquiring a grammar with a more adult form. As the 1960s proceeded, the grammars that were postulated at different ages became more sophisticated. They began to take account of the meaning (semantics) and usage (pragmatics) of language as well as its syntactic structure (see Antinucci & Parisi, 1973; Brown, 1973). At the same time, the age range that was studied was greatly broadened. On one hand, investigators began to study the more complex syntactic and semantic rules that are acquired during middle childhood (C. Chomsky, 1969; Fabian-Kraus & Ammon, 1980; Kessel, 1970). On the other hand, they began to study the linguistic and cognitive precursors of the child's first two-word utterances (e.g., Bates, 1976; Scaife & Bruner, 1975). Finally, during the same time period, there was an expansion in the range of linguistic units that was studied. Although the original focus had been on the sentence, this focus was soon narrowed to provide a detailed semantic analysis of individual words (e.g., Clark, 1973; Gentner, 1975), and broadened to include an analysis of higher-order units as well, units such as those involved in conversation (e.g., Olson & Hildyard, 1985), and stories (e.g., Mandler & Johnson, 1977; Stein & Glenn, 1979). As this work proceeded, it became apparent that the underlying principles that govern the acquisition of nonlinguistic knowledge are remarkably similar to those that govern the acquisition of linguistic knowledge (Slobin, 1973). It also became apparent that the rate of acquisition is similar as well; that is, there are parallels between the sort of linguistic knowledge that children possess at any age and the sort of nonlinguistic knowledge they possess (e.g., Bates, 1976; Beilin, 1975; Greenfield, Nelson, & Saltzman, 1976; Pike & Olson, 1977; Sinclair, 1971).

As these parallels were pointed out, it became clear that the acquisition of language could not be consigned to a device that was entirely language specific, as had originally been supposed (McNeill, 1966). Rather, it was more parsimonious to assume that some more general process was operative as well: one that applied to the full range of problem situations which young children encountered. This realization brought the phenomena of linguistic development within the purview of general developmental theory, and required that anyone who proposed a general model in one domain show at least some evidence that the model could account for phenomena in the other domain as well. On one hand, this was an extremely exciting development, because it held out the promise that a truly unified theory of human development might be reached. On the other hand, however, it was also somewhat discouraging, because it was by no means clear that any of the current theories were equal to the challenge. The problems that Bruner's theory had encountered with the data on language development have already been mentioned. The problems that Klahr and Wallace's theory faced were equally serious. Because their theory could not account for the cross-task parallels that were found within either domain, it seemed highly unlikely that it could account for such parallels as were found between the two domains, either. A difficulty of a different sort was encountered by Pascual-Leone's theory. Here the problem was not in accounting for cross-domain parallels in development. In fact, the M-mechanism provided a convenient basis for this sort of explanation (Bödy, 1977; Fabian, 1982). Rather, the difficulty was in explaining how any highly complex set of structures could be acquired with such rapidity between the ages of $1\frac{1}{2}$ and 5 years, with an M-power of only $e + 1$.

In summary, although the data on children's language development did not actually refute any of the general theories of cognitive development, they did pose each one of them a serious challenge. The challenge was that of incorporating a large new body of data within their existing structure, in a heuristically powerful and simplifying fashion.

Studies of Early Cognitive Development

As was mentioned in the previous chapter, the 1960s spawned a vast number of training studies, the goal of which was to show that children could be taught Piagetian concepts at a younger age than they acquired them spontaneously. During the early 1970s, the attempt to show that children could be taught to solve complex Piagetian tasks gave way to an enterprise of a different sort: the attempt to show that children *already* possessed many of the competencies supposedly assessed by Piagetian tasks, but that they could not demonstrate this competence unless more favorable performance conditions were provided. In an effort to substantiate this claim, investigators began to design more and more ingenious methods of experimentation, and to examine children's functioning at younger and younger ages.

One of the leading investigators of this enterprise was Gelman, who probed children's numerical competence during the preschool period (Gelman, 1972, 1978). Another leading investigator was Flavell, who demonstrated that children had the capability for spatial decentering (Flavell et al., 1968), a capability that was not achieved in its mature form until the period of formal operations (Laurendeau & Pinard, 1972). At Carnegie Mellon University, Klahr began to study the planning heuristics that were available to preschool children for solving their everyday problems, while at Yale Nelson began to study the development of their social scripts (Nelson, 1978).

The findings from these various strands of research of course reflected their differing theoretical motivations. Nevertheless, they were highly congruent with regard to the following two points.

1. They all showed that preschoolers were capable of handling complex procedures and concepts—far more complex, in fact, than might have been guessed either from Piaget's characterization of the period as preoperational, or Pascual-Leone's characterization of the period as one where children's mental power is only $e + 1$.

2. Every study that sampled the full age range from 2 to 5 years showed that children exhibit a great deal of progress within the period as well. In fact, there was at least some evidence to suggest that they showed as much progress during the preschool period as they did during the sensorimotor period which precedes it, or the concrete period which follows it (Case, 1976).

3. Finally, there was evidence of a structural parallel across domains as well; that is, there was evidence of development proceeding through a similar sequence of substages, and at a similar rate (Case, 1976; Case & Khanna, 1981; Greenfield et al., 1976).

At the same time as investigators were probing the nature of preschoolers' cognition, a similar effort was underway in the area of infant cognition. Bower (1969), Bruner (1968), and Lipsett (1969) were three of the first to initiate this enterprise. However, they were soon joined by a large number of other investigators, as techniques for exploring infant cognition and foci of interest began to multiply. Again, what these new analyses showed were

1. that infants were capable of more complex functioning during the first few months of life than had originally been suspected (e.g., Trevarthan, 1974; Meltzoff & Moore, 1977);

2. that there was a dramatic change in the level of functioning of which they were capable throughout the infant period (e.g. Bower, 1974); and

3. that there was at least some evidence of a structural parallel in development across different domains (Bates, 1976).

The general dilemma that the findings on preschool and infant cognition
raised, therefore, was closely akin to the one that had been raised by the findings
on the early development of language. On one hand, it was clear that any
general theory would have to account for the considerable complexity of
children's early mental processes, and for the systematic transformations that
these processes undergo across domains. On the other hand, it was by no means
clear how this task was to be accomplished because the existing theories either
(1) attributed a rather low intellectual capability to preschool children,
(2) described this functioning as local rather than system-wide, or (3) did not differentiate functioning during the preschool period from later functioning, in a
satisfactory manner.

Studies of Social Cognition

A third corpus of empirical data that was gathered during the 1970s concerned the development of children's social cognition. The theoretical motivations for gathering these data varied. One group of investigators approached the
topic from a Piagetian perspective, viewing their efforts as filling a gap that had
been left in Piaget's work, but which could be approached from a similar structuralist perspective (see Chandler, 1977; Damon, 1977; Furth, 1980; Selman,
1980; Turiel, 1975; Uzgiris, 1979). Another group adapted a theoretical stance
that either derived from, or was similar to, that proposed by Bruner. Thus, their
emphasis was on humans' biological predisposition for social and linguistic interaction, and the intellectual consequences of mastering complex rule systems
(e.g., Bruner & Sherwood, 1976; Trevarthan, 1974; Olson, 1980). Still another
group drew their inspiration from classical psychoanalytic theory (e.g., Schaffer,
1971; Stern, 1974) or learning theory (Meichenbaum, 1977). A fourth group was
more empirical in their focus, either concentrating on detailed naturalistic
observation (see Abramovitch et al., 1980; Goldman and Ross, 1978; Mueller &
Brenner, 1977; Ross, 1982), or devising new measures with some a priori
ecological validity (e.g., Flapan, 1968). Finally, a fifth group concentrated on demonstrating that—when Piagetian decentering tasks were simplified—they
could be passed prior to the age of concrete operations (e.g., Borke, 1971; Flavell
et al., 1968; Shantz, 1975; Shatz & Gelman, 1973).

Once again, this work posed several challenges for the process theories that
had been proposed in the wake of Piaget's theory. One of these challenges was
how to extend the sort of precise process or strategy analysis that they had
pioneered in the domain of logical cognition to the domain of social cognition as
well. Another challenge was how to model the acquisition of the child's earliest
social rules and strategies—those acquired in infancy and the preschool

period—in a fashion which would do justice to their complexity while at the same time discriminating them from those that were acquired at later stages. Finally, still another challenge was that of explicating the parallels which appeared to exist across the social and nonsocial domains.

Ironically, the investigators who had the greatest success in coping with the latter two challenges were not those who adopted a process approach, but those who preserved and developed the structural approach that had been pioneered by Piaget (see Chandler, 1977; Damon, 1979; Rubin & Everett, in press; Selman, 1978; Turiel, 1975). Nor was this true just for the domain of social cognition. The investigators who had the greatest success in explicating the parallels between linguistic and nonlinguistic cognition, and in differentiating early attempts to master complex linguistic rules from later attempts were also those who adopted a classic or neostructural approach (see Beilin, 1976; Karmiloff-Smith, 1979; Mounoud, 1982; Noelting, 1975; Pike & Olson, 1977). Although at first glance this might seem surprising, it must be remembered that, in spite of its drawbacks, one of the great strengths of Piaget's theory was that it offered a method and a conceptual framework for distinguishing children's cognition across broad periods of time. Moreover, it did so, in effect, by postulating that there was a natural grain to human cognition, that is, children at different stages of life operated at different epistemic levels, and that their approaches to tasks had to be analyzed in light of this fact. That some sort of structural analysis might be necessary in order to introduce order into the newly emerging data bases, therefore, was not really so surprising. In effect, structural analysis was best suited for describing the forest of cognitive development, while process analysis was suited for describing the trees. This being the case, a number of investigators began to suggest that the two forms of analysis should not be treated as antithetical, but should in fact by synthesized in some fashion (Beilin, 1983, 1984; Case, 1982; Cellerier, 1972; Inhelder *et al.*, 1974; Kuhn, 1983; Pascual-Leone, 1976; Stone, 1975).

STATE OF THE FIELD BY THE LATE 1970s

By the end of the 1970s the field of cognitive development was faced with an intriguing dilemma. On one hand, each of the post-Piagetian theories that had been proposed had solved many of the problems which had plagued Piaget's theory, and had offered an important new perspective on children's intellectual functioning. Moreover, each of the new theories had done so, in its own fashion, by focusing on the *process* of intellectual development rather than its *structure*. On the other hand, as time had passed, it had become apparent that each one of the new process approaches possessed some important problem of its own. In addition, there was also the common theoretical problem of how to organize the new data on linguistic and social cognition at all ages, and on cognitive development prior to the age of 5 years, in a coherent and heuristically powerful fashion. This problem was aggravated by the absence of any principled method of determining the subjectively appropriate grain of analysis for different cognitive tasks, and was in fact handled more successfully by classical structural theory, or variants of it.

The challenge with which the field was faced, therefore, was to develop a theory that would somehow incorporate the strengths of *both* previous sorts of theory—that is, of both structural and process theories—while at the same time eliminating each of their respective weaknesses.

The work that is reported in the present volume was initiated in direct response to this challenge. The work began as an attempt to incorporate the information-processing notion of an executive strategy and the Brunerian notion of a cultural tool, into the general theoretical framework that had been proposed by Pascual-Leone (Case, 1970, 1974). As the difficulties with this first version of the theory became apparent—particularly the difficulties posed by the data on overlearning of basic operations and logical competencies prior to the age of 5 years—a tentative revision of this theory was proposed: one that shared certain features in common with the notions that had been proposed by Klahr and Chi (Case, 1976, 1978a). Finally, as an attempt was made to use this theory to integrate the newly emerging data on linguistic and social development, and as the above-mentioned theoretical and empirical problems were further clarified, the theory was reworked a second time, and a stronger structural element was added (1978–1983).

It is the results of this second reworking that are reported in the present volume. In the next chapter, the metaphor of the young child that underlies the theory is described, together with the general approach to which this metaphor has given rise. Then, in the chapters which follow, the theory itself is described. Finally, in the last chapter, the problems that have been outlined in the past few chapters are re-examined—and a set of solutions is proposed. The present theory is also compared to several other theories that have emerged in the past few years in response to essentially the same dilemma (e.g., Fischer, 1980; Halford & Wilson, 1982), and several directions for further research are suggested.

CHAPTER 5

Toward a Resolution
of the Current Dilemma: Some Preliminary
Assumptions and a General Direction

In an attempt to resolve the dilemma that was described in the previous chapter, two sets of changes will be introduced in the chapers that follow. The first set is designed to improve the process analysis to which young children's thinking is subjected. The second set is designed to improve the structural analysis, and to permit it to be integrated with the process analysis.

In the present chapter, each of these sets of changes is described. Then, in the chapters that follow, the theory to which they have given use is presented.

THE CHILD AS A PROBLEM SOLVER

As was pointed out in preceding chapters, each developmental theorist has preserved a number of postulates from the theories that preceded him, deleted or altered others, and added a new set of his own. To some extent, this process has been goverened by an attempt to overcome the theoretical and empirical problems that previous theories have encountered. However, to some extent it appears to have been governed by another desire as well: the desire to capture some additional dimension of young children's mental functioning, one which previous theories may have foreshadowed, but did not really develop.

For Baldwin, (1895), the most important dimension of children's mental functioning was biological. He viewed the young child in a Darwinian fashion, as an organism whose intellectual development recapitulates that of the species from which it has evolved. For Piaget, the most important dimension of children's mental functioning was its internal logic. Piaget viewed the child as a young scientist, who constructs successively more powerful models of the world by the application of successively more powerful logico-mathematical tools. Each post-Piagetian theorist has accepted Piaget's basic image, but supplemented it with a new image of his own. For Pascual-Leone, the most important aspect of children's mental functioning is their mental energy. He sees the young child in a dynamic fashion, as an organism that is endowed with many sources of energy, and that encounters recurrent internal conflicts as a consequence. Each child is presumed to resolve these conflicts in his or her own characteristic style, but at higher and higher epistemic levels with each successive increase in M-power. For Bruner, the most important dimension of children's mental functioning is their adaptation to their social world. Like Vygotsky, Bruner's predominant image of the young child is as an inheritor and user of cultural tools. Finally, for Klahr and Wallace, the most important aspect of children's mental functioning is their information processing. Klahr and Wallace view the young child as a sophisticated computational system: one that is capable of modifying the programmes with which it has been endowed, in a fashion that is responsive to the environment in which it finds itself.[1]

In the theory that is proposed in the present volume, each one of the above dimensions of children's mental functioning is given at least some degree of attention. However, the aspect of children's functioning that is considered most directly and consistently is their problem-solving. Problem solving is not a topic that has been ignored in the previous developmental literature. Since the time of Baldwin, the standard procedure for testing developmental hypotheses has been to present children of different ages with small problems, and to model their responses to them. Nor has problem solving been a topic that has been ignored in the field of psychology in general. The interest in problem solving can be traced back from the work of Siegler (1983), Klahr and Wallace (1976), and Newell, Shaw, and Simon (1958): through that of Polya (1945), Dunker (1945), and Maier (1931): to that of Tolman (1932) and the Wurzburg school (see Humphrey, 1955).

Although children's problem solving has not been ignored in previous developmental theories, however, it has never been given quite as central an emphasis as it is given in the present volume. In the area of social development, the situation is somewhat different. The image of human beings as travellers, who have certain naturally occurring problems to overcome at each

---

[1] For an analysis of the epistemological assumptions that underlie these different metaphors, and their historical roots, see Case (in press).

stage of their journey, is a recurrent and a well-developed one (see Erikson, 1950; Levinson, 1978). In the area of intellectual development, however, this image has never played such a central role. For example, to be a problem solver is to be an organism that is capable of formulating its own objectives, and actively pursuing them in the face of such obstacles as the world may interpose. Yet, in spite of Baldwin's call for a "purposive" developmental psychology, the role of children's objectives or purposes in their intellectual development has rarely been considered in much detail.

In the present volume, this deficiency will be corrected. The overriding image of the young child which will be adopted will be that of an organism that is endowed with certain natural desires, and that encounters certain natural barriers to their realization, but which also has the capability for overcoming these barriers by refining and re-combining the inborn procedures with which it comes equipped. The image of the developmental process that will be adopted is similar. The developmental process will be construed as one in which higher-order purposes or objectives, as well as higher-order strategies for pursuing them, arise out of the refinement and coordination of lower-order objectives.

Of course, it must be admitted that the objectives which young infants set themselves at the outset of their developmental journey are of a very low order indeed. They include such modest goals as not losing sight of the interesting object that is circling above their crib, sustaining the smiling game in which they are engaged with their caretaker, or getting a pesky thumb back in their mouth. The solutions that infants fashion to these problems are likewise very modest, both in their structure and in the process by which they are generated. Yet what I will attempt to show in the present volume is this: it is in the solution of such simple and apparently unrelated problems that infants become capable of conceiving higher-order problems, and that they develop the competence to tackle such problems in a successful fashion. In effect, what I will attempt to show is (1) that by solving the simple problems which they encounter during the first stages of their lives, young children open up new vistas for themselves, new goals and challenges which they can then pursue at later stages, and (2) that in their pursuit of these goals lies the mainspring of their cognitive development.

Models of Children's Problem Solving:
Strategic Versus Prestrategic Processes

In an attempt to describe the young child's intellectual functioning, one must come to some decision as to the analytic tools one will employ, and the mental units one will impute to the growing child. For Baldwin, the basic mental unit at birth was the *circular reaction*. As these basic units were coordinated, higher-order units called *schemes* were believed to be assembled. Piaget preserved these two terms in analyzing infant cognition. However, he introduced a new unit for the analysis of higher-order cognition, namely the *logical structure*. Pascual-Leone analyzed children's mental functioning at the same two levels as had Piaget, at the level of the scheme and at the level of the logical structure. However, Piaget's distinction between figurative and operative schemes was given a more prominent position, and an additional set of higher-order constructs was introduced as well. These were the *metaconstructs* or *scheme boosters* such as F,M,A, and C. As will no doubt be obvious, the type of unit which each of these theoriests employed was not just compatible with the basic image of the young child which he held. In a sense, it may be said to have been derived from it. The same may be said for Klahr and Wallace, whose basic analytic unit was the production system, and for Bruner, whose basic analytic units were the cognitive strategy and the representational system.

What sort of analytic unit might be appropriate for describing the changes that take place in children's problem solving, as they move from one point in their development to the next? At first glance, it might appear that the most appropriate unit would be the executive strategy. As it is normally defined, an *executive strategy* is a mental procedure or plan for solving a particular class of problems. By very definition, this construct would appear to be an appropriate one to use in analyzing the developmental changes that take place in children's problem solving.

There are, however, two important weaknesses with this construct when it is used in this fastion.

1. The first is that the description it provides is incomplete. Although it does describe the set of steps that a subject performs to solve a particular class of problems, it does not describe the process by which the subject arrives at the insight that such a set of steps is appropriate in the first place. In a sense, what the strategy captures is the outcome of the problem-solving process, not the process itself.

2. The second weakness is that, very often, the strategies that children have in their repertoire do not change very much over considerable periods of development. Rather, what changes are the conditions under which an appropriate rather than an inappropriate strategy can be deployed. In fact, even when a clear developmental progression is apparent, younger children can often be taught to execute the strategy which older children deploy spontaneously, so that what remains is the developmental difficulty that they still experience in applying the strategy to complex or novel situations. If one wishes to capture the aspect of children's problem solving that changes most strongly with development, therefore, it would appear that one must examine the mental processes that are involved in analyzing novel situations, and in selecting or assembling an appropriate strategy for dealing with them, not just in the strategies which are used per se.

To say that one must model these prestrategic processes is not to say that the strategy has outlived its utility as a tool for developmental analysis. As a way of describing the intellectual tools which children acquire from their culture, the strategy remains an excellent device. Moreover, it is one that can be used to provide a powerful description of the developmental process. As a number of investigators have pointed out, development can be conceived as a process in which strategies are first mastered in highly contextualized and socially facilitated situations, and then expanded with regard to the range of situations in which they can be applied, and the degree of contextual or social support that they require (see Brown *et al.*, 1983; Bruner, 1979; Donaldson, 1978).

To say that we must model prestrategic processes as well as strategic ones, however, is to say that we must not stop our description of development at this point. For although terms such as decontextualization and generalization may well capture what is taking place from the viewpoint of the adult observer, they say relatively little about what is taking place from the viewpoint of the developing child. Note that when one interviews children to discover what their intentions were in approaching a particular task, one rarely hears comments such as "I was trying to think of something I had learned somewhere else, which I could apply to this different task." Rather, one hears comments such as "Well, I knew I wanted to get this, so I decided that first I had to do this." In short, what appears to be a problem of generalization or decontextualization from an adult point of view—and what is, in fact, just such a problem—may not appear to be such a problem from the point of view of the children whose mental life one is trying to model. From the children's perspective, the mental acts leading up to the deployment of a particular strategy may not involve any apprehension of the connection between the particular situation in which they find themselves and some other situation. Rather, they may simply involve an analysis of the current situation in its own terms, and the assembly of the most likely set of operations which will change this situation in a desired direction.

How might one model this sort of situational analysis? The most obvious method would simply be to back up and to describe the child's prestrategic processes in the same general fashion one already used for describing the strategic ones. Thus, one could describe a child's prestrategic processes as a sequence of mental steps, in each of which some operative scheme applied on a set of figurative schemes, under a specified set of affective and perceptual conditions. An example of such an analysis is presented in Table 5.1. The task is one that is normally solved around the age of 9 months, namely, that of removing a barrier which blocks the path to an object one wishes to pick up and manipulate. As may be seen, the number of prestrategic steps is considerably larger than the number of strategic ones. Moreover, by the time children make their first move toward the barrier, they have already solved the problem from a conceptual point of view; that is, they have already grasped the general structure of the problem, and what they must accomplish if they are to solve it. Thus, the sec-

TABLE 5.1

Sequence of Operations Required for Solving the Barrier Task

Step	Operation	Schemes (or productions) required to execute operation	Number of such schemes
1	Scan visual field	(i) SCAN. An operative scheme directing the movement of the infant's eyes across the visual field.	2
		(ii) OBJECT. 1, 2, etc. A sequence of figurative schemes representing the particular objects or areas of potential interest noted.	
2	Notice foreground object	(i) OBJECT. A figurative scheme representing the object placed in the foreground by the experimenter, and noticed by the infant.	1
3	Notice internal features of object	(i) FIXATE. An operative scheme directing the movement of the infant's eye within the contours of a single object.	2
		(ii) PROPERTY. 1, 2, 3. A sequence of figurative schemes representing the particular properties of the object that are noted.[a]	
4	Encode object as possibility for play (i.e., as a toy)	(i) TOY PLAY. A figurative scheme acquired early in the secondary circular period. The releasing features of this scheme are a set of properties such as "small, brightly coloured, etc. The effecting features are a set of pointers to possible actions such as picking up, tasting, throwing, etc.	1
5	Set goal of playing with object.	(i) GOAL SET. An operative scheme of the sort described by Klahr and Wallace as being at Tier 2. This scheme takes a set of pointers	2

to action possibilities as input, and establishes the translation of these possibilities into action as a goal. The sort of multiple-source boosting process described by Pascual-Leone would have to intervene prior to the activation of this operator; otherwise the infant would act on every possibility, regardless of mood, context, etc.

(iii) PLAY 1, 2. Figurative subschemes generated at previous step, indicating action possibilities.

6	Check conditions necessary for executing goal.	
	(i) PLAY EXECUTIVE. An operative scheme representing a conventional sequence of play actions, which is now functioning as an executive (i.e. which is now directing the overall flow of the infant's activity).	2
	(ii) CONDITION 1, 2. A set of figurative schemes representing the preconditions for play, such as that the object be in the hand.	
7	Set subgoal of reaching for object.	
	(i) PLAY EXECUTIVE. As above (Step 6).	3
	(ii) SUBGOAL SET. A Tier 2 operator that takes an unfulfilled condition as input, and sets its fulfillment as a subgoal.	
	(iii) OBJECT NOT IN HAND. A figurative scheme representing the unfulfilled precondition which must be met, for play to become possible.	
8	Check conditions necessary for reaching subgoal.	
	(i) PLAY EXECUTIVE. As above (Step 6).	3
	(i) REACH EXECUTIVE. An operative scheme representing the conventional sequence of reaching schemes, which was accessed and set as a subgoal in previous step, and which is now directing the flow of the infant's activity.	

(Continued)

TABLE 5.1 (*Continued*)

Step	Operation	Schemes (or productions) required to execute operation	Number of such schemes
		(iii) CONDITION 1, 2. A set of figurative schemes representing the preconditions for reaching.	
9	Notice barrier.	(i) PLAY EXECUTIVE. As above (Step 6).	3
		(ii) REACH EXECUTIVE. As above (Step 6).	
		(iii) BARRIER. A figurative scheme representing object in front of toy, and encoding it as a barrier to reaching.	
10	Notice internal feature of barrier.	(i) PLAY EXECUTIVE. As above (Step 6).	3[b]
		(ii)[b] FIXATE. See above (Step 3).	
		(iii) PROPERTY 1, 2, etc. See above (Step 3).	
11	Encode barrier as movable.	(i) PLAY EXECUTIVE.	2
		(ii) BARRIER MOVE. Figurative scheme whose releasing features are size and distance from hand, and whose effecting features is a pointer to the action of swiping, and the reaction of movement.	
12	Set subgoal of moving barrier.	(i) PLAY EXECUTIVE. As above (Step 6).	3
		(ii) SUBGOAL SET. As above (Step 7).	
		(iii) BARRIER MOVE. As above (Step 11).	

13	Check conditions necessary for activating subgoal (i.e., for moving barrier).	(i) PLAY EXECUTIVE. As above (Step 6).	3
		(ii) MOVE EXECUTIVE. An operative scheme representing the conventional sequence of action schemes associated with object movement (swiping, pushing). This scheme was set as a subgoal in the previous step, and is therefore now directing the flow of activity.	
		(iii) CONDITION 1, 2. A set of schemes representing the preconditions for moving an object.	
14	Set subgoal of reaching out to barrier with nearest hand.	(i) PLAY EXECUTIVE. As above (Step 6).	4
		(ii) MOVE EXECUTIVE. As above (Step 3).	
		(iii) SUBGOAL SET. As above (Step 7).	
		(iv) OBJECT NOT TOUCHING HAND. As above (Step 7).	
15	Check conditions necessary for reaching.	(i) PLAY EXECUTIVE. As above (Step 6).	4
		(ii) MOVE EXECUTIVE. As above (Step 3).	
		(iii) REACH EXECUTIVE. As above (Step 8).	
		(iv) CONDITIONS 1, 2. Set of schemes representing conditions necessary for reaching.	
16	Encode conditions as attainable.	(i) PLAY EXECUTIVE. As above (Step 6).	4
		(ii) MOVE EXECUTIVE. As above (Step 3).	

(*Continued*)

65

TABLE 5.1 (*Continued*)

Step	Operation	Schemes (or productions) required to execute operation	Number of such schemes
		(iii) REACH EXECUTIVE. As above (Step 8).	
		(iv) CONDITIONS OK. Scheme representing product of previous step (i.e., realization that subgoal can be achieved).	
17	Reach out toward barrier.	(i) PLAY EXECUTIVE. As above.	5
		(ii) MOVE EXECUTIVE.	
		(iii) REACH EXECUTIVE.	
		(iv) REACH. Operative scheme taking visual position of object as input, and moving hand toward it.	
18	As hand reaches barrier, sweep it sideways.	(i) PLAY EXECUTIVE.	4
		(ii) MOVE EXECUTIVE.	
		(iii) SWIPE. Operative scheme taking visual appearance of hand and object as input, and moving hand in strong lateral fashion.	
		(iv) OBJECT HAND. Figurative scheme representing relative position of object and hand.	

19	When barrier has moved, check toy availability (i.e., conditions necessary for executing play).	(i) PLAY EXECUTIVE.	3
		(ii) SCAN. Operative scheme directing eyes toward toy, to see if it can now be reached.	
		(iii) TOY POSITION. Figurative schemes representing position of toy.	
20	If toy available, set subgoal of reaching (if not, return to 17).	(i) PLAY EXECUTIVE. As above (Step 6).	3
		(ii) SUBGOAL SET. As above (Step 7).	
		(iii) OBJECT NOT IN HAND. As above (Step 7).	
21	Reach for toy.	(i) PLAY EXECUTIVE.	4
		(i) REACH EXECUTIVE. As above (Step 17).	
		(iii) REACH.	
		(iv) OBJECT POSITION.	
22	Play with toy (Hurray!).	( ) PLAY EXECUTIVE.	2
		(ii) TASTE, SHAKE, THROW, etc.	

[a] For evidence that such properties of the object are differentiated from each other by 4 months of age, see Bower (1974).
[b] Note that reaching need not be retained as a subgoal because it can be regenerated from play executive if barrier is successfully dealt with.

67

ond change that will be introduced in the present volume is the use of this sort of prestrategic analysis of children's problem-solving processes, along with a strategic analysis.

FORMAT OF THE PRESENT PROBLEM SOLVING ANALYSIS

Although the sort of analysis in the table appears to represent a step in the right direction, and should improve the process analysis to which children's cognition is subjected, it actually intensifies the major dilemma which was mentioned in the previous chapter, namely, describing the "forest" of cognitive development in a fashion that is faithful to what we have learned in the last 15 years about the "trees." Because if one were to model all of the problems that children master in the course of their development in the sort of fine-grained fashion that is indicated in the table, there is a good chance that one might expire before the task was completed. And, even if one did not, it is by no means certain that any overall pattern would emerge as a result of one's efforts.

The reason for this was also hinted at in the previous chapter. It is a natural property of such process analyses that they provide a better description of the details of children's problem solving on particular tasks than they do of the overall pattern which obtains across different tasks, or across different age levels. Similarly, it is a natural property of structural analyses that they provide a better description of the overal pattern of mental functioning across different tasks at different age levels, than they do of any task-specific process. If one wishes to model both the forest, *and* the trees, therefore, one must heed the advice of contemporary developmentalists such as Beilin (1983). One must stop treating structural analysis as an outmoded approach, and process analysis as the "new wave". Instead, one must find a method of analysis that combines these two perspectives in some sort of productive fashion. A second major goal that will be pursued in the present volume, then, will be the attempt to forge such a synthesis.

The higher-order unit that will be used for this purpose is the *executive control structure*. By definition, an executive control structure is an internal mental blueprint, which represents a subject's habitual way of construing a particular problem situation, together with his or her habitual procedure for dealing with it. In the present volume, all executive control structures will be presumed to contain at least three components: (1) a respresentation of the problem situation, that is, a representation of the conditions for which the plan is appropriate, and in which children sometimes finds themselves; (2) a representation of their most common *objectives* in such a situation, that is, the conditions which they desire, and toward whose achievement their plan is directed; and (3) a representation of the *strategy* they employ, that is, the set of mental steps that they develop for going from the problem situation to the desired situation, in as efficient a manner as possible.

As long as one focuses on the executive control structures that children possess at different points in their development, one ensures that the mental activity which precedes the assembly or application of any particular strategy, as well as the strategy itself will be described. If one is going to preserve the advantages of both structural and process analysis, however, it is not sufficient simply to change the nature of the higher-order mental unit in this fashion. In addition, one must change the way in which one *describes* that unit. Somehow, one must describe the unit in a fashion that specifies both the process by which that unit is assembled in particular situations, and the final structure which it takes.

In an attempt to achieve both of these objectives, a new form of notation will be adopted for the balance of the present volume. The simplest way to introduce this notation is by means of a concrete example. Consider, therefore, the executive control structure on which successful solution of the barrier removal problem depends. Using the form of notation that is employed throughout the present volume, this executive control structure would be represented as follows:

PROBLEM SITUATION	OBJECTIVES
• Interesting object (toy) at X	• Play with object at X
• Second object on path to X	• Move second object out of path
• Second object within reach at Y	• Move hand from Z to Y

STRATEGY

1. Move arm in direction Y.
2. Push object at Y with hand, until it moves.
3a. Check availability of object at X. If available, go to 3b; otherwise, return to Step 2.
3b. Move hand toward object at X.
4. When hand touches toy at X, pick it up and begin to play with it.

A process description of the mental acts that are involved in solving the barrier-removal problem may be obtained by reading in the direction indicated by the arrows. When read in this fashion, the notation suggests that the children's work on the problem begins when they first spot the toy that interests them, and set themselves the goal of playing with it. As they look at the toy, or as they stretch out their arms to reach for it, they catch sight of the object that is blocking the path. Once they spot this object, they set themselves the subgoal of removing it, which in turn requires that they notice its position relative to their hand, and set themselves the second subgoal of moving their hand in the appropriate direction. It is at this point, that the problem is solved from a psychological point of view. That is, it is at this point that children can mentally see their way through the problem, from the ultimate goal they want to achieve, to the first step that is necessary to set out on that path. Once children can envision the general form of a problem solution, all they need do is work their way back up the list of objectives: unpacking each subgoal one at a time, and achieving it by means of the appropriate motor movement. The order in which the steps of the strategy unfold, therefore, is the reverse of that which is indicated in the list of objectives.[2]

The above notation can also be used to provide a structural description of the set of mental elements on which the problem solution depends, and their interrelationship. First, it should be clear that there are three different kinds of elements: one relating to the problem representation, another relating to the subject's goals, and a third relating to the set of operations for bridging the gap between the two.

Within the category of problem representations, it may be seen that there are three basic subelements that are critical to the problem, and which the child must apprehend. These are: (1) that there is an interesting object in the environment, (2) that access to this object is blocked by a barrier, and (3) that the barrier is within arm's reach. Within the category of task objectives there are also three subelements. The relationship among these elements — which is one of subordination — is indicated by indentation. Thus, the structure of the objective list may be read as follows: Children must move their hands to the barrier *in order to* move the barrier, *in order to* play with the toy behind it. Finally, the strategy for achieving these objectives involves four basic steps, whose structure is indicated by enumeration.

The above model of children's mental processes is somewhat global, as is the form of notation with which the model is represented. No indication is provided of the blind alleys children might take en route to attaining their final objective. No indication is provided, either, of the perceptual and affective factors that might influence them in this process. Finally, no indication is provided of the declarative knowledge which the above model presupposes: knowledge such as the fact that small objects can be moved, that they exhibit "fun" reactions when manipulated, and so on.

Although it constitutes a somewhat global model of children's problem solv-

---

[2] Note that there is no necessary connection between the number of objectives and the number of strategic steps.

ing, the preceding type of analysis does have a number of advantages. The first of these has already been mentioned; namely, that the notation permits one to represent information which is of relevance both to the structure of children's mental operations, and to the process by which these operations are applied. A second advantage has also been hinted at; namely, that one can represent this information in a compact fashion (i.e., in a form that will maximize the possibility of extracting features of children's development which are general from those which are task specific). A third advantage is that the notation implicitly embodies all four of the central assumptions on which the image of the young child as a problem solver depends; namely,

1. that young children are capable of respresenting the elementary perceptual features in the world around them, from an early age,

2. that young children are capable of representing familiar states or actions which are not currently present, as well as those that are,

3. that young children have affective reactions to the perceptual or motoric states which they represent, and

4. that young children have some control over which particular cognitive and affective states they experience: (i.e., that they are capable of setting desirable states which they are not currently experiencing as goals, and of working towards them).

Finally, two additional advantages of the above form of modeling should be mentioned. These are:

1. that it permits one to model higher-order goals such as playing with an object, as the nested combination of two lower-order goals such as touching an object and watching it react, and

2. that it allows one to represent organizational changes that occur with time or practice in prestrategic as well as in strategic processes.

The importance of the latter two features will become apparent when children's problem solving is modeled at several different points in time, and the question of stage transition is considered. For the moment, however, it is important to consider the general use to which the above form of analysis will be put, and the type of content to which it will be applied, in the rest of the present volume.

CONTENT TO WHICH THE NEW FORM
OF ANALYSIS IS APPLIED

The general use toward which the preceding form of analysis will be put is to clarify the sort of thinking that children exhibit at different points in time, and the relationship of that thinking to the sort of thinking that precedes and follows it. In order to accomplish this objective, however, it is not sufficient merely to have an appropriate analytic device, one must also apply this analytic device to the appropriate sort of task. This means that one must come to some decision regarding what sort of content one will analyze (i.e., which of the many problems children encounter at different points in their lives one will take as significant and choose to consider). Two conventional criteria will be used to guide the selection which is made in subsequent chapters. The first criterion is simply ecological validity. Other things being equal, the tasks that are analyzed will be those which children encounter in their day-to-day lives, across as wide a variety of human cultures as possible.

The second criterion will be equally conventional, namely the availability of detailed empirical data. Other things being equal, the tasks which will be analyzed will be ones where sufficient data exists to specify the features of the problems to which children attend, and the strategies which they employ in solving them.

The third and final criterion is less conventional. Other things being equal, the tasks that are analyzed will be those for which reasonably detailed success data exist, both across and within stages.

As recently as the 1960's this third criterion would have been impossible to implement. At each stage of children's lives, the content of the most salient problems they can solve changes considerably. During infancy, the most salient problems which children master are those having to do with the use of their limbs and the manipulation of the objects in their environment. In the preschool period, the most salient problem children master is that of cracking the symbolic code on which communication in their culture is based. During the elementary school period, the most salient problems which children master are those having to do with the work-related skills of their culture. Finally, during adolescence, the most salient problems which children master are those having to do with abstract systems of thought, whether in science or in morality. Until very recently, therefore, it was the preceding four types of problems which were studied most intensively at each of the stages in question.

A problem arises with this general form of proceeding, however, when it comes to the analysis of stage transition, for although it is relatively easy to describe the transitions which take place within a stage, it is quite difficult to describe the transitions which take place across stages. The appearence of new structures at each stage appears to have a certain mysterious quality, as though they arose out of the depths of the child's intrapsychic life, by some little-understood transformation of the cognitive system as a whole. At the very best, one can suggest that the emergence of language has to await the construction of a world in which there are permanent objects to refer to (Gopnik, 1983; Piaget, 1951), that the emergence of concrete logic has to await the internalization of a language with which to represent logical problems (Bruner, 1964; Vygotsky, 1934/1962), and that the emergence of formal-operational groups has to await the consolidation of more concrete operational groupings (Inhelder & Piaget, 1958).

Although there may well be a transformation of the system as a whole at each stage, however, it is important not to obscure the nature of this transformation by confounding a change in the complexity of the problems which children can solve with a change in the content. And, with the recent investigations of infant and preschool cognition as a guide, it is now possible to separate these two factors. If there is one trend that has characterized almost all the empirical research that has been done since the mid-1960's it has been that the age in which positive examples of particular types of thinking have been found has been extended "downwards" (see, Bruner *et al.*, 1966; Flavell *et al.*, 1968; Gelman, 1969, 1972). This has been true not only for logical competencies, whose study had previously been restricted to middle childhood, but for linguistic competencies (e.g., Bates, 1976; Scaife & Bruner, 1975) and scientific competencies as well (Noelting, 1975; Seigler, 1976). A parallel trend has emerged in the opposite direction, with certain investigators examining the development of sensorimotor skills after infancy (see Todor, 1979) and others investigating the development of language after the age of 5 years (Beilin, 1975; C. Chomsky, 1969; Kessel, 1970).

What this work allows one to do therefore, is to adopt the criterion of holding task content or problem domain constant, and to look at the development of children's executive control structures within a particular domain from one stage to the next. And, as will be shown in the ensuing chapters, the picture of development that emerges when this criterion is applied is considerably different from the picture which emerges when it is not. Although the problem solving of one stage may still be identified as being qualitatively different from that of the previous stage, and although many of Piaget's general statements regarding stage transition may still be seen to have some validity, the executive structures of one stage no longer appear to emerge mysteriously, or to have only tenuous links to the executive structures of previous stages. Rather, they may be seen to be clearly rooted in the structures of these earlier stages, and to emerge by a process which can be specified in considerable detail.

MANNER IN WHICH RESULTS
OF ANALYSES ARE AGGREGATED

If one's ultimate objective is to describe the overall pattern or structure of children's intellectual development, one can obviously not stop with the analysis of children's development in one particular problem domain. Rather, one must go on to analyze their development in several different problem domains, and determine what similarities and differences exist.

This was the major methodological innovation that was introduced by Piaget. Baldwin, too, had used what came to be known as the *clinical method* in studying the development of his own children. However, he had never presented his children with such a wide range of problems as did Piaget, and he had therefore not been able to draw any firm conclusions with regard to the generality of the pattern he observed. From the time in which Piaget began his studies of his own children, this was the procedure he adopted. He almost never examined a sequence of developmental changes that took place on one task or in one problem domain in isolation. Rather, he considered several such developmental sequences at once, and searched for commonalities in underlying structure among them.

Still, given that one is going to adopt this strategy, one still has the problem of how to do so, that is, of how to aggregate the results of one's individual analyses, so that any overall pattern in development will be apparent. In the present volume, the following procedure will be used. In the first chapter of the next section (Chapter 6) the sequence of executive structures that children assemble in one particular content domain will be analyzed, from 1 or 2 months to full maturity. This will permit a preliminary description of the way in which children's control structures at one point in time relate to those at other points in time, without confounding developmental changes in problem complexity with developmental changes in problem domain. With such a description in hand, the period of infancy will then be reconsidered, and the sequence of control structures which emerge in a variety of other problem domains will be considered as well. This will permit two further questions to be addressed (1) to what extent do children apply the same type of control structure across different domains, at any given age (i.e., to what extent does infant development reveal a common *horizontal structure*; see Flavell, 1982)?, and (2) regardless of whether or not horizontal structure exists, to what extent do children develop a similar sequence of structures in different domains (i.e., to what extent is there a common *vertical structure*; see Flavell, 1982)? Once these questions are answered for the period of infancy (Chapter 7) they will be re-posed for each subsequent period of development in turn, with one additional chapter devoted to the analysis of children's control structures during early childhood (Chapter 8), middle childhood (Chapter 9), and adolescence (Chapter 10). Finally, in the last chapter of the section (Chapter 11) several general conclusions will be drawn and some new data will be reported which have been gathered to test them.

Before embarking on the next section, one final comment is in order, with regard to the possible difficulties the reader may encounter, in working through the large number of task analyses that are presented.

For the general reader, or for the reader whose background is in structural analysis, the most likely difficulty will be that the details of the various analyses will appear as impediments to apprehending the overall pattern of development. The general reader may also feel that little is being asserted with regard to this pattern that was not already asserted by Piaget, and so there is little to be gained from scrutinizing the analyses in a detailed fashion.

To some extent, it must be admitted, this point of view is valid. There is a strong similarity between the picture of development that will emerge in the next few chapters, and that which was painted by Piaget. And it is not necessary to scrutinize the details of every analysis in order to apprehend the general nature of this pattern. I would urge the general reader, however, to scrutinize the details of at least some of the analyses, because the further one progresses in the book, the more the general pattern which emerges will diverge from that described by Piaget. And the more it does diverge, the more it will be necessary to understand the details of the task analyses—not just to explain the overall pattern of development but simply to apprehend it.

For the reader who is a specialist, or whose background is in process analysis, a problem of a different sort may be encountered. For such a reader, the problem may be that the task analyses that are presented will not appear to be sufficiently detailed. Alternatively, they may not appear to be supported by a sufficient data base. Thus, the reader with this sort of background may feel that the theory to which the analyses give rise is either too global or too speculative.

Once again, it must be admitted that there is some merit to this point of view. Given the data that are currently available, it is not possible to generate a highly detailed analysis of every important problem which children solve, during each major period of their development. Nor is it even possible to generate global analyses that are open to no counterinterpretation. It is therefore quite possible that certain analyses will contain errors, either in their general form, or in certain specific details.

Here I would make a request of a different sort. I would ask readers who feel that such errors exist to ask themselves one further question: are the errors or difficulties consistent, that is, do they re-appear across all the various analyses which are presented? Or are they unique to one particular task or one particular age level? Because it must be remembered that the objective of conducting these analyses is to present an accurate picture of the overall pattern of children's development. And it is only if such errors or difficulties as exist are consistent that the overall pattern which emerges will be inaccurate. As long as the errors are not consistent they will tend to cancel each other out, and leave the overall picture unaltered—much as they do in the study of evoked cortical potential, or any other set of data in which both signal and noise are present.

SUMMARY OF PART I AND CONCLUSION

The two questions with which theories of intellectual development have historically been concerned are (1) how best to describe children's intellectual functioning at different points in their development, and (2) how best to explain the process by which they move from one of these points to the next. A third question has often been addressed as well, namely (3) how to create an optimal educational environment, so that each individual child can realize his or her full developmental potential. In the ensuing chapters, a new theory of intellectual development will be presented, one that suggests a revised answer to each of these questions. The exposition of the theory will be divided into three further sections, with one section corresponding to each of the questions mentioned above.

In the preliminary section that has just been completed, I have attempted to set the stage for the theory which will be outlined, by describing the tradition out of which this theory has grown, and to which it will hopefully contribute. This tradition began at the turn of the century with the work of Baldwin. It was continued and developed by Piaget, whose most important work was completed during the years from 1920 to 1960. And it has been further developed and refined by a number of post-Piagetian theorists, including Bruner (1964), Pascual-Leone (1969), and Klahr and Wallace (1976). Each generation of theorists has preserved many of the postulates which it inherited from its predecessors. In addition, however, it has also added others, and modified or deleted still others. The result has been a succession of theoretical systems, each one building on the one before it, but possessing a distinctive structure and coherence of its own.

A number of factors have no doubt contributed to the process of successive restructuring. As is illustrated in Figure 5.1, however, three of the most important appear to be the following: (1) the discovery of some theoretical or empirical problem with the existing theory, often as a result of comparing it to some other theory; (2) the discovery of a new corpus of data, one which was not incompatible with the existing theory, but which was not organized or simplified by it either; and (3) the development of some new conceptual tool, one which permitted children's cognition to be modeled in a more sophisticated fashion, and the existing problems to be resolved.

Barely 20 years have passed since the first generation of post-Piagetian theories was proposed. During this short time period, however, the level of activity in the field has increased considerably. The result is that a set of conditions now prevails which is similar to that which motivated the construction of this generation of theories in the first place. In particular, (1) sufficient theoretically based research has been completed to reveal that each one of the major post-Piagetian or process theories faces some significant theoretical or empirical problem of its own; (2) a large corpus of new data has been gathered—on children's linguistic and social development at all ages, and on children's cognitive functioning in infancy and early childhood—which none of the newer theories appears capable of organizing in as powerful or generative a fashion as did Piaget's; and (3) finally, although no new conceptual tool has been developed, it has been suggested that the tools that are already available can be used in a more productive

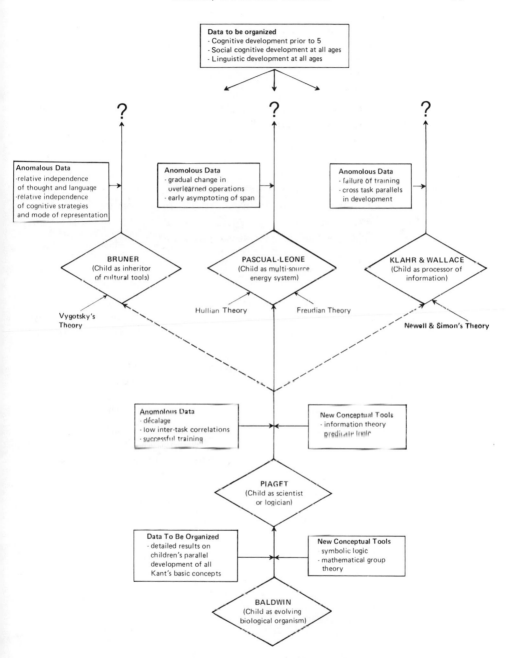

Fig. 5.1. Summary of major developments in the field, from its inception to the present time.

fashion, one which permits the advantages of both process and structural approaches to be preserved, and perhaps even to be improved upon.

It is this sort of synthetic approach that I have taken over the past few years, and whose results I shall report in the chapters that follow. The basic image of the young child will be that of a problem solver; that is, an organism which is endowed with certain natural desires and which encounters certain naturally occurring barriers to their realization, but which is also endowed with the capability for overcoming at least some of these barriers, via a sequence of problem-solving acts. The type of process analysis to which the young child's thinking will be subjected will be one that attempts to capture the essence of these problem-solving acts, as well as the strategies to which they give rise. Finally, the basic analytic unit that will be used is the executive control structure, a tripartite entity that includes a representation of the situation in which children find themselves, the objectives they hope to accomplish, and the strategy which they apply for doing so.

In order to capture the general structure of the changes that take place in children's executive processing with age, their problem solving will first be examined from birth to adulthood within a particular content domain. Various within-domain analyses will then be pooled, in order to determine whether any cross-domain parallels exist, either in the general sequence of changes that is observed (vertical structure), or in the form of structure that is observed across domains at particular age levels (horizontal structure). Then, once children's problem-solving structures at different ages have been described in this fashion, a model of stage transition will be presented.

Finally, in the last chapter, the problems that originally motivated the construction of the present theory (i.e., the problems posed by structural or process theories in isolation) will be reconsidered. A solution to each one of these problems will be proposed, and several directions for further research will be suggested.

PART II

Intellectual Functioning at Different Stages of Development

CHAPTER 6

The Four Stages of Development: A Reconceptualization

INTRODUCTION

In the previous section, it was suggested that the first question which must be addressed by any theory of cognitive development is a descriptive one, namely, how best to characterize children's thinking at successive points in time. In the present section, one possible answer to this question is proposed. The object of this first chapter is to introduce that answer by describing the control structures that children use in one particular problem domain, from the first few months of life through to the time of full maturity.

The particular domain that has been chosen for this purpose is the domain of *causal reasoning*. The goal of problems in this domain is simple, to figure out why things happen the way they do. In a typical experiment, children are presented with some piece of scientific apparatus, and invited to explore it. Then, after this exploratory period is over, they are posed a series of more standardized problems, in order to determine what aspects of the apparatus they are able to understand.

An apparatus that has been used quite extensively for this purpose in recent years is the balance beam. This apparatus was first introduced into the developmental literature by Inhelder and Piaget (1958), who presented it to children from 3 to 18 years of age. With the development of information-processing theory, it became possible to characterize children's understanding of the balance beam in more precise terms. This task was first undertaken by

Siegler (1976). Drawing on the clinical data which Inhelder and Piaget had reported, Siegler formulated a more precise description of the hypotheses or rules that children develop at different ages, concerning the way in which a balance beam operates. He also described the sequence of decisions they make in applying these rules to any given balance beam problem, and a set of problems that would allow an experimenter to determine which particular rule any given child was using.

In recent years, Siegler's work has been followed up by Furman (1981), who has replicated his basic findings, and provided a finer-grained description of the hypotheses that are developed during adolescence, under conditions where feedback is provided. In our own research group we have refined and extended Furman's procedures still further, and used them to build models of the control structures that can be assembled by children during each of the classic stages of development. It is on the results of these studies therefore, that our first description of children's development will be based.

THE DEVELOPMENT OF SENSORIMOTOR
CONTROL STRUCTURES IN INFANCY

In order to study the executive control structures that young infants are capable of assembling, Sonia Hayward and I designed a sequence of extremely simple balance-scale problems, in which the goal was simply to make some interesting event recur (Case & Hayward, 1983). As might be expected, there was a clear difference in the problems that infants were able to solve at different age levels.

Substage 0: Operational Consolidation (1–4 Months)[1]

In the balance task that we gave to our youngest subjects, infants were seated in their mothers' laps, about 18 inches away from the apparatus that is illustrated in Figure 6.1, and directly in front of one of the balance arms. When the infants were comfortable, we placed one of the blocks on the balance arm directly in front of them, and gently rocked the armature in an up-and-down fashion. Following this, the infants were moved to the other end of the apparatus, and the procedure was repeated.

What we observed under these conditions was this. By the age of 2 months,

---

[1]This substage corresponds to Piaget's Substage 2. Successive substages correspond at least approximately to his Substages 3, 4, and 5. The reason that different labels and numbers have been used is to bring out the parallel with development at higher stages.

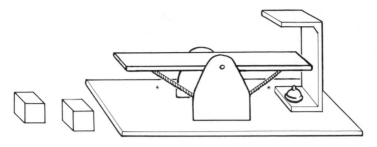

Fig. 6.1. Balance beam designed to investigate infant control structures. (* = springs.)

babies would orient toward the block as it was placed on the balance arm.[2] Often their eyebrows would go up slightly and their eyes would widen as it was set in motion. They would then track the block as it went up and down, sometimes moving their entire head in order to do. For a few babies at this age, tracking the moving block seemed to be too difficult a task. These children would stare resolutely at the spot which the block had just vacated, as though waiting for it to return to this point. By the age of 4 months, however, these difficulties had disappeared, and virtually all of the infants tracked each block with ease.

These results are hardly surprising. What they illustrate, however, is that infants develop control structures for exploring their visual world during the first few months of their lives which apply to a wider range of situations than they can handle at birth. Using the notation that was introduced in the previous chapter, the particular control structure that would be necessary for tracking the block on a balance beam could be represented as follows:

PROBLEM SITUATION   OBJECTIVE
- Interesting object moving out of   - Return pattern of stimulation to
  view, in downwards (or upwards)   its original focal state.
  direction.

STRATEGY
1. Move head and eyes in a
   downward (or upward) direction,
   probably using peripheral input
   from the block as a guide.

[2]To assist the infants in focusing, the blocks were painted a pale green, which made them stand out quite sharply from the bright red of the balance.

In Bruner's (1968) analyses of infant development, he suggested that each of the above components might be localized in a different part of the cortex, citing evidence from Bernstein (1967) in support of this claim. The present claim, however, is not that each one of the components is neurologically distinct (though they may well be), but simply that they are psychologically distinct. If children were incapable of representing the slow movement of the balance arm out of their focal field of view, they would have no basis for tracking it smoothly. Similarly, if they were incapable of setting themselves the objective of refocusing on this object, they would either not track it at all, or track it in some sort of reflexive fashion, continuing until muscle fatigue set in or the apparatus was removed from view. Finally, if children did not have a well-coordinated motor strategy, they would exhibit some sort of trial-and-error search every time the beam began to move, or reached the apogee or epogee of its movement cycle. That they exhibit none of these behaviours may be taken as evidence that each of the above components is represented in at least some fashion in their psychological systems, and can be coordinated with each other component in an on-line fashion. In effect, each one of the components must be psychologically discrete, while the whole set of components must function as a single psychological unit.

Another task that has been presented to children during the first few months of life involves manual rather than visual exploration. As Bower (1974) has shown, infants during this age range will reach out to grasp a small object, if that object is suspended at an appropriate distance from them (i.e., just within reach), and if they themselves are supported in a position where their arms are free to move. During the early part of the stage the infants' "hit rate" in this sort of situation is not particularly high (40%). However, by the age of 4 months it is quite respectable (about 80%).

Using the present notation, the control structure on which this early reaching behaviour depends might be represented as follows.

PROBLEM SITUATION   OBJECTIVE
- Small object within reach at   - Make contact with object
  position X.   with hand.

STRATEGY
1. Move arm from current position
   (Y) to X, using original visual
   input as a guide.

As may be apparent, the above control structure is similar to that for visual exploration in at least two respects. First, it involves the same number of components. Second, the components are of the same general nature. The first component represents an item of spatial information about the external world. The second component represents an objective which is occasioned by this information, and which involves making contact with the object at a particular point in space. Finally, the third component represents a motor movement that is designed to move the appropriate sense organ (in this case the hand, not the eye) in such a fashion that this objective can be reached. It is presumably as a result of applying such structures that infants acquire their first knowledge of the objects in their physical environment, and of the laws that govern their behaviour.

Substage 1: Operational Coordination (4–8 Months)

Although infants become increasingly capable of executing a series of voluntarily directed movements with their eyes or hands during the first few months of their lives, they show few signs of being able to coordinate these two forms of activity, in any sort of on-line fashion. The balance beam task that we designed to reveal this inability was presented by first seating the infant in the mother's lap, at arm's length from the apparatus, and with its feet astride its central post. The experimenter then sat on the opposite side of the beam. When the infant was paying attention, the experimenter reached out and initiated a rocking motion of the beam with her hand, and encouraged the baby to imitate. If the infant did not respond, the experimenter waited five or six seconds for the oscillation of the beam to subside[3] and then repeated the demonstration for a maximum of five trials.

In response to this demonstration, the 3-month-old infants in our study showed clear signs of an affective reaction, and watched the results with fascination. However, they almost never reached out and pushed the beam themselves. This finding was extremely robust, and was not altered even when the experimenter placed the babies' hands on the beam and showed them how it would respond, giving every form of social support she could muster. By contrast, infants in the age range from 4 to 8 months did reach out and make contact with the beam. Moreover, only a small minority needed as many as five demonstrations before they did so. The infants at this substage also initiated a variety of forms of manual exploration on their own, such as touching the springs and tugging at them.

A second task that was presented involved the same basic format, but auditory input as well. A desk bell was placed underneath one of the balance arms. The experimenter then showed how, when the balance arm was depressed to its full extent, the bell would make a ringing sound as the balance struck it. Infants exhibited a stronger affective reaction to this sound than they had to the sight of the beam by itself. Some were quite exhuberant and struck the beam

---

[3]The oscillation was produced by springs that were attached to the beam, in the fashion indicated in Figure 6.1.

with vigor, producing a series of ringing sounds as they did so. Others appeared a bit taken aback, and explored the new feature somewhat timidly, first looking up at the experimenter for encouragement. In almost all cases, however, some form of further exploration was witnessed at the 4- to 8-month-old level, together with some further ringing of the bell, whereas none was witnessed at the 1- to 4-month level.

What sort of control structure would be necessary for producing movement of the balance beam in this sort of intentional fashion? As both Baldwin and Piaget suggested, the structure would have to be one in which the infant's initial circular reactions were differentiated from each other, and coordinated into some form of secondary circular reaction. Using the present form of notation, the new control structure for moving the balance might be represented as follows:

PROBLEM SITUATION   OBJECTIVE

- Balance beam exhibits interesting ——▶ • Re-initiate pattern of movement.
  change in movement (plus
  sound).

- Experimenter's hand made   • Move own hand to balance
  contact with beam at X just   beam at X.
  previously.

STRATEGY

1.   Move arm from current position
     (Y) to X.
2a. Strike or touch beam with hand.
2b. Monitor change in beam which
     results.

There are several things to note about the above structure.

1. The first is simply that the structure has been assembled out of two qualitatively distinct precursor structures, each of which was already available at the previous substage, but each of which previously served a different function.

2. The second is that the integration that has taken place involves the subordination of one structure to the other, in the sense that one structure (hand reaching) is now used as the means toward the achievement of an end that is specified by the other (visual tracking). This subordination is indicated in the above notation by the indentation of the second objective under the first.

3. The third point to note is that—in the course of or prior to this integration—a number of subtle changes have taken place in the components of each structure itself. The original event is now represented in a more differentiated fashion, as a movement of the beam which follows the movement of the experimenter's hand. In addition, the motor movement of the hand has become

more differentiated as well, in that the infant now reaches out to the beam and exerts force on it, in two clear steps.[4]

4. A final point to note is that, accompanying this sort of differentiation and coordination of the child's original control structures, is a large and qualitative change in behavior. This change is noticed by parents and researchers alike. Parents often remark on "what a little person" their infant becomes at around this age, or "how active." From the time of Baldwin, researchers have also commented on the intellectual changes which take place. In fact, Baldwin no longer used the term sensorimotor to describe children's intellectual functioning at this age. Instead, he used the term *ideomotor*. Whatever term one uses, it is clear that the infant's behavior now has an insightful or thoughtful quality which it previously lacked. Previously, infants were capable of adapting their ongoing motor activity to a change in their sensory environment. Now, however, they can combine two different motor activities which were previously quite discrete. In effect, they can now put things together in their heads, often quite suddenly.

The first three characteristics mentioned above, namely, the combination of qualitatively distinct structures into a new structure where the goal of one is subordinated to the goal of the other, and where the internal elements of each are subtly altered, recur at regular points in children's development. And, as will be shown, at each point when these three features do recur, the fourth characteristic recurs as well. That is, there is some large and stage-like shift in their behavior. It seems reasonable to suggest, therefore, that the first three changes may be linked to the fourth in some sort of causal fashion.

An analogy from the inorganic world may be useful at this point. Hydrogen and oxygen are two elements which share certain general formal properties in common, yet which are qualitatively distinct, both in terms of their specific properties, and in terms of their internal structure. Under certain conditions, however, they can combine into a superordinate structure. When this takes place, the internal structure of each is subtly altered. In addition, the new entity which results is qualitatively distinct from either of the components which went into it, and can itself function as a unit in a variety of further chemical reactions. What is being proposed with regard to children's thinking is that an analogous change can take place, as the basic mental elements that children consolidate at one stage of development are combined with each other, to form the new units which will be observed at the next.

It is because children's control structures undergo this sort of transformation at the age of about 4 months, and because their behaviour undergoes a concomitant qualitative shift, that I have used the numeral 0 to refer to the substage of operational consolidation, and the numeral 1 to refer to the substage of opera-

---

[4]For relevant behavioral evidence on this change, see Bower (1974, Chapter 6).

tional coordination. What this notation is intended to imply is that, although sensorimotor operations are consolidated during the first few months of life, sensorimotor thinking and structures do not appear until 4 to 8 months of age, when the first mental coordination of these operations takes place.[5]

Substage 2: Bifocal Coordination (8–12 Months)

Although infants show a variety of coordinated primary reactions from 4 to 8 months of age, they show little evidence of coordinating two such reactions with each other. As a consequence, they rarely focus on more than one object at a time in any situation where they must also execute a voluntarily directed manual action. One task that requires this sort of bifocal coordination on the balance beam is introduced by moving the desk bell from its position under the balance arm in front of the infant, to a position above the arm at the other end. The experimenter then demonstrates how the bell can still be rung, by pushing down on the beam in front of the infant. Finally, the experimenter encourages the infant to ring the bell by him or herself. If the infant fails to push the beam, five further trials are presented in a row, in each of which the experimenter pushes the balance arm in front of the child, and encourages the child to try as well.

As may be apparent, the requirements of this task are extremely similar to those of the previous task. In fact, the motor movement that is required remains virtually identical, because the only change that is introduced involves the location of the bell. Although the change is subtle, however, the task is sufficiently different to place it beyond the capabilities of infants in the 4- to 8-month range. Infants from 4 to 8 months are, of course, capable of pushing the balance arm in response to the experimenter's encouragement. As was demonstrated by their performance on the previous task, they are also capable of responding to a ringing bell, and of engaging in efforts to ring it on their own. Finally, they appear to be capable of noticing the bell at the other end of the balance, and of focusing on it when it rings. However, they do not appear capable of putting all these elements together. Some of the children pushed half-heartedly at the beam, but not hard enough to ring the bell. Others did not push at the beam at all. And none of the children looked over at the bell in any sort of purposeful fashion, as they executed their motor movements.

The behaviour of infants in the 8- to 12-month range was markedly different.

---

[5] In his analyses of children's higher-order thought, Piaget reserved the term operation for the elements of a complex and well-elaborated intellectual structure: one with such systemic properties as reversibility and compensation. In the present volume, however, the term is used to refer to any mental structure, no matter how simple or complex it may be. If a structure is defined as a set of elements and relations, the simplest structures—by definition—are those that involve two elements and a single relation. It is this sort of structure which first appears at Substage 1.

First of all, they would monitor the ringing of the bell with interest. Then they would reach out toward the beam in front of them, turn their eyes toward the bell, and give the beam a push. Some of them even deliberately made this push a slow one or took a little wind-up, scanning their eyes back and forth between their end of the beam and the bell at the other end as they did so. Finally, when they did ring the bell, they would often spontaneously repeat their procedure, with clear evidence of delight at the results produced. The new control structure which they had assembled might therefore be represented as follows:

PROBLEM SITUATION   OBJECTIVE

- Bell rings at other end of $\longrightarrow$ • Ring bell at other end.
  balance beam.

- Ring produced by movement of $\longrightarrow$ • Re-initiate beam movement.
  beam.

- Experimenter's hand made $\longrightarrow$ • Move hand to beam, at X.
  contact with beam at position
  X just previously.

STRATEGY

1. Move arm from current position (Y) to X, monitoring its approach.
2a. As hand approaches or touches beam, turn head and look at other end.
2b. Strike or push beam as hand makes contact.
3. Monitor results at other end.

As was noted in the previous chapter, it is often not a subject's strategy for solving a problem per se, which shows the greatest change with development. Rather, it is the circumstances under which this strategy can be deployed. The above structure illustrates this point. What has changed is not so much the children's motor strategies as their understanding of the situation in which this strategy can produce an interesting result. This change appears in the above notation in the representation of the problem situation and in the objectives more prominently than in the strategy. An extra element representing the occurrence that takes place at the other end has been added to the problem situation. As a result of this addition, a new subgoal has also been established, and represented in the subject's list of objectives. Finally, as a result of these two changes, a subtle change has been introduced into the subject's motor strategy as well. This change is a visual flick of the eyes, to monitor the changes that take place at the other end, as the pushing strategy of the previous substage is executed. It is this flick of the eyes, of course, and the attendant expression on the children's faces, which makes it clear that they are solving the task with insight.

Because the notion of insight is one that has been discussed quite frequently in the developmental literature, it is important to be clear from the outset regarding the assumptions that the above model entails concerning the nature of an insightful solution. In the above model, the children are presumed to have attained a genuine insight into the problem's solution at the moment when they make a connection between the top-level goal which they hope to achieve, and a subgoal which is immediately attainable. In effect, it is at this point that they are assumed to "see their way through" the problem and to connect the first action they will produce to the final outcome in a meaningful fashion. It is this capacity for seeing one's way through a task, then, or for grasping its overall structure that is assumed to change most dramatically with development, not the subject's ability to string together a set of isolated motor components in some sort of successful sequence.

Substage 3: Elaborated Coordination $(1-1\frac{1}{2}$ Years)[6]

As children reach their first birthday they become capable of representing an additional feature of an apparatus such as a balance beam and dealing with it in an insightful fashion. As a consequence, they can now solve tasks which, although they are still of the same general nature, are a good deal more complex. A test item that reveals this change is presented by placing the bell below the arm at the other end of the scale, instead of above it. The experimenter then shows the infants how the bell can be rung by reversing their earlier actions (i.e., by lifting the balance arm up instead of pushing it down). When children in 8- to 12-month range are presented with this task, they show virtually no indication of success and continue to push the balance arm down. This behaviour persists even when the experimenter repeatedly says the word "up." Nor does it change when the balance arm is fitted with a little handle to make it easier for the infants to pull up. All that happens under these conditions is that the children appear frustrated or confused that the bell will not ring when they push the balance arm down.

At first glance, this sort of behaviour might appear quite bizarre. After all, on the previous task, many of the same children appeared to study the action of the beam against the bell at the other end, and to show evidence of understanding the relationship between the two events. And they are quite capable of lifting objects of this weight by the age of 8 months. It is one thing to understand that

---

[6]The preceding ages are only approximate. A more accurate set of ages might be 13 months to 20 months. However, even these would still be debatable, and thus the figures have been rounded off to even numbers.

an action here produces a reaction over there, however, and it is another thing to understand that the particular nature of one's action must be tailored to the particular nature of the effect that is desired. In order to arrive at this latter insight, one must assemble a more complex or *elaborated* control structure. This new control structure might be represented as follows:

PROBLEM SITUATION   OBJECTIVE

- Bell rings at other end of balance ⟶ • Ring bell at other end.
  beam.

- Ring produced by downward   • Make beam go down at
  movement of beam at other end.   other end.

- Experimenter pulled this side of ⟶ • Pull this side of beam up.
  beam up.[7]

- Experimenter made contact   ⟶ • Move hand to beam at X.
  with beam (or handle) at X.

STRATEGY

1. Move arm from current position
   (Y) to X, monitoring its
   approach.
2a. As hand approaches beam, turn
    head and monitor other end.
2b. Move the beam up, after hand
    makes contact.
3. Monitor direction of beam (if
   it is not going in desired
   direction, reverse).
4. Monitor contact of beam with
   bell; if it does not ring, repeat
   2b with more vigor.

The above sort of control structure, with the attendant capability that it produces for operational reversibility, marks the pinnacle of what Piaget labelled the sensorimotor stage in children's development. Our own experimental procedures for distinguishing among the various types of sensorimotor structure on the balance beam are reported by Case and Hayward (1983). The percentages of children who were functioning at each level in our study are given in Table 6.1. For the moment, however, the main point that needs to be made is not empirical, but theoretical: The models that have been presented meet the two basic

---

[7]This feature of the situation is demonstrated. However, several subjects appeared to re-discover it in the course of solving the problem. They started to push, then saw that this raised the beam at the other end, and reversed their action.

TABLE 6.1

Percentage of Children Capable of Performing at each Level of Sensorimotor Thought during the Period from Birth to $1\frac{1}{4}$ Years[a]

Theoretical age range (Mean age of sample)	Level 0: Tracks block and arm up and down when placed in front of it (%)	Level 1: Pushes beam and watches arm go up and down (%)	Level 2: Pushes beam at one end, watching bell at other (%)	Level 3: Raises beam at one end, when bell is placed under the other (%)
1–4 mo (3 mo, 7 d)	89[†]	11	0	0
4–8 mo (6 mo, 4 d)	100	89	26	0
8–12 mo (10 mo, 5 d)	100	100	83	0
12–18 mo (16 mo, 11 d)	100	100	100	89

[a]From Case and Hayward (1984).
[†]Number of subjects per age group = 19; one subject dropped from third group.

criteria which were proposed in the previous chapter for a successful account of intellectual development. First, they present a view of the global organization or *structure* of children's mental activity at successive points in time. Second, they provide a glimpse of the more detailed processes which occur at each successive point in time.

From the point of view of structure, the general hypotheses that flow from the above models are the same as were advanced by Baldwin and Piaget. These are (1) that children are either born with, or very early develop, a basic repertoire of voluntary action schemes; (2) that more complex mental structures are assembled by the differentiation and coordination of these schemes; (3) that each successive coordination leads to a qualitative shift in behaviour; and (4) that by the age of $1\frac{1}{2}$ years children are capable of assembling complex sensorimotor structures in which the effect of one operation reverses the effect of another. To these four points might be added a fifth: (5) that children's knowledge of, or insight into, the external world reflects the nature of the mental structures which they have available for exploring it.

This latter point has not been stressed in the foregoing analysis, and thus deserves elaboration. Both Baldwin and Piaget maintained that the child's knowledge of the external world of objects was not simply given by exposure to this world, but had to be constructed. Accordingly, they both suggested that the kind of knowledge children acquire as a result of any given encounter with the world should reflect the nature of the mental operations which they have available at the time of that encounter. The foregoing models suggest just how strong this sort of influence can be. A child who is at the preliminary substage of the sensorimotor period, on exposure to a balance beam, can not hope to learn much more about it than that it is a brightly coloured object which moves in a particular up-and-down fashion. Children at the first substage of sensorimotor development can learn more, namely, that a balance beam is an object whose movement is affected by their own manual actions in a variety of interesting ways. Children at the next substage can learn that the balance is an object which moves at one end, when it is manipulated at the other. Finally, children at the last substage can acquire the kind of sensorimotor knowledge that any adult takes for granted, that a balance beam is an object which moves in the reverse direction at one end from the one in which it is moved at the other.

What about the process by which such structures are assembled and such insights are attained? If the foregoing models are on the right track, then the conclusions which may be drawn are similar (although not identical) to those advanced by Simon (1962) and Klahr and Wallace (1976). (1) Much of children's early intellectual activity results from the desire to experience or to repeat certain interesting sensory experiences. (2) In the course of working toward this goal, children must often work backwards from the state they hope to achieve. (3) Insight into how a particular top-level goal can be reached—and hence how a particular object works—often comes by establishing a set of pointers to a particular set of subgoals or intermediate states, which link the current state as experienced with the one that is desired. (4) As children move from one substage to the next, they become capable of taking account of one additional task feature, and of setting themselves one additional subgoal which relates to it. (5) As a consequence, they also become capable of constructing new strategies, or of employing existing strategies in more complex situations.

For readers in the structural-developmental tradition, the first set of points will not come as a surprise. For readers in the information-processing tradition, the second set of points are unlikely to come as a surprise either. The primary contribution of the above analyses, therefore, is that they permit the two sets of points to be synthesized, and a more integrated picture of children's development to be provided. The utility of this sort of integration will hopefully become apparent in ensuing chapters. For the moment, however, it is important to track children's continued development as they move into the period which is often referred to as early childhood.

THE DEVELOPMENT
OF RELATIONAL CONTROL STRUCTURES
IN EARLY CHILDHOOD

Neither Baldwin nor Piaget analyzed the changes that take place during early childhood in the same painstaking detail as they had analyzed the changes that take place during infancy. Nor did Piaget focus such analyses as he did conduct on the same sort of task. Rather than posing children problems concerning the operation of simple manipulable objects, he posed them problems concerning objects that they could only observe at a distance, such as the clouds, the sun, and the moon (Piaget, 1926b).

As a result of this difference in methodology, the picture that emerged of children's reasoning was also somewhat different. Although it was acknowledged to be symbolic, reasoning during this period appeared to be characterized by such properties as animism, artificialism, and participation, rather than by any attempt to induce simple physical or mechanical laws. And it did not emerge from this state until the somewhat mysterious appearance of concrete operations at around 8 years of age.

In principle, of course, there is no reason why the same sort of detailed analysis of children's problem solving could not be conducted for early childhood as was conducted for infancy. Nor is there any reason why the same sort of problem sequence could not be presented. In fact, as Berzonsky (1971) has noted, children's reasoning is not animistic during the preschool years when they are asked simple causal questions about physical objects with which they have some first-hand experience. Although their animistic reasoning is real, then, it appears to constitute a form of fall-back response, that is, a response on which they fall back when they are set tasks which are beyond their current capabilities. It does not indicate the sort of knowledge or reasoning of which they are capable under optimal conditions.

In an attempt to probe the nature of preschoolers' causal reasoning under optimal conditions, therefore, and to provide more detail on the link between the operative structures of infancy and those of middle childhood, Peter Liu and I decided to construct a series of problems of our own (Liu & Case, 1981). Once again, the task we employed involved a balance scale.

Substage 0: Operational Consolidation ($1-1\frac{1}{2}$ Years)

The task we presented to children who were still in the sensorimotor stage was the final one in the infant balance beam series: that is, the one that requires that one side of the beam be pushed or pulled, in order to ring a bell that is placed either above or below the beam on the other side. From the perspective of children's sensorimotor development, success on this task represents a complex and sophisticated achievement. From the viewpoint of the development which follows, however, it may be considered a rather elementary achievement. In fact, from the perspective of what will be termed *relational* development, all the task requires is the representation of a single unit, the inverse relationship between the action at one end of a lever and the action at the other. For the sake of simplicity, therefore, the following abbreviated notation will be adapted for describing the control structures on which success on this task depends.

PROBLEM SITUATION	OBJECTIVE
• Far end of beam must be moved up using this side of the beam.	• Move far end *up*, by moving this end down.

STRATEGY

1. Reach out to this end, and move it sharply *down*, monitoring reaction at other end.

The above operation is not the only one that children acquire at this substage, which requires the understanding of a single relationship. Another relational operation that they acquire is one for moving a set of barriers which block their access to some goal. During the period from 8 to 12 months, infants can remove one such barrier. During the period from 12 to 18 months, they can remove two or more. A full sensorimotor description of the structure that is required for removing a barrier was presented in the previous chapter. The relational representation of the same structure would be as follows:

PROBLEM SITUATION	OBJECTIVES
• Movement to goal object blocked by barrier(s).	• Move barrier(s) out of way to reach goal.

STRATEGY

1. Move barriers out of the way in order to reach goal.

Substage 1: Operational Coordination (1½–2 Years)

Although children can represent a relationship between two objects or actions between the ages of 1 and 1½ years, and manipulate that relationship in a variety of fashions, they show no signs of being able to combine two different kinds of relationship, or to utilize one relationship as a means for effecting a change in another. Such a shift does occur, however, between the ages of 1½ to 2 years.[8] The balance beam task that we used to reveal this shift is illustrated in Figure 6.2. After the children were introduced to the apparatus, and it was established that they could solve the sort of simple relational items already mentioned, the experimenter introduced a new type of item in which the supports had to be removed before the balance arm was pushed or pulled. After an initial warm-up period, six trials were presented. In order to be classified as having passed the task, the child had to succeed at least four times out of six. The control structure that is necessary for doing so might be represented as follows:

PROBLEM SITUATION	OBJECTIVES
• Beam at far side must be moved down.	• Move far end *down* by moving this end *up*.
• Movement of arm at far side blocked by supports.	• Move support *out* to move arm *down*.

STRATEGY

1. Move out supports from under arms.
2. Lift right arm sharply up, monitoring effect on other side.

As may be apparent, success at this level requires children to focus on two different types of relationship, (1) the instrumental relationship between their actions on one end of the beam and the reaction at the other, and (2) the preventative relationship between the blocks and the beam. As may also be apparent, both of these capabilities were already present in the child's repertoire, in isola-

---

[8]Or, somewhat more precisely, between 20 and 27 months.

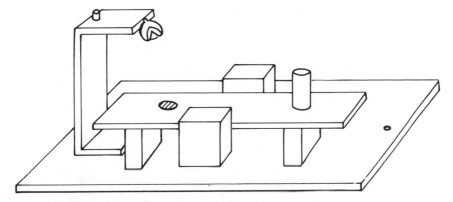

Fig. 6.2. Balance beam designed to investigate preschool control structures. (From Liu, 1981.)

tion, at the previous stage. Finally, it may be seen that the sort of integration that is required is one of *subordination*, or *hierarchical integration*, with some concomitant differentiation or alteration of the component elements. In short, the sort of integration that takes place is similar to that which took place earlier, as children moved from the preliminary substage of the sensorimotor period (1–4 months), to the substage of sensorimotor coordination (4–8 months).

Given that there is a parallel between the structural changes that take place from Substage 0 to Substage 1 in the relational period, and those that took place from Substage 0 to Substage 1 in the sensorimotor period, one might expect that there would be a parallel in children's behaviour as well, and also in the insights that they appear capable of acquiring. In fact, this is the case. Between the ages of $1\frac{1}{2}$ and 2 years, a second major qualitative shift in children's thinking and behaviour takes place, and they become capable of acquiring a new class of insights. The most commonly noted shift is that which takes place in children's language. Prior to this stage, vocalization is used much as any other motor activity, as an instrument for the attainment of basic needs in an indirect fashion. Children can even differentiate certain words from each other. However, they can not use language qua language because they can not utilize two different kinds of words (and hence control two different kinds of relationships) simultaneously. Once they can focus on two different kinds of relationships, they can for the first time begin to control their interrelationship with each other, and hence to use language as a device with a set of rules or structure of its own.

The change in children's language at this age will be considered in more detail in Chapter 8. For the moment, however, the point is simply that the shift which takes place in the child's thinking about the balance beam is also a large one, which bears a parallel to that which is observed in language. Prior to the age of $1\frac{1}{2}$ years children can execute isolated relational operations, and differentiate certain keys operations from each other. However, they cannot coordinate two such differentiated relations with each other, and thus cannot apprehend the workings of an interrelational structure. Between the age of $1\frac{1}{2}$ and 2 years, they become capable of this sort of thinking for the first time, and can thus begin to understand the set of higher-order rules which relate different forces to each other in a physical system. The ability to remove the supports as a means to operating the balance lever is a demonstration of one such change. What it indicates is that children can now understand how the downward force of the lever and the blocking action of the support are interrelated.[9a]

Substage 2: Bifocal Coordination ($2-3\frac{1}{2}$ Years)[9b]

During the second substage, the child's focus expands to include two systemic interrelations rather than one. One task that we designed to reveal this change was introduced by having the experimenter set the balance in front of the child, with its supports in place; then take a peg and place it in the slot on the opposite arm of the balance from the bells. The peg was heavy enough that the arm moved sharply down when the supports were removed, thus ringing the bells. As before, the experimenter then turned the operation of the apparatus over to the child, and changed the position of the bells on every trial. Thus, in order to succeed, the child had to genuinely grasp the principle which was involved, rather than just imitate the experimenter's specific action of putting the weight on the beam.[10] The executive control structure that was required might be represented as follows:

PROBLEM SITUATION   OBJECTIVES

- Beam at far side must be moved up.
- Move far end *up*, by moving this end *down*.

- Movement of arm at far side blocked by supports.
- Move supports *out* to move arm up.

- Movement of arm also blocked unless peg is used.
- Place peg *in* hole on this arm, to *move arm down*.

STRATEGY

1. Place peg in hole on this arm.
2. Remove supports.
3. Monitor effect on far side.

[9a] Note that this is the same age at which children exhibit surprise when the supports of an arch are removed, and it remains standing (Keil, personal communication, October 6, 1983).

[9b] A more exact specification might be 27–40 months.

[10] Children who failed the item often did place the peg on the beam. However, they put it consistently on one side, or consistently on the same side as the bells.

Substage 3: Elaborated Coordination ($3\frac{1}{2}$–5 Years)

During the substage that was just described, the children could succeed on a variety of peg tasks. They could place a peg on either side, and they could do so whether it was heavy or light. They even appeared to develop an intuitive expectation that heavy pegs would exert a dramatic effect, whereas light pegs would not. What they showed no evidence of doing, however, was apprehending the relationship between heavy and light pegs to each other, and coordinating this with the action of the arm once the supports were removed. During the third substage, this final elaboration appeared. The task that we designed to highlight it required the experimenter to hand the children the lighter of two weights, and ask them to ring the bells by placing both weights on the beam. To succeed on this task, children had to reverse the first operation they had executed at the previous level, and place the light weight on the side of the beam they wished to go up, not down. They then had to follow this placement by setting the heavier of the two weights on the opposite side (which they wished to go down). The executive control structure that was required may be represented as follows:

PROBLEM SITUATION	OBJECTIVES
• Left side must be moved up.	• Right side must be pushed down to move left up.
• Supports block beam action.	• Move supports out from under arm.
• Heavy weight at Z.	• Place heavy weight on right to move it down.
• Light weight in hand.	• Place light weight on left, to leave right free.

STRATEGY

1. Set light weight in place on left.
2. Set heavy weight in place on right.
3. Remove supports.
4. Monitor movement of arm towards bells.

The preceding structure marks the pinnacle of what I have labeled *relational* thought and what Piaget termed preoperational thought. The procedures for discriminating the various forms of this thought from each other on the balance beam task are given in Liu (1981) and Marini (1984). The percentage of subjects at each level in the two studies are given in Table 6.2. Once again, however, the main points that need to be made are theoretical, not empirical.

TABLE 6.2

Percentage of Children Capable of Functioning at each Level of Relational Stage during the Period from 1 to 5 Years[a,b]

Theoretical age range (mean age of sample)	Level 0: Uses beam to hit bells (%)	Level 1: Removes supports; then uses beam (%)	Level 2: Places weight before removing support (%)	Level 3: Places both weights before removing support (%)
$1\frac{1}{2}$ yr (1 yr, 6 mo)	100	30	0	0
$1\frac{1}{2}$–2 yr (2 yr)	100	95	20	0
2–$3\frac{1}{2}$ yr (3 yr, 1 mo)	100	90	55	10
$3\frac{1}{2}$–5 yr (4 yr, 2 mo)	100	100	90	55

[a] Data averaged from Marini (1984) and Liu (1981).
[b] Number of subjects per age level = 40.

As may be apparent, the general pattern of development during the relational stage is quite similar to that during the sensorimotor stage. From a structural viewpoint, the essential elements of the pattern are as follows: (1) by the age of $1\frac{1}{2}$ years children have acquired structures for understanding and controlling a variety of well-differentiated (and reversible) relational operations; (2) these structures then serve as the elements from which more complex structures (i.e., structures representing interrelations) are assembled; (3) there is a major qualitative shift that accompanies the first such higher-order structure, and a mini-shift that accompanies each successive structure; (4) by the age of 5 years, children are capable of assembling their relational structures into higher-order structures which are in themselves complex, and in which the effect of one inter-relationship can be compensated for, or reversed, by that of another; (5) children's knowledge of, or insight into, the physical systems in the external world reflects the nature of these underlying structures.

From a processing viewpoint, children's thinking during this period may be described as follows: (1) the goal of much of children's problem solving during the period is to repeat or master interesting relational operations, whose effects have just been observed; (2) in the course of working towards this goal, children must often work backward from the operation that they hope to execute to some other operation; (3) insight into how a particular goal may be achieved, and how a particular operation works, often comes by establishing a set of pointers to a particular set of subgoals, which will link the current state to the state that is desired; (4) movement from one stage or substage to the next is ac-companied by an increase in the number of task features that can be taken into account and subgoals that can be set; (5) as a result, it is also accompanied by a change in the strategy that can be executed, and/or an expansion in the range of contexts in which an existing strategy can be applied.

The only real difference between the first two stages of development, therefore, lies in the nature of the operations that form the basic units of thought. In the period from birth to $1\frac{1}{2}$ years, the basic units of thought are sen-sory objects and motor actions. In the period from $1\frac{1}{2}$ to 5 years, the basic units become relationships between such objects and actions.

THE DEVELOPMENT OF DIMENSIONAL CONTROL STRUCTURES IN MIDDLE CHILDHOOD

Substage 0: Operational Consolidation ($3\frac{1}{2}$–5 Years)

Determining what will happen when two pegs of different weights are placed on opposite sides of a balance beam is a complex achievement when considered from the viewpoint of relational development. However, it is a rather elementary achievement when considered from the viewpoint of the development that follows. In fact, from the perspective of what I have termed *dimensional* development (Case, 1984), all the task requires is the representation of a single unit, namely, the dimension of weight. For the sake of simplicity, therefore, I have adopted the following abbreviated notation for representing the control structures on which this achievement depends.

PROBLEM SITUATION   OBJECTIVE

• Balance beam with an object on   • Determine which side will go
  each arm.   down.

STRATEGY

1. Look at each side. Predict that
the one which looks *heavy* will go
down, the *light* one up.

At about the same time as they focus on the dimension of weight as a cue for predicting the tilt of a balance beam, children focus on a number of other polar dimensions which can be used to make similar predictions. Polar dimensions such as long–short, big–little, hot–cold, and more–less are all used in this fashion during the same age range. They also become differentiated from each other for the first time in the child's language (see Clark, 1973).

Of the various dimensions on which children focus during this period, one of the most important is number. Number is a particularly interesting dimension because the operation on which it depends (i.e., counting) can be clearly specified, and has been extensively studied in recent years. As will be shown in Chapter 8, the development of children's counting goes through the same four substages during the relational period as the development of polar operations. Although the form and function of the operations that are responsible for children's understanding of the number system are quite different from those that are responsible for their apprehension of physical systems, their underlying complexity is similar, as is the age at which they are first observed. They may also be represented in a similar abbreviated fashion, as follows:

PROBLEM SITUATION   OBJECTIVE

• Set of objects at X and Y.   • Determine which set has the
                               big number.

STRATEGY

1. Count each set; note one with
big number

Substage 1: Operational Coordination (5–7 Years)

Although preschoolers can focus on weight or number in situations where only one of these dimensions is of importance, they cannot focus on both dimensions, or use one as a means to drawing a conclusion about the other. Such a capability does emerge, however, between the ages of 5 and 7 years. The balance beam task that highlights this shift is the one designed by Siegler (1976), which is illustrated in Figure 6.3.

On the surface, the question children are asked in Siegler's problems is an easy one: which side of the balance beam will go down, when the supports are removed? Indeed, if there is a gross perceptual difference between the stacks of weights, or if children know in advance which stack is heavier, they can answer this question at the age of $3\frac{1}{2}$ to 5 years (Liu, 1981). In the form that is illustrated, however, there is no such gross perceptual difference, and children do not know in advance that one weight stack is heavier than the other. The only way they can answer the question, therefore, is by coordinating their focus on the dimension of weight with a focus on the dimension of number. The new structure they must assemble might therefore be represented as follows.

PROBLEM SITUATION   OBJECTIVES

- Balance with stack of objects on ⟶ • Predict which side will do down.
  each arm.
- Each stack composed of a number ⟶ • Determine which side has
  of identical units.   larger number of units.

STRATEGY

1. Count each set of units; note
   which side has the bigger
   number.
2. Pick side with bigger number as
   the one which will weigh more
   (and therefore go down).

As was the case at the two earlier stage transition points that were described, there are several things to note about the preceding structure.

1. The first is that the new structure has been assembled out of two qualitatively distinct precursor structures, each of which was already available, but each of which previously served a different function.

2. The second is that the integration that has taken place involves the subordination of one structure to another, in a means-end fashion.

3. The third is that—in the course of or prior to this integration—a number of subtle changes have taken place in the components of each structure.

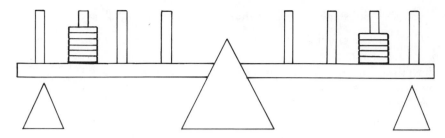

Fig. 6.3. Balance beam designed to investigate school-age children's control structures (Siegler, 1976).

4. Finally, the last point is that accompanying this sort of differentiation and coordination is a large and qualitative change in children's behaviour, and the insights of which they are capable.

Depending on their particular theoretical orientation, developmentalists have referred to the 5- to 7-year-old shift in various terms. For Piagetians the shift has been taken to imply the acquisition of functional logic, that is, a logic in which one variable (x) can be seen as being a function of another (y) (Piaget *et al.*, 1977). For Brunerians, the shift has been taken as evidence that children's thought now has the potential to be dominated by the structure of their symbolic rather than their ikonic processes (Bruner, 1964). For information-processing theorists, the shift has been taken as evidence that the first scientific or quantitative rules can now be constructed (Siegler, 1978). Finally, for parents and laypeople, the shift has been taken as evidence that the child is now ready for a different and more formal sort of schooling.

The present point is not any of these previous descriptions is incorrect. Indeed, if the present model is accurate, each one of the previous descriptions may be seen to be valid, within its own particular context. Rather, the present point is that the underlying changes that are responsible for producing this shift are similar to those which took place earlier, during the two prior points in time at which some form of major cognitive reorganization was generally acknowledged.

Substage 2: Bifocal Coordination (7–9 Years)

Although children can focus on a variety of quantitative dimensions by the age of 5 to 7 years, they can only focus on one such dimension at a time. During the second substage of the period, they begin to focus on a second quantitative dimension as well. On the balance beam, this may be seen in the situation where an equal number of weights is placed on each side of the balance. By the age of 7 or 8 years children no longer predict that the beam will balance. Instead, they *decenter*, and compute the distance from the fulcrum of each weight. They then predict that the weight that is at a greater distance from the fulcrum will go down. The executive control structure for arriving at this conclusion may be represented as follows:

PROBLEM SITUATION

- Balance beam with stack of objects on each side.
- Each object stack composed of a number identical units.
- Each object at a specifiable distance from fulcrum.

OBJECTIVES

- Predict side which will go down.
- Determine side with greater number of objects.
- Determine side with weight at greater distance.

STRATEGY

1. Count each set of weights; note which side has greater number.
2. Repeat 1 for distance pegs.
3. If the weights are about equal, predict that the side with the greater distance will go down. Otherwise predict that the side with greater weight will go down.

Once again, the preceding structure contains one more feature in its problem situation than did its predecessor. It also contains one additional subgoal in its list of objectives. Finally, it contains one additional subroutine in the strategy, an iteration of Step 1 for distance instead of weight.

Substage 3: Elaborated Coordination (9–11 Years)

Although the strategy of Substage 2 is more powerful than that of Substage 1, it does not always lead to success because weight and distance are never related to each other directly. On problems where there is a difference both in weight and in distance from the fulcrum, children must choose between the two. What they do as a consequence is simply to fall back on weight as the basis for prediction (Siegler, 1976). This of course leads to failure on a great many trials.

At the third substage, children become aware of this problem, and no longer base their decisions entirely on weight when the two are in conflict. On the other hand, because they cannot yet compute torque, they have to make a more intuitive compensation between the action of the two variables. Siegler has not specified the strategy that is used for effecting this compensation. However, Inhelder and Piaget (1958) have suggested that addition and subtraction strategies are common during this age range. Moreover, Karplus and Peterson, (1970), Wollman (1973), Furman (1981), and Marini (1984) have all obtained data which show that the majority of children in this age range do apply one of these two strategies to the task.

The addition strategy is quite simple. Children merely add the number of weight and distance units on each side, and pick the one with the greater total value as the one which will go down. The subtraction strategy is more complicated, but follows the same basic logic. Children first compute the difference between the two weights, and the difference between the two distances. They then base their decision on the dimension with the greater difference. For example, if the weights are 2 and 8, and the distances are 4 and 3, they pick the side with the greater weight to go down, because the difference along this dimension is greater than that along the distance dimension. The executive control structure for executing this sort of strategy may be represented as follows:

PROBLEM SITUATION   OBJECTIVES

- Balance beam with stack of   ⟶ • Predict which side will go down.
  weights at various distances.

- Action of weight and distance in   • Determine whether weight or
  opposite directions.[11]   distance has a greater effect.

- Each weight stack composed   • Determine relative number
  of equal amounts.   of weights on each side.

- Each distance composed of   • Determine relative distance
  number of equal units.   on each side.

STRATEGY

1. Count each distance; note size as
   well as direction of difference.
2. Repeat step 1 for weight.
3. Compare the magnitude of the
   results in steps 1 and 2.
   Notice which is bigger.
4. Focus on dimension of greater
   difference. Pick side with higher
   value as one which will go down.

The above compensation strategy marks the pinnacle of what Piaget labeled "concrete operational thought", and what is labeled "dimensional thought" in the present volume. The procedures for discriminating among the various forms that this thought takes on the balance beam are given in Marini (1984). The percentages of children who functioned at each level in his study are given in Table 6.3.

---

[11] Note that this feature must be encoded by applying the strategy of the previous substages, that is, by counting both weight and distance.

TABLE 6.3

Percentage of Children at Each Substage on the Balance Beam Task, During the Period from $3\frac{1}{2}$ to 10 Years of Age[a]

Theoretical age range (mean age of sample)	Level 0: Perceptual assessment of weight (%)	Level 1: Assessment of weight by counting (%)	Level 2: Assessment of distance by counting when weight equal (%)	Level 3: Weight and distance compensation via addition or subtraction (%)
$3\frac{1}{2}$–5 yr (4 yr, 5 mo)	75	25	0	0
5–7 yr (6 yr, 10 mo)	100	95	5	0
7–9 yr (9 yr)	100	100	65	15
9–11 yr (10 yr, 10 mo)	100	100	95	55

[a]From Marini (1984).

As may already by apparent, children's progress from substage to substage during the dimensional period takes an identical course to that which was observed during the previous two periods. The general form of the structural progression is the same, as are the processing principles by which each successive structure operates. Finally, the result of the changes is also the same. By the end of the stage, children can assemble flexible control structures for solving dimensional problems, particularly those which require insight into the compensatory or reversible effects of different dimensions.

THE DEVELOPMENT OF ABSTRACT CONTROL STRUCTURES IN ADOLESCENCE

The changes that take place during the final stage of children's development have not been researched as extensively as those which take place earlier. On at least one task, however, children's further progress has been charted in considerable detail. Fortunately, the task in question is once again the balance beam, which was first analyzed in detail for this age group by Furman (1981), and which has been studied further in our own research group by Marini (1984).

Substage 0: Operational Consolidation (9–11 Years)

Children who compare the magnitude of one quantitative dimension with that of a second may be said to be executing a second-order or abstract dimensional operation. They are no longer comparing quantities that are calculable by enumerating the objects in front of them. Rather, they are comparing quantities that must be calculated by executing a second operation on the product of each of these primary ones (i.e., subtraction). In effect, children are no longer focusing on either of the two concrete dimensions separately. Rather, they are focusing on a more abstract dimension: the vector that results from their opposition. For the sake of simplicity, I shall refer to these *second-order dimensional operations* as *vectorial* operations. I shall also represent the particular vectorial operations underlying 10-year-old performance on the balance beam in abbreviated form as follows:

PROBLEM SITUATION   OBJECTIVE
- Weight and distance in opposi- ⟶ • Determine relative magnitude.
  tion.

STRATEGY
1. Compare weight difference to distance difference. Pick larger as more potent.

At about the same time as they develop primitive vectorial operations on the balance beam, children develop primitive vectorial operations in other domains as well. In the verbal domain, one such operation is analogy. To perceive an analogy, one must perceive a higher-order vector along which two lower-order dimensions may be compared ($A:B::C:D$). In the quantitative domain, one such operation is ratio. In order to understand the equivalence of two fractions, one must again focus on a second-order dimension (ratio) that remains constant, while two lower-order dimensions change.

Ratio is an operation that plays an extremely important role with regard to the development of abstract thought in science and mathematics. In fact, the role it plays is directly analogous to that of counting in the development of concrete thought. Like counting, ratio is used to bring a quantitative precision to relationships that were previously perceived in only a rough, qualitative fashion. Ratio also has a long developmental history, which can be traced well back into the prior stage. Teachers report that they can teach children to add and subtract by the age of 5 to 7 years. They can teach them to multiply and divide by the age of 7 to 9 years. Finally, they can teach them to understand the equivalence of certain multiplications and divisions by the age of 9 to 11 years. The control structures on which these various skills depend have been described elsewhere (Case, 1979). For the moment, it is sufficient to note that ratio is an abstract or second-order dimensional operation that is similar in complexity to that of variable-compensation, but which has a different function, and a different internal form. The earliest problems children can solve with this operation (about grades 3 or 4) are as follows: "For two dollars you get eight francs. How many francs will you get for one dollar?" The control structure on which successful solution depends may be represented in abbreviated form as follows:

PROBLEM SITUATION	OBJECTIVE
• 2 dollars = 8 francs. 1 dollar = ?	• Determine number of francs for one dollar.

STRATEGY

1. Divide up the number of francs (8) among the dollars (2). Note how much each one gets (4).

Substage 1: Operational Coordination (11–13 Years)

Although children can execute isolated vectorial operations by the age of 9 or 10 years, they cannot coordinate two such operations. As a consequence, they cannot assemble abstract *structures,* and their thought does not yet appear to be qualitatively different from that which is observed at younger ages. By about the age of 11 to 13 years, however, such a qualitative shift is observed. Children are now reported as showing their first glimmerings of abstract reasoning, or scientific thought. For example, faced with a problem where 2 weights on the left are opposed by 1 weight on the right, while 2 distance pegs on the left are opposed by 4 distance pegs on the right, they no longer note that the left side has only one more weight than the right, whereas the right side has two more distance pegs than the left. Thus, they no longer predict that the right side will go down. Instead, they note that there are twice as many weights on the left or "two for one", and that there are twice as many distance pegs on the right[12] as well. They therefore conclude that the two sides will balance. This sort of reasoning does not appear if the subjects have no experience with the balance beam, that is, if they have no feedback that the reasoning of the previous stage is inadequate. Presumably it would also not appear if they had no experience in thinking in terms of ratios. Given that these two conditions are met, however, the reasoning does appear to emerge with considerable regularity (Marini, 1984). The control structure underlying it may be represented as follows:

PROBLEM SITUATION   OBJECTIVE

- Weight and distance in opposi- ⟶ • Determine relative magnitude.
  tion.

- Left side has 2 weights, for 1   • Convert distances to com-
  unit on right, distances "per unit"   parable unit form.
  not known (4 right, 2 left).

STRATEGY

1. Divide up the distance pegs on
   the right, to see how many each
   distance peg on the left "will
   get" (2).
2. Compare the two resulting unit
   ratios. If equal, predict that the
   beam will balance; otherwise pick
   the stronger as more potent.

Note that, as was the case at the previous stage-transition points, the above structure involves two operations which were available at the previous stage as components. Note further that these operations, although they were available earlier, previously served quite different functions, and were used in very different contexts (i.e., science or causality problems versus math or sharing problems). Note finally, that one of the two operations has been subordinated to the other, in the sense that its end state now serves as a means to resolving a dilemma which the application of the other structure presents. In all these respects, therefore, the nature of the transition that takes place at 11 years is

[12]Sometimes this "2 for 1" is depicted graphically, by drawing lines connecting each two on the left with one on the right.

similar to the one which took place at 5 years, or earlier still at $1\frac{1}{2}$ years or at 4 months.

Substage 2: Bifocal Coordination (13–15 Years)[13]

Although 11–13-year-olds can utilize some notion of ratio or "dividing things up" when reasoning about two opposing dimensions, they can do so only when this operation has a single and very simple focus. In the problem that has just been considered, one of the dimensions was already stated in simple unit form, and the other could be reduced to such a form by a single division-operation. If children are given more complex problems, what happens is that they either "fall back" on the subtractive reasoning that they utilized at the age of 9 or 10 years, or they introduce some simple ratio into the problem of their own (Furman, 1981; Marini, 1984). By the age of 13 to 15 years, however, they are capable of taking a second division operation into account as well. One of the problems that they can solve as a consequence is one where the distances on the two sides are 5 and 2 and the weights are 2 and 1. As might be expected, the behaviour that emerges is that children take the quantity which is "left over" after 2 is divided into 5 (i.e., 1) and divide it up as well. They therefore end up comparing the unit ratio of the weights which is given (2:1), with the unit ratio in the distances which they have computed ($2\frac{1}{2}$:1). The control structure for doing so might be represented as follows:

PROBLEM SITUATION   OBJECTIVES

- Weight and distance in opposi- ⟶ • Determine relative magnitude.
  tion.
- Weights "per unit" known, dis-
  tance not (5 right, 2 left).   • Convert distance dimension
  to unit form.
- 5 does not divide evenly among
  2 (Answer: 2 with remainder 1).[14]   • Divide remainder evenly
  to generate nonunitary ratio.

STRATEGY

1. Divide remaining distance on the right (1) among pegs on the left ($\frac{1}{2}$) (Answer $\frac{1}{2}$).
2. Add this value to the whole number of pegs for each one on the left (Answer $2\frac{1}{2}$).
3. Compare this value to the unit ratio for the weights (2). Pick the larger ($2\frac{1}{2}$) as more potent.

---

[13]Or, more precisely, 13 to $15\frac{1}{2}$ years.

[14]Note that this feature can only emerge by applying the strategy of the previous substage (i.e., by dividing 5 among 2).

Although the above structure is one that emerges at this substage, a variety of others appear as well, depending on the specific numbers which are used, and the way in which the subject construes the problem. What all these approaches share in common is that they require that a greater number of elements be represented, and a greater number of subgoals be established, than at the previous substage.

Substage 3: Elaborated Coordination (15–18 Years)[15]

As might be expected, the elaboration that is introduced at the final substage is that the particular set of operations that were used to adjust one of the dimensions into a new ratio at the previous substage can now be executed for the second dimension as well. The subject can therefore deal with a problem in which neither quantity is stated in unit form, and in which neither set of quantities can be transformed in any fashion into a ratio that is directly comparable to the other. What the subjects do to solve this problem is to convert both ratios into a new form. For a problem involving seven weights and three weights, at distances of 2 units and 5 units, they may therefore reason that 2 distance pegs and five distance pegs is the same as 1 for $2\frac{1}{2}$, while three weights and seven weights is the same as 1 for $2\frac{1}{3}$. Thus, the weight factor should predominate, and the balance beam should tilt in the direction of the greater weight. This thinking has a truly abstract quality, because neither of the entities that the children end up comparing has any direct visual counterpart in the physical world, yet one of these entities can be pitted against or seen as reversing the effect of the other. One control structure for executing this sort of thinking might be represented as follows:[16]

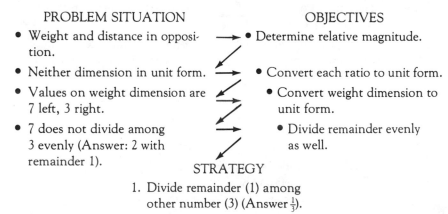

PROBLEM SITUATION

- Weight and distance in opposition.
- Neither dimension in unit form.
- Values on weight dimension are 7 left, 3 right.
- 7 does not divide among 3 evenly (Answer: 2 with remainder 1).

OBJECTIVES

- Determine relative magnitude.
- Convert each ratio to unit form.
- Convert weight dimension to unit form.
- Divide remainder evenly as well.

STRATEGY

1. Divide remainder (1) among other number (3) (Answer $\frac{1}{3}$).

---

[15] Or, more precisely, $15\frac{1}{2}$ to $18\frac{1}{2}$ years.

[16] Other structures have the same basic form, but utilize such strategies as converting to decimals, or using a "lowest common denominator" algorithm, for comparing the two ratios.

2. Add to answer from whole
   number division (2) (Answer $2\frac{1}{2}$).
3. Repeat division for other
   dimension, that is,
   a. Divide 5 among 2 (2
      remainder: 1).
   b. Divide 1 among 2 ($\frac{1}{2}$).
   c. Add fraction to answer from
      whole number division (2)
      (Answer $2\frac{1}{2}$).
4. Compare results from 2 divisions,
   pick large ratio ($2\frac{1}{2}$) as more
   potent.

The sort of thought that is observed on the problems at this substage represents the pinnacle of what Piaget termed formal operational thought and what is here termed abstract-dimensional or vectorial thought. The percentage of children at each age level who were functioning at each substage in Marini's study is indicated in Table 6.4. As may be seen, the majority of children did reach the higher levels of the stage. In this respect, the results are unlike those in many other studies. However, it must be remembered that the children were presented the problems in a sequence of ascending complexity, and that they were shown how the beam really reacted for the first few problems at every level. The percentages thus represent estimates of the complexity of the control structures that adolescents can assemble at each age level, *when they have access to all the facts about a given domain which are relevant*. In effect, they present an estimate of the sort of knowledge adolescents are capable of creating under optimal conditions, not the sort of knowledge they bring to the task spontaneously.

SUMMARY AND CONCLUSION

The preceding analyses complete my preliminary account of the changes that take place in children's executive control structures from birth to adulthood. As the reader will no doubt have realized, each of the control structures that has been described has actually been a cognitive model. That is, it has been a hypothetical account of the mental processes that underlie behaviour, and which may be presumed to control it. Taken together, therefore, the various models may be considered a cognitive theory. The theory does not attempt to specify how children get from one stage of development to the next. That task is taken up later. What the theory does attempt to do, however, is to specify the way in which children's mental processes are structured at each stage and

TABLE 6.4

Percentage of Children Capable of Functioning at Each Level of Vectorial Stage during the Period from 9 to 18 Years

Theoretical age range (mean age of sample)	Level 0: Comparison via addition or subtraction (%)	Level 1: Comparison of unit ratio with simple multiple of it (%)	Level 2: Comparison of unit ratio with nonintegral ratio via two-step reduction (%)	Level 3: Comparison of two nonintegral ratios, with reduction of both (%)
9–11 yr (10 yr, 10 mo)	85	10	5	0
11–13 yr (13 yr, 2 mo)	100	80	30	5
13–$15\frac{1}{2}$yr (15 yr, 8 mo)	100	95	75	25
$15\frac{1}{2}$–$18\frac{1}{2}$ yr 18 yr, 5 mo)	100	100	95	65

[a]From Marini (1984).

substage of their development, and the way in which the processes and structures of one stage relate to those of the next.

Throughout the present chapter I have attempted to point out ways in which the theory that is being proposed builds on previous theories, of both a structural and processing variety. I shall now conclude by making this relationship more explicit.

The following five postulates, all of which were implicit in Baldwin's theory, are preserved in the theory that was advanced in the present chapter.

1. Children are born with a set of innate motor operations, which they gradually bring under voluntary control during the first few months of life.
2. These first voluntary control structures (Baldwin's term was circular reactions) are then coordinated with each other.
3. Whenever voluntary control structures are coordinated, a recognizable shift or accommodation in the child's pattern of thought takes place.
4. Four major accommodations may be identified in children's development, each of which gives rise to a distinctive stage of thought, and a different type of knowledge of the objective world.
5. Within each stage, a number of more minor accommodations may also be identified, each of which gives rise to a distinctive substage.

The following five postulates, all of which were implicit in Piaget's theory, were also preserved.

1. The four major stages of child development correspond approximately to the following chronological periods: birth to $1\frac{1}{2}$ years, $1\frac{1}{2}$ to 5 years,[17] 5 to 11 years, and 11 to $18\frac{1}{2}$ years.
2. The final operations of each stage are organized into stable systems, which permit the child a great deal of flexibility at that particular epistemic level.
3. The operational systems that are the products of one major stage, when differentiated and coordinated, serve as the building blocks for those of the next.
4. In infancy, four types of control structures (circular reactions) appear in sequence: (1) primary, (2) secondary, (3) coordinated secondary, and (4) tertiary operations.
5. The same general progression is observed in subsequent stages.[18]

The following further postulates, all of which were originally advanced by information processing psychologists, were also preserved.

1. Executive control structures may be parsed into at least three components: representations of existing states, representations of desired states (goals),

---

[17] Actually, the age for the onset of concrete questions is normally set at 8 or 9 years, not 5 years However, because Piaget identified a precursor of the full concrete logic during his later work (i.e., the logic of functions) and because this precursor logic is first observed at 5 years, (see Piaget et al., 1977), I have adjusted the age down to fit this new conceptualization and data.

[18] Piaget, it will be remembered, referred to this as vertical décalage.

and representations of the operations or strategies for getting from one of these to the other (Newell *et al.*, 1958).

2. When children can set up an internal set of pointers that trace the route from their current state to a more desirable state via an intermediate set of states or operations, they have the experience of insight into how their current problem can be resolved (Newell *et al.*, 1958).

3. Children are born with the capacity for representing certain elementary properties of their current situation. They are also born with the capacity for setting certain recently experienced and desirable states as goals, and working towards their attainment (Klahr & Wallace, 1976, p. 220).

4. Many of the stage-like phenomena in intellectual development can be accounted for by presuming that children acquire new procedures for bridging the gap between current and desired states, and that these procedures are inserted into their existing procedures in some fashion (Simon, 1962).

Finally, the following five postulates were added to those advanced by previous theorists.

1. Major shifts in thinking are brought about by the coordination of executive structures whose complexity is similar, but whose function and internal form are different. Minor shifts are brought about by the coordination of executive structures whose complexity, form and function are all similar.

2. The same four changes take place during any major cognitive shift: (*a*) the top-level objective of one structure is nested within the other,(*b*) the feature of the situation which requires this nesting is added to the problem representation, (*c*) the operation or operations associated with the subordinate structure are added to those of the superordinate structure, where they function as a new *loop* or *subroutine*, (*d*) a number of modifications are made in the internal structure of each element, in order for the overall structure to function smoothly.

3. The cross-stage parallels in development (vertical décalages) are quite precise. Both the nature and the number of substages in each period is the same.

4. The period from 2 to 5 years of age is not just a precursor of concrete operational development. It is a distinct stage of its own, with its own sequence of operative structures and its own final operational system.

5. The four major classes of intellectual operation are sensorimotor, relational, dimensional, and vectorial (or abstract-dimensional).

In the chapters that follow, the generality of these postulates is examined. In each chapter, two questions are addressed. The first concerns what has been referred to as the *vertical structure* of development (Flavell, 1980). To what extent does the theory as so far elaborated, describe the prototypic way in which children's initial mental structures are assembled into more complex structures, each with a set of emergent properties of its own? That is, to what extent do all the complex forms of human thought have their basis in the sort of genetic progression that has been described? The second question concerns what has been called the *horizontal structure* of development. To what extent do those mental functions which do develop through the sequence that has been specified, do so at a common rate? That is, to what extent can the type of executive structure that has been described at any given level be said to capture the general form of all children's thought at that particular point in time?

These are important but difficult questions. To draw an analogy from chemistry, the questions are equivalent to asking whether the theory can function as a sort of periodic table of cognitive development: that is, as a device for (1) interpreting the existing developmental data which are available, (2) revealing the internal structure and periodicity of the data, and (3) predicting the existence of new data, at ages or for tasks where none is currently available.

In order to address these questions, it is necessary to return to the sensorimotor stage, and to examine children's executive structures across a broader range of situations.

CHAPTER 7

Development in Infancy:
The Underpinnings of
Thought and Language

INTRODUCTION

Baldwin, Gesell and Piaget all studied children's intellectual development during infancy quite intensively. However, for many years their pioneering work was not followed up by other psychologists. One reason for this may have been that so little of interest appeared to take place prior to the child's acquisition of language. Another reason may have been the great technical difficulty associated with studying intellectual development prior to that time. Until infants can follow verbal directions, they cannot participate in the normal sorts of experiments that psychologists are used to conducting. Moreover, until their motor skills have developed, it is hard to devise alternative methods for examining their mental functioning.

Since the early 1970's, however, there has been a renewed surge of interest in infant cognition. In part, this has been due to the renewed interest in cognition in general, which was mentioned in Chapter 4. In part, it has been due to the realization that a great deal of importance does occur prior to the acquisition of language, including developments vital for the acquisition of language itself. With the renewed interest in infant cognition has come an explosion of ingenious methods for studying it. Thus, what once appeared to be a black box has now been rendered, if not transparent, at least visible with appropriate supplementary lenses.

In the present chapter, no attempt is made to present all the fascinating details that the recent studies of infant cognition have revealed. However, at least one sequence of competencies is analyzed from each of the major domains of infant development that has been investigated, beginning with those studied by Piaget and moving on to those studied by more recent investigators. These analyses have two main objectives. The first is to determine whether infants' competencies progress through the same four substages as were described in the previous chapter, in each of the various domains which has been investigated. The second is to determine whether—for those domains for which infants' competencies do show a similar progression—the progression takes place at the same rate. Using the terms that were introduced at the end of the previous two chapters, the object of the present chapter is to determine whether there is any vertical or horizontal structure in infant development. For the purpose of exposition, infants' competencies are divided into two broad categories: those involving interaction with inanimate objects, and those involving interaction with other human beings.

CONTROL STRUCTURES FOR INTERACTING WITH INANIMATE OBJECTS

Exploring Objects in the Immediate Environment

One of the most salient traits of young infants is that they like to explore the objects in their immediate enviroment. And one of the most salient changes that takes place during the first 2 years of their lives is in the structures they can assemble for doing so. The infants' growing competence in this area was first studied by Baldwin. It was later probed in greater detail by Piaget, under the heading of the means-ends scheme. In most of the tasks which Piaget invented to investigate the means-end scheme, infants were engaged in some activity whose ultimate aim was exploring the properties of a nearby object. What varied from task to task was the complexity of the means they had to devise, in order to achieve this end.

Substage 0: Operational Consolidation (1–4 Months)

Many of the tasks that Piaget presented to very young infants involved visual rather than manual exploration. In one of these tasks, a lighted match was moved across the infants' field of vision, to see whether they would track it as it moved in various directions. In another task, a mobile toy was suspended over the infants' basinette, to see how they would respond to it when it was set in motion and allowed to come to rest. The trend that was observed on both these tasks was similar. During the first few months of life, infants became progressively more adept at scanning the features of objects that were at rest, and at tracking objects that were moving. A standardized situation in which this latter capability may be observed is the ring-tracking task, which appears on developmental scales such as the Bayley (1969) and the Griffeths (1954). A small ring is suspended in front of an infant at a distance of approximately 10 cm, and is moved across his or her field of vision in a variety of directions. By the end of the substage, the infant is capable of tracking the ring along a variety of trajectories, including a horizontal path (2 months), a vertical path ($2\frac{1}{2}$ months), and a circle $3\frac{1}{2}$ months). In the present context, the control structure for tracking an object in this latter fashion might be represented as follows:

PROBLEM SITUATION   OBJECTIVE

- Interesting object disappearing   • Relocate interesting object
  from view in lateral direction.   in center of visual field.

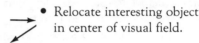

STRATEGY

1. Move eyes from current position (X) to a new position (Y), perhaps using peripheral input as a cue to location.

Note that this structure develops during the same time period as the structure for scanning the various parts of a teetering object such as a balance beam, and that it has essentially the same components. There is a representation of some moving object in the environment which has temporarily disappeared from focal vision. There is a representation of the goal of re-establishing contact with this object. Finally, there is a representation of an occulomotor strategy for doing so, one which probably draws on peripheral visual input as a cue.

Another structure which infants develop during this same time period is one for putting their thumbs or fingers in their mouths. This structure of course serves more than an exploratory function. It serves a soothing function as well. However, from the present perspective, what is of interest is the nature of the underlying control structure which enables the infant to reach this objective, not the nature of the objective itself. One of Piaget's best known anecdotal examples of the change that takes place in this structure came from an observation which he made of his young son, Laurent, whose thumb happened to have been removed from his mouth by his nurse. Immediately following this event, Laurent made 13 attempts in a row to put his hand in his mouth, until he gradually perfected the movement. Later, he managed to raise his hand to his mouth even when it was placed on the bed near his waist. Following Baldwin,

Piaget referred to such strategies as primary circular reactions, because they involve a direct feedback loop between the attainment or nonattainment of a desired goal, and the action which is executed. In the present context, the structure for controlling such a reaction would be represented as follows:

PROBLEM SITUATION   OBJECTIVE
- Pleasant sensation from mouth ——→ • Reinstate pleasant sensation.
  eliminated.

STRATEGY
1. Move arm from current position (X) to mouth (Y), using feedback from the arm as a cue.

Although the preceeding structure is different in its content, it is similar to the ring-tracking structure in its underlying form. In each case, the problem situation is that a pleasant source of stimulation has temporarily disappeared: either one that infants want to learn more about, or one which they want to re-experience in order to alter their current arousal level. In each case, too, the objective is to reinstate this sensation. Finally, in each case, the natural response is to experiment with various motor movements, until the desired objective is achieved, and a well-integrated motor strategy is consolidated.

Substage 1: Operational Coordination (4–8 Months)

Although infants become increasingly adept at executing voluntarily directed actions during the preliminary substage of the sensorimotor period, they show few signs of being able to coordinate two different forms of such action, and hence few signs of what a casual oberver might term active exploration. At 4 to 8 months, however, a qualitative shift in their performance takes place, and this sort of coordination now appears.

On the balance beam scale, the task which was used to demonstrate this change involved placing the beam in front of the child and setting it in motion by striking one of its arms. What was observed under these conditions was that, after infants had observed the action of the beam, they would reach out and strike it themselves, watching the reaction which this produced with great interest.

What sort of competencies are observed on Piaget's means-ends tasks during the same time period? Most of the competencies are quite similar to the one observed on the balance; in fact, so much so that the balance could actually be considered as a candidate for an item in a Piagetian scale. There is one task that was designed by Piaget which is particularly revealing, however, because it does not require any demonstration by an adult, and because the particular form of means-ends connection is novel. What the experimenter does is to suspend a mobile over a baby's crib, and to tie his or her arm to it with a ribbon. During the period from 1 to 4 months, the infant will watch the mobile move intently, when some chance movement of its arm happens to set it swinging. However, the baby will make no attempt to reinstate the action of the mobile once it stops, by repeating the same movement. By the age of 4 to 8 months, however, the infant's behaviour changes dramatically. The infant now repeats the arm movement almost immediately, watching the reaction it produces with great delight. The new control structure that has been developed may therefore be represented as follows:

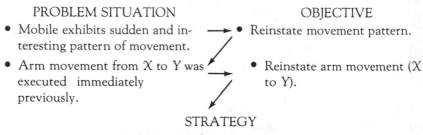

PROBLEM SITUATION
- Mobile exhibits sudden and interesting pattern of movement.
- Arm movement from X to Y was executed immediately previously.

OBJECTIVE
- Reinstate movement pattern.
- Reinstate arm movement (X to Y).

STRATEGY
1. Move arm from X to Y.
2. Track mobile movement carefully, noting its response.

There is a slight difference between the above motor strategy and that used on the balance task, in that the movement of the infant's arm on the balance task includes two subcomponents (i.e., a stretching out component and a hitting component), whereas in the above task one action is often sufficient. In all other respects, however, the above control structure is virtually identical to the one which is exhibited on the balance beam during the same time period. In each case, infants must notice an interesting movement in a stationary object, as well as the action which immediately preceded it. In each case they must also set themselves the object of reproducing the first action in order to reproduce the second one. Finally, in each case they must actually generate this action, and monitor the reaction that takes place.

Substage 2: Bifocal Coordination (8–12 Months)

During the next substage, the competence which is observed on the balance beam is that of making an interesting event occur on the left hand side of the balance (i.e., ringing a bell), by hitting the balance on the right. The structure for achieving this goal was referred to as bifocal because it required the infant to sustain a focus on two different objects while executing a voluntarily directed manual action.

In Piaget's means-ends scale, the competencies that emerge during this same time period are different in their specific content. However, they are once again quite similar in their general form. One task that reveals this similarity is the barrier-removal task, which was described in Chapter 5. If a barrier is placed in front of an object which infants at 4 to 8 months desire, they will make no attempt to remove it. By the age of 8 to 12 months, however, infants will solve the same problem with ease. The control structure which they must assemble for doing so was described in detail in Chapter 5. As may be seen, this control structure is similar to that required to solve the bifocal balance task in a number of important respects. In each case, the infants must notice an object at one position, and set themselves the goal of acting on that object in some fashion. In each case, they must then focus on a second object, and set themselves the subsidary goal of acting on that object as well. Finally, in each case they must establish the particular action they wish to execute as a further subgoal, and actually generate it. They must then monitor the changes which take place both with respect to the object on which they are acting directly, and the other object which is their primary focus of interest. In all these respects, then, the requirements for the barrier removal task and for the bifocal balance beam task are identical.

Substage 3: Elaborated Coordination (12–18 Months)

An additional feature that is introduced in the balance beam task during the age range from 12 to 18 months is that the bells are alternated in their location, being placed either above or below the left hand side of the beam. This new task feature requires that children incorporate a corresponding new element in their representation of the problem situation. It also requires that they incorporate a new goal in their list of objectives, and a new loop in their motor strategy as well: one for moving their arm in the reverse direction from the direction in which they want the arm of the beam to move.

On the means-ends scale, the next task that children are required to solve involves focusing on an additional feature of a similar sort, namely, the relative position of the object on which the child wishes to have an effect, and the object which will be used as a means to achieving this effect. The particular task in question is sometimes called the blanket-and-keys task. Once again, it is a task which was originally invented by Baldwin, but which Piaget put to excellent use in studying his own children. An interesting toy (e.g., a set of keys) is placed out of an infant's reach, on a napkin or a light blanket. In order to play with the toy, the infant must notice that the keys are on top of the napkin, and pull in on the napkin until the toy is within reach. Prior to the age of 12 months, children rarely solve this problem. Somewhere between the age of 12 and 18 months, they show their first signs of success. They also succeed on other tool-using tasks, such as Kohler's famous banana and stick task (Kohler, 1921).

In order to solve this sort of problem, an executive control structure of the following sort must be assembled.

PROBLEM SITUATION   OBJECTIVES

- Interesting object (e.g., keys) at ⟶   • Explore object at Y.
  Y.

- Object out of reach.   ⟶   • Move object within reach.

- Object is on top of cloth.   • Pull cloth closer.

- Cloth is at Z.   • Hand to Z.

STRATEGY

1. Move arm from X to Z.
2a. Grasp cloth.
2b. Pull cloth from Z to Z^1.
3. Monitor new position of keys;
    if within reach, go to 4; other-
    wise repeat or adjust type of
    pull on cloth.
4. Repeat 1 and 2 for keys instead
    of cloth (i.e., explore object)

Once again, the above structure bears a close resemblance to the structure which is developed for the balance beam during the same time period, and which was described in the previous chapter. From a qualitative point of view, it is similar in that it involves the understanding of the relationship between two objects, and the effects of different types of action on this relationship. From a quantitative point of view, it is similar in that it involves an identical number of elements in its representational structure, and an identical number of goals in its goal structure. Even the nature of the loop that must be added in the motor strategy is similar, namely a routine for monitoring the change in position of two distal objects and adapting the particular nature of the hand movement which is used in order to produce this change, in an on-line fashion.

In summary, therefore, it may be said (1) that the general sequence of structures for solving means-ends tasks is similar to that for solving the balance scale tasks, and (2) that the transition from one structure to the next in each sequence also occurs during the same approximate age range. Using the terms that were introduced earlier, one could say that the two developmental sequences show a high degree of both vertical and horizontal structure.

The next set of structures to be considered also involve procedures for dealing with inanimate objects. However, the procedures differ considerably in their focus.

Locating Objects that Have Disappeared from View

A great deal of infants' time during the first few years of life is spent in visual exploration, either scanning stationary objects or tracking moving ones. Not surprisingly, infants develop an increasingly complex understanding of the laws governing the appearance and disappearance of objects in their visual field during this time period, and an increasingly complex set of strategies for locating objects that have disappeared from view. These strategies were also studied by Piaget, under the heading of object permanence.

Substage 0: Operational Consolidation (1–4 Months)

At the beginning of the substage, when an infant's eye is caught by a moving object that disappears and reappears from behind a screen, its eyes will wander each time the object disappears. The absence of the stimulus appears to imply the absence of any organized response. By the end of the substage, however, the infant's eyes will continue to hover around the point of the object's disappearance, apparently waiting for it to reappear (Piaget, 1954; Uzgiris & Hunt, 1975). Using the notation developed in the previous chapter, the executive control structure for controlling this behaviour might be represented as follows:

PROBLEM REPRESENTATION   OBJECTIVE

- Interesting object disappears at ⟶ • Relocate interesting object.
  point X.

STRATEGY

1. Direct gaze in general vicinity of
   X, moving eyes in zigzag
   pattern.

Note that this structure is once again similar to that which is involved in the visual tracking of an object such as a block on a balance beam. In each case, the feature of the environment which must be represented is the temporary disappearance of an object at a particular point in space. In each case, the objective that must be established is also similar, namely, making renewed contact with the object. Finally, in each case the strategy involves the same motor system. The only real difference is that in one case the search can consist of a single jump of the eyes in the direction of movement, while in the other case it must take the form of a series of such jumps, or a steady gaze.

Substage 1: Operational Coordination (4–8 Months)

Although infants become increasingly adept during the first few months of life at searching for an object with their eyes when that object has disappeared from view, they show no sign of being able to coordinate this activity with any other activity. This is true even if the second activity is one which is very similar to the first, and which involves the same sensory and motor systems.

Perhaps the most interesting task on which this limited capacity appears is the one mentioned in Chapter 1. An object is slowly removed from the infants' view on the left side of their visual field. It is then brought back into view on the right side of their visual field, after having been moved around behind their heads. When the object disappears on the left side, infants at the end of first substage engage in active search for it. Then, when the object reappears on the other side, they catch sight of it and begin to track it again. However, even if the activity is repeated several times, they show no sign of making any connection between the disappearance on the left side and the reappearance on the right side. As a consequence, they do not learn to anticipate the rearrival of the object.

Between the age of 5 and 8 months, however, this task is quickly mastered (Uzgiris & Hunt, 1975). After one or two disappearances at X, infants will shift their gaze directly to Y, to await the arrival of the object at that point. The executive control structure that is responsible for producing this behavior might be represented as follows:

PROBLEM REPRESENTATION   OBJECTIVES

- Interesting object disappears at ⟶ • Relocate interesting object.
  X.

- Same object reappears regularly ⟶   • Find Y.
  at Y.

STRATEGY

1. Move eyes from left to right
   until Y is located.
2. Move eyes in a zigzag pattern in
   the vicinity of Y.

Although its content is somewhat different from that of the control structures that emerge on the balance beam or the means-ends scale, the general form of the above structure is once again quite similar. Infants must first notice two events that take place in immediate sequence, and grasp the connection between them. This is analogous to noticing the experimenter touching the balance, and grasping the connection between this and the pattern of movement which the balance beam exhibits immediately thereafter. Next, they must set themselves a major goal and a minor goal which are related to each one of these events. This is analogous to setting the subgoal of moving their arm, in order to move the balance beam. Finally, they must actually execute the action in question, and monitor the results which are produced. In each of these respects, therefore, the operational coordination that is required on the object-location scale is similar to that which is required on the balance scale, although the particular motor operation (eye rather than hand movement) is quite different.

Substage 2: Bifocal Coordination (8–12 Months)

Although infants can learn to anticipate the arrival of an object at one point after they have seen it disappear at another by the age of 8 months, they show no signs of success on tasks that require manual rather than visual search. One such task is Piaget's classic hidden-object task, which has become known as the test of object permanence. In this task, a desirable object is covered by a cloth or some other screen. The child's searching behaviour is then observed. Interestingly, it is not until the age of about 9 months that infants show any sign of actively trying to remove the cloth (see Griffiths, 1954; Piaget, 1954).

On the surface, this task would appear to be a very simple one. The understanding involved does not appear to be any more complex than that involved in the earlier disappearance–reappearance task. In fact, as Bower (1974) has shown, children are capable of anticipating an object's re-arrival from under a cloth by the age of about 5 months, providing they do not have to actively uncover it themselves. The problem would therefore appear to lie with infants' motor system.

As has already been mentioned, however, infants at this age are quite adept at reaching out and pushing or pulling at objects, to see how they react. In fact, one of the objects they may be observed to pull in their daily life is precisely the sort of napkin which they fail to pull in the hidden object task. Thus, on close inspection, the problem does not appear to lie with their motor system after all.

As with many apparently simple tasks that are not solved until a relatively late age, the real problem probably lies—not with the individual components which are necessary for success on the task—but with their coordination and control by means of an appropriate executive structure. In effect, an infant would need a structure such as the following in order to solve this task.

PROBLEM REPRESENTATION   OBJECTIVES

- Interesting object disappears at ⟶ • Relocate interesting object.
  point X.
- Point X occupied by napkin   ⟶   • Remove napkin.
- Edge of napkin is at Y.   • Move hand to Y.

STRATEGY

1a. Reach with arm from current
    position to Y.
1b. Grasp napkin.
2. Pull napkin.
3. Move eyes in zigzag pattern at
    X.

The similarity between this structure and that required to solve the barrier removal and bifocal balance scale tasks will no doubt be apparent. All three tasks require the child to hold in mind a top-level goal relating to one object, while they focus on a subgoal that is related to a second object. All three tasks also require the child to represent some information about the spatial position of the second object. Finally, all three tasks require the child to reach out to the second object, and physically displace it. That all three tasks should be mastered during the same age range is therefore understandable.

If one interprets the child's problem on the object permanence scale in this fashion—that is, as a problem in assembling a bifocal control structure—then one can explain a finding which would otherwise appear quite anomalous. This finding is that children do not solve the object permanence task even if the cover which is used is transparent (Bower, 1974). Why an infant should think an object has ceased to exist simply because it is occluded by a transparent barrier—which is the object permanence interpretation—is not apparent. However, why an infant would not reach out to remove a barrier even when it is transparent—which is the present interpretation—is apparent. To do so would require a problem representation, a goal structure, and a strategy which are of exactly the same complexity as those involved in the case of an opaque barrier, or for that matter any other task which requires some form of intentional manual action, while focusing on two external objects.

Substage 3: Elaborated Coordination (12–18 Months)

Although infants can locate an object behind or under a screen by the age of 8 to 12 months, they cannot succeed at tasks which involve hiding and displacing an object. One such task is a version of the ancient shell game. In this task, two handkerchiefs are placed on the floor. A small object is moved under one of them, but then brought out the other side and placed under the second. Prior to the age of 12 months, children attempt to locate the hidden object under the incorrect cover. That is, they look at the place where the object disappeared, remove the handkerchief which is there, and exhibit surprise when the object is no longer under it. By the age of 12 to 18 months they solve the problem with ease. Clearly, the errors that children produce at Substage 2 result from applying the same structure that yields success on the standard hidden object task. Equally clearly, their ultimate success results from being able to take account of the new element that is added, namely, object displacement. The executive control structure that is required may be represented as follows:

PROBLEM REPRESENTATION   OBJECTIVES

- Interesting object disappears at ⟶• Relocate interesting object.
  point X.

- Interesting object then moved ⟶ • Locate new position of object.
  to point Y.

- Point Y occupied by napkin #2.⟶ • Remove napkin #2.

- Edge of napkin #2 at point Z. ⟶   • Move hand to Z.

STRATEGY

1. Reach with arm from current
   position to Z.
2a. Grasp napkin.
2b. Pull napkin.
3. Move eyes in zigzag pattern in
   the vicinity of Y.

Note that no new element has been added to the motor strategy. As was mentioned in Chapter 5, it is very often the case that the strategies which children employ do not change over rather long periods of time. What changes are the conditions under which they can employ them. And, as may be seen, the present situation involves the representation of one more element than at the previous stage, and the setting of one additional subgoal, namely, that related to the further displacement of the desired object under a second barrier. It is in these latter two respects, then, rather than in any further modification of the motor strategy per se, that the object permanence structure during this age range remains parallel to that which is observed on the balance beam or the means-ends scales.

Consider finally a behavioral sequence of a rather different sort, namely, that involved in drinking and eating.

Drinking and Eating

From a biological perspective, two of the most vital sensorimotor functions in which infants engage are drinking and eating. As might be expected, their structures for engaging in these activities also undergo a considerable transformation during the first 2 years of life.

Substage 0: Operational Consolidation (1–4 Months)

What happens during the first substage of development is that the operation of nursing passes from reflexive to voluntary control. Piaget noted this change using a variety of informal methods (Piaget, 1952). Bruner and his colleagues studied this development more formally, by feeding neonates with a bottle that was capable of delivering milk in various types of spurts, and recording the degree of pressure they applied to the nipple under these various conditions (Bruner, 1968). What they found was that the infants' sucking becomes increasingly well adapted to changes in the nature of the milk flow during the first few months of life.

A parallel change that takes place is in the infants' ability to decrease or eliminate the flow of milk when they are *not* hungry, or have had enough. They do this by actively twisting their heads away from their mother and the nipple. What this avoidance operation reveals is the infant's ability to adjust their motor systems, not just to the problem situation presented by a nipple, but to their own objective in that situation. In short, what it reveals is that their first structures for controlling the intake of food have the same three sorts of components as their first structures for controlling the intake of visual stimulation. In the case of the particular behaviour pattern studied by Bruner *et al.*, these three components might be represented as follows:

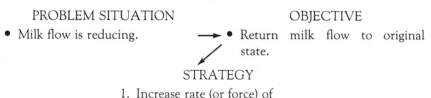

PROBLEM SITUATION   OBJECTIVE
- Milk flow is reducing.   ⟶ • Return milk flow to original
                                      state.
                  STRATEGY
        1. Increase rate (or force) of
           sucking.

Substage 1: Operational Coordination (4–8 Months).

Although infants become increasingly effective at adapting their sucking to the nature of the milk flow and to their own objectives during the first few months of life, they show few signs of being able to coordinate the structures which they develop for nursing with any other structure. For example, if an interesting visual stimulus is presented while they are sucking, they will often stop sucking in order to track it. Alternatively, if they are extremely hungry, they will shut their eyes rather than suffer the interference in sucking which monitoring the stimulus would entail (Bruner, 1968).

Another activity that infants cannot coordinate with nursing is intentional movement of the hands. They may reach for interesting objects which are a few inches away or they may nurse, but they do not appear capable of coordinating these two activities. By the age of 4 to 8 months, however, this capability emerges. Its presence is most clearly evident when infants are placed in the presence of finger food. With clear evidence of intentionality, they will reach for the food and bring it directly to their mouths. The executive control structure for doing so might be represented in abbreviated form as follows:

PROBLEM PRESENTATION   OBJECTIVES

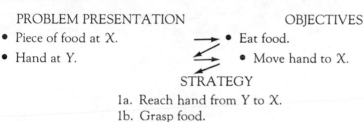

- Piece of food at X.   • Eat food.
- Hand at Y.   • Move hand to X.

STRATEGY

1a. Reach hand from Y to X.
1b. Grasp food.
2. Bring it to mouth.

For babies who are bottle fed, another clear indication of this sort of voluntary manual–oral coordination is that they will now actively hold their bottle while being fed, and can often prevent it from falling out of their mouths on their own (Brazelton, 1969). The executive control structure which is required for regulating this latter behaviour might be represented as follows:

PROBLEM REPRESENTATION   OBJECTIVES

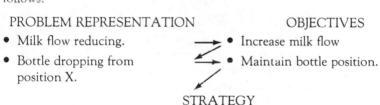

- Milk flow reducing.   • Increase milk flow
- Bottle dropping from   • Maintain bottle position.
  position X.

STRATEGY

1. Hold bottle tightly with arms.
2. Recommence sucking with
   increased force.

Substage 2: Bifocal Coordination (8–12 Months)

During the next substage, infants become capable of attending to two different visual stimuli, and of coordinating information from both of these sources with the action of their hands and mouths. One example of this may be seen in the infant's manipulation of a spoon. During the previous substage, infants learn to reach out and pick up small spoons, much as they learn to pick up any other object of comparable size (Griffiths, 1954). They may also bring a spoon to their mouth to explore it. Because their focus is on the spoon as a global entity, however, they will not necessarily put the appropriate part of the spoon in their mouths. Nor will they distinguish between a spoon which has food on it and one which does not. Hence, they will show no sign of using the spoon as a tool for eating.

By the age of 8 to 12 months, however, the first preliminary use of the spoon in this fashion may be observed. Infants will not yet use a spoon spontaneously. However, if it is preloaded with food, and placed in their hands, they may successfully use it to bring the food to their mouths, and get at least some of the food to its intended destination (Brazelton, 1969). What success in this task requires is that the infants integrate a new element into their structure for bringing an object to their mouths and opening their mouth as it approaches. The new element is a representation of some part of the object, and an adjustment of the movement of the overall object so that this part arrives at their mouth. The executive control structure for effecting this coordination might be represented as follows.

PROBLEM REPRESENTATION   OBJECTIVES

- Edible substance in view.   ⟶ • Eat substance.
- Substance on cusp of spoon.   ⇄ • Bring cusp to mouth.
- Hand on spoon handle (i.e., to   ⇄ • Bring handle to side of
  side of cusp).   mouth.

STRATEGY

1. Lift hand to side of mouth.
2. Track spoon cusp, adjusting movement so cusp approaches center of mouth.
3. As food arrives, open mouth and taste it.

As was the case at previous substages, the above behaviour is not the only sign of bifocal coordination which emerges during the period. Another one is that children show their first preliminary success at drinking from a cup—providing that the cup has very little milk in it, and that their caretaker is prepared to tolerate a good deal of dribbling as the milk is actually drunk (Brazelton, 1969; Griffiths, 1954). A food-avoidance strategy of similar complexity is also observed. For the first time, children will actively twist their head and blow out air as a spoon arrives at their mouth, if they observe that the spoon contains food which they do not like (Piaget, 1952). What both these latter achievements require is the ability to sustain a focus on two external objects. Like the bifocal balance task, the barrier-removal task, or the object-permanence task, therefore, these responses may also be said to be bifocal, and may be modeled by means of an executive control structure with the same general format.

Substage 3: Elaborated Coordination (12–18 Months)

A number of elaborations are introduced into the structures of the previous substage, as infants enter the final substage of the period. One of these, as might be guessed, is that infants can now spontaneously use a spoon, even if it is not already in their hands, or preloaded with food (Griffiths, 1954). The control structure that is required for executing this behaviour is perhaps most similar to that which is required to solve the blanket and keys task. Both tasks require that the child first reach for one object, and then use it to transport a second object to its intended location. However, at a more global level, the task is similar to all those which have been described for this age range. The executive control structure for independent spoon use might be represented as follows:

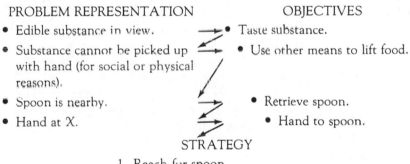

PROBLEM REPRESENTATION   OBJECTIVES

- Edible substance in view.
- Substance cannot be picked up with hand (for social or physical reasons).
- Spoon is nearby.
- Hand at X.

- Taste substance.
- Use other means to lift food.
- Retrieve spoon.
- Hand to spoon.

STRATEGY

1. Reach for spoon.
2. Grasp spoon and pick it up.
3. Dip spoon in food; lift to mouth.
4. Open mouth and taste food as it arrives (and if it arrives).

In summary, children's structures for eating and drinking go through the same sequence of four substages as they do for the balance tasks, the means-ends, or the object-permanence tasks. They also go through the sequence at the same rate. It may therefore be concluded that—at least in the domain of nonsocial cognition—children's early development reveals a substantial degree of both vertical and horizontal structure.

CONTROL STRUCTURES FOR INTERACTING
WITH OTHER HUMAN BEINGS

The human infant does not grow up in a world populated entirely by in-animate objects. Bottles and nipples do not mysteriously appear and disappear out of nowhere, and food is not presented by Skinnerian machines. The human infant grows up in a world populated by other humans, and is nurtured by them. Clearly, if development is to be fully understood, the infant's interactions with these other humans must be taken into account.

For many years, speculation concerning the processes of early social development was left largely to clinical psychologists. The first theories were constructed on the basis of childhood recollections of adults in therapy (Freud, 1953). These early theories were then elaborated, refined, or altered by later theorists, on the basis of observations of children in institutions or in therapy (Bowlby, 1969; Freud, 1949; Klein, 1957; Spitz, 1950). Finally, as investigators became interested in the process of mother-infant attachment, experimental methods began to be employed, using normal rather than abnormal infants (Ainsworth, 1964).

Since the early 1970's it has become increasingly apparent that there is a strong cognitive component to human social development as well. Thus, investigators whose background is in cognitive developmental psychology have become interested in children's early social development (See Flavell, 1968, 1981; Seraficia, 1982). And, at the same time, investigators whose background is in child psychiatry have become interested in cognitive development (See Sander, 1977, 1983; Stern, 1977, 1983). As social and non-social cognition have been examined for the first time side by side, one of the issues that has arisen is whether the two types of development proceed at the same rate. The first studies that were conducted suggested that children's development took place more rapidly in the social domain than in nonsocial domains (See Bell, 1970). More recent studies, however, have called this finding into question, and suggested that certain concepts in the two domains actually develop at a very similar rate, when all the relevant task factors are controlled (Jackson, Campos, & Fischer, 1978). It seems quite possible, therefore, that at least some degree of vertical and horizontal structure may be present in the domain of social cognition as well.

Nonverbal Interaction with the Primary Caretaker

Of all the changes that take place in the infants' social behaviour during the first $1\frac{1}{2}$ years of life, probably none are as well documented as those involving their nonverbal interaction with their primary caretaker. Early research on this interaction concentrated primarily on establishing what sort of visual stimulus would elicit a social response such as smiling (see Spitz &

Wolfe, 1946). More recent research has looked at the infant and caretaker as a social system, and documented the changes which take place in each member of this system as time passes (see Stern, 1974, 1977; Bruner, 1977; Trevarthan, 1977; Fafouti-Milenkovic & Uzgiris, 1979; Als, 1979).

Substage 0: Operational Consolidation (1–4 Months)

From the age of about 1 month, infants exhibit a response to the human face which is quite distinctive. Rather than gazing at it intently and engaging in visual scanning as they might with an inanimate object, they alternate between brief moments of eye contact and eye aversion. During the periods of contact, they exhibit a distinctive pattern of motor responses, including smiling, cooing, and bicycling with the arms and legs. What happens during the first few months of life is that their eye aversion becomes less frequent, and is replaced by monitoring the mothers' response. Also, the motor responses become more energetic and better organized (Als, 1979). By the middle of the period, the infant is often seen to engage in a prolonged and delightful pattern of interaction which has been labeled protocommunication (Fafouti-Milenkovic & Uzgiris, 1979). In response to a smile from their mothers, infants will kick, flail their limbs, coo, and smile energetically, giving the impression of joyful exhuberance. They will then monitor their mothers' response, which more often than not will include reciprocal expressions of warmth and delight. The whole pattern will then repeat itself, in a cyclic manner that has been likened to a dance (Stern, 1977).

By the end of the period, infants' responses to their own mothers is clearly different from their response to others. It also contains a clear intentional component: if the mother is coached to respond in a different fashion from normal, the infant will notice the change immediately, and after repeated attempts to engage in the normal pattern, will turn away and engage in thumb-sucking or some other activity for comfort (Brazeltin et al., 1975). What this means from the present perspective is that the infants' first social structures must contain an intentional component. They must engage in their own behaviour at least to some degree, in order to elicit or maintain the parallel behaviour of their caretaker. Their executive control structures for doing so may therefore be represented as follows:

PROBLEM SITUATION	OBJECTIVES
• Caretaker's face with expression X (e.g., eye brows raised, mouth in affectionate smile).	• Produce (or sustain) changes in expressions (e.g., laugh or coo).

STRATEGY
1. Exhibit social behaviours (smiling, cooing, etc.).

Substage 1: Operational Coordination (4–8 Months)

Although infants' nonverbal responses to their mothers become increasingly energetic, sustained, and focused during their first few months of life, they show no signs of coordinating these responses with any other well-differentiated response patterns. During the second substage, a number of such coordinations appear. For example, infants will pull their mothers' hair and laugh for the first time, apparently as an invitation to play (Bates, 1976; Piaget, 1952). For the first time, too, they will stretch out their arms toward their mothers, apparently as a request to be picked up. What both these behaviors share in common is that an activity which originally had one objective is being used as a means of obtaining another objective, namely, some desired form of social interaction. The executive control structure underlying the arm-reaching response could be represented as follows:

PROBLEM SITUATION   OBJECTIVES
- Current field is boring (or   - Produce more interesting (or
  threatening).   secure) state.
- Mother is across room.   - Bring mother near.

STRATEGY
1. Stretch out arms toward
   mother.
2. Smile, coo, etc., as she
   approaches.

Substage 2: Bifocal Operational Coordination (8–12 Months)

During the second substage, infants begin to integrate their structures for interacting with objects with their structures for interacting with their mothers. For example, they may now reach for a small plaything such as a spoon or a rattle and begin banging it, while glancing repeatedly at their mother and exchanging laughs or smiles (Trevarthan & Hubley, 1979). When they are close to their mother but not the object of her attention, they may reach out for an object and present it to her, again smiling and making eye contact as they do so (Bates, 1976). The executive control structure underlying this latter behavior may be represented as indicated at the top of page 137.

As was the case in the domain of inanimate objects, the above structure is bifocal. One focus is on the mother, the other focus is on the object.

Substage 3: Elaborated Coordination (12–18 Months)

Although infants first offer objects to their mothers during the 8 to 12 months range, and although mother also first engage in object-oriented play with their infants during this same period, the infants do not yet imitate the

PROBLEM SITUATION	OBJECTIVES
• Mother's expression = X (e.g., neutral regard).	• Produce expression Y (e.g., laugh, comment).
• Interesting object in sight.	• Present object to mother.
• Object located at point Z.	• Move hand to Z.

STRATEGY

1. Reach for object with nearest hand.
2. Grasp object and extend it to mother.
3. Scan mother's face, smile, etc.

actions which their mothers execute on objects, in what might be termed a reciprocal fashion. Nor do infants execute an action on an object, and invite their mothers to do the same. In fact, they often do not even release it. They hold out a toy as if to say "look at this", but maintain a firm grip on it themselves (Bates, 1976). During the fourth substage, such behaviour is replaced by turn taking. Another change which is seen is that the children will now actively search for and retrieve an interesting object, in order to present it to their mother (or to an experimenter) when they wish to initiate some particular form of interaction (Bates, 1976). Each of these changes indicates an elaboration in the control structures of the previous substage, and could therefore be modeled in the same fashion as the nonsocial elaborations which take place during the same time period.

Verbal Interaction with the Primary Caretaker and Others

Although infants' nonverbal development is of great interest to their mothers and fellow family members, to other members of the community their linguistic development is often of greater significance. For it is children's ability to speak which will most clearly mark their transition from the world of infancy to the world of early childhood, and to the wider cultural community of which they are destined to become a part.

In the burst of theorizing that followed Chomsky's postulation of generative grammar, it was often suggested that the child's acquisition of language was unique in the rapidity of its emergence, and in the complexity of the rules whose mastery it demanded. As a consequence, it was further suggested that there was some genetically programmed and unique language acquisition device (see Chapter 4). Subsequent investigators, however, have pointed out that language development in fact shares a great deal in common with other forms of cognitive development (e.g., Greenfield, Nelson, & Saltzman, 1972; Slobin, 1973), and that it is dependent on the same forms of social interaction (see Bruner, 1979). In addition, investigators have shown that there are similarities in the rate at which this development takes place, with certain important prelinguistic developments taking place during infancy (Bates, 1976; Bruner, 1977; Sinclair, 1971), and certain other developments taking place well into the concrete and formal periods (e.g., Beilin, 1975; C. Chomsky, 1969; Fabian, 1982; Kessel, 1970; Karmiloff-Smith, 1979; Pike & Olson, 1977).

Of course, the above studies do not rule out the possibility that there may be a substantial degree of genetic programming in children's linguistic development. Nor do they rule out the possibility that—in many ways—children's linguistic development may be quite unlike their development in any other domain. What they do rule out, however, is the possibility of treating language as a category entirely unto itself; that is, as a form of development which is quite unlike any other sort that is observed. Rather, they suggest that there is an aspect of linguistic development which is quite general, and which stands in need of further elucidation.

It is on this general component, then, which the final section of the present chapter focuses. The object is to determine what sorts of general features children's pre-linguistic control structures may share with the other sorts of control structure that have already been considered.

Use of Vocalization for Social Purposes

Substage 0: Operational Consolidation (1–4 Months)

During the preliminary substage, infants' ability to vocalize develops very gradually. At the beginning of the substage, they are capable of generating only small throaty sounds. By the end of the substage, they are capable of babbling and cooing, and have a small repertoire of vowel sounds (e.g., ah eey). Although infants often vocalize in the presence of an adult, however, their vocalization often appears to be undifferentiated from any of their other activities, such as arm flailing and smiling. Hence, it is often difficult to tell whether or not it is being used in a purposeful fashion. One situation in which vocalization does have a quality which is both differentiated from other activity and purposeful, however, is when infants are alone in their crib, and their stimulation level is low. At this time they will often coo or babble to themselves (Weir, 1962), with the apparent intent of producing interesting stimulation. The executive control structure underlying this behaviour may be represented as follows:

PROBLEM SITUATION   OBJECTIVE
- Perceptual field dull.   ⟶ • Produce interesting stimulation.

STRATEGY
1. Exercise vocal chords (coo, etc.) while opening mouth and monitoring feedback.

Substage 1: Operational Coordination (4–8 Months)

Somewhere between the ages of 4 and 8 months, infants' vocalizations take on a different character. For the first time, vocalization is used as a means toward achieving some objective other than one which emerges in the context of an ongoing activity. For example, if their mother disappears from view, or if she remains in view but ceases to pay any attention to them, infants will often babble loudly and in an insistent tone, until she approaches them again or shows renewed interest. The executive control structure underlying this behaviour might be represented as follows.

PROBLEM SITUATION   OBJECTIVES
- Adult not near.   • Cause adult to approach.
- Perceptual field still quiet.   • Generate noisy activity.

STRATEGY
1. Babble loudly (or force a cry).
2. Monitor approach of adult.

The similarity between this structure and the hand-raising structure which was mentioned in the previous section is no doubt apparent. Both involve the hierarchical integration of two schemes that previously served quite different functions. Both also serve the same ultimate goal, namely, producing a change in the behaviour of the caretaker. The major difference is that the vocal strategy works when the mother is looking elsewhere or is in a different room, whereas the hand-raising strategy works only when her gaze is already on the infant.

Substage 2: Bifocal Coordination (8–12 Months)

During the third substage, infants integrate their routines for commanding an adult to pay attention with their routines for obtaining objects. When an interesting object is just out of reach and an adult is near, they will stretch out their hand toward the object, turning their head toward the adult, and babbling insistently. By the end of the substage, they no longer stretch toward the object but merely point (Bates, 1976). The executive control structure underlying this behavior might be represented as follows:

PROBLEM SITUATION   OBJECTIVES
- Object out of reach.   • Get object.
- Adult nearby.   • Cause adult to move to object.
- Adult not attending.   • Secure adult's attention.

STRATEGY
1. Babble loudly at adult.
2. Point to object.
3. Monitor adult's behavior.

Substage 3: Elaborated Coordination (12–18 Months)

Although infants' babbled requests for objects are often understood by adults, they are also not understood under certain circumstances. I once witnessed my nephew at his first birthday party, when he wanted one of the objects on the other side of the dining room table. He pointed toward the group of objects, and began to shout gleefully, turning to his mother as if to say, "Hurray! Bring me one of those." His mother dutifully obliged. Evidently, however, she must have brought the wrong object, for the infant brushed it away, pointing and babbling more insistently. The mother then tried again with three or four more objects. Each time, however, the result was the same. Eventually the infant began to cry. He clearly wanted something from across the table, but could not make his mother understand what it was.

At some point during the period from 1 to $1\frac{1}{2}$ years, infants solve the above dilemma by uttering requests which are object-specific. At first, their verbalizations are quite idiosyncratic. For example, "pu" might mean apple or perhaps doll. By the end of the period, however, they have established a repertoire of up to 40 recognizable words (Nelson, 1973). This does not mean that they use these words in exactly the same sense as adults do. Overextensions and underextensions are common (Anglin, 1979; Piaget, 1951). However, their use of words does mark a clear evolution in their executive structures, which may now be represented as follows:

PROBLEM SITUATION   OBJECTIVES
- Object out of reach.   • Retrieve object.
- Adult near by.   • Get adult to bring object.
- Object in a group with other   • Specify which object must be
  objects.   brought.
- Adult's gaze elsewhere.   • Secure adult's attention.

STRATEGY
1. Babble loudly until adult attends.
2. Utter object name.
3. Point to object.
4. Monitor adult behavior.

The above analysis demonstrates how children's first words are embedded in their general structures for social interaction. It also demonstrates that their first use of words can have the same instrumental character as many of their nonsocial behaviors during the same period. In effect, the first word can serve as a specific means toward achieving a desired end (see Bates, 1976).

What the above analysis omits, however, is any hint as to how the infants produce a socially appropriate label, as opposed to an idiosyncratic one. One possibility is that they simply generate sounds in a random fashion, until they hit upon one that works for a given object. If this were their only strategy, however, it seems unlikely that their vocabulary would develop at the rate it does. Moreover, by the time infants reach the age of 1 year, there is independent evidence that they already understand the meaning of a number of words. When these words are spoken, they will often orient to the object to which the word refers, or engage in the action with which the word is associated (Nelson, 1973). The question which naturally arises, therefore is how these first word-meanings are acquired.

The Assignment of Meaning to Words

Infants no doubt learn the meaning of words in a wide variety of situations. Because the majority of their early words are concrete nouns (Nelson, 1973), however, one of the most typical situations is very probably having an adult point to or lift up an object, and utter its name. This could occur in a number of different ways.

Infants might point to something they wanted, and an adult might not be sure what. The adult might hold up a possible object and say "Duckie, Do you want Duckie?"

Adults might talk to infants, in the course of presenting them with objects. For example, they might hand an infant a bottle, and say "Here's your bottle. Nice bottle. Hold your bottle."

An adult might be sitting near an infant when an interesting event occurred, and comment on it. For example, when an infant's father came in to the room, the nearest adult might say, "Oh' There's Daddy, See Daddy? Hi Daddy."

An adult might actively try to teach the child words, by holding up objects and saying their name, "Dollie, That's Dollie. Can you say Dollie?"

If children are to profit from any of these experiences, or others like them, they must clearly be able to attend to at least three different patterns of sensory stimulation at once. These are

(1) the pattern of visual stimulation presented by the adult, including the pointing gesture;

(2) the pattern of auditory stimulation presented by the adult's voice, in particular the part of the pattern which is most strongly accented, and which has been underlined in the above examples; and

(3) the pattern of visual stimulation presented by the object or event to which the word refers.

In order to understand how children come to assign their first meaning to words, we must therefore examine the structures in their repertoire which might lead them to focus on these three patterns of stimulation simultaneously, and the efforts of the older members of their culture which might help them to do so.

Substage 0: Operational Consolidation (1–4 Months)

As has already been mentioned, children develop control structures for keeping physical objects in the center of their visual field by the age of 4 months. They also develop control structures for attending to and interacting with their primary caretaker. What about control structures for attending to language?

A good deal of research has been done on this topic during the last 10 years. Eimas *et al.* (1971), Trehub (1973) and others have shown that the infant is capable of distinguishing many of the basic phonetic contrasts from which human languages are formed almost from birth. Bower (1974) has shown that infants will orient their heads toward the source of sound during the first few months of life, and that they do so with increasing efficiency as the period progresses. It seems reasonable to suggest, therefore, that the infant consolidates linguistic control structures during the first few months of life with the following general format.

PROBLEM SITUATION   OBJECTIVE
- Voice at X.   ⟶ • Listen to voice.
                             STRATEGY
                1. Turn head toward sound, and
                   listen.

As a result of applying such structures, infants presumably take their first steps toward learning the basic sound patterns of their parents' language.

Substage 1: Operational Coordination (4–8 Months)

Although infants develop structure for "locking in" on the human voice during the preliminary substage, and for listening carefully, there is no evidence that they coordinate the activity of listening to the human voice with that of scanning the objects or events to which particular sound patterns refer. In fact there is evidence to the contrary. When an adult such as their mother is talking, the place the infants' eyes normally come to rest is on her, not on the object to which she is referring. If infants are to learn the meaning of particular sound patterns, they must of course develop more than the capacity for listening to and recognizing particular sound patterns. They must also develop the capacity for what Bruner has called *shared visual regard* (Scaife & Bruner, 1975). This capacityty first emerges during the period from 4 to 8 months. If a mother turns and looks (or points) at an object which is in her infant's field of peripheral vision prior to the age of 4 months, the infant will let his or her gaze wander aimlessly about the visual field, as though searching for something else of interest to look at, now that eye contact with the mother has been broken. Alternatively, the infant will continue to stare at the mother, as though waiting for her to start looking at him or her again (Scaife & Bruner, 1975).

By the age of 6 or 7 months, however, infants will shift their eyes in the direction of their mother's gaze, and scan the object at which she is looking (Scaife &

Bruner, 1975). Note that the structure of this situation is quite similar to that of the object disappearance-reappearance task which was analyzed at the beginning of the chapter. The mother's turning her head away from the child is analogous to the disappearance of an object at point X, because it means that continued eye scanning in that region will no longer produce a satisfying result. The presence of an object in the peripheral field is analogous to the reappearance of an object at a second point, because that it means that scanning in this region will produce a satisfying result.

In order to acquire the appropriate response, therefore, the infants must somehow coordinate their structure for scanning their mother's face at X with their structure for scanning an object at Y. Presumably they do so by assembling an integrated control structure with a format such as this:

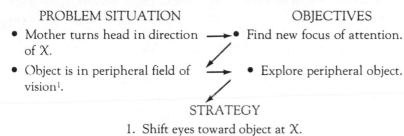

PROBLEM SITUATION   OBJECTIVES

- Mother turns head in direction   • Find new focus of attention.
  of X.

- Object is in peripheral field of   • Explore peripheral object.
  vision[1].

STRATEGY

1. Shift eyes toward object at X.
2. Focus on and scan object.

Substage 2: Bifocal Operational Coordination (8–12 Months)

The sort of coordination that takes place at the third substage is between the infants' structures for attending to and noticing objects pointed out by their mother, and their structures for localizing the source of speech, and attending to what is said. The structure that is responsible for effecting this coordination might be represented as follows:

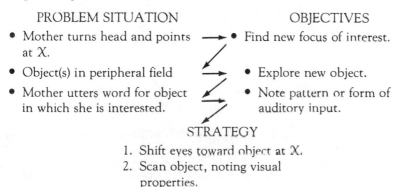

PROBLEM SITUATION   OBJECTIVES

- Mother turns head and points   • Find new focus of interest.
  at X.

- Object(s) in peripheral field   • Explore new object.

- Mother utters word for object   • Note pattern or form of
  in which she is interested.   auditory input.

STRATEGY

1. Shift eyes toward object at X.
2. Scan object, noting visual
   properties.

---

[1] Note that, if there is no object in the children's peripheral field of vision, they will not emit the appropriate response (Butterworth, 1979).

3. Encode element(s) of auditory
   pattern, perhaps rehearsing it (them)
   mentally.

Of course, the third step in the above strategy is an extremely big one, and one might well ask how it is that infants are able to accomplish it. A full answer to this question is beyond the scope of the present volume. Basically, however, it appears that infants are biologically predisposed to pay attention to elements of language which are accentuated in certain ways, either by being uttered more loudly than others, or by appearing at the beginning or end of streams of speech (See Slobin, 1973; Daneman & Case, 1981). Moreover, it appears that adults have a natural tendency, in speaking to young infants, to make the job of isolating relevant aspects of speech more easy. For example, they will speak more slowly and rhythmically. They will accentuate key words or parts of words, as was indicated by the underlying in the above dialogues. They will also speak in shorter sentences. (Snow, 1977, 1970), It is probably as a result of these adult adaptations, then, that infants are able to accomplish the third step in the above strategy with as little effort as they do, and to acquire their first word meanings at such a young age.[2]

The Production of Recognizable Words

Suppose you realized that if you could only generate the appropriate sound you could get your caretaker to bring you the particular object in which you were most interested. Suppose further that you knew which particular pattern of sound was characteristically associated with that object. While both of these realizations would be necessary for you to generate the word in question, they would clearly not be sufficient. For, in addition, you would actually have to produce the appropriate pattern of sound with your own vocal chords. In order to fully understand the emergence of the infants' first word, therefore, we must understand something about their growing vocal competence as well. In particular, we must understand how it is that they manage to tune their own vocal productions to those of the linguistic community in which they find themselves.

Substage 0: Operational Consolidation (1–4 Months)

The two operations which are of most direct relevance to this achievement are the operations of listening to and generating simple sounds. As has already been

[2] In fact, there is some evidence that children can actually acquire certain word meanings a good deal earlier, (i.e., at 4 to 8 months) (Fowler & Swenson, 1979). In keeping with the above analysis, however, this early acquisition appears to be associated with somewhat different social conditions. In particular, it appears to occur only when mothers repeatedly and forcefully utter the names of objects to which their baby is already attending, so that the baby will process the appearance of the object and a characteristic sound, rather than the appearance of the mother's face and a characteristic sound.

mentioned, both of these operations are consolidated during the first few months of life. By the age of 4 months, infants show clear evidence of sustained attention to adult speech. They also develop a repertoire of at least one or two vowel sequences or coos such as ah-ee-ya. (Griffiths, 1954; Uzgiris & Hunt, 1975).

Substage 1: Operational Coordination (4–8 Months)

As might be expected, one of the major developments which takes place during the period from 4 to 8 months is the active coordination of listening with sound production. Prior to the age of 4 months, children's sound production often overlaps or oscillates with that of an adult. Although there is some debate on this point, however, the timing appears to be controlled by the adult more than the child. In effect, adults appear to fit their own sounds into the pauses in the infants' activity. By the age of 4 months, however, infants begin to share this timing function. They now clearly make a sequence of sounds, pause, and listen to the adult's response; then continue to generate sounds when this response ends, as though they are having a conversation. Their speech also begins to reflect what goes on during the listening period, in that certain very general features of the adults' response are preserved (e.g., suprasegmental contour).

A second development that occurs in speech production indicates a coordination of a different sort. This is that the infants' coos, which are essentially made by exercising the vocal chords while the mouth is open, change to babbles, which are consonant vowel patterns that involve a coordination of vocal chord movement with lip movement.[3]

Substage 2: Bifocal Coordination (8–12 Months)

During the next substage, infants generate certain two-syllable utterances such as "MaMa" "DaDa" on their own, and imitate them when they are used by adults. They may also use them in their social interaction for achieving pragmatic purposes, if the consequences of using them are made apparent (Brazelton, 1969).[4] As yet, however, infants cannot imitate a novel adult utterance; that is, one for which they have no production—mechanism already in their repertoire.

Substage 3: Elaborated Coordination (12–18 Months)

During the final substage, children become capable of this latter sort of imitation. Presumably they do so by combining vocal patterns that are already in

---

[3] To verify that these two components are entailed, the reader might wish to articulate one of the consonant vowel patterns which appears in this age range, such as "mah".

[4] Presumably this accounts for the similarity of the name for "Mummy" across language groups (e.g., the Hebrew "eema" and the French "mama"). The adult word is in effect being tuned to the capabilities of the child, rather than the reverse.

their repertoire and producing some sort of best fit to the word used by an adult. "Mama-AY", for example, might be used as an approximation for "Marmalade", the first time such a word was encounterd, or "GAH-MAH" for grandmother. Once children have successfully imitated a word—providing that they already know its meaning—they will also use it in pragmatic contexts such as those discussed in the previous section.

Given our present knowledge, it would be premature to model the executive control structures that are responsible for generating the above sequence of phonetic productions in any detail. Nevertheless, at a global level, it may be seen that they do follow the same pattern as the other structures which have been considered.

THE GENERAL PATTERN OF INFANT DEVELOPMENT

The preceding analysis concludes my account of infants' early linguistic development. What I have tried to show in this analysis, following Bruner, Bates, and others, is that the emergence of the child's first word depends on a number of prior cognitive accomplishments, each of which is quite distinct. It depends, first, on finding social interaction rewarding, and on developing complex structures for engaging in it: either as a means to other ends, or as an end to be achieved by other means. It depends, second, on being able to vocalize, and on substituting patterns of vocalization for other responses in the structures that govern social interaction. It depends, third, on being able to understand the vocalizations of others, when they are embedded in social structures of a similar sort. And it depends, fourth, on being able to tune one's vocalizations so that they match those of the other members of one's linguistic community. The same four abilities were no doubt necessary for primitive humans, at whatever point in evolution their first words emerged.

To say that human beings have these basic abilities, however, and that each one has its own developmental history, is to tell only part of the story. What is perhaps most fascinating about human linguistic development is that—although each characteristic or ability develops independently—it does so in a fashion which parallels the development of each other characteristic. In modeling the structures on which the various strands of children's linguistic development depends, I have not emphasized the cross-task parallels that exist as explicitly as I did for the inanimate competencies which were analyzed. That such parallels do continue to exist, however, will hopefully have been apparent. During the preliminary substage, the structures which are consolidated normally have three basic components: one for representing some ongoing pattern of stimulation, one for representing a desired change in this pattern (often one which will restore it to a previous state), and one for representing the motor strategy that will produce this effect. During Substage 1 a major qualitative shift takes place, as these various different control structures are coordinated with each other. Although a wide variety of coordinations are observed, the three most important ones for children's linguistic development are probably those for coordinating (1) the monitoring of one's own voice with the monitoring of changes in the social world, (2) the monitoring of other people's gestures, with the occurrence of other states or events in the world, and (3) the monitoring of other people's voices, with the monitoring of one's own voice. During Substage 2, these first coordinated structures become bifocal; that is, their focus expands to include some additional element, often one that existed as a structure or a partial structure in its own right, during the previous substage. Finally, during Substage 3, some additional elaboration is introduced, often one which permits the elements of the previous substage to be related to each other in a more direct, ongoing, and active fashion. Finally, not only are there strong parallels in the sequence of developments that are observed in the various strands of linguistic development, and in the timing of these developments, the parallels appear to be formally identical to those that are present in the domain of nonsocial development as well.

As the reader may remember, the two questions that were posed at the beginning of the chapter were (1) is the same four-substage pattern present in every strand of infants' development? and (2) if so, do infants pass through the substages in different domains during the same approximate age range? The answer to both questions would appear to be yes. The four-substage pattern does appear, in every domain which has been subjected to detailed experimental scrutiny, whether it be social or nonsocial. And the progression through the substages does appear to take place at approximately the same rate. In short, there does appear to be a high degree of both vertical and horizontal structure in infant development.

Why there should be such a high degree of structure in infant development is an important and interesting question. Before this question can be pursued, however, we must first determine whether the same degree of structure is present during other stages of development as well, or whether it is unique to the sensorimotor period.

CHAPTER 8

Development in Early Childhood: The Missing Link between Sensorimotor and Logical Operations

INTRODUCTION

As was mentioned in Chapter 3, Piaget's account of early childhood was somewhat less precise than his account of the other major periods in children's development. He did note a decrease in the incidence of egocentric speech, that is, speech uttered in the presence of another, but not serving any communicative function (Piaget, 1926a). He also noted a decrease in magical and animistic beliefs (Piaget, 1926). Finally, he noted an increase in the objectivity of verbal concepts (Piaget, 1951). The data on which these three generalizations were based, however, were largely verbal or anecdotal. Moreover, for the most part, they were gathered rather early in Piaget's career, before he had formulated his hypotheses concerning the underlying structure of children's thought. As a consequence, Piaget was not able to formulate a description of the substages through which children pass during this period which was either as precise or as general as his description of the substages through which they pass during other periods. There is no description, for example, which rivals that of the first three substages of the sensorimotor period, during which time children pass from primary to secondary to coordinated secondary circular reactions. Nor is there any account which rivals that of the late preoperational and early concrete operational years (i.e., 4–10), during which time children pass from partial morphisms to one-way functions to two way functions. In effect, therefore, there is a missing link in Piaget's work. The exact nature of the transition from sensorimotor to logical thought is not clear.

In Chapter 6, a suggestion was made concerning the nature of this transition. It was proposed that the relational operations that form the pinnacle of sensorimotor thought constitute the building blocks from which subsequent structures are constructed. It was further suggested that, having consolidated such operations by the age of $1\frac{1}{2}$ years, children go through a series of three substages which are directly parallel to those observed in infancy. During the first substage they coordinate two different types of relational operations, thus for the first time apprehending the workings of a relational *structure*. During the second substage, they expand their focus, and consider some additional interrelationship of a similar sort. Finally, during the last substage, they introduce some additional elaboration into their existing structures, often one that permits two of the interrelations that were noticed at the previous substage to be coordinated in some more direct or sophisticated fashion. These elaborations are usually complete by the age of 5 years, and in turn function as the building blocks from which the structures of the next stage are constructed.

The object of the present chapter is to determine whether or not this proposal is a viable one. Put differently, the object is to determine the extent to which the developments that were described on the balance beam are prototypic, and can be used as a basis for understanding the general nature of the changes which take place in preschoolers' thought.

Given that Piaget's investigations do not provide a sufficient data base for addressing this question, what other sort of data might one turn to? At least four different sorts of data would appear to be of relevance. The first are the data that have been gathered by psychometricians, in order to assess the intellectual capabilities of children in this age range (e.g., Beery, 1967; Catell, 1940; Gesell *et al.*, 1940; Griffiths, 1970; Terman & Merrill, 1960; Wechsler, 1967). The second are the data that have been gathered by psycholinguistics, in order to explore children's earliest syntactic and semantic development (e.g., Brown, 1973; Clark & Clark, 1977; Ferguson & Slobin, 1973; Menyuk, 1977). The third are the data that have been gathered in the cognitive-developmental tradition, on children's quantitative and social competencies during the preschool period (e.g., Flavell *et al.*, 1968; Gelman, 1978; Rubin & Everett, 1982). Finally, the fourth are the data from our own research group, which have been gathered to supplement the data from these other sources, and to test the proposal which was advanced in Chapter 6 more directly (Bruchkowsky, 1984, Case & Khanna, 1981; Khanna, 1985; Liu, 1981; Marini, 1984).

In the present chapter, all four of these sets of data are considered. For the purpose of exposition, the data are divided into four general categories, as a function of whether they deal with spatial, social, linguistic, or quantitative relations.

THE DEVELOPMENT OF SPATIAL CONTROL STRUCTURES

At the same time as children are learning about relationships of cause-and-effect by playing with mechanical toys such as the balance beam, they are also learning about purely spatial relations, by playing a variety of games that involve the construction and manipulation of geometric patterns.

Figure Drawing

Perhaps the most universal sort of spatial play is drawing. To begin with, children's interest does not appear to lie in drawing pictures, but simply in drawing figures. What excites them is the act of making marks on a flat surface. As parents will readily attest, virtually any flat surface will suffice for this purpose, from a flat stretch of sand to a newly painted wall. The change that takes place in children's spontaneous drawing during this period has been described by Kellogg (1967). It has also been observed under somewhat more controlled conditions by psychometricians. Taken together, the two sets of data provide quite a detailed picture of the developmental progression that takes place.

Substage 0: Operational Consolidation $(1–1\frac{1}{2}$ Years)[1]

By the age of $1\frac{1}{2}$ years, if an adult scribbles on a piece of paper and hands a pencil to a child, the child will also scribble on the paper (Gesell *et al.*, 1940; Catell, 1940). From the viewpoint of sensorimotor development, children's success on this task represents a considerable achievement. As was the case with the balance task, children must first notice the interesting results that the adult produces by bringing one object into contact with another. Next, they must establish a fairly complex set of nested objectives. Specifically, they must plan to extend their arm, in order to pick up an object (the pencil), in order to act on a second object (the paper) in order to produce a desired result (the mark). Finally,

---

[1]Throughout this chapter, the ages that are cited are rounded off to $1\frac{1}{2}$, 2, $3\frac{1}{2}$, and 5 years of age. The reader is reminded, however, that these are only approximate and that a more precise set of ages might be 20 months, 27 months, 40 months, and 60 months.

they must develop a strategy that will allow them to accomplish all of these objectives in a reasonably smooth manner. If one were to characterize the complete executive control structure that is necessary for successful scribbling, therefore, it would look something like this:

PROBLEM SITUATION   OBJECTIVES

- Pencil marks on paper.   • Make a similar pattern.

- Pattern made by moving tip of   • Move tip of pencil across
  pencil.   paper.

- Paper held in experimenter's   • Pick up pencil in hand.
  hand.

- Pencil within reach at point X.   • Move hand to X.

STRATEGY

1a. Move arm from current position
    to X.
1b. Grasp pencil in hand.
2. Pick up pencil.
3a. Move pencil towards paper.
3b. Point tip down.
3c. Push tip against paper.
3d. Move it back and forth.
4. Monitor result produced.

Although producing a mark on a piece of paper is a complex achievement from the viewpoint of sensorimotor development, it may be considered an elementary achievement from the viewpoint of the development that follows. In fact, from the perspective of relational development, it may be considered the most basic sort of achievement that is possible, because all it requires is the representation and reproduction of a single relationship, that between a pencil and a piece of paper. To simplify the exposition in subsequent sections, therefore, the following abbreviated notation will be adopted:

PROBLEM SITUATION   OBJECTIVE

- Pencil marks on paper.   • Make a similar pattern.

STRATEGY

1. Put pencil tip on paper, and move
   it about.

Substage 1: Operational Coordination ($1\frac{1}{2}$–2 Years)

Between the ages of $1\frac{1}{2}$ and 2 years, a clear change takes place in children's performance. Instead of just moving their pencil across the paper with a series of gross motor movements, they now begin to control the type of movement they execute, in order to control the type of mark that is produced. By the age of 2 years, when an experimenter draws a vertical line on a piece of paper, children no longer simply scribble in response. (Beery, 1967; Cattell, 1940). Instead, they carefully push their pencil from top to bottom of the page, thus reproducing the experimenter's production. Presumably they must focus on a second relationship in order to do so, namely, the relationship between the line and the edge of the paper. Presumably, too, their control structure must now subordinate the activity of pushing the pencil across the paper to the aim of reproducing this particular spatial feature. The control structure that is required may therefore be represented as follows:

PROBLEM SITUATION	OBJECTIVES
• Pencil mark (line) on paper.	• Make a similar pattern.
• Line goes from top to bottom of paper.	• Move pencil from top to bottom.

STRATEGY

1a. Place pencil tip near top of page.
2a. Move pencil toward bottom.
2b. Monitor progress, stopping when pencil line has made a pattern resembling the one desired.

Note that, as was the case in the balance task, the new relationship is qualitatively different from the first one, and that children's ability to coordinate the two relations leads to a qualitative shift in their behaviour.

Substage 2: Bifocal Coordination (2–$3\frac{1}{2}$ Years)

At the second substage, children become capable of focusing on a second spatial relation as well. This capability can be demonstrated in two quite different fashions. Children can be asked to copy a circle (Beery, 1967; Catell, 1940; Gesell, 1940; Terman & Merrill, 1960), which requires monitoring both the character of the line (curved) and the desired ending point (back at the place of origin). Alternatively, they can be asked to copy a cross (Gesell, 1940; Case & Khanna, 1981), which requires monitoring the character of the line (straight) while keeping a desired endpoint in mind (the middle of the first line). The executive control structure for drawing a cross might be represented as follows:

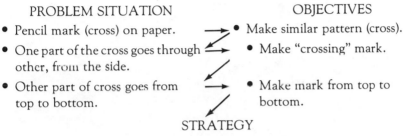

PROBLEM SITUATION

- Pencil mark (cross) on paper.
- One part of the cross goes through other, from the side.
- Other part of cross goes from top to bottom.

OBJECTIVES

- Make similar pattern (cross).
- Make "crossing" mark.
- Make mark from top to bottom.

STRATEGY

1a. Place pencil tip near top of page.
2. Move pencil toward bottom.
3a. Place pencil to the side of straight line.
3b. Move pencil toward it.
3c. When pencil reaches the line, continue toward edge of paper, monitoring progress until overall pattern is produced.[2]

Substage 3: Bifocal Coordination with Elaboration (3½–5 Years)

During the third substage, children become capable of incorporating an additional element into the structures of the previous substage. This new element can be one that was mastered in Substage 1, as is the case with a balloon (i.e., a circle with a line coming out at the bottom) (Khanna, 1984); a "tadpole man" (circle with lines coming out for legs, and dots in middle for eyes); or a "sun" (circle with lines around edge). Alternatively, the new element can be another one which was mastered at Substage 2, as is the case with a mandala (i.e., cross superimposed on a circle) (Kellogg, 1967). The executive control structure for drawing a mandala might be represented as follows:

---

[2]This final step may seem a rather artificial one. The most common difficulty that children have at this substage, however, does appear to be in making the final segment of the line. Often they do not continue, once the vertical line meets the horizontal line.

PROBLEM SITUATION	OBJECTIVES
• Pencil pattern (mandala) on paper.	• Duplicate pattern.
• Most salient element of pattern = cross.	• Make cross.
• One line of cross bisects other.	• Make "crossing" mark.
• Other part of cross goes straight from top to bottom.	• Make line from top to bottom.

STRATEGY

1. Place pencil tip on page.
2. Move pencil straight from top toward bottom.
3a. Place pencil tip at side of first line.
3b. Move pencil line to centre.
3c. As pencil line reaches centre, continue until overall pattern looks like cross.
4. Replace pencil in the middle of one of the pieces of cross, and draw a circle.

In summary, the general nature of the progression that takes place on the figure drawing task is similar to that on the balance beam. Moreover, the rate of progression is similar as well. Of course, the specific operations are quite different. Nevertheless, the general sequence is virtually identical. There is a parallel in the result of this sequence as well. This is that children acquire new forms of production—elements such as a man, a sun, and a balloon—which can function as basic units in the productions that are observed at the next major stage of development, when full-page pictures or "scenes" emerge (Dennis, 1984; Case *et al.*, 1985).

Block Assembly

A second type of spatial activity that preschoolers enjoy is playing with blocks. If given the opportunity, children of this age will spontaneously pile blocks into various configurations, for no apparent reason other than to discover the patterns that result. Once again, this activity has been used as an item on a variety of preschool IQ tests, and these tests thus constitute a good source of information concerning children's capabilities during this age range.

Over the past few years, we have also devised a number of new items in our own research group, in order to clarify the nature of the progression which is observed (Case & Bruchkowski, 1984; Case & Khanna, 1981).

Substage 0: Operational Consolidation (1–1$\frac{1}{2}$ Years)

The simplest block assembly item is the tower—a form which appears in children's spontaneous play during this period, and which can be elicited in a test situation by means of a copying task. To introduce this item, experimenters pick up a block, and set it in front of the children. They then pick up another block, and set it on top of the first. Finally, they remove their own construction, and invite the children to build one just like it with theirs. Another item that is presented at this level is similar but involves the relationship "against" rather than "on top of." In this item, experimenters bring one block up against a second one with a click, and then push the two along for a few inches. Finally, they separate the blocks and invite the children to make one of their own.

The control structures for succeeding on the two items are quite similar. The one for building a tower might be represented as follows:

PROBLEM SITUATION   OBJECTIVE
- Experimenter placed one block   ⟶ • Build a similar construction.
  on top of first block.

STRATEGY

1. Pick up one block and set it on top of a second.

Note that, as with the drawing task, success on these two items requires the children attend to a single relationship, and duplicate this relationship themselves.

Substage 1: Operational Coordination (1$\frac{1}{2}$–2 Years)

During the next substage, children become capable of coordinating two relational operations with each other. One of the block patterns that they can erect as a consequence is the "train with engine" (Catell, 1940), which is illustrated in Figure 8.1. As may be seen, the first relationship is identical to the one in the tower of the previous substage (on top of). The second relationship is identical to the one in the flat train (beside). To construct the train with engine, therefore, children must assemble a structure that contains both of these relations as components. Another item that makes a similar demand is the step, which is also illustrated in Figure 8.1. The executive control structure for succeeding on the first item might be represented as follows:

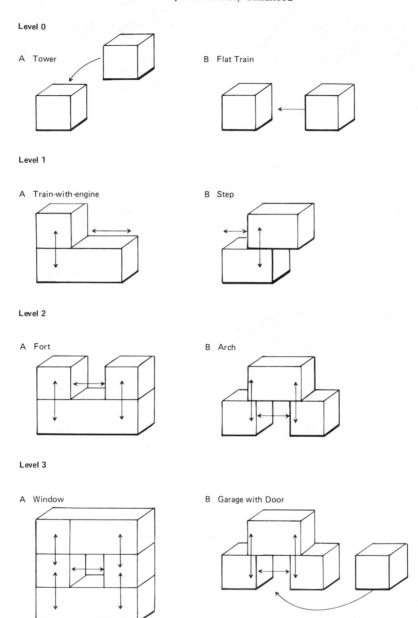

Fig. 8.1. Items used on the preschool block-assembly test.

PROBLEM SITUATION

- Small block placed on top of big, to make a "train."

- Top item is at the side of the block.

OBJECTIVES

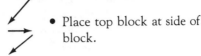

- Make a similar pattern.

- Place top block at side of block.

STRATEGY

1a. Pick up small block, and move it towards big block.

1b. As small block approaches, line it up with one side of big block.

2a. Place small block on top of large one, monitoring overall pattern produced, and making any necessary (sideways) adjustments.

Note that only one of the two relations that must be represented in the above structure is actually signaled by the experimenter's action (i.e., on top of). The other must be apprehended by analyzing the internal structure of the configuration which results. In this sense, the two relations that are coordinated are similar to those which must be coordinated in the drawing task, as is the qualitative change in children's performance which results.

Substage 2: Bifocal Coordination (2–3½ Years)

During the next substage, children become capable of constructing the arch that is illustrated in Figure 6.3 (Terman & Merrill, 1960). A similar item that we have used in our own studies is the *fort*, which is illustrated in the same figure. Both these constructions are bifocal, in that they require the child to focus on two spatial interrelationships rather than one. To construct such items is beyond the capabilities of 2-year-olds. By the age of 3½ years, however, children can sustain such a dual focus with ease. The control structure for building the fort might be represented as follows:

PROBLEM SITUATION

- Blocks assembled to make a fort.

- Top element on left is "at the side".

- Top element of right is "at the side".

OBJECTIVES

- Duplicate overall pattern.

- Build left side.

- Build right side.

STRATEGY

1a. Pick up small block and move it toward the long one.

1b. As small block approaches, line
it up with right edge.
2. Place small block on top of large
one, continuing to monitor the
fact that it is "at the side"
and making any necessary
adjustment.
3. Repeat 1a and 1b for left side,
checking overall pattern which
results.

As may be seen, each component of the preceding structure contains one more element than at the previous stage. An additional feature has been added to the representation of the problem situation. This has required the addition of an element to the list of problem objectives. And this in turn has required the addition of a third subroutine (itself a two-step iteration) to the strategy for solving the problem.

Substage 3: Elaborated Coordination ($3\frac{1}{2}$–5 Years)

During the final substage, children become capable of introducing a number of elaborations into the patterns which they could construct at the previous substage. As was the case with drawing, some of these involve the integration of elements that were mastered at Substage 1, and some involve integration of elements that were not mastered until Substage 2. Two elaborations of the latter sort are illustrated in Figure 8.1. The data for each item are presented in Table 8.1, together with the data from the earlier items. As may be seen, the general pattern of the results is the same as for figure drawing and balance beam tasks.

THE DEVELOPMENT OF SOCIAL CONTROL STRUCTURES

At the same time as children are learning about the spatial and mechanical relationships in their physical world, they are also learning about a variety of social relationships as well. In recent years, a good deal of research has been devoted to exploring the social changes that take place during this period (see Flavell & Ross, 1981; Krasnor & Rubin, 1983; Rubin & Everett, 1983). In the present section, two strands of this work will be considered. One of these focuses on children's social interaction and role taking. The other has focused on their diagnosis and manipulation of other people's feelings.

TABLE 8.1

Percentage of Children Passing the Block Items at Different Age Levels[a]

Approximate theoretical age range (Empirical mean in sample tested)	Items[b] at Level 0: Consolidation of relational operations (%)		Items at Level 1: Coordination of relational operations (%)		Items at Level 2: Bifocal coordination (%)		Items at Level 3: Elaborated coordination (%)	
	Tower	Train[c]	Engine	Step	Fort	Arch	Window	Garage[d]
12–20 mo (18 mo)	83	50	0	0	0	0	0	0
20–27 mo (26 mo)	100	100	90	60	10	10	0	0
27–40 mo (37 mo)	100	100	90	80	90	80	50	20
40–54 mo (49 mo)	100	100	100	100	100	100	90	100

[a] From Bruchkowsky (1983). Number of subjects per cell = 10.

[b] All items are first demonstrated by experimenter then knocked down. Child is then asked to build one just the same. Pass = ability to construct design on first or second trial.

[c] One block is banged against other, and pushed for a few inches extra.

[d] Last block referred to as "back door" for garage.

Social Interaction and Role Taking

Preschoolers are highly social creatures. Whether they are in an environment that contains only their principal caretakers, or whether they are in an environment that includes a wider variety of adults and peers, it does not take them long to initiate some form of social interaction. The type of interaction in which they engage, however, changes dramatically as they move through the preschool period.

Substage 0: Operational Consolidation (1–1½ Years)

Children imitate their peers and their caretakers long before they are 1 year old. The distinctive feature of imitation between the ages of 1 and 1½ years, however, is that it can centre on objects, because children are capable of focusing on the particular action that someone executes with an object, and duplicating the action themselves. When their companions are peers, this can lead to a form of object-centred *parallel play*. For example, each child may bang a stick on a drum, while pausing to observe the other from time to time, and exchanging laughs or smiles (Mueller & Lucas, 1975; Mueller & Vandell, 1979).

With their caretaker, the same sort of imitation can lead to a variety of activities in which the experimenter models the use of an object or toy, gives it to the child for a turn, then takes it back and repeats the action (Bates, 1976). Again, these activities are often accompanied by an exchange of glances and affect, as if to say, "Hurray! we're both doing it."

One consequence of this sort of object-centered turn taking is that children learn the function of a variety of objects in their environment, whose particular use they might not otherwise discover. It is during this period, for example, that objects such as rakes, tennis rackets, and teacups are first used in an appropriate fashion in cultures where these objects play some important role. The structure for mastering the use of a tool such as a rake might be represented as follows:

PROBLEM SITUATION   OBJECTIVE
- Parent moves rake across lawn   - Duplicate parent's action (or
  building a pile of grass.   participate in activity).

STRATEGY
1. Pick up rake after parent puts
   it down and move it across lawn,
   monitoring results.

Substage 1: Operational Coordination ($1\frac{1}{2}$–2 Years)

At the age of $1\frac{1}{2}$ to 2 years, a qualitative shift takes place, and children for the first time engage in object-centered operations that are *complementary* or *reciprocal* to those being executed by someone else, rather than identical (Mueller & Brenner, 1977; Mueller & Lucas, 1975; Mueller & Vandell, 1979). In the area of peer play, for example, an observer may see one child pulling a wagon, while the other child rides in it. In the area of adult–child interaction, an observer may see a child going to get a rake, while the child's parent is cutting the grass. Even activities where the actions appear identical take on a more complementary or cooperative character at this age. For example, one child may push a chair up to a table and sit down, motioning to a playmate to sit down as well. Alternatively, one child may pick up a tennis racket, and start swiping at a tennis ball, motioning for another child to join in the fun.[3]

When one sees this sort of interaction, it is hard to resist the inference that the

---

[3]The specific examples are taken from my own son, Jonathan, at play in the back garden with a peer at the age of 22 months. That the phenomena are general has been suggested by the studies of Mueller and his colleagues (see Mueller & Brenner, 1977). While carefully controlled studies have revealed the existence of certain cooperative patterns earlier (Ross, 1982), they are all patterns which either involve no object, or else involve identical actions (as in "you chase me, I chase you").

children are developing their first tentative sense of cooperation, and hence their first tentative insight into the workings of an elementary social system. The basis for this acquisition has been clarified by a recent study by Fenson and Ramsay (1981). What these investigators did was to demonstrate certain culturally appropriate actions on objects, such as pouring water from a teapot to a cup, or picking up a cup and drinking from it. By the age of 15 months, the majority of the children in their study were able to imitate each one of these actions individually. If the actions were combined, however (e.g., first pretending to pour water into the cup, then pretending to drink from it), the children would imitate only one of them. By contrast, children at the age of 19 months would imitate both actions, in the culturally or pragmatically appropriate sequence. It seems reasonable to presume, therefore, that it is the ability to coordinate two object-oriented actions that leads children to engage in object-centred cooperation during this period. This being the case, the control structure for getting a rake when the parent gets out a lawnmower might be represented as follows:

PROBLEM SITUATION   OBJECTIVES

- Parent gets out lawnmower, and $\longrightarrow$ • Join in activity.
  starts to cut grass.

- Next action in sequence is   • Get rake and start moving it
  normally raking the grass.   on grass.

STRATEGY

1. Pick up the rake, and begin to
   move it across the lawn,
   monitoring the parent as one
   does so.

Note that the preceding control structure constitutes another example in which the actual strategy that children use does not change with age. Rather, what changes is their apprehension of the conditions under which this strategy is appropriate.

Substage 2: Bifocal Coordination (2–$3\frac{1}{2}$ Years)

Between the ages of 2 and $3\frac{1}{2}$ years, children become capable of focusing on two social interrelations simultaneously. For the first time, therefore, they become capable of playing *circle games*, e.g., games in which they retrieve a ball bounced to them by someone on their left, and then turn and bounce it to the person on their right (Khanna, 1984; Sparling & Lewis, 1979). They can also engage in activities involving more than one person around the house, providing that sufficient direction is provided. For example, they can learn to get a basket to collect the grass their sibling is raking, in order to help their parent who is cutting the grass. The control structure for engaging in this latter activity could be represented as follows:

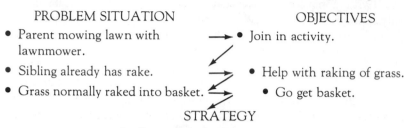

PROBLEM SITUATION　　　　　　　　　OBJECTIVES

- Parent mowing lawn with　　⟶ • Join in activity.
  lawnmower.
- Sibling already has rake.　　　　　• Help with raking of grass.
- Grass normally raked into basket.　　• Go get basket.

STRATEGY

1. Go retrieve basket.
2. Hold it near place where grass is
   accumulating.

A bifocal function that has been studied more systematically at this age is what has been called the *behavioural role* (Fischer *et al.*, in press; Kuhn *et al.*, 1978). Acquiring the understanding of a behavioural role presumably requires a form of dual focusing as well. As a minimum, it would appear to require focusing on a particular behavioural interrelationship and the characteristics of one of the participants (e.g., a doctor examines you and wears a white coat).

Substage 3: Elaborate Bifocal Coordination ($3\frac{1}{2}$–5 Years)

A number of elaborations are observed during the final substage of the period. In the area of role taking, the most salient change is that children become capable of sustaining a particular role and acting out the appropriate actions, while simultaneously monitoring the role being played by a peer. If a peer deviates from his or her role in a doctor-and-patient game, for example, the child at this stage who is playing the doctor may say something like, "No, you're not the doctor; you're supposed to be sick" (Garvey, 1976). It is also at this age that childen will make two dolls (e.g., a doctor and a nurse), engage in activities that are both role specific, and appropriately complementary (Fischer *et al.*, in press). Finally, it is at this age that children can answer questions about what mother will do as a function of her child's behavior, and what the child will do as a function of her mother's behavior (Goldberg, 1984). This basic insight (i.e., the insight concerning the way in which one behavioral role and another complement each other) is a vital one, if children are to deal with the more complex social systems in which they will have to participate in the years to come. It thus marks the pinnacle of their relational thought in the social domain, in a way which is not unlike that which is observed in the mechanical or spatial domains.

Diagnosis and Manipulation of Other People's Feelings

The first studies that were designed to assess children's understanding of other people's feeling utilized complex decentering situations of the sort that were originally designed by Piaget (see Chandler, 1977). Perhaps not surprisingly, therefore, these studies showed that children were not very good at diagnosing other people's feelings until well into the elementary school years. In keeping with the zeitgeist, however, later studies showed that some understanding of other people's feelings can be demonstrated a good deal earlier, providing that the task situation is simplified, and that the feelings in question are ones with which young children are familiar (e.g., Borke, 1971). In order to trace the ontogeny of this capability in a somewhat more fine-grained fashion, we have recently conducted two studies in our own research group. The first one involved the manipulation of other people's feelings (Marini, 1984). The second involved the diagnosis of other people's feelings (Bruchkowsky, 1983). The results from both studies were quite similar.

Substage 0: Operational Consolidation (1–1½ Years)

During the preliminary substage, children appeared to react with genuine feelings themselves, to puppet shows in which one of the protagonists expressed some particular feeling. In the study by Bruchkowsky, for example, one puppet was given a big smile and a happy face, and made to hop around saying such things as, "Oh, it's such a nice day, I'm so happy," in a joyful sing-song voice. Under these conditions, 1½-year-old children seemed genuinely delighted. They would play with the puppet in a happy fashion, and exhibit a great deal of positive affect themselves.

Next a puppet was brought on the stage who had a big frown on her face, and who crept about saying such things as, "Oh, I'm so unhappy, I think I'm going to cry. Sniff. Sniff. This is such a terrible day." Again, these expressions were uttered with all the unhappy affect the experimenter could muster. Under these conditions, the majority of the children became quite subdued. Some then brightened again, looking at the experimenter behind the puppet, as though to assure themselves that things were really all right. A few children, however, were sufficiently affected that they actually began to cry themselves, and wanted the game to stop.

Given that children of this age can treat a puppet as they would a human, and "catch" its feelings in this fashion, it is of interest to know whether they can also learn to manipulate such feelings. In the study by Marini, children were taught how to pat a Muppet (Kermit the Frog) in order to stop him from being unhappy, and to make him happy. They were also taught how to "tweak" another Muppet (Fozzy-the-Bear) in order to elicit an expression of mock anger or protest. The children had little difficulty in learning how to engage in either of these sorts of interactions, and appeared to enjoy both immensely.

From the viewpoint of sensorimotor development, the ability to produce the sort of affective reaction that one wants in a Muppet represents a considerable achievement. In order to succeed, one must reach out to the Muppet, and either pat or tweak it, as a function of whether its current mood is sad (and therefore needs brightening) or neutral (and therefore can be teased). One could therefore represent the underlying control structure as a complex and nested set of sensorimotor schemes. From the viewpoint of relational development, however, the same achievement can be seen as requiring the representation of a single relation, namely, that between the action of the experimenter, and the reaction of the Muppet. It may therefore be represented as follows:

PROBLEM SITUATION   OBJECTIVE
- Kermit looking sad.   ⟶ - Make Kermit happy.
STRATEGY
1. Reach out and place hand on
   Kermit's back, stroking him until
   he begins to smile.

Substage 1: Operational Coordination ($1\frac{1}{2}$–2 Years)

It is one thing to engage in a sensorimotor action in order to cheer someone up. It is quite another to understand the social conditions that have led to someone else's unhappy state, and to manipulate these conditions. This latter capability implies some rudimentary understanding of a social system, or a structure that involves two different relationships as components. At the age of $1\frac{1}{2}$ to 2 years, a qualitative change takes place, and these latter sorts of capabilities begin to emerge.

In the study by Bruchkowsky, the focus was on the conditions that might lead to a mood of happiness or sadness. Each of two puppets was brought on the stage, and turned so that they were facing away from the child. The experimenter then delivered a present to each one. The first puppet got a toy bicycle, the second one got an identical toy that had been broken into several pieces. The experimenter then asked how each one of the puppets felt, and whether one of the puppets might start to cry. The $1\frac{1}{2}$-year-olds were unable to answer either of these questions, or to demonstrate by pointing that they understood. The 2-year-olds, however, quite readily identified the puppet who might cry as the one who got the broken toy.

Were these the only data available, one might presume that the $1\frac{1}{2}$-year-olds' difficulty was purely linguistic (i.e., that they did not understand the affective terms that were used in the question). The experiment by Marini, however, used a very similar set of conditions, in a situation where no understanding of feeling terms was necessary. After he had taught each age group how to make Kermit and Fozzy happy or angry, Marini introduced two props: a blanket that would make the Muppets happy, and a brush that could be used to tease them and make them angry. The 2-year-olds were able to imitate these actions quite easily, and to apply them appropriately when the experimenter introduced a new Muppet. By contrast, the $1\frac{1}{2}$-year-olds were not. Instead, what they did was to operate on the unhappy Muppet directly, as they had done at the previous level. Presumably the reason that the $1\frac{1}{2}$ year-olds had this trouble was that they were not yet capable of assembling a control structure in which an event involving the receipt of an object was linked to an affective reaction on the part of the person receiving it. In short, they could presumably not assemble a control structure with the following format:

PROBLEM SITUATION	OBJECTIVES
• Kermit is crying.	• Make Kermit happy.
• Kermit's blanket is nearby.	• Pick up Kermit's blanket and give it to him.

STRATEGY

1. Reach out for Kermit's blanket.
2. Pat him with the blanket.

Presumably, too, it was the capability for assembling this sort of coordinated relational structure that made the task so straightforward for the older children.

Substage 2: Bifocal Coordination (2–3½ Years)

In the study on the diagnosis of other people's feelings, the new element that was introduced at the bifocal level was information about a second internal characteristic of each puppet, namely, what each one wanted for a birthday present. The children were told that each of the puppets wanted a bike, and were questioned until they could successfully answer the question, "What did they want?" After they had answered this question successfully several times, they were then shown what the puppets actually received. One puppet did receive a bike. However, the other received another toy. This toy was very appealing in its own right (a doll). However, it was of course not what the puppet in question wanted. The experimenter then asked the same questions as had been asked at the previous level, namely, which puppet might be expected to cry, and which puppet might be sad. The 2-year-olds tended to say that each puppet would laugh and that neither would cry. By contrast, the 3-year-olds were able to understand that the puppet who did not get what it wanted might be sad and cry (Bruchkowsky, 1984).

In the study on the manipulation of feelings, a new element was introduced at this level as well. Now children were told that, when Kermit was sad, it was not enough simply to pat him with his blanket, in order to make him happy. To feel happy, Kermit needed his best friend Fozzy as well, and Fozzy had to do the blanket-patting. The experimenter then demonstrated how Fozzy might go and get Kermit's blanket, and pat him with it, thus making him happy.

After several different bifocal interactions of this sort had been demonstrated, the children were asked to play the game themselves. As might be expected, the 3-year-olds were able to execute the appropriate actions with ease. However, the 2-year-olds were not. Presumably the reason was that they could not assemble a control structure with the following format.

PROBLEM SITUATION   OBJECTIVES
- Kermit is sad.   • Make Kermit happy.
- Kermit likes his blanket.   • Get Kermit his blanket.
- Kermit needs his friend, too.   • Get Fozzy too.

STRATEGY
1. Pick up Fozzy.
2. Move him toward the blanket, and make him pick it up.
3. Bring the two to Kermit, and make Fozzy pat Kermit with the blanket.

Whether or not the above structure indicates a true understanding of other people's feelings or true *empathy* depends on how these two terms are defined. In the present context, however, the point is simply that the child's behaviour indicates a growing understanding of the way in which other people's actions are intertwined (i.e., the way in which a simple system of social relations can operate). It also indicates an ability to put this knowledge to use, in order to achieve simple goals involving changing someone's affective state. Lest it be thought that the above structure is purely a creation of the psychological laboratory, it should be mentioned out that one often sees children getting a blanket or bottle to comfort their peers in daycare centres during this age range, and that adults are often approached to help in the process.

Substage 3: Elaborated Coordination ($3\frac{1}{2}$–5 Years)

At the final substage, the element that was added in the feeling-diagnosis study was a differentiation between the object that each of the two puppets desired. Although one puppet wanted a bike, for example, the other puppet wanted a doll. Moreover, on one trial each puppet got what it wanted whereas on the other trial the two presents were reversed. In order to pass both items the subject therefore had to consider the particular desires of each particular puppet in question, and determine whether or not the toy he received would fulfill them.

In the feeling-manipulation task, the new element that was added was another person. This time the reason that Kermit was unhappy was that his little baby (Baby Kermit) was crying. In order to make Baby Kermit stop crying one needed to bring Fozzy and the blanket to Baby Kermit's aid. After this basic plot had been introduced, children were placed in front of big Kermit, and told to make him happy. As might be expected, the 3-year-olds approached the unhappy Muppet in front of them (i.e., big Kermit). By the age of 5 years, however, the children were able to understand that big Kermit's feelings stemmed from the feelings of his baby, and that the actions in question had to be applied to his baby instead.

The data from Marini's and Bruchkowsky's studies are summarized in Table 8.2. As may be seen, the general progression that was observed, as well as the percentages of subjects at each age level who were functioning at each cognitive level, were quite similar to those reported for the balance beam and for the blocks.

THE DEVELOPMENT OF LINGUISTIC CONTROL STRUCTURES

Perhaps the most dramatic development that takes place during the preschool period is the acquisition of language. In fact, this acquisition is often considered the hallmark of preschool thought. At the beginning of the stage, children experience considerable difficulty in articulating single words, and can make their wants known only in familiar contexts. By the end of the stage, they have mastered many of the major semantic and syntactic distinctions in their native tongue, and can make their wants known with considerable ease, even in completely novel contexts.

Given the importance of language for human culture, and the rapidity of its onset during this period, it is hardly surprising that most preschool IQ tests include a number of linguistic items. Nor is it surprising that the acquisition of language has been the subject of intense scrutiny in developmental psychology from the time of its inception.

As has already been mentioned, Chomsky's (1957) theory of generative grammar triggered an explosion of theoretical and empirical work in the field. In the present section, no attempt is made to summarize the entire literature that resulted from Chomsky's pioneering work, with its rich and fascinating detail. Instead, the focus is on the global pattern of children's linguistic development, and the parallels this development shares with developments in other domains.

TABLE 8.2

Percentage of Subjects Passing each Task in the Feeling Studies[a]

Theoretical age range (mean age of sample)	Level 0		Level 1		Level 2		Level 3	
	Diagnosis (responds to doll's affect) (%)	Manipulation (changes doll's affect by direct sensorimotor action) (%)	Diagnosis (predicts receipt of broken toy will lead to negative affect) (%)	Manipulation (changes doll's affect by bringing suitable object) (%)	Diagnosis (predicts receipt of toy that is not what was desired will produce negative affect) (%)	Manipulation (uses object and "friend" to change affect) (%)	Diagnosis (predicts results when each of two puppets desires a different toy) (%)	Manipulation (object and friend used to comfort baby, to make father happy) (%)
$1\frac{1}{2}$–2 yr (18 mo)	87[b]	70[c]	0	30	0	0	0	0
$1\frac{1}{2}$–2 yr (24 mo)	100	100	85	85	0	30	0	0
2–$3\frac{1}{2}$ yr (37 mo)	100	100	90	95	80	60	30	5
$3\frac{1}{2}$–5 yr (4 yr)	100	100	100	100	100	90	45	55

[a] From Marini (1984) and Bruchkowsky (1984).
[b] n = 11.
[c] n for all other cells = 20.

Two sorts of study are considered: those that have focused on children's spontaneous utterances, and those that have focused on more contrived laboratory tasks.

Spontaneous Utterances

Substage 0: Operational Consolidation (1–1½ Years)

As was mentioned in the previous chapter, children first begin to use words to achieve pragmatic purposes between the age of 1 and 1½ years, at least in cultures where their caretakers actively encourage this. The executive structures on which this development depends are similar to those of many other sensorimotor activities, and can be modeled as a complex sequence of sensorimotor acts (see Chapter 7). Alternatively, they may be modeled from a relational perspective, as an attempt to manipulate a single relationship, that between a listener and an interesting event. This representation would have the following format.

PROBLEM SITUATION   OBJECTIVE

- Interesting event in distance   - Share interesting event with
  (Daddy hitting a ball with a bat).   listener (Mummy)

STRATEGY

1. Name salient feature of event
   (e.g., actor = "Daddy").

Substage 1: Operational Coordination (1½–2 Years)

It is as children move from Substage 0 to Substage 1 that their speech takes on the first appearance of language as we normally think of it. It is at this substage, for example, that words are first used in the absence of their referents (Piaget, 1951). It is at this stage, too, that a sudden change takes place in word phonology and morphology (Dromi, 1985). Finally, it is at this stage that children's first two-word utterances appear. Common utterances include sentences that refer to a person and an action (e.g., Daddy hit), an action and an inanimate object (hit ball), or a person and an object (Daddy ball) (Bowerman, 1973; Brown, 1973). Clearly, children's speech cannot yet be understood without reference to the context in which it is uttered, because any single utterance could have several possible meanings. The important point, however, is that the children's speech now focuses on a relationship that is inherent to an event itself, not just on a relationship between a globally experienced event and a listener. The expression of this sort of relationship marks the child's entry into language as a system, in much the same way that the changes which have already been considered mark his entry into the world of spatial, social or mechanical systems.

Different investigators have classified the various types of relationships which children express in their first two-word utterances in different fashions (e.g., Fillmore, 1968; Schlesinger, 1974). However, as Brown has pointed out, there is a good deal of overlap among their classification schemes, and the total set of relational categories that are suggested remains small, regardless of which particular scheme is used. Brown's own preferred set includes agent–action (e.g., Daddy gone), action–object (e.g., hit-ball), agent–object (Daddy ball), possession (my block), attribution (big shovel), recurrence (more ball), negation (allgone juice), and location (Mummy out).

Whether or not children employ grammatical categories or devices at this substage in order to signal the relationships that they express is not clear. What is clear, however, is that in languages where any of the preceding relationships are signaled by a particular word order, children will use this same word order during the great majority of their utterances by the end of the period, whereas in cultures where word order is more variable, children's word order remains variable as well (see Brown, 1973). This being the case, one might represent the child's control structure for generating a sentence such as "Daddy hit" at this stage as follows:

PROBLEM SITUATION   OBJECTIVES

- Mummy not looking at interesting   • Share interesting event (involving
  event (Daddy hitting a ball in the   Daddy) with Mummy.
  garden).

- Event is Daddy executing   • Indicate action.
  interesting action.

STRATEGY
1. Name actor in event ("Daddy").
2. Name action, ("Hit").

Note that—unlike most of the strategies that have been described so far—the steps in the above strategy do not necessarily unfold in the reverse order in which children set up their goals and subgoals. Rather, they unfold in the same order as they are used in adult speech. Note, too, that the ordering requirement is not represented in the child's control structure as any sort of problem feature. Although re-orderings that are designed to signal particular types of relational features must be represented, it is presumed that the preservation of word order is simply a capability for which the organism is biologically designed.

Substage 2: Bifocal Coordination (2–3½ Years)

As children move into the next stage of linguistic development, their control structures become bifocal in two senses. The first is what might be called a grammatical sense. Expressions begin to appear in their speech in which one of the words they utter is qualified in some fashion, to signal some additional semantic feature. In English, this additional feature may be signaled lexically, as is the case with such features as noun specificity (hit *the* ball) or noun location (Daddy *in* garden). The additional feature may also be specified syntactically, as in the case with verb modifications indicating continuity ("Daddy sleep*ing*,") or tense (Daddy hit*ted*). These latter sentences are of course incorrect but indicate the generative nature of children's productions at this stage. The underlying control structure for generating such an utterance might be represented as follows:

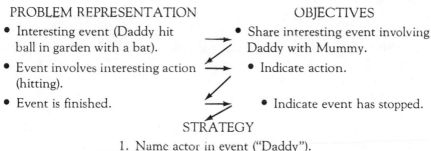

PROBLEM REPRESENTATION

- Interesting event (Daddy hit ball in garden with a bat).
- Event involves interesting action (hitting).
- Event is finished.

OBJECTIVES

- Share interesting event involving Daddy with Mummy.
- Indicate action.
- Indicate event has stopped.

STRATEGY

1. Name actor in event ("Daddy").
2. Name action, adding *ed* ("Hitted").

A second way in which children's sentences become bifocal during this stage is related less directly to form than to content. At the same time as they are acquiring structures to qualify relationships, they are also acquiring structures to express two such relationships, rather than just one. As a consequence, the two sentences "Daddy hit" and "hit ball" may now be expressed in a single utterance, with the conventional subject–verb–object structure (Daddy hit ball). Finally, as children's capabilities in both areas become automated, they begin to utter sentences that are more complex in both respects at once. By the end of the stage, they can generate sentences such as "Daddy hitted the ball" with little difficulty.

How it is that children's attention can become bifocal both within and across units simultaneously is a topic that is beyond the scope of the present volume.[4] For the moment, however, it is sufficient to point out that it can, as long as the domain is one in which the particular within-unit elements appear regularly, and where the structural form for within-unit and across-unit combinations can be learned separately. It is also perhaps worthwhile to mention that this capability is not limited to the domain of language learning, but appears in other domains as well (e.g., art).

---

[4] For an explication of this phenomenon, see Case *et al.* (1985).

Substage 3: Elaborated Coordination ($3\frac{1}{2}$–5 Years)

During the final substage of the period, children begin to use well formed sub-ject–verb–object sentences that have some elaboration attached to one of the components. Actually, if one examines utterances that are not fully formed dur-ing the previous substage, one sees that most of these elaborations can be observed during this time period as well (Menyuk, 1977). Nevertheless, their ap-pearance in fully formed sentences is a characteristic of the final substage of the relational period, and one which is again directly parallel to developments in other domains. Another parallel is that the elaborations can be quite simple or quite complex. An example of a simple elaboration would be "Daddy kicked the ball hard." An example of a more complex elaboration would be "Daddy kicked the ball in the garden." A final parallel to developments in other domains is that the fully formed sentences children generate at the end of the stage can then form elements in constructions of a higher order still, which appear during the next major stage of their development. These constructions include stories with well-formed episodic structure (McKeough, 1982), and complex sentences in which one complete clause is embedded within the center of another (Olson, personal communication, February, 1983).

Performance on Laboratory Tasks

The advantage of studying children's spontaneous utterances is that one ob-tains a sense of their linguistic capabilities in the sort of natural settings for which these capabilities were biologically designed, and in which they are nor-mally deployed. The disadvantage is that one cannot always separate the effects of linguistic factors from contextual factors. Two laboratory tasks that can be used to circumvent these problems are the tasks of executing commands and repeating sentences. The first of these has often been used to assess linguistic comprehension, both on IQ tests and tests in the psycholinguistic literature (see Chomsky, 1969; Terman & Merrill, 1960). The second has often been used to assess linguistic production (see Slobin & Welsh, 1973; Terman & Merrill, 1960). In spite of its apparently rote nature, the task of repeating sentences can serve as an index of children's productive capabilities, in the same way that the task of executing commands can serve as a test of their capability to com-prehend. In two recent studies, therefore, we administered both these measures, in order to assess the generality of the pattern that appears in children's spon-taneous utterances (Case & Khanna, 1981; Khanna, 1984). In constructing the commands test, we took care to insure that the verbs could not be predicted from a knowledge of the nouns, or vice versa. This meant that the most of our sentences had rather unusual meanings (e.g., "Roll the truck with the spoon"). However, it also meant that each element we were counting would actually have to be represented by the child in an on-line fashion. In constructing the set of objects from which the children had to choose in executing the commands, we also took care to insure that we included a number of items which shared certain general perceptual or functional properties with those in the sentences (e.g., truck versus car, and spoon versus fork). This precaution was designed to insure that children would also have to process the meaning of each major element of the sentence.

The results that were obtained in the first study have already been published (Case & Khanna, 1981). The results that were obtained in the second study (Khanna, 1985) are presented in Tables 8.3 and 8.4. As may be seen, of the 54 entries in the Table 8.3, only three were not in accord with the predictions. These items all involved sentence repetition, and the form verb + ing, which we

TABLE 8.3

Percentage of Children Capable of Repeating Sentences at Various Levels of Complexity[a]

Theoretical age range (mean age of sample)[b]	Level 0: Doggie Daddy Crying Missing (%)	Level 1: Kiss doggie. Daddy cry. Two frogs. Johnny smells. (%)	Level 2: Daddy smelled the doggie. Johnny kissed the keys. Jane paints quietly. The rabbit is crying today. (%)	Level 3: Jane is crying with the doggie today. The rabbit was smelling Johnnie quietly Mummy was painting the truck with a stick. Doggies like to smell new keys sometimes (%)
1–1½ yr (18 mo, 9 d)	48	13	0	0
	48	17	0	0
	17	8	0	0
	13	4	0	0
1½–2 yr (23 mo, 9 d)	96	75	22	4
	92	70	30	0
	90	63	9	9
	83	59	9	4
2–3 yr (30 mo, 3d)	100	100	61	27
	100	96	70	4
	100	96	61	9
	100	100	40	0
3–4½ yr (45 mo, 3 d)	100	100	96	79
	100	100	95	70
		92	88	67
		83	96	63

[a] From Khanna (1985).
[b] Number of subjects per group = 24. Mean IQ is approximately 110 in each group.
[c] Deviations from predictions.

TABLE 8.4

Percentage of Children Capable of Executing Commands at Various Levels of Complexity[a]

Theoretical age range (mean age of sample)[b]	Level 0 (Where is the *ball*). Kiss (the Teddy). Throw (the Teddy). (Where is the *car*). (%)	Level 1 Kiss the ball. Smell the key. Throw the car. Pat the truck. (%)	Level 2 Throw the truck into the cup. Hit the bed with the flower. Pat the cup with the key. Roll the truck with the spoon. (%)	Level 3 Hit the ball on the bed with the key. Pat the kleenex on the chair with the spoon. Smell the ball in the cup on the chair. Throw the cup onto the box on the bed. (%)
12–20 mo (18 mo, 9 d)	88	36	0	4
	74	28	8	0
	73	26	4	0
	52	18	0	0
20–27 mo (23 mo, 9 d)	100	71	39	17
	96	67	35	8
	96	70	33	8
	83	71	39	0
27–40 mo (30 mo, 3 d)	100	96	75	58
	100	96	62	17
	100	79	54	17
	100	92	42	17
40–54 mo (45 mo, 2 d)	100	100	96	42
	100	100	92	46
	100	88	75	38
	100	91	83	33

[a] From Khanna (1985).

[b] Number of subjects per group = 24. Mean IQ in each group approximately equal to 110.

had presumed could be processed in a passive fashion and repeated as a single item. Had we followed the generative analysis of the previous section more closely, of course, we would have analyzed these items as involving two morphemes, and would have successfully predicted the entire pattern. In Table 8.4 the only prediction failures were at the upper levels, where children ran into unanticipated problems with the particular relationships that were signaled by the various prepositions.

In spite of these few prediction failures, the general point of the data will, I hope, still be clear. It is that there is a strong parallel between the pattern that appears in various laboratory tests of children's linguistic functioning and that which appears in their spontaneous utterances. Moreover, this parallel is the same—both with regard to its general form and with regard to its timing—as that which appears on tests of children's mechanical, spatial, or social functioning.

That some sort of parallel exists between linguistic and nonlinguistic development has of course been known for some time (Baldwin, 1894; Piaget, 1951). It is important to realize, however, that the nature of the parallel that is being suggested here is somewhat different from the one which was suggested by Piaget. Piaget's point was that children's language bears a parallel to their make-believe play and their gestural imitation, in that all three types of activity involve symbolization. What distinguished the preschooler from the infant in Piaget's system was the general capacity for symbolization. The present point, however, is that preschooler's capacity for symbolization is just one of their distinctive cognitive characteristics. That is, symbolic activity itself is part of a capability that is more general still, the capability for coordinating two relationships and thus coming to apprehend the workings of relational structures and systems. While this capability is observable in the symbolic domain, it is observable in many other domains as well. The same point could perhaps be made with regard to higher versus lower primates. What distinguishes higher primates such as apes from lower primates such as dogs and cats may not just be that they can be taught to use symbols (Gardner, & Gardner, 1980; Premack, 1983), or that they can use tools in an imitative fashion. Rather, it may be a more general property of their mind: that they can comprehend two relationships simultaneously, and thus come to a preliminary understanding of a variety of interrelational systems.

THE DEVELOPMENT OF CONTROL STRUCTURES IN OTHER DOMAINS

There are a number of other domains in which a similar pattern is observed during early childhood, including children's gross-motor play. For present purposes, however, the only remaining domain which needs to be considered is the domain of quantification, because the developments in this domain pave the way for a great many of the further developments that take place during the next major stage of development, and which have been studied under the headings of scientific and logical reasoning.

The Development of Counting

Counting is one of the skills that has been studied by neo-Piagetian investigators, in an attempt to demonstrate that children acquire a number of basic logical capacities well before the age of concrete operations (Gelman, 1978). It has also been studied by information-processing psychologists, whose interest has been in specifying the elementary processes and structures that underlie human cognition (see Klahr, 1973) and by educational psychologists with an interest in the child's first attempts to master addition and subtraction (Davydov, 1982; Fuson, 1982).

Our purpose in studying counting was somewhat different from that of these other investigators. What we wanted to do was to compare the development of counting to developments in other domains. Accordingly, the type of task we presented, and the type of analysis we conducted, were also somewhat different. The general pattern of our data, however, was congruent with that which has been obtained by other investigators.

Substage 0: Operational Consolidation ($1-1\frac{1}{2}$ Years)

The first item on our counting scale required the assembly of a control structure representing a single relation, that between an experimenter's index finger and a set of objects. The experimenter set out a group of dolls in a line. She then placed a finger on one of them, saying "nice, dollie" and turned to the child, inviting her or him to do likewise. The control structure that this requires might be represented as follows:

PROBLEM SITUATION   OBJECTIVE
- Experimenter placed finger $\longrightarrow$ • Imitate experimenter's action.
  on doll(s).

STRATEGY
1. Focus on a particular doll,
   and place finger on it.

Clearly, the preceding task bears little relationship to counting as we know it. The control structure that it requires, however, does form one of the two basic relational components on which counting is based. The other basic component is generating a word, a capability that is also mastered at this substage.

Substage 1: Operational Coordination ($1\frac{1}{2}$–2 Years)

At the second substage, the experimenter set out two dolls, and touched each one of them in sequence. On the surface, this task required nothing more difficult than at the previous substage. In fact, however, it required the same shift in focus as is required by other tasks at the first substage in the relational period. It demanded a coordination of the relationship between the counter and the dolls, with that between one doll and the next. The control structure for executing this operation might be represented as follows:

PROBLEM SITUATION   OBJECTIVES
- Experimenter placed finger on   • Imitate experimenter's finger
  dolls.   action.
- Finger went from one doll to the   • Place finger on a particular
  next.   doll.

STRATEGY
1. Focus on a particular doll (e.g., left one), and touch it with finger.
2. As hand withdraws, switch focus to the next doll, and repeat Step 1.

As may be seen, the action that the child executes at Step 1 is identical to that at the previous substage. However, it has now become subordinated to the larger object of touching both the objects, and as such must be coordinated with a second operation of the same sort. A second task that we presented at this substage was identical to those presented in our sentence imitation battery. The experimenter asked the child to repeat the words he or she was about to say, and then said: "one–two". Both tasks were mastered between the ages of $1\frac{1}{2}$ and 2 years.

Substage 2: Bifocal Coordination (2–$3\frac{1}{2}$ Years)

During the next substage, children became capable of focusing on a pair of number words and a pair of touching acts simultaneously. By the beginning of the substage they could therefore count two objects. By the end of the substage, providing they had been taught and could repeat the appropriate number words by heart, they could extend this competence to counting an array of four or five objects in a line. In the present context, the executive control structure for performing this act would be represented as follows:

PROBLEM SITUATION   OBJECTIVES

- Experimenter placed finger on dolls.
- Finger went from one doll to the next.
- Different number word uttered as each pointing act was executed.

- Imitate experimenter's actions (i.e., count dolls).
- Touch each doll.
- Say appropriate number word at same time.

STRATEGY

1. Focus on left most doll. Place finger on it.
2. As hand touches doll, say appropriate number name.
3. Remove hand from doll, switching focus one to the right. Repeat 1 and 2, using next number word in sequence (if known).

Substage 3: Elaborated Coordination ($3\frac{1}{2}$–5 Years)

A number of elaborations were introduced in our items at the final level. One was to have the children count a set of dolls that were spread out in a random arrangement. Another was to have them count only the "boy dolls", in a set which contained both boys and girls. Each of these elaborations thus required the addition of a new loop in the preexisting structure. The control structure for executing the latter task might be represented as follows:

PROBLEM SITUATION   OBJECTIVES

- Experimenter placed finger on dolls.
- Finger went from one doll to the next.
- Different number word uttered as each pointing act was executed.
- Only the boy dolls were touched.

- Imitate experimenter's actions (i.e., count dolls).
- Touch each doll.
- Say appropriate number word at the same time.
  - Isolate the boy dolls from the girls.

STRATEGY

1. Focus on left most doll, decide if it is a boy or a girl.
2. If it is a girl, skip it. If it is a boy place finger on it.

3. As hand touches doll, say
appropriate number name.
4. Remove hand from doll,
switching focus one to the right.
Repeat steps 1–3, using next
number word in sequence.

What appears to be the case, then, is that the modifications that take place in children's procedures for counting are similar to those that occur in their other routines in the same period. They also appear to take place at the same general rate.

THE GENERAL PATTERN OF DEVELOPMENT IN EARLY CHILDHOOD

As was the case in the previous chapter, the control structures whose development was described in the present chapter were quite diverse. Included were structures for dealing with spatial, social, linguistic, and quantitative relations. Despite the surface diversity of the structures, however, the underlying pattern was quite similar. Not only did children pass through the same sequence of substages, they did so at the same rate. In both these regards, then, the data on children's development during early childhood are similar to the data on their development during infancy. In the terms introduced by Flavell, what the data indicate is a substantial degree of both *vertical* and *horizontal* structure.

At the beginning of the chapter, it was pointed out that Piaget's description of early childhood was not as precise as his description of other stages. Thus, the question was raised as to whether the model of children's performance that was presented for the balance beam could serve to supplement Piaget's description, and to characterize the general set of changes which take place during this period.

The answer to this question would appear to be affirmative. The set of substages through which children pass in their apprehension of simple mechanical systems such as a balance beam appears remarkably similar to the set of substages through which they pass in their apprehension of spatial, social, linguistic, or numerical systems. There is a preliminary substage, during which the relational operations of relevance are consolidated (1–$1\frac{1}{2}$ years). This is followed by a major qualitative shift, during which two different sorts of relational operations are coordinated with each other, to form an interrelational structure ($1\frac{1}{2}$–2 years). Finally, there is a further progression during which these structures first become bifocal (2–$3\frac{1}{2}$ years), and then become more fully elaborated ($3\frac{1}{2}$–5 years). Often the elaboration is one that permits a better integration of the previous interrelations, and/or an appreciation of how the relationships in the system can be reversed.

There is one final parallel to the trend that is observed on the balance beam during this period, and to the trend that is observed in other domains. This is that, as children approach the end of the stage, and begin to apprehend the full workings of an interrelational system, the products of their thought can once again serve as new units on which further development can be based. That is, they can serve as elements whose coordination can give rise to another major qualitative shift in their thinking.

One such shift is observed in the area of logical or scientific reasoning. As defined by Piaget, such reasoning normally entails the coordination of causal reasoning of the sort that is demonstrated by 5-year-olds on a balance beam, with counting of the sort that is observed at the same age. Another emerging competence is the ability to acquire logical insights such as class inclusion. As is shown in the next chapter, this requires the coordination of classification with counting. Perhaps the most important consequence from a cultural point of view, however, is one to which Piagetian and neo-Piagetian researchers have unfortunately given little attention. This is that children become ready for formal schooling. In fact, if one were building an organism that had to be ready for formal schooling by the age of 5 to 7 years, it would be hard to imagine how one could improve on the design that nature has already created.

Consider the following simple example. In order to profit from formal instruction in arithmetic, children must be able to understand the social context in which instruction takes place. In addition they must be able to obey simple instructions such as, "Sit down. Take out a pencil and paper". Finally, they must also be able to count an array of objects (e.g., the classic array of apples), and to copy numerals with their pencils, numerals such as 8 and 9. The remarkable thing is that all these competencies develop in parallel during early childhood, and reach the required level at about the same time. Most simple commands, for example, like the one mentioned above, require the assembly of control structures with 3 or 4 relational components. As has just been shown, counting also requires a control structure of this complexity. Finally, each numeral also requires a similar control structure if it is to be formed correctly. The numeral 9 must be formed by drawing a circle and a straight line. As was shown in the section on drawing, both of these are Level 2 accomplishments. Hence, their integration can only occur at Level 3.[5]

The full picture of development in early childhood, therefore, is not just one of increasing complexity in a number of unrelated executive control structures. The full picture is one of increasing complexity in a number of discrete executive

---

[5]Getting the circle on the right side of the stick is a different matter, and represents a dimensional attainment. It is often not mastered until 5 to 6 years of age.

control structures, whose consolidation at the end of the stage and integration at the beginning of the next stage will permit a qualitatively different type of learning to take place. The preschool period is thus a linking one in the most literal sense of the word. It connects the sensorimotor thinking of infancy, which reaches its most advanced state in means–end behaviour and tool use, with the logical thought of middle childhood, on which formal schooling depends. It is thus no coincidence that groups around the world begin to initiate their young into the industrial skills required by their culture somewhere around the age of 5 to 7 years (White, 1975). Nor is it a coincidence that children respond very well to this initiation. Clearly, although the transition from the informal learning of the home to the more formal learning of the school is a major one, it is by no means unnatural. On the contrary, it is an event for which children's entire lives to that point have been a preparation and for which, in the most literal sense of the word, they are ready.

CHAPTER 9

Development in Middle Childhood: Abstracting the Dimensions of Significance in the Physical and Social World

INTRODUCTION

Of all the major stages of development, none has been studied as intensively as the period of middle childhood. One reason for this is purely practical. It is during this period that experimental subjects are easiest to obtain. Children have arrived at the stage where they spend much of their day in school. However, they have not yet arrived at the stage where they are streamed by ability, or where they must devote all of their classroom time to their studies. An added benefit is that they are eager to cooperate in the sorts of experiments that psychologists are interested in conducting, and are able to persist at them for reasonably long periods of time. Hence, it is relatively easy to obtain large, representative samples of children, and to present the children with tasks that require a good deal of time and concentration.

Another reason this period has been studied so intensively is theoretical. It was for this age group that Piaget developed his most explicit set of logical models, and his most provocative set of logical tasks (seriation, classification, conservation, etc.). Hence, when his theory became the focus of wide scale interest and experimentation, it was to this age group that further attention was devoted. Perhaps not surprisingly, the first theoretical question that was examined was the one that has been considered in the last two chapters, namely, whether or not there is any evidence of general stages in children's thought. Although this proposition seemed reasonable for infants and very young children—given the rapidity, the scope, and the universality of their early achievements—it seemed a good deal more questionable for school aged children. By the same token, however, the proposition also seemed a good deal more important to investigate for this age group because, if it turned out to be correct, the implications would be far reaching, both for psychological theory and for educational practice.

As was mentioned in Chapter 3, the first studies that were conducted seemed to favor Piaget's claim. What they demonstrated was that children did indeed fail a wide variety of logical tasks prior to the age of 7 or 8 years, and that attempts to teach them the underlying concepts were relatively unsuccessful (Flavell, 1963). As new methods of assessment and instruction were invented, however, and as more data were gathered, it became clear that the overall picture was considerably more complex. In particular, it became clear that different tests of the same logical concept were passed at widely different ages, some being passed as early as 3 or 4 years, and some not being passed until 9 or 10 years of age (e.g., Gelman, 1972, 1979). By the end of the 1970's, therefore, a new consensus had begun to emerge. This was that Piaget's assertions concerning the constructive nature of children's thought were correct, but that his assertions about general stages and structures were not, or at least not for the period of middle childhood (see Brainerd, 1978; Fischer, 1980; Flavell, 1980; Gelman, 1979; Klahr & Wallace, 1976; Kuhn, 1983).

Although this conclusion had a solid basis in experimental data, it is important to realize that the sort of finely graded task sequence that was reported in the previous two chapters was just beginning to be perfected at this time. It is also important to realize that the data that these task sequences revealed showed a substantial amount of consistency across domains (cf. Case, 1981; Siegler, 1978, 1981). As the presence of these new-found consistencies began to become known, then, a number of investigators began to soften their claims about the absence of horizontal structure in children's development. Instead, they began to suggest that there might be a substantial degree of horizontal structure as well as décalage in development, and that the tasks for future investigators would be (1) to determine the extent of this structure, and (2) to provide new descriptions and explanations for it (cf. Fischer & Bullock, 1981; Flavell, 1981).

It was with these general objectives in mind that we undertook a new series of studies in our own research group, and that we began to collate and re-analyze the results that were being obtained elsewhere. Although we were not certain just how much vertical or horizontal structure we would discover, we felt that the issue of general stages was still an open one. We also felt that the conclusions that emerged when children's executive control structures were analyzed might be considerably different from those which had emerged earlier, when their logical abilities had been analyzed from a purely structural perspective (Case, 1982).

In the present chapter, the results of our investigations are reported. For the purpose of exposition, the studies are grouped into three categories, as a function of whether they deal with children's scientific, social, or spatial reasoning.

DIMENSIONAL CONCEPTS IN THE DOMAIN OF SCIENTIFIC REASONING

Mixing Juice

Although Siegler's study of the balance beam is the best-known example of structural microanalysis, a number of similar analyses were conducted at the same time. One particularly revealing analysis was done by Noelting (1975, 1980, 1982). Following up on his well-known work with the chemical yellow task, in which he collaborated with Inhelder and Piaget, Noelting examined children's understanding about what happens when orange juice and water are mixed together. The task he presented was as follows.

The dark beakers in Figure 9.1 contain orange juice. The clear beakers contain water. When the beakers are poured into pitchers, which mixture will taste more strongly of juice, A or B? Or will they taste the same?

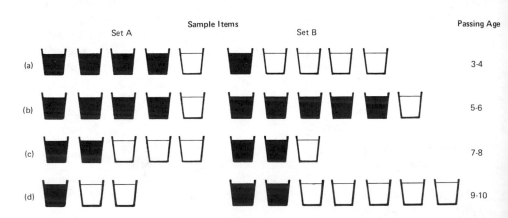

Fig. 9.1. Items used on Noelting's juice problem.

Substage 0: Operational Consolidation ($3\frac{1}{2}$–5 Years)

During the first substage, children correctly assume that if side A gets a lot of orange juice, and side B gets very little, then side A will taste more strongly of juice. From the viewpoint of relational development, this is a complex achievement, involving the coordination of a number of different relations. From the viewpoint of dimensional development, however, the same achievement can be viewed as a rather elementary one, involving the abstraction of a single polar dimension. The executive structure that is involved may therefore be re-represented as follows:

PROBLEM SITUATION   OBJECTIVES

• Two pitchers, each of which will   • Determine which one will taste
  be filled with liquid from beakers.   "juicier".

STRATEGY

1. Check each perceptual array; pick
   set with a lot of juice.

Substage 1: Operational Coordination (5–7 Years)

During the next substage, children begin to coordinate their evaluation of the size of each array with an evaluation of number. When the two arrays appear to be about the same size, they now count the number of juice cups in each set, and predict that the set with the greater number will taste juicier. Their executive control structure may be represented as follows:

PROBLEM SITUATION   OBJECTIVES

• Two pitchers each of which will   • Determine which set will taste
  be filled with liquid from beakers.   juicier.

• Each juice set looks the same size,   • Determine which set has the
  but has a particular number of   greater number of juice
  beakers in it.   beakers.

STRATEGY

1. Count the number of juice in
   each set. Note bigger number.
2. Pick the set with the bigger
   number as juicier.

Note that this change involves the coordination of two routines that are qualitatively distinct, and which have not been used for the same purpose before, namely counting and size estimation. Note, too, that the change results in liquid quantity being treated as having an infinite number of potential points, not just two poles and a middle. Note, finally, that the new type of coordination permits the child to set a new goal, that of searching for the quantitative regularities or rules that govern the operation of the physical world.

Substage 2: Bifocal Coordination (7–9 Years)

During the next substage children's focus expands to include a second quantitative dimension, namely, the number of water cups in each set, When the number of orange juice cups is the same, childrens decenter, and count the number of water cups as well. Their new executive structure may be represented as follows:

PROBLEM SITUATION

- Two pitchers, each of which will be filled with liquid.
- Each juice set looks about the same size, but has a particular number of juice beakers.
- Each set has a particular number of water beakers in it as well.

OBJECTIVES

- Determine which set will taste juicier.
- Determine which set has greater number of juice beakers.
- Determine which side has greater number of water beakers.

STRATEGY

1. Count juice in each set. Note relative number.
2. Count water in each set. Note relative number.
3. If juices are approximately equal, pick the set with more water as less juicy. Otherwise pick the set with more juice.

Substage 3: Elaborated Coordination (9–11 Years)

During the final substage, children develop a strategy for dealing with the troublesome situation where the relative amount of juice suggests that one side should taste juicier, whereas the relative amount of water suggests that the other side should taste juicier. Either they note which side has the greater excess of juice over water, or else they note which dimension has the greater difference, and make their decision on this basis. The executive control structure for the latter strategy may be represented as follows:

PROBLEM SITUATION	OBJECTIVES

- Two pitchers each of which will be filled with liquid from beakers.
- One set has more juice; the other more water.[1]
- Each beaker set has a particular number of juice.
- Each beaker set has a particular number of water.

- Determine which mixture will taste juicier.
- Determine which factor (juice or water) will be "stronger".
  - Determine magnitude of "water factor".
  - Determine magnitude of "juice factor".

STRATEGY

1. Count each water set. Note size of difference.
2. Repeat 1 for juice.
3. Compare magnitude of results in steps 1 and 2.
4. If juice difference is larger, pick set with more juice as "juicier". If water difference is larger, pick set with more water as "less juicy".

As may be apparent, there is a close parallel between the sequence of substages through which children pass on Noelting's juice task and the sequence through which they pass on Siegler's balance task. The structure for global juice evaluation is formally identical to the structure for global weight evaluation on the balance. Similarly, the structure for quantitative juice evaluation, quantitative juice and water evaluation, and juice × water compensation are formally identical to the structures for quantitative weight evaluation, weight and distance evaluation, and weight × distance compensation, respectively. The age at which each structure in the sequence emerges is also very similar.

Assessing Liquid Quantity

A second task that taps children's understanding of their physical world is even simpler than Noelting's. In this test, children are presented with two beakers of water such as those indicated in Figure 9.2. The question they are asked is, "Which beaker contains more water?" In an unpublished study in our own research group,[2] we used a similar methodology to that used by Siegler and Noelting, in order to determine what strategies were used by different age groups (See Figure 9.2).

---

[1]Note that this feature can only be detected once the strategy of the previous substage is available.

[2]This study was conducted with the assistance of Libby Wyatt.

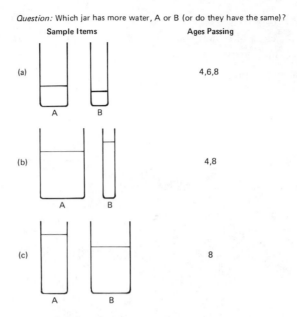

Question: Which jar has more water, A or B (or do they have the same)?

Sample Items   Ages Passing

(a)   A   B   4,6,8

(b)   A   B   4,8

(c)   A   B   8

Fig. 9.2. Items used on liquid quantification task.

Substage 0: Operational Consolidation. ($3\frac{1}{2}$–5 Years)

During the preliminary substage, children realize that the size of the liquid column in each beaker is a dimension that can be used in predicting amount. They therefore solve problems such as those illustrated in Figure 9.3, giving justifications such as "It looks bigger," or "This one is small. This one is big." Not surprisingly, they fail all items where a careful quantification of either height or width is necessary (e.g., item c).

Their executive control structures may be represented as follows:

PROBLEM REPRESENTATION   OBJECTIVE

- Two beakers, partially filled with water.

- Determine which beaker has more to drink.

STRATEGY

1. Scan area covered by the water in each beaker; say one which looks bigger has more.

Substage 1: Operational Coordination (5–7 Years)

Somewhere between the age of 5 and 7 years, children change their strategy. They now coordinate their global evaluation of size with a systematic quantification of height. Their new strategy is revealed quite clearly by their language, which now refers to the height of the two columns explicitly (e.g., This one has more because it's taller.) Their new strategy is also evident in their choice of beakers, particularly on items such as are shown in Figure 9.2b. Whereas they passed these items at an earlier age, they now fail them, due to their preoccupation with the dimension of height.

Obviously, subjects' quantification of the column heights is not done by counting. However, the operation that is involved appears to be quite similar. It appears to involve a sequence of fixations along the extent of each column, and some sort of mental summation, either of the number of such fixations or of their cumulative duration in time. The executive control structure may be represented as follows:

PROBLEM REPRESENTATION   OBJECTIVES
- Two beakers, partially filled with   • Determine which beaker has
  water.   more to drink.
- Each side has a liquid column   • Determine which side has
  with similar height.   greater height.

STRATEGY

1. Track eyes along extent of
   column A and column B; note
   which is higher.
2. Pick the one which is higher as
   the one which has more.

Substage 2: Bifocal Coordination (7–9 Years)

During the next substage, children's focus expands to include the dimension of width as well as height. As a consequence, they get problems such as that in Figure 9.1b correct again, but give a much more differentiated reason when asked to justify their responses (e.g., it's shorter, but it's much wider). They also get items such as that in Figure 9.1c correct. The executive control structure underlying their responses may be represented as follows:

PROBLEM REPRESENTATION   OBJECTIVES
- Two beakers, partially filled with   • Determine which beaker has
  water.   more to drink.
- Each beaker has a liquid column   • Quantify the heights.
  of similar height.
- Each beaker has a liquid column   • Quantify the widths.
  of similar width.

STRATEGY

1. Scan column A and column B for
   height; note if one is higher.

2. Scan surface A and surface B for
   width; note if one is wider.
3. If heights are about the same, pick
   the wider as having more. Otherwise pick the higher.

Substage 3: Elaborated Coordination (9–11 Years)

Unfortunately, our work on liquid quantification was done in the early 1970s,
prior to the publication of Siegler's and Noelting's studies. Because we did not
have the benefit of their analyses, we did not discriminate between items where
the two liquid columns were identical in height, and those where they were not.
Nevertheless, our older subjects did appear to have a higher success rate, and
justified their responses in the sort of compensatory fashion mentioned by
Piaget (e.g., "this one is a bit higher, but this one is much wider"). It seems quite
possible, therefore, that they were using the strategy of finding the dimension of
greater difference, and making their response on this basis. The executive control structure that would be involved would be as follows:

PROBLEM REPRESENTATION   OBJECTIVES

- Two beakers, partially filled with   • Determine which beaker has
  water.   more to drink.

- Taller beaker is also narrower.   • Determine whether the height
                                                   difference is greater than the
                                                   width difference.

- Each side has a column of a par-   • Evaluate the magnitude of
  ticular width.   the width difference.

- Each side has a liquid column of a   • Evaluate the magnitude of
  particular height.   the height difference.

STRATEGY

1. Scan column A and B for height,
   note magnitude of difference.
2. Repeat 2 for width.
3. Compare results of 1 and 2; note
   greater difference.
4. If height difference is bigger, pick
   taller as having more. Otherwise,
   pick wider.

Projection of Shadows, Distance, and Probability

In a recent series of studies, Siegler (1981) investigated children's responses to
three additional problems, all of which share the same structure as the tasks that
have been described so far, and all of which were refined versions of tasks

originally designed by Inhelder and Piaget. In the first of these problems, children were asked which of two rods (differing in size) would throw a larger shadow on a screen, when a light is placed at a particular distance away from each one. In the second task, children were shown two sets of black and white marbles. They were asked to pick the set for which they would have the greater chance of picking a black marble when blindfolded. In the final task children were shown two trains which went different distances and which stopped at different times, and were asked which train they thought had gone faster (Siegler & Richards, 1979).

Clearly, all three of the preceeding problems require children to focus on two separate dimensions. Moreover, all three problems require a careful quantification along each of these dimensions, and some sort of compensation of the results. Perhaps not surprisingly, Siegler reported that children passed through a sequence of substages on each task that were similar to those he had observed previously on the balance beam task. They also did so at a similar (though not identical) rate.

In summary, it seems reasonable to conclude that the pattern for the dimensional stage is similar to that for the sensorimotor and relational stages, at least for the domain of elementary concepts in science. Children pass through a fairly similar sequence of substages on different tasks. Moreover, they do so at a similar rate. Thus, their thinking has a considerable degree of both horizontal and vertical structure.

DIMENSIONAL CONCEPTS IN THE DOMAIN OF SOCIAL COGNITION

A second domain that has been studied quite intensively in recent years is the domain of social cognition. On the surface, the problems that a child encounters in the social world are quite different from those that he or she encounters in the physical world. As was demonstrated for the previous two stages, however, there is often a direct parallel, not only in the nature of the problems, but in the nature of the reasoning that must be used to solve them. During the past few years, a similar parallel has become apparent for the dimensional period as well, as the pioneering work of Piaget (1932) and Kohlberg (1963) has been extended and revised by a new generation of developmental psychologists (e.g., Chandler, 1977; Damon, 1979; Turiel, 1975).

Attribution of Feelings to Others

In the previous chapter, mention was made of children's ability to label their own feelings, and to diagnose and manipulate the feelings of others. In a recent

Fig. 9.3. Display used in Marini's birthday party task.

study in our research group, the development of this ability has been followed through the dimensional stage, by means of the task that is illustrated in Figure 9.3 (Marini, 1981, 1984).

The story that accompanies the pictures in Figure 9.3 is as follows:

> This is a picture of David. This is a picture of Bill. They live in different cities. Today each one of them had a birthday party. Bill was hoping that he would get this many marbles for a present (the experimenter takes out a set of cardboard discs at this point, representing the marbles the child had hoped for, and places them in the "cloud" above his or her head). Here's what he got at the party (the experimenter then takes out a set of real marbles, and places them under the picture of the child). Now David was hoping he would get this many marbles (again, a set of cardboard discs is placed above the character in question), and here's what he got (again, a set of real marbles is placed under the picture). The question is, who do you think was happier at his party, or was each boy just as happy as the other?

Substage 0: Operational Coordination ($3\frac{1}{2}$–5 Years)

During the preliminary substage, children focus on the global appearance of the marbles that each child received. If one child received a great deal more than the other, that child is assumed to be happy. If they both got about the same, they are both assumed to be happy. The control structure on which these responses are based may therefore be represented as follows:

PROBLEM SITUATION   OBJECTIVE

• Children with presents.   ⟶ • Determine happiness.

STRATEGY

1. Scan each set of presents: if one has a lot more, say that he is happier.

Substage 1: Operational Coordination (5–7 Years)

During the first major substage, children coordinate their evaluation of the size of each gift with an evaluation of number. They now say that the child who gets the greater number of marbles is the happier. Their new control structure may be represented as follows:

PROBLEM SITUATION   OBJECTIVES

• Children with sets of presents.   ⟶ • Determine relative happiness.

• Size of sets similar, but each has a   • Determine relative quantity.
particular number.

STRATEGY

1. Count each array, notice who has more.
2. Assert that the child with more is happier.

Of course, no claim can be made that the preceding control structure is a universal one. That is, no claim can be made that it would emerge in societies where less value is attached to physical commodities than in our own, or where the quanity of one's possessions is deemed of little importance. Nevertheless, at least for societies where these factors are deemed important, the emergence of this sort of reasoning during this age range is of considerable interest.

Substage 2: Bifocal Coordination (7–9 Years)

During the second substage, children's focus expands to include a second quantitative dimension, the number of marbles each child was hoping for. A common response is as follows: "David is happier because he got more than he wanted. Bill didn't." The executive control structure which underlies this response could be represented as follows:

PROBLEM SITUATION	OBJECTIVES

- Children with sets of presents. ⟶ • Determine relative happiness.
- Sets of same size, but each has a   • Determine relative number
  particular number.   received.
- Children also wanted a different   • Determine relative number
  number.   wanted.

STRATEGY

1. Count the number of marbles each child wanted.
2. Count the number of marbles each child actually got.
3. If child got as many marbles as he wanted (or more), assume he is happy; otherwise, assume that he is not happy.

Once again, no claim can be made for the universality of this structure. It does seem possible, however, that the general form of the structure may be universal. That is, whatever external dimensions are of value in a particular culture, it seems possible that people's hopes along this dimension will be seen as an important determinant of their satisfaction with what actually occurs.

Substage 3: Elaborated Coordination (9–11 Years)

During the final substage, children take account of the size of the discrepancy between each boy's desires and what he receives. Thus, if the two boys both received less than they wanted, children now note how *much* less each received, and conclude that the child who came close to getting what he wanted was the happier. Their new executive control structure may be represented as follows:

PROBLEM REPRESENTATION	OBJECTIVES

- Children with sets of presents. ⟶ • Determine relative happiness.
- Neither child got exactly what he   • Determine relative amount by
  wanted.   which each fell short.
- Quantities for David given on   • Determine number by which
  left.   David "fell short".
- Quantities for Bill given on right. ⟶   • Determine number by which
                                              Bill "fell short".

STRATEGY

1. Compute size of difference for Bill.

2. Repeat for David.
3. Compare results of 1 and 2. Note larger.
4. Predict boy with larger deficit will be more unhappy.

As may be apparent, both the nature of the substages that are observed on this task, and the rate of children's progression through them are identical to those observed in the domain of physical cognition.

Attributions of Intelligence

As children grow older, they learn to make inferences about the thoughts and intellectual capabilities of others, as well as their feelings. In a study by Chandler, Mangione, and Moss (1977), this sort of attribution was examined in some detail. The problem with which the children were presented was one that showed two children, each holding up some artwork. The question was "Who do you think does better in school, the boy who drew this picture, or the boy who drew this picture?" The two boys differed in age, and the two pictures differed in their degree of articulation.

Substage 0: Operational Consolidation ($3\frac{1}{2}$–5 Years)

At the first substage, children responded to the question by picking one of the two boys, and giving justifications which the authors classified as irrelevant. In general, these responses were based on some tangential association (e.g., my brother is good in school), or some salient perceptual feature (that boy looks like my brother).

At first glance, the preceding responses look quite different from the responses to the other tests that have been mentioned so far. On most of the other tests, 4-year-olds indicate at least some rudimentary understanding of the dimension in question, yet on this test they do not. The reason for this difference may well be that the specific items that were used in Chandler's test did not include any problems in which a global preceptual evaluation would yield a correct answer. In fact, when such items have been excluded from other tests, children's responses have appeared just as irrelevant (See Siegler, 1976). Whether or not children's responses to this task would appear more relevant if such items were included can of course only be determined empirically.[3] However, the important

---

[3] One possible item would be as follows: Picture A: big boy succeeding in assembling a puzzle. Picture B; a small boy failing at the same task. The question would remain the same: Who do you think does better in school?

point is that, even in their present form, many of children's responses indicate that they are scanning each of the photographs rather globally, and looking for some salient feature which will indicate the presence or absence of success (e.g., he looks like my brother). This is essentially the same strategy as they employ on all the other tests that have been considered so far, and may be represented as follows:

PROBLEM SITUATION   OBJECTIVE
- Two photographs, each depicting   • Determine which of the boys does
  a boy and a drawing.   better in school.

STRATEGY
1. Scan each photograph, for an
   indication of achievement.

Substage 1: Operational Coordination (5–7 Years)

During the first substage, children coordinate their evaluation of success with an evaluation of age. They now carefully scan each picture, and note which boy appears to be older. They then pick the older boy as the one who does better in school: Their executive control structures may now be represented as follows:

PROBLEM SITUATION   OBJECTIVES
- Two photographs, each depicting   • Determine which of the boys does
  a boy and a picture.   better in school.
- Two boys of different ages.   • Determine which of the boys is
                                 older.

STRATEGY
1. Assess the age of each boy. Note
   who looks older.
2. Assert that the older boy does
   better in school.

Substage 2: Bifocal Coordination (7–9 Years)

During the second substage, children's focus expands to include the picture the two boys have drawn as well as their appearance. If the two boys appear to be about the same age, children carefully evaluate the two pictures, and pick the boy who has drawn the more differentiated picture as the one who does better. Their executive control structures may now be represented as follows:

PROBLEM REPRESENTATION	OBJECTIVES

- Two photographs, each depicting a boy with a drawing.
- Boys differ in age.
- Drawings differ in quality.

- Pick the boy who does better in school.
- Find out which boy is older.
- Find out which boy did better picture.

STRATEGY

1. Assess the appearance and size of each boy. Note if one looks older.
2. Assess the quality of each drawing. Note which looks better.
3. If the boys are about the same age, pick the one who drew the better drawing as the one who does better in school. Otherwise pick the older.

Substage 3: Elaborated Coordination (9–11 Years)

During the fourth substage, children form some sort of primitive compensation between the two dimensions. Their executive control structures may now be represented as follows:

PROBLEM REPRESENTATION	OBJECTIVES

- Two photographs, each depicting a boy with a drawing.
- Better drawing was done by older child.
- Two boys differ in age.
- Two drawings differ in quality.

- Determine which of the boys does better in school.
- Determine which boy did better for his age.
- Determine which of the boys is older, and by how much.
- Determine which picture looks better, and by how much.

STRATEGY

1. Assess the age of each boy, note difference.
2. Estimate how good each picture is, note difference.
3. Compare results of 1 and 2.

4. Whichever difference is bigger,
   pick boy with higher value on
   this dimension as smarter.

In summary, children progress through the same four substages on this test as on tests of physical cognition. They also do so at the same rate. In fact, Chandler *et al.* demonstrated this by administering a test of physical cognition to the same children, and showing that the norms on the two tests were the same at each age level.

Judgments of Fairness

In addition to making judgments about people's feelings and capabilities, children of course learn to make judgments about the social situations in which they participate. One of the most important dimensions along which such situations are judged is their fairness. In a study by Damon (1973), children's judgments of fairness were examined by presenting them with hypothetical problems in which a set of valuable but limited resources had to be distributed. The children were asked what would be the fairest way to distribute them. Damon's work was followed up by DeMersseman (1976) who presented children with a set of hypothetical situations and a set of real life situations as well.

In one of DeMersseman's situations, all the children in a particular school were asked to help a volunteer assemble greeting cards for children in hospital. Then, when each child's turn came, he or she was taken off by the volunteer (actually the experimenter) to a room where the materials for the greeting cards were kept. After the children had completed two cards, the volunteer thanked them and said that she wanted to give a treat to all the children who had helped her that day. Taking out a box containing three elaborate cards, she said, "These were done by a child just your age." Then, taking out one rather sloppily constructed card, she said, "This was done by a child younger than you." The children were then handed nine wrapped candies and asked to distribute them in a fair way. The children were allowed to keep the candies they allotted to themselves. The others were put away "for the other children."

Interestingly, DeMersseman found that children's reasoning in this real-life situation was identical to that which they displayed when presented with a different (but analogous) situation in a hypothetical format. The behavior they exhibited was also the same. That is, the number of candies they kept for themselves was the same as they said would be fair in the hypothetical situation.[4] Several substages of reasoning were identified, which included the following.

[4] The two sessions were separated by a 2-3 week interval and presented by different testers. Order of presentation was counterbalanced.

During Substage 0, children made sure every child got some candy, but saw nothing unfair with giving themselves the most. During Substage 1 children coordinated their evaluation of whether or not each child got a share of the rewards, with an evaluation of quantity. Each child was given exactly the same. During Substage 2, children expanded their focus to take account of the amount each child had helped (i.e., the quality and or quantity of the cards they had produced). Finally, during Substage 3, children took each child's age into account as well. Thus, they no longer penalized the younger child for not helping as much, "Cause he was just a little kid."

Clearly, the preceeding four substages parallel those in the other social tasks that have been reviewed quite closely. At each substage, one new feature of the problem is identified, one new subgoal is established as a consequence, and one new subroutine is included for reaching this subgoal. The general pattern in the domain of social cognition is therefore quite similar to that in the domain of physical cognition.

DIMENSIONAL CONCEPTS IN THE DOMAIN
OF SPATIAL REASONING

A third general domain that has been studied quite intensively in recent years is the domain of spatial reasoning. In one sense, the sort of reasoning that has been considered so far may already be said to be spatial in nature. To figure out which direction a balance beam will tilt, or to determine which distribution of rewards will be more fair, one must analyze the spatial arrays with which one is confronted. When psychologists speak of spatial reasoning, however, they normally mean reasoning in which the only relations to be analyzed are spatial ones, and where no verbalization of the rationale for one's response need be given. When defined in this latter manner, spatial problems for elementary school children form a particularly interesting class of tasks, because they have been studied by three quite different groups of psychologists: psychometric theorists, learning theorists, and developmental theorists.

Spatial Analogies

A task that has been of great interest to psychometric theorists is the spatial analogy (Raven, 1958). In its most complex form, the spatial analogy is a problem which can challenge the most sophisticated adult. In less complex forms, however, it can be solved by children as young as 3 or 4 years.

In the early 1970s, a good deal of work was directed toward specifying the strategies that adults employ on spatial analogies (Hunt, 1974; Sternberg, 1977). Then, in the late 1970s and early 1980s, investigators began to focus their attention on young children, and examine the differences between their strategies and those used by adults (See Sternberg & Rifkin 1979; Bereiter & Scardamalia, 1979). For present purposes, the clearest data are those gathered in a study by Wagner (1981). Wagner's data are of particular interest because he provided subjects with experience plus feedback on one set of analogies, thus giving them a chance to assemble an appropriate executive structure. He then examined their transfer to a set of items involving different perceptual dimensions. The series of substages he identified were as follows.

Substage 0: Operational Consolidation ($3\frac{1}{2}$–5 Years)

During the first substage, children succeed in recognizing that the items in the patterned set on the left side of the page share a group of features in common. They also succeed in using these features as a guide in selecting from the unpatterned set on the right. They therefore succeed on the "degenerate" analogies illustrated in Figure 9.4 (a). Their executive control structures may be represented as follows:

PROBLEM SITUATION
- Two sets of shapes, one patterned, one unpatterned.

OBJECTIVE
- Find member of unpatterned set which belongs in patterned set.

STRATEGY
1. Scan patterned set, extract common perceptual features in form of an image. Scan unpatterned set. Select item which matches this image.

Substage 1: Operational Coordination (5–7 Years)

During the next substage children coordinate their identifications of the commonality in the patterned set with the identification of a dimension of difference. As a consequence, they can pass a qualitatively different item, one that no longer looks like a pattern completion test but which has the beginnings of an analogical format (See Figure 9.4b). The executive control structure for solving this sort of item may be represented as follows:

Analogy Items Passed by Children at Different Ages, After Familiarization with Analogy Format

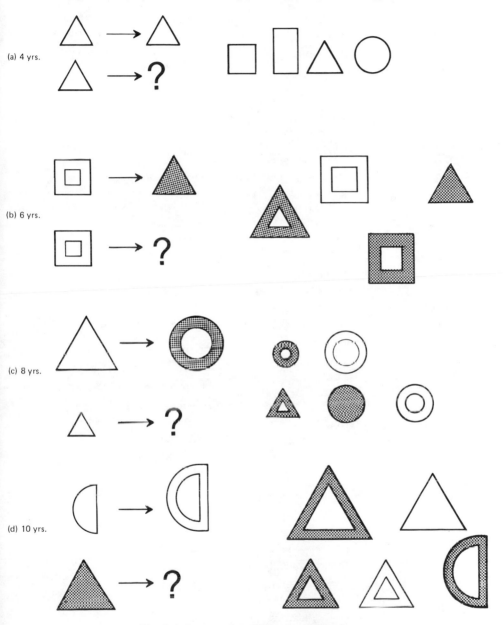

Fig. 9.4. Items used on Wagner's analogy test.

PROBLEM SITUATION   OBJECTIVES

- Two sets of shapes, one pat-   • Find member of unpatterned set
  terned, one unpatterned.   which belongs in patterned set.

- Top pair in patterned set show a   • Isolate dimension of difference
  pronounced perceptual dif-   that distinguishes top pair.
  ference.

STRATEGY

1. Scan top pair, noting difference
   and forming image of right-
   most member.
2. Scan unpatterned set, looking for
   one which will look like image
   of right-most member.

Substage 2: Bifocal Coordination (7–9 Years)

During the second substage, children's focus expands to include the dimension along which the top and bottom items differ, as well as that along which the
left and right members differ. As a consequence, they now show their first success on items such as 9.4c. Their new executive control structures may be
represented as follows:

PROBLEM SITUATION   OBJECTIVES

- Two sets of shapes, one pat-   • Find member of unpatterned set
  terned, one unpatterned.   which belongs in patterned set.

- Top pair in patterned set show a   • Isolate dimension which
  perceptual difference.   distinguishes top pair.

- Vertical pair at left also show a   • Isolate dimension which
  difference.   distinguishes left pair.

STRATEGY

1. Scan vertical pair at left; isolate
   dimension of difference and label
   property X of bottom member
   (e.g., small).
2. Scan top pair, note pattern difference and store image of right
   member.
3. Scan unpatterned set, and select
   one which has property X
   (e.g., small), but in all other

respects matches image of right
hand member.

Substage 3: Elaborated Coordination (9-11 Years)

During the final substage, children succeed on items where the vertical pair at the left differs along two dimensions rather than just one. The increased difficulty of this sort of item may at first glance appear surprising, because it makes little difference along how many dimensions the horizontal pair differs (Wagner, 1981). One possible reason for this asymmetry, however, is this: As long as children are dealing with only one axis of the matrix—either horizontal or vertical—they can simply store an image of the second member of the pair. As soon as they must deal with a second axis, however, they must encode this difference in a digital rather than an analogue fashion. In effect, they must supply the equivalent of a verbal label. The reason is that they can not look for an item that matches two disparate patterns at once. As a consequence, the addition of a second feature along the second axis adds a serious additional burden. In effect, it requires them to encode two digital features or labels rather than one. Presumably they do so by adding an elaboration or "loop" to the control structure of the previous substage. This loop could be of two forms, depending on what feature of the task cued subjects to its additional complexity. (1) If subjects noticed the additional vertical feature while scanning that pair, then the loop would be a simple one, which encoded the second feature that was noticed as well as the first. (2) If subjects failed to notice the second feature on their first pass through the problem, the loop would be of a different sort. As they scanned the response set, they would discover that two answers were equally possible. Thus, their new loop would involve returning to the original problem, and iterating through all the previous steps until an extra distinguishing feature was found.

Of the two possibilities, the latter is probably closer to the process which takes place on the balance beam and other bidimensional physical problems in which the feature of *dimensional conflict* can not be noticed until the entire set of steps from the previous substage are applied. On such problems, children must repeat their previous steps, adding an extra quantification loop, in order to resolve the conflict. Whichever sort of loop children employ on the analogy task, however, it should be apparent that their new structure involves an elaboration of the one that was observed at the previous substage, and that it requires (1) noticing an additional task feature, (2) setting up an additional subgoal, and (3) adding an additional subroutine for accomplishing this subgoal. Thus, in this general sense, their final structure on this task may be said to be parallel to their final structures on the physical and social tasks that are passed during the same age range.

Concept Learning Tasks

A spatial problem that has been of great interest to learning theorists is the *concept learning task*. In the concept learning paradigm, the experimenter presents children with two stimulus objects such as those illustrated in Figure 9.5. He or she then tells them that one of the objects is correct, and that their job is to guess which one. A large number of further trials is then presented, with the specific pairs of objects varying from trial to trial. The underlying rule that determines the correct member of the pair, however, remains constant, and normally involves some elementary spatial dimension (e.g., the larger is correct, or the dark shape is correct).

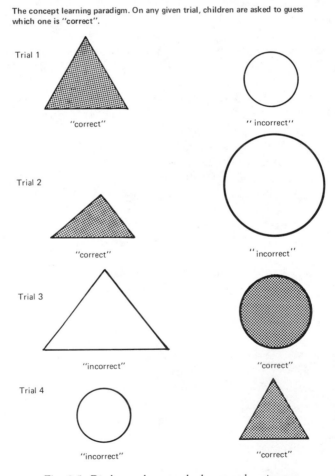

The concept learning paradigm. On any given trial, children are asked to guess which one is "correct".

Trial 1

"correct"   " incorrect"

Trial 2

"correct"   "incorrect"

Trial 3

"incorrect"   "correct"

Trial 4

"incorrect"   "correct"

Fig. 9.5. Display used on standard concept-learning test.

For some time it has been known that the children of 6 to 8 years of age solve this task in a qualitatively different fashion from younger children. When this fact was first discovered, neobehaviourists took it as an indication that 6- to 8-year-olds could use *verbal mediation*, whereas younger children could not (See Kendler, 1963). More recently, however, this view has been called into question. In 1966, Levine focussed on the strategies subjects use in the concept formation paradigm, rather than on their success or failure (Levine, 1966). He did so by inserting a number of trials with no feedback among those with feedback. By carefully selecting these *blank trials*, he was able to diagnose the rule or hypothesis subjects had generated at any point in time, in much the same manner as Noelting and Siegler did on the orange juice and balance beam tasks.[5] This technique has since been used by Gholson to determine children's strategies at a variety of age levels (see Gholson, 1984; Gholson & Beilin, 1979). The results of Gholson's studies may be summarized as follows:

Substage 0: Operational Consolidation ($3\frac{1}{2}$–5 Years)

During the preliminary substage, children focus on the perceptual properties of the first object that is declared to be correct. They then use these properties as a guide for guessing the correct object on subsequent trials. If they are told that they are wrong, they either shift to a new object, or else they use the position of the correct object as a cue to guide their further decisions (e.g., the correct ones are always on the right)

PROBLEM REPRESENTATION   OBJECTIVE
* Objects at X and Y.   ⟶   * Pick the winning object.

STRATEGY

1. Pick the object that looks like the
   last one labeled correct.
   If wrong, remember the
   appearance (or position) of
   the new correct object.

Substage 1: Operational Coordination (5–7 Years)

By the age of 5 to 7 years, children begin to utilize their ability to classify to aid their hypothesis formation. Now, if they are told that the object at X is the winner, they will focus on some particular dimension such as colour, and consistently pick objects with the same attribute on this dimension on subsequent

---

[5] For example, if trials 2 through 4 were given without feedback, and the subjects' choices were left-right-right one could assume that their hypothesis was "the dark one". If their choices were left-left-right one could assume their hypothesis was the "the triangle". If their choices were right-left-right one could assume their hypothesis was "the large one". Finally, if their choices were left-left-left, one could assume their hypothesis was "the left one".

trials (e.g., the red ones). If they are wrong, they will make a *reversal shift*. That is, they will maintain their focus on the dimension, but will start picking the other colour as the winning one. The result is that a qualitative shift in their performance is noted, and that it now appears for the first time to be *rule bound*. The executive control structure that is responsible for producing the shift may be represented as follows:

PROBLEM SITUATION   OBJECTIVES

- Objects at X and Y.   • Pick the winning object.
- Each object has a particular value   • Check to see if there is a winning
  on the most salient dimension   colour.
  (e.g., colour).

STRATEGY

1. Notice colour on each side.
2. Pick object with colour last
   labeled correct. If wrong, shift
   to other colour.

Substage 2: Bifocal Operational Coordination (7–9 Years).

Although the strategy of Substage 1 works very well if children happen to select the correct dimension by chance, it does not work at all if they do not, because it contains no provision for a shift to some other dimension. During the second substage, children expand their focus to consider a second dimension as well. Thus, if they are told that they are incorrect, they shift to a new dimension, and pick a value on it. This of course decreases their solution time considerably, and introduces a new element of flexibility into their thought. Their new executive control structure may be represented as follows:

PROBLEM SITUATION   OBJECTIVES

- Object at X and Y.   • Pick the winning object.
- Each object has a particular value   • Check to see if there is a
  on one dimension (e.g., colour).   winning colour.
- Each object has a particular value   • Check to see if there is a
  on another dimension (e.g.,   winning shape.
  shape).

STRATEGY

1. Notice colour on each side.
2. Pick object with colour X; if
   wrong shift to other colour; if
   wrong again go to 3.
3. Repeat 1 and 2 for shape.

In summary, then, it may be seen that the progression on the concept learning task is very similar to the progression on the spatial analogies task. The rate of progression is also quite similar.

Tests of Basic Logical Operations

A number of spatial tasks have been of interest to psychologists in the Piagetian tradition, particularly those designed to assess logical operations such as seriation and classification. The progression that is observed on both these tasks is very similar. In the interest of brevity, therefore, only one of the tasks will be considered, namely, classification.

Substage 0: Operational Consolidation ($3\frac{1}{2}$–5 Years)

During the preliminary substage children consolidate the operation of classifying an array according to some particular dimension. Given a set of objects such as that illustrated in Figure 9.6, they can execute commands such as "Put all the squares here, and all the circles here" or "Put all the black ones here and all the white ones here. In the former case, the dimension of shape must be used to determine the physical placement of objects. In the latter case, colour must be used. The executive control structure underlying the latter performance may be represented as follows:

PROBLEM REPRESENTATION   OBJECTIVE
- Objects of different colours, in a   - Place red ones on left, blue one on
  group.   right.
                         STRATEGY
              1. Pick up the red ones, place them
                 on the left. Pick up the blue ones:
                 place them on right.

Fig. 9.6. Display used in a typical classification study. Questions answered correctly are as follows:

    Substage 0: "Can you put all the black ones here, and all the white ones here?" or "How many black ones are there?"

    Substage 1: "Are there more black ones or white ones?" or "Can you put all the white squares in one pile, and all the black circles in another?"

    Substage 2: "Are there more black ones, or squares?"

Substage 1: Operational Coordination (5–7 Years)

Although children can use-colour or shape as a basis for classification during the preliminary substage, they cannot coordinate these two operations with each other. Hence, they cannot execute commands such as "Take the squares and put the black ones here, and the white ones here." They can also not coordinate a single classification with quantification. Hence, they cannot answer questions such as "Are there more red ones or more blue ones?", unless the shapes have already been divided into two piles for them. By the age of 5 to 7 years, neither of these tasks presents a problem. The executive control structure that underlies the latter performance might be represented as follows:

PROBLEM REPRESENTATION   OBJECTIVES

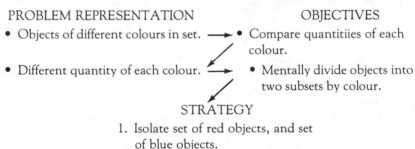

- Objects of different colours in set. ⟶ • Compare quantitiies of each colour.

- Different quantity of each colour. ⟶ • Mentally divide objects into two subsets by colour.

STRATEGY

1. Isolate set of red objects, and set of blue objects.
2. Quantify each set; pick larger.

Substage 2: Bifocal Operational Coordination (7–9 Years)

At the next substage, children become capable of sustaining a focus on two different dimensions of an array while executing a quantification operation. Hence, they can now answer questions such as "Are there more square ones or red ones?" Presumably, they do so by assembling a control structure such as the following:

PROBLEM REPRESENTATION   OBJECTIVES

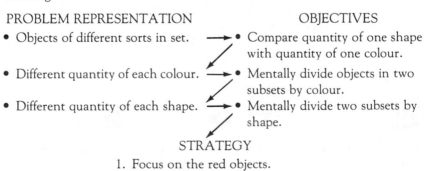

- Objects of different sorts in set. ⟶ • Compare quantity of one shape with quantity of one colour.

- Different quantity of each colour. ⟶ • Mentally divide objects in two subsets by colour.

- Different quantity of each shape. ⟶ • Mentally divide two subsets by shape.

STRATEGY

1. Focus on the red objects.
2. Focus on the squares.
3. Quantify each subset and compare.

Once again, then, both the sequence and the rate of progression which are observed are similar to those observed on other spatial tests.

THE GENERAL PATTERN OF DEVELOPMENT
IN MIDDLE CHILDHOOD

Three different types of development were analyzed in the preceding sections: the development of physical or "scientific" concepts, the development of social concepts, and the development of spatial concepts. In spite of surface differences in content, however, the underlying structural changes in each domain were the same. In each case, some sort of complex relational structure was consolidated during the period from $3\frac{1}{2}$ to 5 years of age. In each case, a major qualitative change was observed between the ages of 5 and 7 years, as different structures of this sort were coordinated with each other. Finally, in each case a new type of thinking emerged, one which entailed *dimensional* as opposed to *relational* thought. The cross-task parallels then continued as children moved through the stage, progressing form a consideration of only one dimension at 5 to 7 years, to a consideration of two dimensions at 7 to 9 years, and to some further elaboration between the ages of 9 to 11 years. Often this further elaboration was one that permitted children to relate the two dimensions in question to each other in a more sophisticated or integrated fashion.

As readers worked their ways through the various models that were proposed in the chapter, they may have found themselves more forcefully struck by the parallels among the tests of physical and social cognition than between these tests and the tests of spatial cognition. There is a good reason for this. The tests of physical and social cognition that were described in the first two sections not only showed a parallel in *complexity* from stage to stage. They also showed a parallel in *form*. Using the sort of notation employed by Piaget, one could say that the four substages of significance for each group of tasks were as follows: Substage 0: A or not A = f (B or not B). Substage 1: Quantity (A) = f (Quantity (B). Substage 2: Quantity (A) = f (Quantity (B) or (Quantity (C). Substage 3: Quantity A = f (Quantity (A) × Quantity (B). In short, one could say that all the tasks in the first two domains led to a common Piagetian grouping, that of multiplicative compensation. By contrast, those in the last section led to more than one type of grouping.

The question of how many, and what forms of grouping the human mind can apprehend is an interesting one. It is also one that may have been too lightly dismissed in the face of the difficulties that Piaget's theory originally encountered, and which should be pursued further as our tools for structural analysis become more sophisticated. For the moment, however, my point is simply that a general pattern exists during the period from 5 to 11 years, which transcends any particular form of grouping or content domain, and that this pattern is essentially the one that was suggested by the analysis of the balance beam in Chapter 6.

Given the presence of this pattern, one might well ask how the data that were mentioned at the beginning of the chapter are to be explained. That is, one might ask how to explain the fact that different forms of the same logical test (e.g., conservation) are often passed at very different ages, as a function of what appear to be rather trivial variations in the stimulus materials, or in the testing context. On the surface, these findings would appear to be directly at variance with those that have been reported in the present chapter, where the pattern is not one of the décalages but of synchrony.

A detailed answer to this question is presented in Chapter 11. First, however, it is necessary to complete the task that was begun in Chapter 7, and to consider the final changes that take place in children's reasoning as they enter the period of adolescence.

CHAPTER 10

Development in Adolescence: The Emergence of Vectorial Operations and Abstract Systems of Thought

INTRODUCTION

From the time of Baldwin, developmental psychologists have acknowledged that the thinking processes of adolescence are qualitatively different from those of middle childhood. From the time of Binet, psychometrists have acknowledged the same fact, and have included different types of items for this age group in their batteries (e.g., Raven, 1958). Although the general characteristics of adolescent thought have been known for some time, however, they have not been investigated in any sort of systematic fashion until quite recently. Once again, the major influence has been the work of Piaget and his colleagues in Geneva (Inhelder & Piaget, 1958).

Although Piaget's work has dominated the field of adolescent development in the same way as it has dominated the field of child development, it has not stimulated nearly the same volume of research. One reason for this may be that Piaget's research on this period was done rather late in his career. There was therefore less time for a body of data to accumulate, and for experimental methods to be refined. Another is that his findings were not very startling. Nothing was found that adolescents could not do, and that people would have supposed they could do. This was in marked contrast to middle childhood, where the finding of nonconservation among children who could add and subtract took researchers and teachers by surprise, and stimulated a great deal of interest. Still another factor may have been the tasks which Inhelder and Piaget devised for probing adolescent thought. These tasks were drawn almost exclusively from the area of physics. Moreover, the analysis of their underlying logic was extremely complex. For this reason as well, then, they may have had less general appeal.

Although the literature on adolescence has been less extensive than the literature on middle childhood, the general trend has been the same. The earliest studies concentrated on clarifying the nature of Piaget's theoretical formulations, on replicating his empirical findings, and on extending them to new domains (e.g., Lunzer, 1965; Lovell, 1961). Then came a number of studies aimed at challenging certain of Piaget's assumptions. The ones that were challenged most directly were the impossibility of training (Case, 1974; Siegler, Robinson, Liebert, & Liebert, 1973; Stone & Day, 1978), the cross-task generality of performance (Martarano, 1977), and the universiality of the behaviours exhibited. These studies were answered by studies aimed at supporting the same general assumptions (e.g., Allaire-Dagenais, 1977; Black, 1976; Fortin-Theriault, 1977). Finally, attempts were made at synthesis (Brainerd, 1980; Neimark, 1975). The general conclusions were (1) that some moderate degree of trainability is possible, (2) that there is a wide variation in performance across different tasks, and (3) that the structures which are acquired are by no means universal, at least not as measured by Piaget's instruments.

In the past few years, there has been a shift in focus that has also been similar to that which was described for earlier periods. Under the influence of developments in mainstream cognitive psychology, investigators have begun conducting fine-grained analyses of preadolescent, adolescent, and adult reasoning strategies. Two of these studies were mentioned in Chapter 5, namely Furman's and Marini's studies on the balance beam. These data were interpreted in the same fashion as Siegler's data had been for the earlier period. It was suggested that there is a preliminary substage of *operational consolidation*, which extends from about 9 to 11 years of age. During this substage, children can reason in terms of compensating variables. Alternatively, they can reason in terms of ratio, and can compute the missing term in a simple ratio equation (e.g., $\frac{1}{4} = \frac{5}{?}$). However, they cannot execute both operations simultaneously, or use one as a means to drawing a conclusion about the other. During the next substage (11 to 13 years), which was labeled *operational coordination*, this becomes possible. The strategy that emerges is one of using a simple ratio to compare the magnitude of the weight and distance variables. During the next substage, children become capable of *bifocal coordination* (13 to 15 years). They can now focus on the problem of how to convert a complex ratio (e.g., 5:2) into a simple one, as well as the problem of how to use a simple ratio in resolving the conflict between weight and distance. The final substage was labeled *elaborated coordination* (15 to $18\frac{1}{2}$ years). In this substage children become capable of adjusting both ratios into new forms, such that they will be directly comparable.

In the present chapter, the question that is addressed is whether any parallel sort of progression has been found in the other recent studies where adolescents' reasoning has been examined at a similar grain of analysis.

THE EMERGENCE OF VECTORIAL OPERATIONS IN CAUSAL REASONING

As was mentioned in the previous chapter, one of the first investigators to build a bridge between the global structural analyses of the Piagetian tradition and the finer-grained process analyses of contemporary cognitive psychology was Noelting (1975, 1980, 1982). The task he used was called the *juice mixing task*.

Noelting's Study of the Juice-Mixing Task

In virtually all respects, the juice mixing task is directly analogous to the balance beam task. Hence, if a cross-task parallel in children's development were to appear anywhere, one would expect it on this task.

Substage 0: Operational Consolidation (9–11 Years)

In actual fact, the data from the two tasks are strikingly similar. Prior to the age of 11 years, children are capable of reasoning in terms of two opposing factors, and of effecting a quantitative compensation between them. The strategy that they employ, however, is additive or subtractive. A typical response is that given by Louise (10.0 years), who picks the left side as juicier in Figure 10.1(a). Her reasoning is as follows: "The left side has one glass of water more [than juice], while the right side has two more." The details of this *variable compensation* structure were outlined in the previous chapter. For present purposes, it may be represented in abbreviated form as follows:

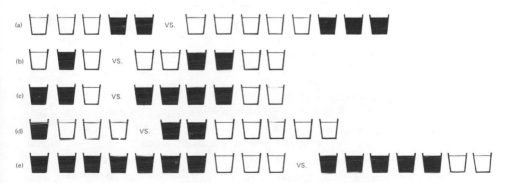

Fig. 10.1. Higher-level items on Noelting's juice problem.

PROBLEM SITUATION   OBJECTIVE
- More water than orange juice on ──→ • Determine relative dilution.
  each side.

STRATEGY
1. Subtract juice from water on each
   side. Pick side with greater excess
   as more diluted.

Substage 1: Operational Coordination (11–13 Years)

At the next substage, children become capable of combining the operation of variable-compensation with the operation of ratio equivalence. As a consequence, a qualitative shift in their thought is observed. A typical protocol is that of Christianne (12 years), who says that the two mixtures will taste the same in Figure 10.1(b). Her reasoning is as follows: "In both there is double the water there is of juice". Note that no mention is ever made of first-order dimensions, such as the number of juice or water on either side. Reasoning appears to be exclusively in terms of second order dimensions such as "double" or "half". The new executive control structure may therefore be represented as follows:

PROBLEM SITUATION   OBJECTIVES
- More water than juice on each ──→ • Determine relative dilution.
  side.
- Left has 1 juice with 2 waters;   ──→ • Convert juice and water on
  water "per unit" juice on   right to comparable unit form.
  right unknown (4 water
  2 juice).

STRATEGY
1. Divide water on right equally
   among juice, until number of
   waters for juice is known.
2. Compare this number to that on
   the right, and pick the larger as
   the more diluted.

Interestingly enough, when children such as Christianne encounter problems for which the above strategy will not work, they fall back on the strategy of the previous period. That is, they calculate the excess of water over juice on each side, and pick the side with the greater excess as more diluted. One might therefore describe their behaviour as *transitional*. While they are clearly capable of abstract thought, they can only demonstrate this capability on relatively simple or concrete problems (see Collis, 1975).

Substage 2: Bifocal Coordination (13–15 Years)

At the next substage, children become capable of maintaining a focus on ratio even when the ratios that are present are not directly comparable to each other, and one ratio must therefore be adjusted into a new form. A typical response is that given by Nicole (13 years) to the problem in Figure 10.1(d): "The mixture on the left will taste more, because in B [on the right] there is a glass of juice for $2\frac{1}{2}$ glasses of water, while on the left there is 1 glass of juice for 3 glasses of water." If it were not for the fact that the quantities being discussed are juice and water rather than distance and weight, this protocol would be indistinguishable from the ones cited by Furman for the balance beam during the same period. It may also be modelled in the same fashion:

PROBLEM SITUATION

- More water than juice on each side.
- Left has 1 juice with 3 waters; water per unit juice on right unknown (3 water, 2 juice).
- 5 cannot be divided by 2 evenly (Answer 2, remainder 1).[0]

OBJECTIVES

- Determine relative dilution.
- Convert juice and water on right to comparable unit form.
- Divide "left over" amount as well.

STRATEGY

1. Divide number of leftover water on right (1) by number of juice (2) (Answer $\frac{1}{2}$).
2. Add this number to the result of whole number division (2) (Answer $2\frac{1}{2}$).
3. Compare this value to water and juice ratio on left (3); pick larger as more diluted.

Substage 3: Elaborated Coordination (15–18 Years)

During the final substage, children become capable of answering the question if neither side is in unit form. As might be expected, many of them do so by adjusting the ratio of juice to water on each side so that it is in unit form. The executive control structure for solving a problem such as the one in Figure 10.1(e) might be represented as follows:

---

[0] Note that this feature can only emerge once the strategy of the previous substage (division) is applied.

PROBLEM SITUATION   OBJECTIVES

- More water than juice on each ⟶ • Determine relative dilution.
  side.

- Neither ratio in unit form.   • Convert each ratio to
                                                    comparable form.

- Right side has 5 juice, 2 water.   ⟶   • Determine number of juice
                                                    per water on right.

- 5 cannot be divided among 2   • Determine exact unit ratio
  evenly (Answer 2 remainder 1).   of juice/water on right.

STRATEGY

1. Divide number of juice remaining
   on right (1) by number of
   water (2) (Answer $\frac{1}{2}$).
2. Add to answer from whole number division (2) (Answer $2\frac{1}{2}$).
3. Repeat steps 1 and 2 for left
   (Answer $2\frac{1}{3}$).
4. Compare two results, pick larger
   ratio ($2\frac{1}{2}$) as more diluted.

Not all subjects adjust one ratio down into unit form at Level 2, or both ratios down into unit form at Level 3. Some subjects adjust one ratio up to the form of the other at Level 2, matching either the juices or the waters, as a function of the particular numbers involved. Then, at Level 3, they adjust both ratios up into common form, a strategy that is often called finding the lowest common denominator. The general form of the structure for these methods, however, is identical to that for the unit or decimal method. It is just that the particular features, objectives, and calculations are somewhat different. Moreover, these alternative methods are also observed on balance problems (Marini, 1984). In virtually all respects, therefore, the executive structures that children assemble to solve Noelting's juice problem are similar to those they assemble to solve the balance beam problem at the same age.

THE EMERGENCE OF VECTORIAL OPERATIONS
IN VERBAL REASONING

An important abstract operation in the verbal domain is analogy. Verbal analogies are used in the literature of most societies, as well as in day-to-day interaction. Moreover, from a purely logical point of view, they have the same structure as ratios. That is, they express a higher-order equivalence between two pairs of terms, each of which is itself a vector composed of two items.

Studies of Reasoning on Verbal Analogy Problems

The first psychologist to analyze the logical structure of analogies from a Piagetian perspective was Peel (1960), who suggested that analogical reasoning should require the same intellectual structure as bivariate multiplication of classes because its underlying form is identical (i.e., A_1: A_2:: B_1: B_2). It seemed reasonable to suggest, therefore, that the capability for solving such problems should not emerge until the complete system of concrete operations was in place, that is, until the age of 9 or 10 years.

This suggestion was first tested by Lunzer (1965), who found that while certain elementary analogies could be solved by this age, many more could not. Since that time, analogical reasoning has been taken as a sign of formal reasoning in the verbal domain that is parallel to that of reasoning by ratio in the scientific domain. Piaget and his colleagues have themselves investigated this sort of thinking (Piaget, Montagero, & Billetier 1977), as have subsequent researchers in both the Piagetian and the information-processing traditions (Gallagher 1978; Sternberg, 1977).

Substage 0: Operational Consolidation (9–10 Years)

Although Peel was wrong with regard to the structure required for solving complex analogies, he appears to have been right with regard to the basic operations from which these more complex structures are constituted. Virtually all studies which have included simple analogies (i.e., analogies where the relationships between the items are straightforward, and the items themselves are concrete nouns) have found evidence of analogical reasoning by the age of 9 or 10 years. Two problems that Lunzer (1965) found to be passed at this age level were the following:

black: white:: hard:_____(steel/stone/solid/soft/blue)
_____: see:: knife: cut (fork/eye/look/shape/blue)

At first glance, it might appear that the above problems could be solved simply by picking the most common association to the term adjacent to the blank space (e.g., eye: see). Although this is a reasonable suggestion for these two items, it is less reasonable for the following five items, which are also passed by the majority of children in this age range.[1]

1. ink: pen:: paint:_____(i) color (ii) spray (iii) brush (iv) paper
2. god: white:: devil::_____(i) red (ii) angel (iii) black (iv) horns
3. wet: dry:: warm::_____(i) desert (ii) cool (iii) damp (iv) cold
4. hate: friends:: love:_____(i) marriage (ii) partners (iii) enemies (iv) dislike

---

[1] The data in question were collected by Debra Sandlos and myself. Criterion for passing was $\frac{3}{5}$. The percentage of subjects passing was 72%.

5. beautiful: ugly:: true:_____(i) justice (ii) false (iii) lying (iv) facts

It seems reasonable to suggest, therefore, that Peel was correct. Simple analogies such as these can be solved by the elaborated bidimensional processes of middle childhood. The full control structure for solving such items has been detailed by Sternberg and Rifkin (1979). It may be represented in abbreviated form as follows:

PROBLEM SITUATION
- Two parallel relations belong on each side of double dots (::).

OBJECTIVE
- Determine which word from the given set will complete the second relation.

STRATEGY
1. Note relation 1 (*A:B*). Check relation 2(i), 2 (ii), etc. until one is found which is the same.[2]

Substage 1: Operational Coordination (11–13 Years)

Although children can solve simple analogy problems by the age of 9 to 11 years, this does not represent a major qualitative shift in their performance. A number of very similar (though simpler) items are present on verbal IQ tests, and are solved in the age range from 5 to 11 years.

At the age of 11 or 12 years, however, a qualitative shift does appear. Investigators in the psychometric, Piagetian, and information-processing traditions have all remarked on the change, and taken it as evidence that the child is entering a new stage in development (Lunzer, 1965; Piaget, Montagero, & Billetier, 1977; Raven, 1966; Sternberg & Rifkin, 1979). The shift can be seen on two quite different kinds of items: (1) problems in which the relationships between the terms are not obvious at a glance, but must be abstracted, and (2) problems in which the response alternatives are not obvious at a glance, but must themselves be constructed.

Consider first the latter type of item, in which the difficulty lies in the abstractness of the problem form. Two examples of this sort that were used by Lunzer were as follows:

lion: lair::_____(set/burrow/dog):_____(rabbit/kennel/fox)
sheep: flock::_____(herd/pack/soldier/swarm):_____(cow/bee/
regiment/wolf)

At first glance, it might appear that the greater difficulty of the above items stems from the fact that neither member of the second pair is provided in either

---

[2]There is some debate as to whether children search only until they find a match or whether they search the entire set and pick the best match (Sternberg, 1977). Of course, the strategy, may well change with development.

case. That this is not the whole story, however, is revealed by the fact that 9- and 10-year-olds can solve certain items of this type providing each alternative is presented as a pair, and need not be generated. Thus, a more probable explanation is that subjects can only solve such problems if they are capable of generating and examining the possible pairings of response items, in some sort of systematic (e.g., combinatorial) fashion (Lunzer, 1965).

Interestingly enough, combinatorial reasoning is very much like reasoning via ratio or reasoning by analogy in two important respects. (1) In its simplest form, it can be reduced to a bivariate problem (C_1D_1, C_2D_2, C_1D_3, C_2D_1, C_2D_2, etc.) and (2) when it is reduced to this form, it is passed spontaneously by the age of 9 or 10 years (Scardamalia, 1977). The structure for forming all combinations from a set of two response classes may therefore be represented as follows:

PROBLEM SITUATION   OBJECTIVE

- Set of items $C_1C_2C_3\, D_1D_2D_3$ ⟶ • Generate all possible pairings of C_x with D_y.

STRATEGY

1. Pick value 1 along dimension C, pair it with values 1,2,3 on dimension D. Repeat for values C_1 and C_3.

The structure for generating all pairs of possibilities as a means to solving analogy problems may be represented as follows:

PROBLEM SITUATION   OBJECTIVES

- Two parallel relations belong on either side of double dots.   ⟶ • Find pair of words from those provided that complete the second relation.

- A number of possibilities are provided for C as well as for D.   ⟶ • Generate all possible pairings of C_x with D_y.

STRATEGY

1. Beginning with C_1, form all possible CD pairs (C_1, D_1, C_1D_2 etc.)[3]

2. Compare each CD pair to AB, until a match is found.

As may be apparent, the preceding control structure is similar to that which appears on the juice or balance problems, in the sense that it involves the coor-

---

[3] Another possible procedure is to focus on the general properties of the given pair (e.g., animal home, then to (1) go down the first set looking for an animal, and (2) go down the second set, looking

dination of two different types of operation, each of which was mastered at the previous substage, and each of which is in some sense bivariate.

A second type of item that is passed at this age is one in which the individual terms are concrete items such as lion and lair, but where the relationship between these items is not obvious at a glance. An example of such an item is as follows:

food: body:: water:_____(storm/coat/ground).

At first glance, this analogy may appear a good deal easier than the combinatorial items used by Lunzer. In fact, from the viewpoint of its form, it is. There is another source of difficulty in this item, however, which the combinatorial item does not contain. This is that the relationship between food and body—unlike that between food and eating, or food and taste—is not one that can be noticed in one's everyday experience or seen at a glance. It must be abstracted by realizing the function that food serves for the body. The same is true for the relationship between water and ground. Unlike that between water and coat or water and storm, it must be abstracted, it cannot be seen directly. Unfortunately, a detailed analysis of the steps in abstracting such a relation is beyond the scope of the present volume. However, at a global level, it may be seen to be rather like the bivariate combinatorial operation, in that a number of pairings must be examined (namely, those between the semantic properties of item A and item B) until a matching relation is found. By the age of 9 or 10 years, children can execute such dimensional abstractions, as is indicated by their performance on the Wechsler Intelligence Scale. What they cannot do, however, is to combine this sort of dimensional abstraction with the operations for selecting an appropriate analogy. It is this capability that marks the qualitative shift in their analogical reasoning, and that emerges at age 11 to 13 years. The underlying control structure might be represented as follows:

PROBLEM SITUATION   OBJECTIVES

- Two parallel relations belong on either side of double dots.
- Relationship between A and B not obvious at a glance (or most obvious relation has no CD match).

- Find word from set which will complete the second relation.
- Find relationship between A and B.

STRATEGY

1. Think of properties of A. Think of properties of B. Extract common property $A_x B_x$.

---

for its home. While the specific procedure is different the general point remains the same. The subject must solve the search problem, as a prerequisite to solving the analogy problem.

2. Check the relations CD_1 CD_2
until one is found which matches
it.

Once again, the transition to a more abstract form of thought is brought about by the coordination of two second order dimensional operations, each of which was available at the previous stage, but each of which previously served a different function and had a different internal form.

Substage 2: Bifocal Coordination (13–15 Years)

Although children can solve items involving abstract relationships between concrete nouns by the age of 11 or 12 years, it is not until the age of 13 to 15 years that they can solve items that involve abstract relationships between entities which are themselves abstract. An item that appears on Lunzer's battery and which is not solved until this age is the following:

task:_____:: problem: solution
(attempt/completion/work/end/question)

An analysis of children's construction of meaning for abstract nouns is also beyond the scope of the present chapter. Once again, however, it seems reasonable to suggest that understanding the meaning of such items must involve—as a minimum—a comparison of the semantic properties of at least two exemplars of the term, and the eduction of an abstract relationship which links the two. As with other abstract tasks of this sort, the first signs of success appear at about the age of 9 or 10 years. It is at this age, for example, that children are first able to give an accurate, if somewhat concrete, definition of abstract terms such as *pity* on the Stanford Binet. One could therefore model the control structures which are required for solving abstract analogies as follows:

PROBLEM SITUATION

OBJECTIVES

- Two parallel relation belong on either side of double dots.
- Relationship between A and B not obvious at a glance.
- Meaning of A and B not obvious at a glance.

- Find word from set that will complete second relation.
- Find relationship between A and B.
- Assign a meaning to A and B.

STRATEGY

1. Think of meaning of abstract terms A and B.
2. Search for and extract common property between them.
3. Scan the alternatives CD_1, CD_2 etc. until the best match to AB is found.

Once again, this control structure bears no relationship in content to those used for the balance or juice problems at this age. However, it does bear a certain general resemblance in form. Just as children could focus on two equivalence relations at this period as a means to deciding whether two opposing vectors were or were not equivalent, so children can now focus on two semantic abstraction operations, as a means to determining whether or not two semantic vectors are or are not equivalent. Of course, further elucidation of these parallels must await a more detailed analysis of what is involved in the process of semantic abstraction itself.

Substage 3: Elaborated Coordination (15–18 Years)

Few developmental studies have provided age norms for analogies that are more complex than those cited above. In order to test the model of development implied in Chapter 6, therefore, we decided to administer the following second-order analogies.

1. Bert and Ernie are to friendship as   relatives
Romeo and Juliet are to _____   love
                                            make believe
                                            lovers

The instructions that we provided were as follows: "The problems in this set are all two-stage analogies. To solve them, you must first find the relationship between the words in brackets, as you would in a one stage analogy." For example:

Stage 1
    Bert and Ernie are famous *friends* (in Sesame Street)
    Romeo and Juliet are famous *lovers* (in Shakespeare)
Stage 2
    Friends are to friendship as lovers are to _____
    (the correct answer is love)

As we had expected, items of this sort were not answered correctly until the age at which items such as Noelting's most complex juice problems were answered correctly, which in the sample in question was about 15 to 18 years.[4]

THE EMERGENCE OF VECTORIAL OPERATIONS IN SPATIAL REASONING

A spatial operation that has the same basic structure as ratio equivalence or verbal analogy is matrix completion. In fact, matrix-completion problems are often referred to as spatial analogies. While developmental psychologists have

[4]The subjects were a group of university-bound adolescents at a laboratory school. The items were designed and administered by Debra Sandlos.

become interested in such problems in recent years (e.g., Inhelder & Piaget, 1964; Sternberg & Rifkin, 1979), the problems actually have their origin in the psychometric tradition, with the work of Spearman, and Raven (see Jensen, 1980, p. 645). Moreover, the clearest item progression is still to be found on the psychometric test that was mentioned in the previous chapter, Raven's Progressive Matrices.

Substage 0: Operational Consolidation (9–11 Years)

Several of the items that are passed at the 9- and 10-year-old level on the Raven Matrices have the structure of simple bivariate classification problems.[5] For example, on item B11, the two top figures in the matrix differ along one dimension (cross in center vs. no cross in center), while the two left-hand figures differ along a second dimension (shape of figure = rhombus vs. square). The subjects' task is to detect each dimension of difference, and to figure out what the missing element in the matrix (i.e., the bottom right figure) should look like. The details of the control structure for solving problems of this sort were outlined in the previous chapter. They may be summarized as follows:

PROBLEM SITUATION | OBJECTIVE

- Top pair differ along dimension X. Bottom pair look different, but must differ along the same dimension. ⟶
- Find item D from response set such that this will be true (i.e., A: B:: C D).

STRATEGY

1. Note dimension along which A and B differ. Select D such that $C = D$ in all respects, except along this dimension.

A second type of item which children solve at the age of 9 or 10 years is similar to the first one, except that the relationships involve a progression rather than a simple cross-classification. For example, on item C4, a three-by-three matrix is presented, with the top row containing one, two, and then three horizontal lines, and the left-hand column containing one, two, and then three vertical lines. In Piagetian terms, one could say that this item involves bivariate seriation rather than bivariate classification. The structure for solving these problems might be represented in abbreviated form as follows:

[5] I am indebted to John Raven for supplying the raw data on which the norms mentioned in this section are based.

PROBLEM SITUATION

- Rows go from 1 to 3 horizontal lines; column goes from 1 to 3 vertical lines.

OBJECTIVE

- Find item D from set such that both top and side will match matrix.

STRATEGY

1. Select D, such that both top and side have 3 items.

Substage 1: Operational Coordination (11–13 Years)

Although the preceding items require the recognition of the vertical and horizontal relations in the matrix, these relationships are usually obvious at a glance. Moreover, the correct answer may be found simply by combining the properties of the top right and bottom left figures, and scanning the response alternatives. At the age of 11 or 12 years, children become capable of solving items that require a good deal more reflection. It is at this point which Raven classifies their performance as abstract. One item[6] that requires such reflection is particularly interesting in that it requires a coordination of the two types of structures which were available at the previous stage, namely bivariate classification and bivariate seriation. In fact, although this item was created independently from (and prior to) Piaget's work on formal operations, it would be hard to find a more direct instantiation of his claim that formal reasoning often involves the coordination of the groupings for classification and seriation. In order to solve the item children must note a progression from 0 to $\frac{1}{2}$ to 1 along both axes (seriation). In addition, they must note two different types of hatching (left versus right diagonal) which are making this progression in each case, and figure out the way these two types are combined (cross-classification). Only then will they be able to select the appropriate item from the given set.

THE USE OF VECTORIAL OPERATIONS IN SOCIAL REASONING

Although adolescents tend to think about interpersonal situations in a more abstract fashion than do younger children, no test exists which documents the transition that takes place in such a fashion that the social reasoning which children exhibit at each substage can be compared to their nonsocial reasoning,

---

[6]The item in question is item C8.

in any sort of precise fashion.[7] As a step in this direction, therefore, Marini and I decided to design a measure that would have these general characteristics.

The basic rationale behind our new measure was quite simple. Children begin to develop a reasonable understanding of abstract traits such as intelligence at the end of the dimensional period (see Chapter 9). They also begin to analyze social situations along abstract dimensions as well (see Chapter 9). It follows, therefore, that as they move into the final period of their development, they should be able to combine these two sorts of analysis. That is, they should be able to make the analysis of someone's personality the means, toward the end of predicting what the person will do when placed in a social situation with a certain set of characteristics. Then, as they move into the second substage of the period, they should be able to take account of more than one personality trait in making such a judgement. Finally, by the end of the period, they should be able to introduce some additional elaboration, such as taking account of the subject's mood, in deciding which of two opposing personality characteristics is likely to predominate in a particular situation. On the basis of this general set of considerations, then, we constructed the following types of items.

Substage 0: Operational Consolidation (9–11 Years)

The sort of item we designed for children at this age range was as follows:

> Jack needed a new book for school so he went into the store and joined the line to pick one up. There was only one book left for each person in the line. While he was counting his money someone grabbed the last book that should have gone to him. As the other person went to pay for the book Jack left the store. What type of person is Jack? Why?

As a dimensional task, this item may be seen to be quite complex. In order to make a decision about how to characterize Jack, it is not sufficient to focus on Jack's unwillingness to engage in confrontation: Otherwise one might simply characterize him as "calm." In addition, one must focus on his right to the book, and his need for it, thus coming up with some sort of judgment as "shy" or "afraid to stand up for his rights." In fact, these are the sorts of characterizations which children during this age range do suggest. The process that leads them to this conclusion may be represented in abbreviated form as follows:

PROBLEM SITUATION   OBJECTIVE
- Jack says nothing, when his book ⟶ • Find way of characterizing Jack.
  is taken unrightfully by a stranger.

STRATEGY
1. Search vocabulary for word or set
   of words which capture both his

---

[7] An exception is the work of Fischer and his colleagues (in press) which has recently been brought to our attention.

reluctance, and the social
situation under which it is
observed.

A second sort of item that was designed for this age did not require a description of a person, but simply a prediction as to what he would do in a particular situation. A sample item was the following:

> The class was coming to an end and Bill was still trying to finish his painting. As the bell rang the art teacher asked the students to take their art supplies back to the cupboard. Because Bill had not finished his painting, he decided to work on it after lunch. When Bill went back to the art room, he found an older student using his art supplies without permission. What do you think Bill did? Why?

Note that the structure of the preceding item bears a direct resemblance to the first one. Someone's rightful possession has been taken, under conditions where he needs it, but where there may possibly be some awkwardness or difficulty in retrieving it. The difference is that this time the children are simply asked to predict what will happen. Most children at this age predict that Bill will demand his supplies back. They also often suggest that he may have to get the teacher because the person who has taken his supplies is older and may resist. The reasoning that leads to this conclusion may be characterized in abbreviated fashion as follows:

PROBLEM SITUATION   OBJECTIVE
- Bill's supplies have been taken ⟶ • Predict Bill's action.
  by an older student.

STRATEGY
1. Analyze the basic dimensions of
   the situation, and give the
   response that you yourself would
   exhibit.

Substage 1: Operational Coordination (11–13 Years)

The sort of item that was presented at the next level was as follows:

> Lisa wanted a new dress for a dance. She heard about a half-price sale at a local store, so she decided to go. At the sale, Lisa found a nice dress and joined the line of people waiting to be served. Lisa laid the dress on the counter and while she was counting her money another customer grabbed the dress. As the other person was checking the dress, Lisa left the store. That afternoon when she arrived home, Lisa found that a person had taken her gardening tools and was using them. What do you think Lisa did? Why?

This new item requires that one combine the two sorts of analysis that were re-quired at the previous level. If one ignores the information about Lisa's behaviour in the first situation, then one will be apt to conclude that she will simply ask for her gardening tools to be returned. This is, in fact, the sort of prediction that 9- and 10-year-olds make. If one takes into account the first situation, however, and perceives its structure as similar to that of the second situation, then one will be likely to give a different answer. In effect, one will be able to treat the problem as a sort of abstract social analogy. The sort of reason-ing that would lead to a correct response might be characterized as follows:

PROBLEM SITUATION   OBJECTIVE

- Lisa's garden tools have been ——→ • Predict Lisa's behaviour.
  taken by a stranger.

- Previously Lisa did nothing when   • Analyze reasons for previous
  her dress was taken by a stranger.   behaviour.

STRATEGY

1. Consider possible reasons for first
   behaviour. Conclude that Lisa is
   unwilling or afraid to stand up
   for her rights.
2. Note that the present situation is
   similar, and predict that she will
   not ask for her tools back.

Substage 2: Bifocal Coordination (13–15 Years)

The sort of item that was constructed for the next level was as follows:

When Robert was visiting the computer fair, he became very interested in one of the latest models. While waiting to get information on the display model, Robert noticed that several people had been served before him. He told the salesman that he had been waiting for some time and would like to be served. Later that afternoon, as Robert was entering the school, he saw a student carrying a large cardboard box having problems opening the door. Robert offered his assistance by opening the door so that the student could get in. He then went to his class and found an older student sitting in his seat. What do you think Robert did? Why?

In order to give an answer to this question that both is reasonable and takes account of all the information that is given, it would be necessary to go through some sort of reasoning process such as the following:

PROBLEM SITUATION   OBJECTIVES

- Robert finds someone sitting in   ⟶ • Predict his behaviour.
  the seat which is supposed to be
  his.

- Previously Robert helped someone   • Analyze reason for previous
  who needed assistance.   behaviour$_1$.

- Previously Robert demanded   • Analyze reason for previous
  something which he considered to   behavior$_2$.
  be his right.

STRATEGY

1. Consider Robert's first
   behaviour. Conclude that he is
   assertive.
2. Consider Robert's second
   behaviour. Conclude that he is
   considerate.
3. Consider present situation; note
   possible infringement of rights,
   but insufficient information with
   regard to reason or needs.
   Generate response that will be
   both assertive yet considerate
   (e.g., Ask if they need it, etc.).

Substage 3: Elaborated Coordination (15–18 Years)

At the final level the sort of item that was included was as follows:

> Cathy was waiting in line to get her skates sharpened and just as her turn came up they
> announced that the shop was closing. Cathy told the people at the shop that she had been
> waiting a long time and she wanted her skates sharpened before they closed the shop.
> After skating she went over to see her friends. Late in the afternoon she remembered that
> she had to be home because relatives were coming, so she excused herself and started to
> leave when her friend asked her for help in finishing an assignment. Cathy helped her
> friend with the homework and then left for home. On her way home she slipped and
> ruined her favorite pants. When she got off the bus a person approached her asking for
> directions. What do you think Cathy did? Why?

On reflection, it would probably be better to have made the original dilemma
that Cathy confronted and the final one more closely analogous (e.g., both
could involve infringement of rights, but the latter one might have had ex-
tenuating circumstance). Nevertheless, even in its present form, the above item
discriminated quite well between 13- to 15-year-olds and older children, when it

was scored for whether or not they mentioned Cathy's current mood, in balancing off her tendency to put her own needs before others in certain circumstances, and her tendency to put others' needs before her own in others. Some of the students concluded that the episode of the splashing would upset her, but would not affect her willingness to give the directions. Others concluded that her bad mood might cause her to be abrupt in giving the directions, or to refer the person to someone else. In either case, however, it was clear that the respondents went through a process that was formally identical to that at the previous stage, but which took account of the extra information regarding a mood-altering event in arriving at their answers.

The data from Marini's study are summarized in Table 10.1. As may be seen, the general progression was the same as that observed on the balance beam during the same period.

THE GENERAL PATTERN OF ADOLESCENT DEVELOPMENT

As is no doubt apparent, the range of tasks that has been analyzed for adolescence is a good deal more restricted than at previous stages. Moreover, even for these tasks, a number of important gaps exist with regard to the specification of component operations. In spite of these gaps, however, it would appear that at least three general conclusions are warranted.

1. The first is that the change that marks children's arrival at the final stage of development is quite similar to that which signalled their arrival at earlier stages. The major operations on which the development of abstract reasoning depends are consolidated during the final substage of the dimensional period. These include bidimensional classification, seriation, compensation, and combination, as well as ratio, analogy, and trait abstraction. Just as relational operations were in effect second-order sensorimotor operations, so vectorial operations are in ef-

TABLE 10.1

Percentage of Subjects Capable of Performing at each Level
on Marini's Test

Theoretical age range (mean age of sample)	Levels			
	0	1	2	3
9–10 (10.8)	75	30	0	0
11–13 (12.7)	100	75	25	0
13–15 (15.6)	100	100	60	30
15–18 (18.4)	100	100	100	70

fect second-order dimensional operations. Moreover, it is the coordination of two different types of vectorial operation—each of which, was previously used in a different context, and which previously served a different function—which gives rise to the first abstract structure, and which yields the qualitative shift in thought that is observed.

2. The second conclusion is that the *progression* that takes place within the stage is also quite similar to that which took place during earlier stages. Pairs of nested vectorial operations are coordinated during the second substage of the period, and some additional elaboration is introduced during the third substage. The elaboration is often one which permits a more sophisticated coordination of the nested pairs of Substage 2.

3. The final conclusion is that the progression appears to take place during approximately the same age range, across a variety of domains.

Although the preceding three conclusions are reasonable, two caveats must also be noted.

1. Further investigation of the aforementioned pattern is necessary before its generality can be evaluated with any certainty. What is needed is a study in which a parallel set of items is created across a wider variety of content areas, and administered to children aged 9 to 18 years.

2. Even if the results of such a study should prove positive, it must be remembered that the components from which adolescent control structures are assembled are more culturally specific than those at previous substages. Whereas operations such as counting appear to be universal—even if the system of counting varies across cultures (Saxe, 1979)—operations such as multiplication and division clearly are not. Similarly, even for operations that may very well be universal, such as variable compensation, or the abstraction of personality traits, the specific dimensions along which subjects are accustomed to operating at this level may still vary considerably, as a function of the sort of culture in which a child grows up and the amount of support which it provides for this sort of higher-level activity.

These are hardly new points. They have been made by cross-cultural psychologists for some time (e.g., Cole & Scribner, 1973). They have also been suggested by Piaget (1972). What the above analyses do point out, however, and what previous analyses have not been able to specify, is which particular operations or operational components enter into which particular abstract structures. It should therefore be possible to do a better job of predicting the environmental conditions under which subjects will or will not show any development of vectorial structures, and what should be done to train them in instances in which such development is desirable but is not observed. It should also be possible to do a better job of determining whether or not development through the vectorial stage is a cultural universal, or whether certain cultures exist where development stops at the dimensional stage.

CHAPTER 11

Vertical and Horizontal Structure
in Intellectual Development

INTRODUCTION

The conclusions that have been drawn in each of the last four chapters have been identical. In each chapter, it has been suggested (1) that children go through the same sequence of substages, across a wide variety of content domains, and (2) that they do so at the same rate, and during the same age range. In short, it has been suggested that there is a great deal of both vertical and horizontal structure in children's development.

The notion that there is a great deal of vertical structure in children's development is relatively uncontroversial. It is supported both by Piaget's original work and by the more recent work of investigators such as Uzgiris and Hunt (1975), Siegler (1978, 1981), and Fischer (1980). The notion that there is a great deal of horizontal structure in children's development, however, is a good deal more controversial. It suggests the existence of general stages of the sort that were postulated by Piaget and which came under heavy attack during the 1960s and 1970s. Not only were Piaget's general stages criticized on theoretical grounds, as being too abstract, vague, and difficult to operationalize, they were criticized on empirical grounds as well. The data that were most frequently cited as incompatible with the notion of general stages were the data on décalages; that is, the data that showed that the same logical concept (e.g., conservation) could be acquired in different content domains at very different ages.

As was mentioned in Chapter 9, a renewed openness appears to be developing in the field regarding the notion of general stages. Moreover, this renewed openness appears to stem, at least in part, from the sort of data that were presented in the past four chapters. While these data do appear to warrant a re-appraisal of the general stage question, however, it is important to realize that they do not warrant a simple return to the Piagetian position. For the data on décalages are just as strong now as they were in the 1960s and 1970s, and just as inconsistent with Piaget's theory. Before proceeding, therefore, it seems worthwhile to pause and consider these data more closely, and to offer some suggestions concerning how they can be explained, without sacrificing the capability for explaining the stage-like data that have been presented in the past four chapters. Accordingly, in the balance of the present chapter, the following four objectives are pursued.

1. First, the notion of horizontal structure that is implicit in the models of the previous chapters is clarified.
2. Second, this notion is contrasted with the classical Piagetian view.
3. Third, it is shown that—although the data on horizontal décalages are indeed inconsistent with the classical Piagetian view—they are not inconsistent with the present view.
4. Finally, it is shown that the present view can be used to generate new data, data in which décalage becomes the exception, not the rule.

HORIZONTAL STRUCTURE: THE PRESENT HYPOTHESIS

In order to clarify the present hypothesis, it is useful to begin with a hypothetical example. Suppose, therefore, that you could eavesdrop on the conversation of a group of 2-year-olds, by means of some sort of audio recording device. Suppose further that the children were responding to a novel question that had been raised by their teacher, and which had caught their interest. Now suppose that you could eavesdrop on the conversation of a group of 5-year-olds. Suppose that they were discussing a different question, but one which was equally novel and interesting. Suppose finally that you didn't know how old each group of children were. Do you think you could guess the approximate age of each group, in spite of the fact that they were discussing quite different questions?

If you knew nothing about children, you might not be able to. However, if you had any practical experience—whether as a nursery school teacher, a day care worker, or whatever—it seems quite likely that you would be able to. Your experience would enable you to say something like this, "That group sounds just like my toddlers. They must be about 2 years old." Or, "That group sounds just like our kindergarten, they must be about 5 years old."

Now suppose you were able to identify the age of each group. Suppose, further, that you were able to specify the characteristics that had enabled you to do so. The consequence of this would be that you would be able to tell others how to do what you had done. In effect, you would be able to tell others how to develop a scoring system for classifying children's behaviour. Your system might have only two categories, "toddler thought" and "kindergarten thought". It might have one intermediate category ("transition"), or it might have a relatively large number of categories. Regardless of the number of categories, however, it would allow you to score subjects on a theoretically based, ordinal scale.

Now suppose that you used your system to develop several different empirical measures, each in a different content domain. Suppose further that you gave each set of measures to several different age groups. At any given age level, you might expect that individual children would exhibit unique response profiles. As a function of some particular talent, interest, or experience, one child might do a bit better on task sequences A and C than on task sequences B and D. Another child might do a bit better on task sequences B and D than on task sequences A and C. Although there might be a good deal of variability from child to child, however, this variability would disappear if you averaged across children. Averaging across children would eliminate the effects of individual differences, and give you the characteristic thinking pattern of a particular age group, when faced with an interesting and genuinely novel problem. Assuming that this pattern was constant across tasks, the pattern you would see would be the one illustrated in Figure 11.1. Note that the older children perform at one characteristic level across domains, while the younger children perform at a lower but equally characteristic level.

The hypothetical set of data in Figure 11.1 was generated by making four different assumptions.

1. That different age groups exhibit different characteristic forms of thinking when exposed to novel questions.
2. That some sort of general intuitive representation of these patterns of thinking can be developed.
3. That these general intuitions can be articulated, and translated into a set of explicit theoretical models.
4. That a set of empirical scales can be created in different content domains, each of which constitutes a valid instantiation of the theoretical models.

Because the pattern illustrated in Figure 11.1 is the one that would be expected according to these assumptions, it follows that the pattern which was actually obtained should enable one to test the validity of the assumptions. If the expected pattern was not obtained, it would follow that at least one of the assumptions was in error.

The reason that this hypothetical example has been presented may by now be

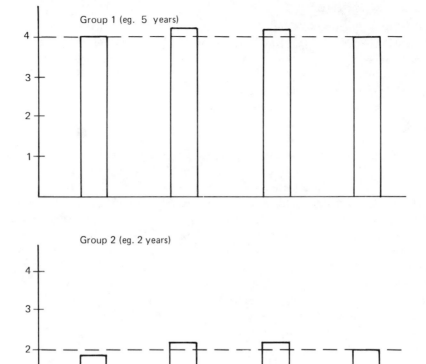

Fig. 11.1. Hypothetical pattern of data that should be obtained, given assumptions about horizontal structure specified in text.

apparent. The position that was suggested by the analyses in the previous four chapters is based on a set of four postulates that are formally identical to the preceding assumptions.

1. The first postulate is that different age groups exhibit different character-istic forms of thought—across a wide variety of content domains—when responding to novel problems with whose basic elements they are familiar.

2. The second postulate is that the intuitions of previous theorists concerning the nature of these thinking patterns are basically correct: four general stages in children's thinking may be isolated, with each stage entailing operations that build upon those of the previous stage.

3. The third postulate is that the thinking of each stage—and of each substage

within each stage—can be adequately characterized by means of a set of executive control structures which differ in their content, but which have a common general form, and a common degree of complexity.

4. Finally, the fourth postulate is that a sequence of tasks can be devised to infer the presence of such control structures. To qualify as an assessment device, the type of operation required by the simplest task must be specifiable. Then, each subsequent task must (1) contain one additional feature, (2) require the establishment of one additional subgoal, and (3) entail the execution of one additional step or set of steps for reaching this goal.

Given that the above set of postulates correspond in their general form to the assumptions which were made in generating the hypothetical example, it follows that the pattern of data which should be obtained if they are correct is the one indicated in Figure 11.1. The problem that must be confronted, therefore, is that the pattern of data that was obtained in the 1960s and 1970s—in response to Piaget's very similar proposal—did not conform to this pattern. In order to understand why it did not, and why this does not constitute a refutation of the present position, it is important to understand the ways in which the present position differs from Piaget's, not just the ways in which it is similar.

DIFFERENCE BETWEEN THE PRESENT VIEW
OF HORIZONTAL STRUCTURE AND PREVIOUS VIEWS

Piaget's View of Horizontal Structure

Both Baldwin and Piaget believed that different age groups employ different characteristic forms of thinking. They also both shared a similar intuition concerning the nature of these forms of thinking at different ages. Baldwin suggested that children's thought progresses through four general stages, which he labeled the stages of sensorimotor, prelogical, logical and hyperlogical thought. Piaget suggested that they pass through four general stages, which he labeled the stages of sensorimotor, preoperational, concrete operational, and formal operational thought. Both theorists also implied that the thinking of one stage was somehow assembled out of elements that were present during the previous stage.

While both theorists shared similar intuitions concerning the general structure of children's thought, it was Piaget who proposed a set of explicit models, and who developed a set of empirical measures for testing the validity of these models. In doing so, he implicitly advanced the following additional postulates.

3a. The form of children's thought at any age can be modelled by means of symbolic logic.

3b. Each type of symbolic logic should give rise to a different type of logical concept.

Before proceeding, it is worthwhile to consider each one of these postulates in turn. In discussing the thought of 5- and 6-year-olds, Piaget (*et al.*, 1977) suggested that the form of this thought could be captured by means of the following formula: $X = F(Y)$. What this formula implies is that children's underlying logic has the form of a functional relation. Children tend to see quantitative variation in one variable (X) as a function of quantitative variation in a second variable (Y). For example, they tend to see variation in the tilt of a balance beam as a function of variation in the relative weight on each side.

In discussing the thought of 9- and 10-year-olds, Piaget suggested that the form of this thought could be captured by means of a variety of formulae, the best known of which is the formula for reciprocal compensation: $X = f(Y \times Z)$. What this formula implies is that children now see quantitative variation in one variable (X) as a function of quantitative variation in two other variables, Y and Z. Moreover, they now understand that these two variables can act in opposite directions, and that one can negate or reverse the effect of the other. For example, the effect of increasing the weight on one side of a balance beam can be reversed by increasing the distance on the other side.

The preceding models represent Piaget's most explicit formulation of his intuitions concerning the nature of children's thought in middle childhood. Before developing assessment devices for inferring the presence of such structures, however, Piaget made the additional assumption noted above, that each type of logic would lead directly to the acquisition of a different type of concept (Postulate 3b). For example, the type of thought captured by the formula $X = f(X \times Y)$ was assumed to lead to the acquisition of conservation. The reason for this was that conservation was presumed to require the insight that quantitative increase in one salient dimension (e.g., height) is compensated for by a quantitative decrease in a less-salient dimension (e.g., width). When it came to designing a set of empirical measures in different domains, therefore, it was concepts such as conservation which were actually assessed, not thinking which could be demonstrated to conform to the logical formulae in some more direct fashion.

While initial attempts to probe children's understanding of conservation were promising, it soon became apparent that the pattern of data that had been expected was by no means the pattern that was actually obtained. For example, whereas conservation of substance was acquired in the predicted age range (i.e., 7 to 8 years), conservation of number was acquired a good deal earlier, (Binet & Simon, 1916; Piaget & Szeminska, 1952) at an age when children's only logic was supposedly the logic of one-way functions (i.e., 5 to 6 years). North American investigators, upon simplifying Piaget's measures further, often found that conservation concepts were acquired earlier still. In one study, for example, Gelman (1972) presented children with a game in which they had to discover that an array of three mice would always be a winner whereas an array of two mice would always be a loser. After children had learned this, she transformed one array so that the line of three mice looked shorter than the line of two mice. What she found was that children still chose the array of three mice, and justified their responses by referring to the number of mice in the line. The pattern of data that was actually found on tests of conservation is illustrated in Figure 11.2. A similar pattern was found for other abilities which were supposed to stem from the 8-year-old thinking pattern, such as the ability to decenter (Flavell *et al.*, 1968). As was mentioned in Chapter 3, this pattern was given the name horizontal décalage, in order to contrast it with the pattern of horizontal evenness which had been expected. And it was acknowledged to be a major stumbling block for Piaget's theory.

Given that the pattern of data was not as expected, it does follow that at least one of the postulates that was advanced in generating it must be wrong. Exactly which postulate was in error, however, is not clear. To begin with, Piagetians often assumed that the problem was strictly one of measurement. That is, they assumed that the problem lay with Postulate 4. They suggested that the measures that had been used to test conservation did not conform to the appropriate theoretical criteria. Straightening out these criteria, and ensuring that they were appropriately applied, took up a good deal of energy in the field during the 1960s. Eventually the point was reached, however, where investigators in both Geneva and North America realized that making the assessment criteria more rigorous would not make the problem go away. Every year it seemed that new tests were devised to assess an understanding that was supposedly the by-product of a particular logical structure, but which was passed at a younger age than had previously been thought possible (Fischer, 1980; Gelman, 1979; Kuhn, 1983). Thus, far from ameliorating the situation, efforts to improve and simplify existing measurement techniques actually made the situation a good deal worse. It became clear that the pattern of data indicated in Figure 11.2 would have to be taken as the rule, not the exception, in human development. Stated differently, it became clear that the problem did not lie with Postulate 4—the measurement postulate—but with one of the others.

The next postulate that was questioned—at least in North America—was the first one (i.e., the postulate that different age groups have different characteristic patterns of thought). As was mentioned at the beginning of the chapter, North American investigators began to challenge the idea that horizontal structure exists at all, and to entertain the notion that development in any one domain occurs independently from development in any other (Fischer, 1980; Flavell, 1980; Gelman, 1979; Klahr & Wallace, 1976).

Although this interpretation certainly fit the data, it of course did not fit the intuition that the thinking of different age groups is discriminable, independently of problem domain. Because the latter intuition was not held just by practitioners, but by many researchers themselves, a more moderate suggestion was soon advanced, which was more in line with the European response to the same

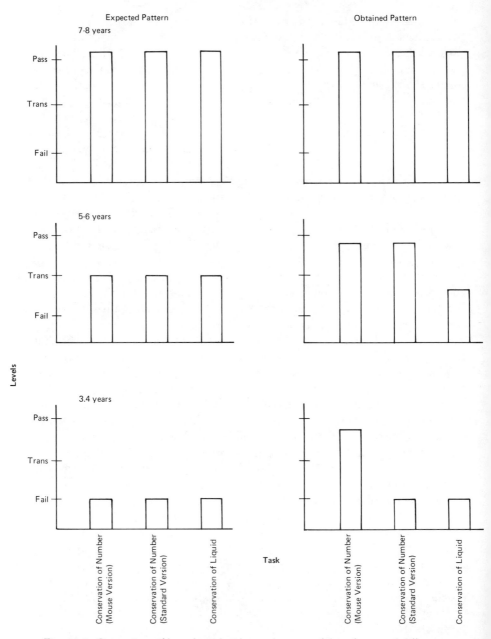

Fig. 11.2. Comparison of hypothetical with actual pattern of data, for several different conservation tests.

dilemma. This was that the horizontal structure in children's thought, if it existed at all, would have to be reconceptualized (Flavell, 1982; Fischer & Bullock, 1981).[1]

That is essentially the situation at the present. While there is still a general wariness concerning the notion that horizontal structure or general stages exist (Postulate 1), there is a growing acknowledgment that the problem may lie either with our intuitions concerning the nature of this structure (Postulate 2) or with the way in which these intuitions have been translated into a set of explicit models (Postulates 3a and 3b).

Piaget's Position and the Present Position Contrasted

At first glance, it would appear that the difference between the present view of horizontal structure and Piaget's lies with Postulate 3a. While Piaget assumed that the form of children's thought at different ages could be adequately modeled by means of symbolic logic, the present position is that a more complex form of modeling is necessary, one which will do justice to the process of children's intellectual functioning as well as to its underlying structure.

While the two forms of modeling are certainly different, however, this difference is not as fundamental as it might appear at first glance. Moreover, it can not be used as an explanation for why the pattern of data that was predicted by Piaget's theory was not the one that was actually obtained. In order to understand why this is so, it is useful to consider the control structure which was proposed in Chapter 6, as a model for how 6-year-olds respond to Siegler's version of the balance beam problem.

PROBLEM SITUATION

- Balance beam with objects on each arm.
- Each object composed of a number of identical weights.

OBJECTIVES

- Find out which side will go down, when supports are removed.
- Find out which side has the greater number of weights.

STRATEGY

1. Count weights on each side; note greater number.
2. Pick side with greater number as the one which will go down.

To say that children assemble a control structure with this format is simply to describe, in greater detail, the internal means by which they establish a func-

---

[1]For attempts to effect such a reconceptualization within the context of Piaget's theory, see Inhelder *et al.* (1974), and Pinard (1975).

tional relationship between the force or action tendency of a balance arm (variable X), and the relative weight on each side (variable Y). Far from being incompatible with the notion that children's thought has the structure of functional logic, therefore, the above model actually constitutes an explication of this claim.

A similar point could be made with regard to 10-year-old functioning. To say that children have a control structure in which two dimensions are represented rather than one and in which these two dimensions can be traded off against each other is not to deny that the underlying form of their logic has changed from $X = f(Y)$ to $X = f(Y \times Z)$. Rather, it is to explicate this claim. Thus, while the models of children's executive functioning that were presented in Chapters 6 through 10 would appear to have a distinct advantage over Piaget's with regard to the information they offer about process, they do convey the same general information about structure. Moreover, there could be many instances in which Piaget's more global formulation might be preferable, simply because it is so economical. Thus, although there are differences between the present models and Piaget's, these differences are not the sort that would lead to differences in predictions regarding the general pattern of children's performance across different tasks—at least in the 5- to 10-year-old age range.

This leaves Postulate 3b. Where the present position departs from Piaget's most significantly is in the assumption that each type of logic necessarily leads to a different type of concept (such as conservation), or a different type of ability (such as the ability to decenter). The present position is that each type of thinking or logic necessarily leads to a different *level* of concept or ability, not a different type.

The difference between a type and a level is subtle but important. To say that children's thinking determines the type of concept they can construct is to say that certain particular concepts such as conservation cannot be acquired until a certain age: when the prerequisite logical structure is available. The same applies for capabilities such as decentration. By contrast, to say that children's thinking determines the level of concept or ability they can acquire is to say that any given type of concept or ability—including conservation and decentration—can be acquired at almost any age. What varies with age is the level of understanding, or degree of sophistication, which children can attain with regard to the concept or ability in question.[2]

---

[2] Actually, Piaget is inconsistent on this point. In discussing causality, for example, he clearly takes a position which is congruent with the present one, that causality is constructed at different levels as a function of the structures available. The same may be said for his position on concepts having to do with space and time. It is only with regard to tests such as conservation, seriation, and classification that he takes the other view, presumably because they seem to tap concrete logical structures more directly.

A NEW LOOK AT THE EXISTING EMPIRICAL DATA

Once Postulate 3b is modified in this fashion, the data which were previously seen as anomolous no longer present such a problem. Consider first the test of liquid conservation. On this test, assessing the relative quantity of the two liquids after one has been transformed does indeed require the ability to make a quantitative comparison along two dimensions, at least under normal conditions. If one could only focus on the salient dimension (height) one would have no basis for determining which appearance was misleading: the apparent equality before the transformation, or the apparent inequality after the transformation (Case, 1977a). Thus, children who apply the logic of one-way functions to the task should not be able to pass it. In fact, this has been demonstrated empirically in several studies conducted in our own laboratory. If one classifies children according to whether they quantify one or two dimensions, one discovers that the unidimensional quantifiers almost never pass the test of liquid conservation, even after training, whereas the bidimensional quantifiers do. A summary of these data is presented in Table 11.1. As may be seen, then, success on this particular task does indeed imply a level of reasoning which is more complex than $X = f(Y)$.

Consider next the standard test of number conservation. Unlike continuous arrays, discontinuous arrays can be quantified by counting. To solve the conservation of number problem, one must simply realize that variation in relative amount (X) is a function of variation in relative numerousity (Y). Thus, on this task, success only requires a logic of the form $X = f(Y)$.

Finally, consider Gelman's conservation test which uses mice as the stimulus materials. Although this test also involves quantification, it does not require quantification along a dimension. The winner is not the array with the greater value along the dimension of height, width, or number. The winner is simply

TABLE 11.1

Percentage of Unidimensional and Bidimensional Quantifiers
Showing Conservation after Training[a]

	Acquired concept (%)	Failed to acquire concept (%)
Unidimensional quantifiers (N = 27)	3	97
Bidimensional quantifiers (N = 29)	64	36

[a]From Case (1977), Studies 1, 2, and 4.

the array that has three mice in it. As a consequence, children do not have to think of number as a dimension along which two objects may be compared, they can think of it simply as a property of a particular set. Moreover, the actual numbers involved (2 and 3) are ones which can be understood directly, via subitizing. The same may be said for winning. Winning does not need to be thought of in terms of amount or degree. It can be thought of more simply as an event which either happens or does not. Thus, success on this task does not imply a logic of the form $X = f(Y)$ but rather a more primitive logic.[3]

When the above three tasks are examined in this fashion, it becomes clear that they do not constitute equivalent (i.e., horizontal) assessment devices, but rather vertical ones. Moreover, the fact that the first test should be passed at 7 to 8 years, the second at 5 to 6 years, and the third at a lower age is not incompatible with Piaget's view of children's logical development. On the contrary, it is entirely compatible with it. The only notion of Piaget's with which the data are not compatible is his Postulate 3b, that the acquisition of certain logical concepts automatically entails a particular type of logical structure.

Demonstrating that the data on conservation do not refute the notion of horizontal structure is of course not the same as demonstrating that they actually confirm it. To acquire data of the latter sort, one would need to present a variety of tasks, each in a different content domain, which do demand the same level of logical thinking. And one would then have to demonstrate that the pattern which emerged was the one in Figure 11.1.

It is precisely this sort of task and this sort of data, however, which were described in the previous four chapters. In discussing the thought of 6- and 8-year-olds, for example, it was noted that 6-year-olds judge the fairness of a particular distribution of rewards in terms of the relative number of candies each person received. They judge the relative success in school of two children in terms of their relative age. They judge the relative size of two shadows which will be projected in terms of the relative size of the objects which will cast the shadows. Finally, they judge the relative juiciness of two orange juice mixtures in terms of the relative number of beakers of orange concentrate placed in each. In short, for each one of these different tasks, 6-year-olds employ a logic of the same form, $X = f(Y)$. The same may be said about 4- and 8-year-olds. For each task, it is the case that 4-year-olds fail to process the task in terms of the appropriate quantitative dimensions, while 8-year-olds focus on a second dimension as well. One could therefore say that 4-year-olds apply a more primitive form of logic than 6-year-olds, and that 8-year-olds apply a more sophisticated form of logic.

Figure 11.3 presents the data from two of the studies cited in previous chapters, rescored according to the following scale; 1 point = predimensional

---

[3] Following in the Piagetian tradition, one could suggest that this logic has the form $x^1 = y^1$ or $x^2 = y^2$, where $X = x^1 + x^2$, and $Y = y^1 + y^2$.

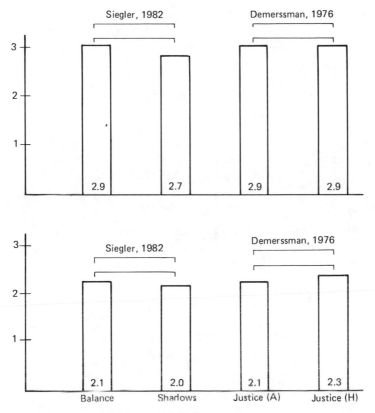

Fig. 11.3. Re-analysis of data from Siegler (1982) and Demerssman, (1976), using present response categories.

thinking, 2 points = unidimensional thinking, and 3 points = bidimensional thinking. As may be seen, the degree of horizontal structure is substantial. In fact, the pattern in this figure is virtually identical to the one illustrated in Figure 11.1. While there may well be the occasional exception to this pattern (e.g., children's understanding of probability, see Siegler, 1981), these exceptions appear to be just that, exceptions and not the rule. The same could be said for development during the sensorimotor and relational periods. Although the developmental data are not consistent with the strongest version of the Piagetian notion of horizontal structure, then, they do appear to be consistent with the weaker version of this position which has been advanced in the present volume. That is, they do appear consistent with postulates 1, 2, 3a, and 4.

Of course, it is one thing to induce a common horizontal pattern across different tasks on the basis of post hoc analyses of data which were gathered on different populations, under differing conditions of administration. It is another thing to predict the existence of horizontal structure for a set of novel tasks, which are to be administered to the same population under the same conditions of administration. In order to meet this latter criterion, and hence to provide a more stringent test of the existence of horizontal structure, we decided to do a series of studies of our own, using the sort of procedures which had been developed by Noelting and Siegler.

NEW DATA OF RELEVANCE TO THE HORIZONTAL STRUCTURE HYPOTHESIS

Study Number 1[4]

The object of the first study was to determine whether children's level of performance on a newly designed task in one domain could be predicted on the basis of what was already known about their performance on a task in another domain.

Subjects

The subjects were drawn from a public school in a middle class neighbourhood in Toronto. Four different age groups were tested. The mean ages of the groups were 4 years, 10 months ($n = 19$), 6 years, 10 months ($n = 28$), 8 years, 10 months ($n = 27$), and 10 years, 10 months ($n = 30$).

Tasks

Two different tasks were used: one from the domain of physical cognition, the other from the domain of social cognition.

The test of physical cognition was Noelting's juice mixing task. As the reader may remember from Chapter 9, this is a task where children are shown two empty pitchers, together with a set of juice and water beakers that are to be poured into each. They are then asked which mixture they think will taste juicier, when the pouring is complete. During the dimensional period, children's strategies go through four distinct substages. At Level 0, the strategy is one of global juice evaluation. Children look at each array, and choose the one that has a large number of juice cups. If the two arrays have approximately the same number of juice cups, they respond that they will both taste the juiciest, or else give an irrelevant answer. At Level 1, children's strategy is one of counting the juice. Children carefully count the number of juice cups in each array, and say

---

[4]This study was conducted by Zopito Marini, as part of his Master's thesis (Marini, 1981).

that the one with the greater number will taste the juiciest. At Level 2, children's strategy is one of counting the juice and counting the water. When the number of juice cups is equal, they predict that the array with less water will taste more juicy. Finally, at Level 3, children's strategy is one of juice versus water compensation. When the side that has more juice also has more water, children pick the side with the greater excess of juice over water, rather than guessing or falling back on the answer which is obtained by counting only the juice.

To parallel Noelting's task in the domain of social cognition, a new task was created which was called the birthday party test. This task was also described in Chapter 9. Children were shown a picture of two boys, each of whom was smiling. They were told that the two boys lived in different cities, but that each was having a birthday party, and that each wanted a set of polished stones for a present.[5] They were then shown how many stones each boy wanted, and how many he actually received. The question they were asked was which child would be happier. The actual items which were presented, and the scoring criteria which were used, were directly parallel to those presented in the juice mixing test. The order of presentation was counterbalanced.

Predictions

In keeping with the horizontal structure hypothesis, it was predicted that children would go through four parallel stages on this task: (1) global gift evaluation, (2) counting of gifts received, (3) counting of gifts-received and gifts-wanted, and (4) gifts-received versus gifts-wanted compensation. It was also predicted that they would go through the four substages at the same rate, and during the same age range.

Results

The mean score on each task at each grade level are shown in Figure 11.4. As may be seen, the mean scores of the 10-year-old group were somewhat lower than expected. However, the results with regard to horizontal structure were as expected. An analysis of variance showed a highly significant age effect, and an insignificant task effect.

Discussion

The results from this study showed that a substantial degree of horizontal structure exists across tasks in different domains, and that the existence of such structure can be used as a basis for making predictions about novel tasks. They also showed that horizontal structure is not just limited to the beginning of the

---

[5]Polished stones were chosen as the gift, they were a highly prized commodity in the school where the testing was conducted.

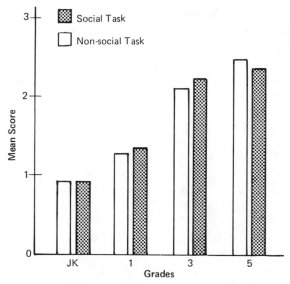

Performance on Social and Non-social Tasks During Dimensional Period

Fig. 11.4. Performance on Noelting's juice task and Marini's birthday party task. (From Marini, 1981.)

dimensional period, as has sometimes been assumed (Flavell, 1982; Siegler, 1981).

Study Number 2[6]

The object of the second study was to replicate the findings of the first study, across a slightly broader range of ages and tasks.

Subjects

The subjects were again drawn from a public school in a middle-class neighbourhood in metropolitan Toronto. Twenty children were tested at each of four ages: 4, 6, 8, and 10 years.

Tasks

Four different tasks were used, the balance beam task, the birthday party task, the projection of shadows task, and a distribution of rewards task. The first three tasks were described in Chapters 6 and 9. The last task was invented for

[6]The second study was conducted by Zopito Marini, as a part of his doctoral dissertation.

the present study, on the basis of earlier tasks used by Damon (1973) and DeMerssman (1977). The story that was told to each child was as follows:

> A teacher asked some of the kids in her class to come in after school, to make some cards for children who were in hospital. John came in on these days (At this point the experimenter laid down several pieces of paper, each with a day of the week printed on it). And here are the cards he made (At this point the experimenter laid down a set of X Christmas cards, each identical in appearance). Jim came in on these days (as above), and here are the cards he made (as above). Now here are some candies (at this point the experimenter pulled out a bag of candies) which the teacher decided to give to John and Jim as a reward. Tell me. Do you think John should get more candies, or Jim should get more candies? Or should they get the same?

As is no doubt apparent, the above task has the same structure as the first three, and can therefore be scored in the same fashion. The four levels that were used were as follows: Level 0, global output evaluation (i.e., cards produced); Level 1, quantification of each child's output; Level 2, quantification of output and input (i.e., number of days worked); Level 3, output versus input compensation.

Results

The mean scores on each task at each age level are shown in Figure 11.5. As may be seen, the mean scores at the first two age levels were virtually identical, with the greatest difference between any two tasks being two tenths of a point. At the upper two grade levels, the range in mean scores widened to four tenths of a point, with the children doing significantly better on the two social tasks than the two nonsocial ones. However, it was still the case that the majority of children performed at the predicted level on each task.

Discussion

The overall pattern of the results in the second study was still in accord with the horizontal structure hypothesis. The difference between the social and nonsocial tasks at the upper grade levels is an interesting one, however, because it is in accord with the suggestion that the magnitude of décalage may increase as children progress through any given stage (Fischer *et al.*, in press; Flavell, 1981; Siegler, 1981).

Study Number 3

While the results from the first two studies indicate a substantial degree of horizontal structure (even allowing for some variation between the social and nonsocial tasks at the upper age levels) they still have two clear limitations. The first is that they apply only to the dimensional stage. The second is that they ap-

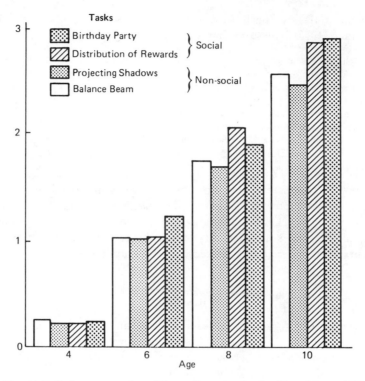

Fig. 11.5. Performance on four different dimensional tasks. (From Marini, 1984.)

ply only to tasks that entail a common underlying operation, counting. To counteract these two limitations, a third study was done, using preschoolers as subjects and two tasks that differed in the operations they required.[7]

Subjects

The subjects were drawn from two daycare centers serving middle-class neighbourhoods in Toronto. Four different age groups were tested, $1\frac{1}{2}$ years (n = 16), 2 years (n = 19), 3 years (n = 17), and 4 years (n = 10) years.

Tasks

Two different tasks were used. Again, one was from the domain of physical cognition, the other from the domain of social cognition.

The test of physical cognition was the preschool version of the balance beam

[7] This study was also done by Zopito Marini as part of his doctoral dissertation (Marini, 1984).

task, which was described in Chapter 5. As the reader may remember, this is a task where children are shown a balance beam, which is set up so that one of its arms has a bell immediately above or below it. To parallel the preschool balance task in the domain of social cognition, the Muppet test, which was described in Chapter 8, was created. Children were presented with a small set of Muppets called Kermit (a frog), Fozzie (a bear), and Baby Kermit (a baby frog). They were then asked to make one of the muppets happy or angry, under a variety of conditions. At Level 0, the task was simply to make the muppet happy or angry by patting it or tickling its stomach. At Level 1, the task was to select an appropriate object (a blanket or a brush) in order to achieve the same results. At Level 2, the task was to select an appropriate friend (Bear or Kermit) to get the appropriate object and achieve the same result. Finally, at Level 3, the task was to make Daddy Kermit happy or angry, by executing the Level 2 actions on baby Kermit instead.

Predictions

In keeping with the horizontal structure hypothesis, it was predicted (1) that children would go through the four levels on each task and (2) that they would do so at the same rate, and during the same age range.

Results

The mean scores on each task at each age level are shown in Figure 11.6. As may be seen, the results were as predicted. An analysis of variance once again showed a highly significant effect due to age, and an insignificant effect due to task.

Discussion

Once again, the results showed that a substantial degree of horizontal structure exists across tasks in different domains, and that the existence of this structure can be used as a basis for making predictions about novel tasks. Note that this time the two tasks shared no common operation. What they did share was the requirement for focusing on a set of relations with a common structure, and setting up a goal stack with a common number of relational objectives.

Study Number 4[8]

The object of the fourth study was to replicate the results of the third study, using children from the vectorial rather than the relational stage.

---

[8] The fourth study was also conducted by Zopito Marini, as part of his doctoral dissertation (Marini, 1984).

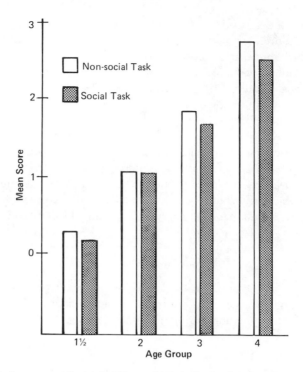

Performance on Social And Non-social Tasks During Relational Period

Fig. 11.6. Performance on balance task and muppet task during relational period. (From Marini, 1984.)

Subjects

The subjects were selected from academically streamed classes in two public schools in Metropolitan Toronto. Twenty subjects participated at each of four age levels, 10, 12, 15, and 18 years.

Tasks

Two tasks were used, the balance beam task and the social dilemma task, which was described in Chapter 10. Both tasks were scored on a common scale, as follows: Level 0, no evidence of using an abstract vector (ratio in one case, and an abstract personality trait in the other), to make a prediction about what will happen in a specified situation; Level 1, use of a single abstract vector, to make such a prediction; Level 2, use of two such vectors, but without any independent operation to combine them; and Level 3, use of two vectors, with an independent operation involved in their comparison.

Procedure

The social dilemmas were read to subjects in the fashion indicated in the previous chapter. The balance beam problems were administered after four warm-up problems had been presented, in which children received feedback on whether their first guesses were or were not correct.

Results

The results are presented in Figure 11.7. As may be seen, the degree of horizontal structure remained substantial. The greatest difference between the two tasks at any age level was only two-tenths of a point. An analysis of variance revealed no significant effect due to task, but a highly significant effect due to age.

Discussion

The results from the fourth study strengthen the conclusion that was reached in the first three studies concerning the existence of horizontal structure and the utility of the present theory in conceptualizing it. The only obvious objection

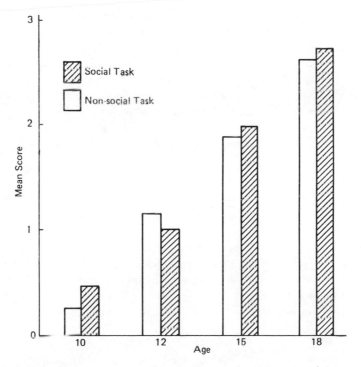

Fig. 11.7. Performance on balance task and character trait task during adolescence. (From Marini, 1984.)

that could still be raised is that all of the tasks considered so far have a rather artificial laboratory character, and that the degree of horizontal structure under such constrained conditions may misrepresent the degree of horizontal structure in children's everyday functioning. To examine this latter possibility, a final study was conducted.

Study Number 5

The fifth study began as two separate experiments that happened to use the same population of subjects. It was only after both experiments were completed that we realized their relevance to the issue of horizontal structure.

Subjects

The subjects were selected from a public school that served a middle-class neighbourhood in metropolitan Toronto. They were pre-screened to insure that they were of average intelligence.

Tasks

In the first experiment,[9] children were administered several tests of general cognitive ability. Immediately afterward, they were asked to tell the experimenter three stories. The instructions were as follows: "Now I want you to tell me a story about (for instance) a cute little lamb, kind of like you'd tell it to a boy or a girl littler than you are."

The second experiment was conducted several days after the children had participated in the story-telling task. Each child was presented with a set of coloured pencils and paper, and given the following instructions. "Draw me a picture which shows a little girl (or boy) your age, doing something that makes her (or him) happy."[10]

Results

On the story-telling task, children's productions fell into one of four general categories. At Level 0, children told a story that had the structure of some sort of everyday event or script. Although some action invariably took place, and successive events bore an appropriate temporal and causal relationship to each other, no problem or unusual event was introduced that would serve as the focus for the story, and give the overall production a sense of thematic unity. At Level 1, children's stories underwent a clear qualitative shift. Some sort of prob-

---

[9]The first experiment was conducted by Anne McKeough, as a part of her Masters' thesis (McKeough, 1982).

[10]The second set of data was analyzed by Sonja Dennis (Dennis, 1984).

lematic event or state was described early in the story, which was then immediately resolved. The balance of the story then consisted of a description of a sequence of (usually happy) events that took place after the problem had been resolved. The result of this shift was that the overall story could be classified as having some sort of conventional story plot or theme (e.g., loneliness ended, or villainy nullified). At Level 2, there was another shift, although it was more of a quantitative than a qualitative nature. Now children embedded a minor plot within their major plot. Moreover, they tended to do so in such a fashion that the minor plot was juxtaposed against the major one, thus presenting the major character with some additional difficulty (e.g., authority intervening in an attempt to establish friendship, and preventing it). At Level 3, some additional elaboration was introduced, which often produced a novel and satisfactory resolution to both the plot and the subplot.

On the picture drawing task, children's productions fell into four clear categories as well. At Level 0, children drew a monochromatic outline of a human figure, together with an irregular shape indicating some other object. While the various parts of the figure usually bore an appropriate spatial relationship to each other, the object rarely had any discernable parts and both the figure and the object appeared to be hovering in space. At Level 1, a major qualitative shift took place. Some sort of brightly coloured context was introduced, and both the person and the object were placed within it. As a consequence, the drawing now appeared to be a unified and conventional scene in which each object was depicted as occupying an appropriate position with regard to the vertical axis (e.g., sky at top, ground at bottom, person and plants on grass, birds or sun in the middle of the sky). At Level 2, another set of changes took place, which were of a more minor but nevertheless significant nature. Now children introduced a second dimension into their pictures in addition to *height*, the dimension of *depth*. They did so by a variety of artistic techniques, such as bringing the sky down to the ground (and hence making it look behind the figure) or occluding some part of the body with a limb (thus making the limb look in front of it). Finally, at Level 3 the children introduced an additional set of elaborations, which integrated the depth dimension and the height dimension in a more satisfactory fashion.

In writing up their experiments, both McKeough (1984) and Dennis (1984) conducted detailed structural analyses of each of their four levels, and related them directly to the stages described for the dimensional period in Chapter 9. In addition, they developed a reliable coding system, and tested a number of predictions concerning performance on each of their tasks and the more general cognitive measures which were administered. What is of interest for the present purpose, however, is the global set of levels in each domain, and their relationship to each other.

The mean scores on each measure are presented in Figure 11.8. As may be seen, development in each domain took place at a common rate. An analysis of

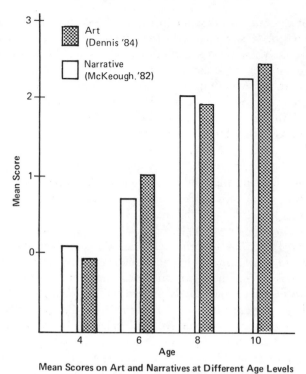

Mean Scores on Art and Narratives at Different Age Levels

Fig. 11.8. Performance on spontaneous drawing and story-telling tasks. (From McKeough, 1982, and Dennis, 1984.)

variance revealed a highly significant effect due to age, and an insignificant effect due to task.

Discussion

When taken together with the results from the first four studies, the results from the fifth study suggest quite strongly that—when tasks are analyzed from the point of view of the present theory—décalage is by no means the rule. To the contrary, it is the exception. The standard pattern that emerges, whether task conditions are highly constrained or relatively open, is that development proceeds through a formally equivalent set of stages in different domains, at a common rate.[11]

---

[11] For data on individual differences and the way in which these differences are conceptualized within the present theoretical framework, see Case *et al.* (1985).

DESCRIPTIVE VERSUS EXPLANATORY ACCOUNTS
OF HORIZONTAL STRUCTURE

The argument that has been advanced so far may be summarized as follows: although the data that were gathered in the 1970s showed that décalage was the rule when viewed from the classic Piagetian perspective, they did not demonstrate that it was the rule when viewed from any perspective. Moreover, it turns out that—if a slight modification is made in the classical Piagetian position—a very different conclusion is reached. The slight modification is to delete the claim that horizontal structure should manifest itself in the type of concept children can grasp, or the type of ability they can display, and to replace it with the claim that horizontal structure should manifest itself in the level of problem solving of which children are capable. Once this modification is made, the existing data no longer constitute a refutation of the general Piagetian claim. To the contrary, they actually support it because they show that every time one simplifies a task, and hence the level of problem solving which it requires, one also reduces the age at which it is passed. Moreover, if one uses Piagetian formulae to characterize the new level of problem solving that is required, one can even explain the amount by which the passing age is reduced, at least in the age range for which Piaget's structural formulae are applicable. With the present (neo-Piagetian) theory as a supplement, one can extend this range to the full period from birth to adulthood.

Such an explanation is, of course, post hoc. However, as was shown in the new experiments that were reported, it can also be used to make a variety of novel predictions. Providing that the task sequences are designed in an appropriate fashion, successful predictions can be advanced for a variety of new content domains, test formats, and age levels. It follows that—in spite of the criticism which has been directed against it in the past—the general Piagetian claim about the existence of horizontal structure remains essentially intact; all that needs to be altered is the way in which that claim is interpreted.

One important caveat must be entered before concluding. To say that Piaget's theory is adequate to describe the structure of children's thinking at different ages—or even that it is adequate once important modifications are made—is not to say that his theory is adequate to explain this structure, or to account for the process by which children move from one form of structure to the next. As the reader may remember, Piaget's explanatory theory runs as follows: the reason that tasks with the same underlying problem structure tend to be solved at the same age is that children have general mental entities that correspond to this structure, psychological *structures of the whole*. When exposed to a new situation or problem, children assimilate this task to their current structure of the whole and respond accordingly. With time, the limitations of this structure gradually become apparent to them. Then, via an autoregulative process which involves both equilibration and reflective abstraction, they create a more powerful general structure. At this point, this general structure once again serves to define their view of the world and to determine the strategies which they will apply to a wide range of cognitive tasks.

As was pointed out in Chapter 3, Piaget's explanatory theory leads to predictions about learning and intertask correlations that are simply not borne out. The prediction about learning is that children should not be able to learn how to solve problems beyond their current level of functioning, unless they are already in a state of transition (i.e., unless they have already begun to detect the limitations in their current general structure). The prediction about intertask correlations is that they should be high, because the same general structure is used to solve all manner of different problems. Given that these predictions are not borne out, and given that Piaget's explanatory theory is less well worked out than his descriptive theory in any case, it seems reasonable to suggest that a different explanatory theory is necessary, if the horizontal structure in children's problem solving is to be explained.

In the chapters that follow, such a theory is presented. Before this is done, however, it is worthwhile to make one final point. This is that there would be good theoretical reasons for abandoning Piaget's explanatory theory, even if no empirical reasons dictated it. Because if the present theoretical description of children's intellectual functioning is correct, the particular operative and figurative schemes that comprise any given structure are quite specific. They are specific not only to broad general domains such as linguistic, spatial, or causal reasoning. They are specific to particular problem types within these domains as well. This being the case, it follows that the reason children's thinking has a common general form at any age cannot be sought in the structures which exhibit this form themselves. In effect, there can not be any such entity as a structure of the whole. Rather, the reason must be sought in some common process by which the structures are assembled, or some common constraints to which the process is subject.

It is to the search for these sorts of commonalities, then, that Part III of the present volume is devoted.

PART III

The Process of Stage Transition

CHAPTER 12

Basic Processes and Regulatory Mechanisms

INTRODUCTION

In the previous section, a rather detailed answer was provided to the question of how to conceptualize children's thinking at different stages of development. In the present section, a somewhat less detailed answer is provided to the question of how to conceptualize the stage transition process. The two questions are of course closely linked. It is not a coincidence that Piaget conceptualized the process of stage transition as one of equilibration, nor that behaviourists conceptualized it as one of modeling and reinforcement. The former notion fits well with the idea that development can best be described as a sequence of increasingly sophisticated general logical structures. The latter notion fits well with the idea that development can best be described as a sequence of increasingly sophisticated specific intellectual skills.

The position that was elaborated in the previous five chapters might best be characterized as neo-Piagetian. It followed Piaget in characterizing children's development as a sequence of increasingly sophisticated mental structures. It also followed Piaget in examining the form and complexity of these structures across a wide variety of content domains. Finally, it followed Piaget in concluding that four broad stages—each with its own set of substages—could be discerned. The account did not follow Piaget, however, in its description of the form and functioning of the structures themselves. The structures of each stage were characterized as domain-specific devices for achieving executive control, rather than as domain-independent systems of logical operations. And, as will be shown in the present section, this change in the way children's mental structures were conceptualized leads to a change in the way in which the stage transition process must be conceptualized as well.

As the reader will no doubt remember, the major stage boundaries that were proposed in the previous section were at 4 months, 20 months, 5 years, and 11 years of age. At each of these points in time, it was suggested that children integrate a variety of their existing control structures, into new structures that are qualitatively different from each of their component parts. In addition, it was suggested that the operation or strategy of one structure very often serves as the means, toward the attainment of an end that is specified by the other. For example, hand reaching becomes a means for producing interesting visual effects at the age of about 4 months. Pencil manipulation becomes a means for producing interesting geometric patterns at about the age of 20 months. Counting becomes a means for generating causal predictions at about the age of 5 years. And ratio computation becomes a means for resolving dimensional conflicts at about the age of 11 years. In all these cases, the process of stage transition may be seen to involve two components. The first is the integration of two previously existing structures, each of which previously served a qualitatively different purpose. The second is the hierarchical subordination of one of these structures to the other. This being the case, the present chapter is concerned with the question of what sort of processes children come equipped with, so that they are capable of hierarchical integration on one hand, and predisposed towards it on the other.

One way this question can be addressed is to consider the component tasks that must be accomplished, in order for this sort of integration to take place. From a purely logical point of view it would appear that the following four tasks must be accomplished.

1. The first task is simply to activate the two different structures at the same time: either simultaneously or in immediate sequence.
2. The second task is to recognize the functional benefits that accrue—either internally or externally—when the two structures are activated in this fashion.
3. The third task is to alter the way in which the two structures are internally represented, so that the newly preceived benefit can be obtained again in the future, in a more intentional fashion.
4. Finally, the fourth task is to consolidate the new representation, so that the two structures can function in a conjoint fashion in the future, in as smooth a fashion as each one functioned separately in the past.

Given that all four of these tasks must somehow be accomplished, it follows that young children must come equipped with some basic mechanism or process which is capable of executing each one of them. In addition, it follows that they must come equipped with some more general mechanism or process as well: one which will orient them toward situations where work on these tasks is likely to bear fruit, and which will orchestrate the overall flow of their mental activity as they pass from one task to the next.

GENERAL REGULATORY PROCESSES THAT CAN LEAD TO HIERARCHICAL INTEGRATION

There are a number of general regulatory processes that appear to meet the foregoing requirements.

Problem Solving

The first of these is problem solving. When faced with an objective which they have no preexisting operational sequence for reaching, young children have a natural tendency to experiment with new operational sequences, in an effort to achieve their objective. Moreover, they have a natural tendency to evaluate the success or failure of any such sequence and to incorporate successful sequences into their strategic repertoire. In the present context, there are two things to note about this general tendency, and the sequence of mental operations to which it gives rise. The first is that, in setting out to solve a problem, a child is orienting to a situation in which there is a least a reasonable possibility that hierarchical integration may take place. The general class of situations in which problem solving is observed is illustrated in Figure 12.1. As may be seen, both the problem situation (situation A) and goal situation (situation B) of a potentially new control structure are already given. What children are missing is the

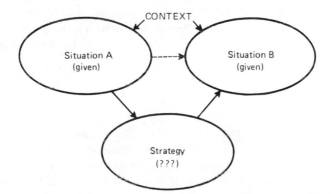

Fig. 12.1. Schematic illustration of situation in which problem solving takes place. Note that situation B is not, strictly speaking, given. It is given only once the subject has encoded the current situation, and set himself a more desirable one as a goal.

strategy that will permit them to bridge this gap. An important function that children's natural efforts at problem solving can serve, therefore, is simply to orient them to this class of situations.

A second thing to note about problem solving is that, at least under certain circumstances, it is capable of accomplishing each one of the four component tasks which were mentioned above.

Schematic Search

The first step that takes place in problem solving is a search for some operation or sequence of operations which may help to bridge the gap between the current and the desired situations. This search presumably requires some sort of fast-acting and automatic subprocess, in which the features of the current and desired situations are matched with the corresponding tags indexing the structures that are already in the child's repertoire, and in which some sort of maximum likelihood or best fit is then computed. Regardless of the specific mechanism by which it is achieved, however, the result of this first step is that the first prerequisite for hierarchical integration is achieved, In short, a novel sequence of operations is generated.

Schematic Evaluation

The second step that takes place in problem solving is an evaluation of each operational sequence which is generated, to determine whether or not it actually does achieve the desired goal. Note that the goal need not necessarily be an empirical one. It can equally well be a cognitive one, such as the resolution of uncertainty or conflict. Thus, the evaluation can involve an external or an internal state. In either case, however, the outcome of the evaluative act is the same, namely a decision as to whether or not the desired end state has been achieved. This decision achieves the second prerequisite on which the process of hierarchical integration depends, a determination of the functional utility of a novel sequence.

Schematic Retagging

There is third step that often takes place in problem solving, but which is usually left out of informal accounts of the process. This is that, after the outcome of a particular operational sequence has been evaluated, the sequence itself is retagged, so that it can be accessed in a more intentional fashion in the future (if it leads to a positive outcome), or so that it can be avoided in a more intentional fashion in the future (if it leads to a negative outcome). In reflective children, this process may occur quite consciously. In other children, the process may be far less conscious. Considerable variation may also be present in the time at which the process takes place. For some children, the process may occur immediately following the application of a novel operational sequence, as the child experiences elation or frustration and reviews the events which led up to this affective state. For others the review may take place at a later point in time, as they reflect on the emotionally salient events that have taken place during their day.[1] That the process takes place in most children, however, in some fashion and at some time, is indicated by the fact that they no longer repeat all their trials-and-errors on subsequent exposures to a problem. Rather, over the course of a few exposures, they begin to execute the successful sequence of operations in a fashion which shows all the earmarks of intentionality. From the present perspective, what is important about this is that the third prerequisite for hierarchical integration is being accomplished: children are retagging the operation in question, so that it is seen as a means to a new end.

Schematic Consolidation

A final subprocess that takes place is apparent only after a problem has been solved in an intentional fashion. With each successive trial, the sequence of operations becomes more and more smooth and automatic. Whether or not this process should be considered a step in problem solving per se is a moot point. From the viewpoint of the experimenter, it does not appear to be a part of the same process, because by definition the problem has already been solved. From the viewpoint of the child, however, it may well be a part of the same process because children appear to return again and again to problems which they have only recently encountered, until they achieve this sort of mastery (White, 1975). At this point, the process that began with their initial interest in the problem seems to come to a natural completion, and they move on to other things. In any case, what is important from the present viewpoint is that children do return to many problems until this sort of mastery is achieved and that, by doing so, they accomplish the final task which the process of hierarchical integration entails, the consolidation of a new executive structure.

In order to understand how the above sequence of steps might unfold, and how it might culminate in the formation of a higher-level executive structure, it is useful to consider a concrete example. Consider, therefore, the case of a particular child, a boy, who has developed a structure for determining relative weight by means of visual estimation, and a structure for determining relative number by counting, but who has not yet integrated these structures into one hierarchical unit. Such an integration might very well take place via problem

---

[1] The existence of a time-line that can be reviewed in this fashion was hypothesized by Klahr and Wallace (1976), and has been documented in the adult memory literature by Murdoch, (Murdoch, 1974; Muter, 1979).

solving on the child's first exposure to a balance beam—simply because the apparatus would present him with a class of problems which he had never encountered before, and which he would try to master. In fact, such an integration might actually take place in the course of being tested by a developmental psychologist.

Suppose, for example, that an experimenter let the child play with a balance beam, until he realized that the side with the heavier object always went down. Suppose that the experimenter then set up a stack of five weights on one side and a stack of six weights on the other, and asked the child which side would go down. In response to this question, the child would no doubt attempt to apply the weight estimation strategy already in his repertoire, namely, visual inspection. In doing so, however, the child would discover that the size of the two objects was about the same, and that it was impossible to be certain what would happen. Siegler reports that young children do, in fact, exhibit considerable uncertainty when faced with this sort of situation, and are reluctant to make an immediate prediction (Siegler, 1976). In effect, the situation poses a problem, and the children recognize this.

Now suppose that the child in our example encountered such a problem, and tried to solve it. How might he do so? The most obvious first step would be to search for some way other than visual inspection for determining which of the two objects weighed more. In the course of this search, the child would be quite likely to access his counting executive because the situation for which this executive is appropriate would already be tagged in a fashion similar to that specified by the problem. That is, it would already be represented as a strategy for reaching the objective of knowing which of two sets of objects had more, in situations where this was not visually apparent.

Once the child did access this strategy, he could recognize its potential usefulness in one of two fashions. He could note that it led to a successful prediction about which side would go down. Alternatively, he could simply note that it allowed him to make a prediction, in a situation in which he had not been able to make one previously. Whichever positive result he noted, the consequence would be the same, The counting strategy would be retagged as one that was of potential use in predicting relative weight when the answer was not visually apparent. On subsequent trials, therefore, the child would be likely to access his counting procedure again. Eventually, he would set himself the subgoal of quantifying the two stacks as soon as he heard the experimenter ask a weight question, without any need for active problem solving. In effect, the consequence of repeated problem solving would be that counting would become a smoothly functioning part of the child's weight determination structure. That is, it would become hierarchically subordinate to, and integrated with, his weight-determination structure.

Exploration

Although problem solving is one general process which could lead to hierarchical integration, it is by no means the only one. A second process that could have the same effect is exploration. When faced with a situation where a particular strategy or operation could be applied, but where the results of such an application cannot be anticipated, young children have a natural tendency to apply the strategy or operation in question, simply to satisfy their curiosity. Moreover, they have a natural tendency to reapply the strategy or operations even if the event produced is in and of itself quite neutral, until such time as they can anticipate the results. As this point, they rapidly lose interest (Biemiller, 1966).

In and of itself, the exploratory application of a single structure would not necessarily lead to hierarchical integration. All it would lead to would be an expansion in the range of situations to which existing structures could be applied, together with an increased understanding of the consequences. Another important attribute of exploration, however, is that it tends to lead to several different executive structures being applied in immediate succession. In fact, when a situation is completely novel, children tend to apply virtually all the executive structures in their repertoire that can be applied to the situation, one after the other (Biemiller, 1966). It is this sequential application of pre-existing structures which could lead to the assembly of a higher-order structure.

In order to see how this might occur, it is useful to begin directly with a specific example. Consider once again, therefore, the case of a young child, a girl, who has two discrete control structures in her repertoire, one for determining the relative weight of two objects via visual inspection, and one for determining the relative number of two sets via counting. Suppose that such a child had the opportunity to explore the properties of a set of marbles or a set of building blocks. One of the operations which she might apply would be counting. Gelman (1978) has noted that 2- and 3-year-olds have a spontaneous tendency to count groups of identical objects, and my own informal observation suggests that 5- and 6-year-olds have a spontaneous tendency to determine which of two sets has more as well. Suppose, therefore, that in the course of such exploration the child focused on two subgroups of marbles and counted the number of items in each set. The consequence would be that she would know which set had the greater number.

Now suppose that, having applied this counting structure, the child decided to move on to some other activity. If the sets in question were marbles, she might place each set in a different bag, and go out to play with the marbles in the yard. If the sets were building blocks, she might transport each set to a different location, in order to assemble two different buildings. In the course of picking up and transporting the two sets, she would be very likely to notice their weight. In short, she would be very likely to apply a weight-evaluation executive as well. Note that this executive would not necessarily have to be applied in an exploratory fashion itself. Although it could well be applied in this fashion, it could also be applied as a part of some broader activity, which was the new focus of the child's curiosity.

Now suppose, finally, that this sort of sequence occurred on a number of different occasions. That is, suppose that the child applied each executive structure in sequence, and thus noticed (1) that set A had more objects in it, and (2) that set A also appeared to weigh more. It seems highly likely that—at some point in time—the child would begin to suspect that there was a connection between these two facts. She might do so on one trial, by actively reviewing a particular event sequence, either at the time it was executed or at some time thereafter. Alternatively, she might do so across trials, thus gradually forming a notion of a prototypic sequence, and the schemes that were active in short-term memory at the end of such a sequence. In either case, the result would be a retagging of the number structure as one that could predict the consequence of applying the weight structure. Very probably there would be some sort of active hypothesis testing associated with this new tag, as the child tested and explored the new relationship that had been discovered. This further exploration would lead to a consolidation of the two newly integrated structures, into a relatively automatic and permanent superstructure.

As with the problem-solving example, there are two important things to note about the process of exploration. The first is that it applies to a very general class of situations, one in which hierarchical integration is a possible outcome. This class of situations is illustrated in Figure 12.2. Note that, in this diagram, the ini-

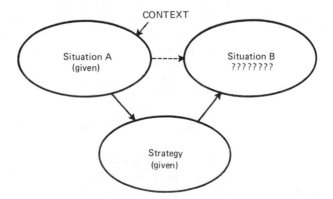

Fig. 12.2. Schematic illustration of situation in which exploration takes place. Note that the strategy is not, strictly speaking, given. It is given only once the subject has encoded the current situation and accessed an operation or set of operations applicable to it.

tial situation (A) is given, as are all the various strategic operations that can be applied. However, the final situation—the outcome of applying these operations—is not. In effect, exploration is the natural complement of problem solving. What problem solving accomplishes in a top-down or goal-driven fashion, exploration accomplishes in a bottom-up or situation-driven fashion.

The second thing to realize about the process of exploration is that, although its details are somewhat different from those of problem solving, the general set of substeps which it entails are similar.

Schematic Search

In the first step the subject searches for interesting operations to apply in the current situation, and generates them, one after another. Note that each search must be guided by an automatic and rapid acting subprocess which is similar to that involved in problem solving. The features of the current situation must be matched to the corresponding tags of the structures in the child's repertoire. The only difference is that this search is not constrained by a simultaneous matching with regard to a desired end state—other than the desire for novelty.

Schematic Evaluation

In the second step, the subject notices the covariance that is implicit in a particular operational sequence, either by active review of the contents of short-term memory on a single trial, or by gradual schematization of a protypic scheme sequence.

Schematic Retagging

In the third step, the subject retags the strategy of the first member of the operational sequence, in a fashion that indicates its connection to the end state of the second member.

Schematic Consolidation

Finally, in the fourth step, the subject tests out the hypothesis inherent in the new tag, experimenting with various possible variations and applications, until the newly assembled superstructure is consolidated.

In effect, then, children's exploration can lead them to tackle the same four tasks they would in problem solving, but in a bottom-up rather than a top-down fashion.

Imitation

A third process that could lead to hierarchical integration is imitation. In most natural environments, there are many situations where young children do not realize what operational sequences can be applied, or what new situations can be reached as a result, but where those who are older or more experienced do realize this. Young children have a strong natural tendency to observe the actions of those around them under these circumstances, and to imitate these actions.

As was the case with problem solving and exploration, imitation is a process which serves to orient the young child toward a very general class of situations, one in which there is a substantial probability that some new integration of his existing structures may be suggested.

The child's state at the outset of an imitative episode is similar to that in exploration, in that situation A is given by the physical context, but does not in and of itself suggest a goal or a strategy. However, the adult's behavior soon serves as a possible model for both. Depending on whether children focus on the end state that the adult produces, and try to produce such a state themselves, or whether they focus primarily on the adult's actions, and try to generate a similar set of actions themselves, one could say that imitation can constitute a social analogue of either problem solving or exploration.

Given that imitation can serve as the social counterpart to either of these two processes, one might expect that it would involve a similar set of results, In fact, this appears to be the case. As the children observe the adult, they presumably activate a set of schemes from their own repertoire which represent the visible components of the adult's behaviour, together with the end result that is produced. Then, if the particular configuration has the right degree of novelty and/or utility, they become interested in generating the sequence on their own. It is at this point that their real cognitive work begins, and that their inner processes begin to resemble those in problem solving or exploration.

Schematic Search

In order to imitate an adult's behaviour, children's first step must be to search for operations in their own repertoire which correspond to the activity they have just witnessed. Presumably this requires some sort of fast-acting and relatively automatic subprocess, in which the features of the visual schemes they have just activated are matched with the corresponding tags in their operative repertoire.

Schematic Evaluation

In the next substep, children must apply the relevant schemes, and evalutate their effectiveness. That is, they must decide whether or not they have generated the desired outcome.

Schematic Retagging

In the next substep, children must retag the operational components they applied as ones which, in combination, will generate the particular result observed. In the case under consideration this often means retagging the operation associated with the first of two executive structures as one that will lead to the opportunity to apply the second structure, and to produce the particular goal that is associated with it.

Schematic Consolidation

Finally, in the fourth substep, children must practice the new sequence until they have mastered it (i.e., until the new relationships are consolidated).

In order to get a better sense of how the process of imitation could lead to hierarchical integration, it is useful to return to the example which has already been considered. In most natural environments there are a number of situations where adults or older children use counting as a means for determining the weight of something, and where younger children have the opportunity to observe them as they do so. In my own youth, such situations used to occur when my friends and I were refilling the wood box. We used to count the number of logs we piled into each other's arms, both as a clue to the weight of individual loads, and as an indication as to which of us could carry the heaviest load. Once we had done so, we would stagger off with our respective loads, groaning and laughing en route. Not surprisingly, our younger siblings were exposed to such situations, and had the opportunity to observe them. Suppose, therefore that a particular 5-year-old boy was exposed to such a situation, and that he was able to encode the actions he observed as counting, followed by groaning and carrying. Suppose further that he decided to do this, too, and thus to act like a "big boy". What he would do would be to stack up a number of small logs or sticks in his arms, counting them in the process, and then to carry them off. As the load increased in number, it would of course, also increase in weight. Moreover, the child would find it very difficult not to notice this covariance, and to realize what all the groaning was about. Over a certain number of trials, therefore, he would be very likely to discover that large numbers were associated with loads that were too heavy to carry while small numbers were associated with loads that were not too heavy to carry. In short, he could discover that counting was a useful cue to use in determining weight.

Mutual Regulation

A final process that could lead to hierarchical integration is mutual regulation; that is, the active adaptation of the child and some other human being to each other's feelings, cognitions, or behaviours. Such adaptation may be an end in itself, as in many forms of affectionate or aggressive transaction. Alternatively, it may be a means to an end, as in many forms of task-based cooperation. In either case, however, each member of the social dyad exerts an influence on, and is in turn influenced by, the other.

A particularly interesting form of mutual regulation from the present viewpoint is instruction. Instruction is a form of interaction that is very much like imitation, in that it involves two individuals, one of whom has a particular control structure and one of whom does not. The difference, however, is that the individual who has the structure takes just as active an interest in the acquisition process as the one who does not.

The general class of situations to which instruction is applicable is one in which models of both the initial and the final situation (A and B) are given, as in imitation. However, the intervening operations are not facilitated just by the presence of the model, but by his or her active efforts to help the child acquire them. In effect, instruction may also be considered as a social counterpart of either exploration or problem solving, depending on whether children have a clear sense of the goals toward which the instruction is oriented from the outset, and actively try to pursue them, or whether they just try to "act like an adult," and see what consequences ensue. Perhaps not surprisingly, the subprocesses that are involved are also quite similar.

Schematic Search

During the first substep, children very probably search for a structure to apply in a particular situation and receive a suggestion from someone who is older or more experienced. This suggestion may be solicited or unsolicited. It may be verbal or non-verbal. The only requirement for it to succeed is that there should be some match between the features the instructor provides and the representation of some structure which is already in the child's repertoire.

Schematic Evaluation

During the second substep, children apply this structure or structural sequence and evaluate the consequence, perhaps with the instructor's assistance.

Schematic Retagging

During the third step children retag the new sequence—again with assistance being provided by the instructor.

Schematic Consolidation

Finally, during the fourth step, children practice the new sequence, either independently or under the guidance or the instructor, until the new structure is consolidated.

When one first thinks of instruction, the image that comes to mind is of a process which is quite different from that which has just been described. One tends to conjure up the image of a teacher at the front of a classroom, lecturing to a group of pupils who are all seated at their desks. It may therefore seem inappropriate for the process to be characterized as one of mutual regulation, or to be described in the same terms as exploration or problem solving. Certainly Piaget's writings contain no suggestion of this sort. For Piaget, instruction was a sort of necessary evil, something that at best was irrelevant to development, and at worst was capable of interfering with it.

When one actually observes good teaching, however, one realizes that the process is in fact a highly reciprocal one. One also realizes that it can involve every one of the steps mentioned above, and that it can indeed lead to hierarchical integration. Data to support these assertions will be presented in Chapter 15. In order to convey a preliminary sense of the way in which good instruction can operate, however, it is worthwhile to consider one final concrete example.

A fourth way in which 5-year-old children might integrate their control structures for weight determination and counting is that an older child or adult might actively instruct them in how to do so. This instruction might be initiated by either member of the dyad. The younger member might see the older member playing with a balance or tecter totter, and ask them how it worked. Alternatively, the older member might see the younger member playing with such an apparatus, realize that the youngster didn't understand how it worked, and set out to show them. Once again, this sort of event might even be promoted by the presence of a developmental psychologist. Two children of different competencies might compare notes about what they were asked and how they answered when they were tested by the psychologist. In the course of such a discussion, they might realize that one of them had a strategy for answering the questions, and the other had to guess. This in turn might trigger a request for, or an attempt at, instruction.

Regardless of the specific situation that led up to the instruction, the instruction itself would very probably unfold in a very similar manner. The younger member of the dyad—either by observation or by being told—would realize that there was a problem he or she did not know how to solve, but which the older member did. The youngster would then pay attention to whatever demonstration or observation the older member provided, and attempt to apply whatever operations were already in his or her repertoire, in order to follow the description or model provided. At the same time, the older member would observe the youngster's attempts, and supplement or modify the instruction accordingly.

While they apply in somewhat different situations, therefore, it should be apparent that problem solving, exploration, imitation, and mutual regulation are actually quite similar. They are similar in that they all orient children toward situations in which novel structural sequences are likely to be generated. They are similar in that they all involve a common set of subprocesses: (1) accessing and experimenting with novel scheme-sequences, (2) evaluating the consequences of those sequences, (3) restructuring valuable sequences so that they can be used in an intentional fashion in the future, and (4) practising these new structures until they become consolidated. Finally, they are similar in that they can all lead, under appropriate environmental conditions, to the same result, the hierarchical integration of structures that are already in the child's repertoire, but which have never previously been combined.

Of course, to say that the processes are similar is not to say that there are no differences among them. As has already been suggested, the four processes may be distinguished with regard to whether or not they are directed toward the achievement of a particular goal (i.e., whether they are driven in a top-down or bottom-up fashion) and whether or not they are socially facilitated. From the viewpoint of the survival of the species, this variability is no doubt essential, for if only one type of process led to development, then development would be too dependent on the existence of a particular type of environment. By insuring that infants will orient toward whatever structural possibilities are in their social and physical environments, even if no specific goal is currently active, nature no doubt ensures that development will take place across as wide a range of domains and circumstances as possible. And, by providing the possibility of focusing on the attainment of particular goals, with the addition of social assistance where this is available, nature no doubt ensures that development will be particularly efficient in those domains which have the greatest utility in the particular culture and environment into which a young child is born.

On both structural and functional grounds, therefore, one would expect that there would be important differences among the four global processes, but a common core as well, one that would insure that existing structures were combined in new ways, that the results of this combination were evaluated, and that some reorganization would take place such that the new sequences themselves became smoothly running executive units.

Of course, to say that the above four processes should have this effect is not to say that they actually do. In order to provide further substance to the foregoing analysis, therefore, it is necessary to examine the available data.

EMPIRICAL EVIDENCE ON THE EFFECTIVENESS OF THE GENERAL REGULATORY PROCESSES

At least three kinds of evidence are of relevance to the question of whether each one of the foregoing processes can actually lead to hierarchical integration: (1) evidence on the age of emergence of each process, (2) evidence on the ecological frequency of each process, and (3) evidence on the consequences of each process, under controlled laboratory conditions.

Age of Emergence

If a process does not emerge until late in the course of human development, it can clearly not exert an influence on stage transition during the early years. In effect, it must be though of as the result of development, rather than a primary cause. The first evidence to consider is therefore data on the age of emergence of the different processes.

Consider first the process of problem solving. By the age of 2 months, this process appears to be reasonably well established. The 2-month-old infant who has just experienced the sensation of having its finger in its mouth will actively work towards reinstating this pleasant state, experimenting with various possible arm movements that might enable it to do so (Piaget, 1952). Similarly, the 2-month-old infant who has just experienced a strange face approaching him or her too closely will actively work at escaping from the sensation which is produced, experimenting with various eye and head movements that may enable it to do so (Schaffer, 1977). Both of these activities involve problem solving, as it was described above.

The situation with regard to exploration is quite similar. As virtually all observers of infant behaviour have noted, the infant is not motivated solely by a desire to reinstate pleasant sensations, or to eliminate unpleasant ones. It is also motivated by curiosity, that is, by a desire for exploration. In the first few months of life, the most obvious form of exploration is visual. The infant will scan any new environment in which it is placed with great interest, until it notices all the salient features in it. By the age of 4 to 8 months, visual exploration is extended to include manual and oral activity as well. Any time a novel object is placed within the infant's reach it will explore its properties in a variety of ways. Moreover, it will repeat these actions—either within or across encounters with an object—until it appears to know in advance what operation will lead to what consequence. As is the case with problem solving, therefore, exploration appears to be a general tendency toward which the infant is oriented from a very young age.

Imitation is also a process that is present from an early age. For some time, it was thought that the process was not present until 6 to 7 months of age (Maratos, 1973), and that it did not emerge in its deferred form until 12 to 18 months (Baldwin, 1894; Bayley, 1969; Piaget, 1954). More recently, however, it has been suggested that both simple and deferred imitation may actually be elicited at birth (Meltzoff & Moore, 1977). The first claims of this sort were greeted with considerable skepticism, on both theoretical and methodological grounds. Subsequent studies, however, have done a lot to counter this skepticism, both by introducing new experimental controls, and by qualifying the original theoretical claims (see Meltzoff & Moore, 1983a, 1983b). It now does appear that, providing the appropriate testing conditions are met, an infant will imitate gestures that are only subtly different from each other, from the first few hours of life.

Actually, from the present perspective, it is not crucial that imitation be present from such an early point in time, as long as it emerges sufficiently early to play a significant role in subsequent development. Nevertheless, the suggestion that the process is innate is certainly congruent with the present position, in contrast to the earlier positions advanced by Baldwin and Piaget.[2]

Finally, *mutual regulation* is a process that emerges at a very early age as well. The first example is the protocommunication, which is observed between an infant and its mother, as was described in Chapter 7. As was noted, infants' smiling and cooing becomes interleaved with that of their mother's during the period from 1 to 4 months (Stern, 1974; Trevarthan, 1974). Moreover, the infant is so well tuned to this regulation that it is disturbed if any deviation in the pattern is introduced (Trevarthan, 1982). Several important forms of mutual regulation are also observed at the age of 4 to 8 months. These include intentional babbling or calling of the mother, and intentional crying. Finally, more complex regulations are observed from 8 to 12 months, and include such activities as pointing and babbling to obtain an object (Bates, 1976) or inhibiting a current activity to avoid material displeasure (Griffiths, 1954). As with the other processes, therefore it appears that mutual regulation is a process that emerges at a very early age, and for which children have both the necessary capabilities and dispositions.

Ecological Frequency

If a process is rarely observed in children's day-to-day functioning, it matters little at what age if first becomes available. It is still not likely to play a major role in intellectual development. Thus, the second sort of evidence that must be examined is evidence on the ecological frequency of the four processes. A study that was concerned with recording the spontaneous activity of young children is relevant in their regard. In this study children from a variety of different social classes were observed in their natual habitat in the Boston area (White, 1975). The data that were obtained are presented in Figure 12.3.

As may be seen, the correspondence between the categories in the table and those that have been used in the present chapter is by no means exact. However, if one assumes that retrieving an object that is not within reach, restoring order, and preparing for an activity, all involve active problem solving, it may be concluded that this activity occupies at least 6% of an average American child's day, at the age of 18 to 21 months. Exploration is listed as a distinct category and involves a further 7% of the child's day. Cooperation, procuring service, gaining attention, and maintaining social contact all involve a strong component of

---

[2] Both Baldwin and Piaget based their explanation for the delayed emergence of the symbolic function at least in part on the delayed emergence of deferred imitation.

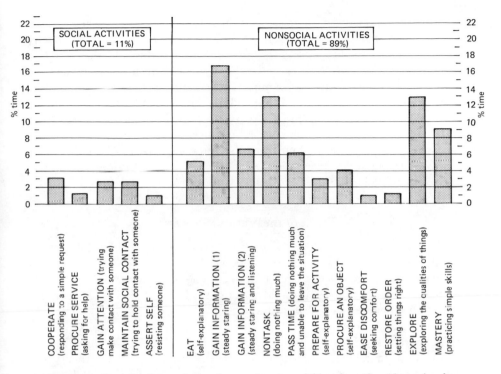

Fig. 12.3. Typical daily experience of young American children from 12 to 15 months of age. N = 19. (From White, 1975.)

mutual regulation. Thus, one can conclude that this sort of social problem solving or exploration involves a further 14% of the young child's day. Finally, mastery, which can be the final step in any one of the general regulatory processes, involves a further 12%.

While the total that is thereby accounted for is less than half of the child's waking hours (42%), it is nevertheless quite substantial. Moreover, it must be remembered that many of the other activities that are cited (such as eating—11%), involve components of exploration, problem solving, and mutual regulation as well, as any caretaker can attest. It must also be remembered that White's information-gaining categories, listening and staring, often form a prelude to one of the other three activities as well. When these considerations are taken into account, what is remarkable is just how much of the average child's day is devoted to tasks that can contribute to cognitive development, namely, 70%.

Of the four processes mentioned in the present chapter, the only one about which no direct inference can be drawn from White's data is imitation. While much of the child's visual exploration may result in subsequent imitation, no quantitative estimate can be made as to just how much from the above table because this was not a category in White's scoring system. Fortunately, Abramovitch and her colleagues have addressed this question directly (Abramovitch et al., 1978, 1979, 1980). Abramovitch studied middle-class preschoolers, both at home and in nursery school, under conditions of free play. In the nursery school, she found that children engaged in imitative acts on an average of 7 to 19 times per hour. At home, younger children imitated their older siblings from 10 to 24 times per hour. On balance, therefore, it seems fair to say that each one of the four regulatory processes that has been described not only emerges at a relatively early point in human development, but is observed with a high frequency as well.

Effect of the Various Processes

Given that each of the four processes emerges at an early point in development, and has a reasonable degree of ecological frequency, the final question is what effect each process has, once it does emerge. What evidence is there concerning the effect of engaging a child in one of the four regulatory processes, as a means to promoting stage transition?

Experimental data on the effectiveness of the processes comes largely from the training studies which were conducted during the late 1960's and early 1970s. As was mentioned in Chapter 3, this period was one in which Piaget's theory was becoming better known in North America, and coming into increasing conflict with the behaviourist view of development that was dominant at the time. The major issue on which the battle between the two schools was fought was the effect of experience on development, and the major weapon was the training study.

By far the most frequently studied developmental structure was the one on which liquid conservation dpends. Initially, the studies that were reported showed very little evidence of success from any sort of intervention (Flavell, 1963). As experimenters became better at adjusting their training procedures to the difficulties that children experience in acquiring conservation, however, results of considerable magnitude began to be reported (Gelman, 1969; Kohnstamm, 1967). Behaviourists, of course, interpreted these results as supporting their position. However, the same results were interpreted by Piagetians in a different fashion. They suggested that the studies had not really succeeded in producing genuine development, but had only produced a sort of pseudo-development (Piaget, 1964). A spirited controversy ensued concerning the criteria that should be used for assessing genuine as opposed to pseudo-development.

As more time passed, there was increasing agreement as to what the criteria for assessing development should be: (1) the absence of any sign of a particular developmental concept prior to training, (2) a clear sign of the concept after

training, (3) broad transfer of the concept after training, and (4) long-term retention of the concept following training. As these criteria were employed in subsequent studies, an interesting picture began to emerge. Contrary to what Piagetians had originally maintained, it became clear that genuine development
could be produced by well-planned laboratory manipulations, in a relatively
short period of time (Beilin, 1971b; Lefebvre & Pinard, 1972). Contrary to what
behaviourists had believed, it became clear that processes such as modeling did
not produce results that were any better than others. Attention then focused on
what sort of intervention would produce optimal development, and whether
this should be construed in a Piagetian or a behaviourist fashion (see Brainerd,
1973; Lefebvre & Pinard, 1972; Strauss, 1972).

This issue was never clearly resolved. Once the issue of whether development
could be produced was settled, and once the difficulties of interpreting successful
results became apparent, the attention of the field switched to other matters. In
particular, it switched to the sort of detailed analyses of children's intellectual
functioning which the newly emerging discipline of cognitive science had made
possible, and which were illustrated in Chapters 5 to 10 (e.g., Siegler, 1981). In
the meantime, investigators who remained within one of the traditional
theoretical camps continued to cite the existing training data as supporting their
own position (cf. see Strauss & Langer, 1970; Zimmerman & Rosenthal, 1974).

While the interpretative question was never resolved to the satisfaction of
either of the traditional theoretical camps, it is worthwhile to re-examine the
particular studies that were conducted, with the advantage that hindsight and a
new prespective can provide. And, from the perspective of the present theory, it
appears that studies were conducted which produced sizeable results in all four
of the categories that have been mentioned. A study by Strauss and Langer
(1970), for example, demonstrated that conservation could result from a
relatively unguided period of exploration, providing that the materials and
transformations that children conducted were of relevance to the conservation
concept. Similarly, a study by Lefebvre and Pinard (1972) demonstrated that
conservation could also be induced by problem solving, that is, by presenting
children with problems for which their current quantification strategy was inadequate, and by encouraging them to tackle the problem of developing a better
one. Studies conducted by Charboneau et al. (1976), following earlier studies by
Sullivan (1967), showed that conservation could be induced by imitation,
whether the actor being imitated was a child or an adult. Finally, studies conducted by Murray (1972) showed that conservation could be induced by mutual
regulation. The technique used by Murray was to have conserving and non-
conserving children engage in discussion. However, in our own work we
demonstrated that direct instruction could be just as effective, providing it
focused children's attention on the appropriate dimensions (Case, 1977a,
1977b).

Thus, while the training studies did not lead to any definitive formulation at the time, the general pattern that they yielded seems relatively clear in retrospect. Stated simply, it is that a wide variety of different interventions can produce stage transition, and that results of impressive magnitude have been associated with all four of the general regulatory processes that have just been described. That is not to say that they should all have equal effects. If the present model is correct, methods that focus children on relevant aspects of a situation, and help them to access, evaluate, retag, or consolidate new sequences more effectively should be more powerful than those which leave these processes up to chance. However, it is fair to say that all four of the general processes that have been described could make an important contribution to the process of hierarchical integration under appropriate circumstances, and hence could contribute to children's development.

SUMMARY AND CONCLUSION

The argument that has been advanced in the present chapter may be summarized as follows. As children make the transition from one major stage of development to the next, the most important change that takes place is that control structures that were originally discrete become integrated in a hierarchical fashion. In order for hierarchical integration to take place, at least four component tasks must be accomplished: (a) an existing set of executive structures must be activated in a novel sequence, (b) the consequences or functional utility of this new sequence must be noticed, (c) the sequence must be retagged or recoded so that it can be activated intentionally in the future, and (d) the newly coded entity must be practiced, until it is consolidated as a new unit in its own right.

There are a number of naturally occurring regulatory processes with which children are endowed, which make it likely that each of these tasks will be accomplished. These include problem-solving, exploration, imitation, and mutual regulation. These processes differ as to whether they are driven in a top-down or bottom-up fashion, and as to whether they do or do not involve social facilitation. However, they are alike in that they all involve a common set of subprocesses: (a) schematic activation, (b) schematic evaluation, (c) schematic retagging, and (d) schematic consolidation. In short, they are alike in that they all accomplish each one of above mentioned tasks in the appropriate order.

As yet, very little empirical work has been done on the above mentioned subprocesses. However, a good deal of empirical work has been done on the general processes themselves. In accordance with the present analysis, this work indicates that all four of the processes emerge at an early point in human development, that they all occur with a relatively high degree of frequency, and that they are all capable of producing stage transition under controlled laboratory conditions. Accordingly, it seems reasonable to conclude that they are all capable of producing stage transition in the everyday world as well.

At the beginning of the present chapter, it was pointed out that Piaget's description of development led him to postulate that equilibration and reflective abstraction were the primary mechanisms on which the process of stage transition depends, and that processes such as modeling and mutual regulation play a relatively minor role. While problem solving is not identical to equilibration, it clearly does share a number of important features with it. Problem solving is essentially the organism's response to disequilibrium, whether this disequilibrium is externally or internally induced. Similarly, although schematic evaluation and retagging are not identical to reflective abstraction, they do share a number of important features with it as well. They are the subprocesses by which the organism recognizes new patterns of functional significance in its own intellectual activity, and then reorganizes this activity so that, with practice, the new patterns can become a smoothly running part of its cognitive repertoire.

Given the relationship between problem solving and equilibration on one hand, and certain of the core subprocesses and reflective abstraction on the other, the present account of stage transition may be said to be broadly congruent with Piaget's, and to constitute one possible way in which it may be explicated. On the other hand, the present account is clearly not congruent with Piaget's contention that the processes he hypothesized were the only ones that were of importance, and that the processes hypothesized by behaviourists (i.e., modeling and imitation) or by Vygotsky and Bruner (i.e., mutual regulation) play a relatively insignificant role. To the contrary, the present account of stage transition suggests (1) that these latter two processes are merely the social analogues of the former two, (2) that the latter two processes share a common set of at least four subprocesses with the former two, and (3) that any one of the four general processes can play an important role in producing the sort of hierarchical integration on which stage transition depends, under appropriate environmental circumstances.

One final comment is in order, concerning the stage transition processes hypothesized by Vygotsky and Bruner. As the reader will no doubt remember, the underlying metaphor that both these theorists employed was that of the child as an inheritor of cultural tools. Both theorists also suggested that the intellectual inventions of the culture were first acquired by young children in the course of some form of mutual regulation, and then gradually internalized to the point where they could function as tools of independent thought. At that point, the new structures were seen to endow their possessors with a new intellectual power, and to permit them to function at a higher cognitive level.

The view of the internalization process that has been offered in the present chapter has been somewhat more detailed, and a good deal more *rationalist* or *constructivist* in its flavor than that offered by either Bruner or Vygotsky. In addition, there has been a good deal less emphasis on the role of language. Nevertheless, it is important to realize that the account does exemplify many of the key points these two theorists made, particularly insofar as the development of children's scientific reasoning is concerned.

As has been shown in the present chapter, the acquisition of dimensional thought on scientific problems such as the balance beam, results from the use of counting as a means toward the end of increased predictive power. Similarly, the acquisition of vectorial thought on the beam was shown in Chapter 6 to result from the use of ratio-comparison as a means toward the end of resolving dimensional conflicts. Thus, in effect, both stage transitions were shown to result from the use of one structure as a tool to increase the power of another.

Now, as will no doubt be apparent, both counting and ratio-comparison are cultural inventions. Moreover, each invention is normally acquired by young children in a socially facilitated context. Counting is normally acquired via imitation, while ratio-comparison is normally acquired as the result of direct instruction. In both cases, then, we have an example of a cultural invention being acquired at one stage of development via a socially facilitated process, and then going on to function as a tool of independent thought at the next, Moreover, in both cases we have an example where the cultural tool is actually instrumental in producing the stage transition to begin with.

Depending on the particular aspect of the present model on which one focuses, then, one can obtain either of two complementary views of the stage-transition process. If one considers only the core intellectual processes and subprocesses that have been hypothesized (i.e., hierarchical integration, via schematic search, evaluation, retagging, and consolidation), one obtains a view that is highly rationalist, and compatible with Piaget's account of the stage-transition process. On the other hand, if one considers the full range of general activities in which these processes can be elicited—both social and nonsocial—as well as the social origins of several of the key structures that are actually integrated hierarchically in particular domains, one obtains a view that is a good deal more historical or cultural in nature, and compatible with the accounts of Vygotsky and Bruner. Just as one does not need to choose between the structuralist and information-processing accounts of children's functioning at each successive stage of their development, then, so one does not need to choose between the structuralist and historical-cultural views of the process by which children move from one of these stages to the next. Each perspective has its own validity. Moreover, for a full account of the stage-transition process to be rendered, each perspective must somehow be taken into account.

CHAPTER 13

Epigenetic Changes

INTRODUCTION

The transition model as so far developed postulates that movement from one stage to the next takes place by means of hierarchical integration, which in turn takes place by the application of a set of general regulatory processes to the particular physical and social environment in which a child is raised. If suitably elaborated, it would appear that this model could be used to account for a wide range of developmental phenomena. These include the following:

1. The fact that, within any given content domain, there is a universal order in which various structures emerge. The explanation for this fact would hinge on the definition of hierarchical integration. Because hierarchical integration involves the assembly of a superordinate structure from previously existing component structures, it is logically impossible for the superordinate structure to emerge at an earlier point in time than the component structures of which it is composed.

2. The fact that processes such as problem solving, exploration, imitation, and mutual regulation emerge at such an early age, and are accompanied by such a high degree of affect. The explanation here would hinge on the function that these processes serve, and its importance for the survival of the species. Because the function of the processes is to produce development, and because development is of such clear survival value, one would expect that the processes and dispositions on which it depends would emerge at an early age, and would be given a high degree of affective priority.

3. The fact that different children in the same environment may differ widely in their overall rate of development, and in the terminal level of development which they achieve. Here the explanation would center on the general regulatory processes, and their efficiency. If one makes the additional assumption that different children are endowed with regulatory processes of different efficiency, then it would follow (a) that they would be able to put the experience to which they were exposed to different use, and (b) that they would develop at different rates, across the full range of content domains to which they were exposed.

4. The fact that, when differences in the rate of general development are taken into account, there still remain individual differences in development which are content or domain specific. Here the explanation would center on the different environments in which different children are raised. Because different children encounter different experience in different content domains, and because they also receive a different amount or type of social support, one would expect that content-specific differences of this sort would emerge as a matter of course as well. Domain-specific differences in talent could also be postulated to help explain the same phenomenon.

5. The fact that different cultural groups also differ in their rate of development in specific content domains (e.g., Price-Williams, 1969). The explanation for this would be that different cultural groups have regulatory processes of equivalent efficiency, but that they differ in the opportunities which they encounter for applying these processes, and the nature of the social support they receive.

6. The fact that certain instructional treatments are far more effective than others in facilitating particular developmental acquisitions. The explanation for such effects would center on the various tasks that must be accomplished, if hierarchical integration is to take place. For example, although a child might well access a relevant sequence of previously existing structures under conditions where the relevant cues were not highlighted (see integration Task 1); he would be far more likely to do so if they were highlighted. Thus, cue highlighting should be one potential variable in developmental-instructional research (see Gelman, 1969). Similarly, because verbal instructions could serve to facilitate the processes of novel sequence evaluation (Task 2) and retagging (Task 3) they should constitute another variable of potential instructional relevance.

PROBLEMS FOR THE THEORY
OF HIERARCHICAL INTEGRATION

Although there are a number of important developmental phenomena for which the hierarchical integration model could provide an account, if elaborated in this fashion, there are a number of equally important phenomena for which it could not provide an account, or at least not in any straightforward fashion. These include the following:

1. The fact that the process of development takes so long. As was shown in Chapters 6 through 10, even the most complex adolescent control structure can be assembled in 12 substages (four stages × three substages). Moreover, at each substage, all that is required is the integration of two substructures, each of which was acquired at the previous substage. Finally, even the most recalcitrant of structures that has so far been studied, that is, conservation, can be produced in the laboratory in about 20 minutes, under the appropriate experimental conditions. Why, then, can one not bring an infant from the earliest sensorimotor structures in some particular content domain to the vectorial structures, in the course of twelve 20-minute laboratory sessions? Is it that any new structure requires a lengthy period of consolidation, before it can serve as the basis for further progress? Perhaps, however, even allowing 1000 practice trials per structure and one minute per trial, one should still be able to produce a full developmental sequence in the laboratory in the course of about 48 half-day sessions. Is the reason for slow development that so many separate components are involved? If every one of the 12 stages involved the integration of completely unrelated components, the number of total components which had to be trained would increase dramatically as one progressed from stage to stage. While this would increase the required training time considerably, however, it is still not likely to be the whole story. For if one uses the number of separate components that are involved in the balance beam as a basis for computation, one still does not arrive at an estimate for total laboratory training time that exceeds 250 half-day sessions (i.e., about 1 year).

The question therefore remains as to why development takes so long. Is it that development in each separate content domain is subtly dependent on development in each other content domain, in ways that are not yet fully understood? Or, alternatively, might some sort of maturational factor be at work, which sets a limit on the maximum rate at which structural progress can take place, regardless of the sort of training that is provided? While the general question is quite clear, the answer is not. Or at least not within the framework of the model as elaborated so far.

2. A second fact that would be difficult for the model to explain is why development appears to stop at about the age of 18 years. Although certain kinds of development do continue to occur in some populations (Commons *et al.*, 1984), this development does not appear to be as universal as that which is observed prior to that time. Why is this so? Clearly, children's opportunities for problem solving, exploration, imitation, and mutual regulation do not cease at the age of 18 years. If anything, they expand. Is it just that universal experience ceases, with the termination of compulsory schooling? Or, alternatively, is the explanation that early development has a maturational component and that the

influence of this component tapers off as the organism reaches the age of biological maturity?

3. A third troublesome fact has to do with the changing rate of development during the years between birth and biological maturity. As is illustrated in Figure 13.1, children's intellectual development during this period decelerates at approximately the same rate as their physical development. What causes this deceleration? Is it that—as structures become more complex—it takes longer to integrate and consolidate them? Or alternatively, does children's rate of maturation play a similar role in intellectual development to the one which it plays in physical development?

4. A fourth troublesome fact has to do with the cross-task parallels in intellectual development. As Fischer (1980) has pointed out, any model that attempts to explain development in terms of specific hierarchical integrations must predict that assynchrony is the rule and not the exception in development. However, as was demonstrated in Chapter 11, quite the reverse is actually the case. Why is this so? Is it that children are exposed to the same number of opportunities for exploration, problem solving, imitation, and mutual regulation in all content domains? Is it that apparently separate domains actually share common component structures? Or, alternatively, does maturation set some sort of ceiling on the rate at which structural progress can take place—regardless of the number of learning opportunities to which a child is exposed?

5. The final troublesome fact is related to the first one, and has to do with the failure of instruction to produce stage transition in certain children. Almost any training study that has been conducted has reported a certain incidence of such failure. As an illustration, consider a series of studies which was conducted in our own laboratory, and which was designed to teach conservation of liquid quantity to children who used a unidimensional quantification structure. Three groups of children participated in the study: one whose mental age was $4\frac{1}{2}$ years, one whose mental age was 6 years, and one whose mental age was $7\frac{1}{2}$ years. In the first study children were exposed to a test–retest control (CONT), or feedback concerning the validity of their unidimensional judgments (TREAT 1). In the second study, they were exposed to a test–retest control, or to feedback plus cues designed to focus their attention on the dimension of beaker width as well as beaker-height (TREAT 2). In the third study, they were exposed to a test–retest control, or to feedback plus cue focusing plus verbal instructions designed to aid them in assembling a bidimensional quantification structure, and applying this structure to the conservation task (TREAT 3). In effect, therefore, the three treatments provided children with an increasing degree of facilitation for the tasks that hierarchical integration entails.

The results from these three studies are illustrated in Figure 13.2. As may be seen, the greater the degree of facilitation, the greater the success rate on the task. In and of itself, this is not particularly surprising. In fact, it is entirely con-

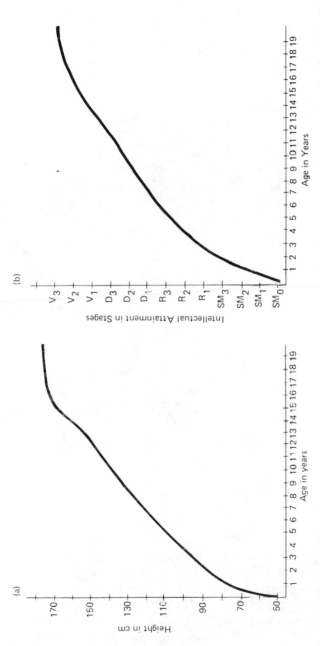

Fig. 13.1. Comparison of growth curves for (a) physical and (b) intellectual development. The physical growth curve is from Tanner (1970). Values of intellectual curve taken from estimates in present text for substages of Sensorimotor (SM) Relational (R), Dimensional (D), and Vectorial (V) periods.

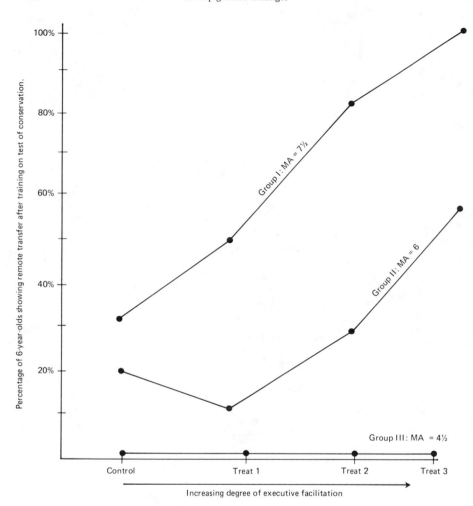

Fig. 13.2. Post-test results from series of conservation training studies (Case, 1977b).

sistent with the model as sketched out in the previous chapter. What is surprising, however, is the fact that the children with the mental age of $4\frac{1}{2}$ years showed
no progress under any of these conditions (Case, 1977b).

Because all three groups initially used the same control structure, one must ask
why one of the three groups failed to show any progress. Was it just that younger
children were slower learners, and needed a longer treatment period? Perhaps.
However, the treatment time was doubled for the lowest group, with no change
in the results. Was it that they were missing some key cognitive component,
which the training failed to diagnose? Again, this is a possibility. However, it is

by no means clear just what such a component might be. Finally, might it be that the children were already at some sort of maturational ceiling with regard to their understanding of liquid quantification, which even adult assistance could not enable them to overcome? Once again, the answer is not clear.

In summary, the problem with the hierarchical integration model is not that it can suggest no explanation whatsoever for the above five types of data. Rather, the problem is that certain of the explanations it suggests seem somewhat unlikely, while those which do seem likely fail to knit together in any coherent fashion, as the phenomena themselves appear to. In short, the problem is that the explanations which the model can suggest seem either implausible or unparsimonious. By contrast, the maturational hypothesis in each case appears both plausible *and* parsimonious.

To say that the maturational hypothesis is both plausible and parsimonious is not to say that it is correct. Nor is it to say that it has no deficiencies of its own. One major deficiency is that it is extremely vague with regard to mechanism. The hierarchical integration model specifies the changes that take place in a child's psychological system over time with reasonable precision. It also specifies how these changes are related to the child's general cognitive processes and to experience. By contrast, the maturational hypothesis, at least as formulated above, specifies very little. It fails to indicate (1) what type of change maturation produces or (2) how this change might affect a child's general cognitive processes. A related problem is that—with the single exception of cross-task generalities in development—the data that the hypothesis is designed to explain are all rather negative in nature. That is, they all have to do with the failure to find rapid learning. In order to test the adequacy of a hypothesis, it is normally necessary to predict what *will* happen, and how it will happen under certain circumstances, not just what will *not* happen. In the absence of either detailed specification or positive predictions, the maturational hypothesis appears to have the status of a *default option*. It appears to be a hypothesis one advances when all other forms of explanation have been exhausted, not one that can form the basis of a positive and progressive research program.

In the face of the preceding difficulties, it would appear that one could choose to follow one of two paths. One could remain within the framework of the hierarchical integration model as so far articulated, and try to explain the above sets of data in a more compelling and parsimonious fashion, without invoking any maturational construct. Alternatively, one could expand the hierarchical integration model to include a maturational construct, then try to explicate the construct in a precise fashion, and use it to generate predictions that are both positive and novel.

Given that so many of the phenomena of development do appear to point to the presence of some sort of maturational influence, and given that the maturational hypothesis has a certain a priori plausibility on purely biological grounds, the path we have chosen to follow in our own research group has been the latter one. And, in searching for a maturational construct to incorporate into the model, we have drawn heavily on the notion of attentional capacity as defined by Pascual-Leone.

As was pointed out in Chapter 4, certain of the data that have been gathered do not appear to support the model of attentional growth in the exact form which Pascual-Leone originally proposed it; the rate of growth does not always appear to be as it should, and growth sometimes appears to asymptote well before the age of physical maturity. As will be shown, however, many of these difficulties can be resolved by slight changes in the way in which the construct of attentional capacity is defined and explicated. And, once these changes are made, it becomes possible to develop a model that is capable of explaining each one of the types of data that are problematic for the hierarchical integration model.

DEFINITION OF TERMS

As was pointed out in Chapter 2, the first theorist to invoke the notion of attentional capacity was Baldwin. The label that Baldwin gave to his construct was *attention span*. In using this term, he did not mean to denote the sort of attention span one speaks of in everyday parlance, that is, the length of time for which a child can sustain attention to one activity. Rather, he meant to denote the maximum number of mental elements (ideas, or schemes) to which a child can pay attention *at any one time*. He assumed that this span was limited by various neurological factors, which he described with the phrase "degree of cortical coordination" (Baldwin, 1895). He also assumed (1) that this span changed with age, in response to biologically regulated changes in the cortex, and (2) that the rate of this change set a limit on the rate of a child's intellectual development.

The label that Pascual-Leone gave to his maturational construct was *mental power*, often abbreviated as *M-power*, or *M-space*. The core meaning of Pascual-Leone's construct remained the same as Baldwin's. A subject's mental power was defined as the maximum number of schemes he or she could activate mentally, at any one point in time (Pascual-Leone, 1970). The same core assumptions were also made about its role in intellectual development. It was seen as a factor that changed very gradually with age—in response either to biologically or to epigenetically regulated changes in the cortex—and which set an upper limit on the rate at which a child's intellectual development could take place.

As the change in terminology suggests, however, several new features were added to the meaning of Baldwin's construct, as a result of its incorporation into Pascual-Leone's system. The first of these was that mental activity was construed as a boosting process; that is, as a process of bringing schemes from a dormant to an active state, by the application of energy (hence the term power). The second was that cognitive or mental energy was distinguished from energy that stemmed from other sources, such as perceptual stimulation or affective arousal. Finally, the third was that each energy source was assumed to have its own quantitative limit. The limits in M-power were thus seen as being specific to *mental* boosting as opposed to boosting via perceptual stimulation or affective arousal. Under sufficiently intense perceptual or affective conditions, Pascual-Leone believed that the number of schemes a subject could activate would increase substantially, because the effects of perceptual and affective energy would be added to those produced by mental energy.

In the present volume, the term *executive processing space* is used to denote a construct that is similar to that designated by Baldwin and Pascual-Leone. The core meaning of the construct is the same. It refers to the maximum number of independent schemes a child can activate at any one time. However, the additional features that are associated with this meaning are somewhat different from those intended by either of these previous theorists. First, although it is acknowledged that schemes can be energized in a variety of different fashions, it is assumed that the maximum number of schemes which can be fully activated at any one moment is a property of the entire psychological system, not of any one energy source. An implication is that, under conditions of intense perceptual or affective activation, the total number of schemes that can be energized should remain constant and the number of schemes that can be activated mentally should decrease.[1] Second, a distinction is made between the mental activity of executing an ongoing operation, and the mental activity of retrieving the product of such an operation. Given that both activities are subject to the same total limitation, it follows that there must be a trade-off between them, and that maturation could exert an influence on either function, independently of whatever influence it exerts on the executive processing space that is available to the system as a whole.

Unfortunately, a full justification for these changes must await a later chapter, when developmental changes in attention span are considered. For the moment, all that can be done is to note that the differences exist, and to define the various terms that will be used in a fashion that will denote their present usage as clearly as possible. To this end, a subject's executive processing space is defined as the maximum number of independent schemes that a subject can keep in a state of full activation simultaneously, while working toward a goal about which some executive decision must be made. A subject's *operating space* is defined as that proportion of a subject's total executive processing space that is currently being devoted to the activation of new schemes. A subject's *short-term storage*

---

[1] For supportive evidence, see Link (1979).

space (STSS) is defined as that proportion of a subject's total executive processing space that is currently being devoted to the maintenance and/or retrieval of recently activated schemes. Finally, two additional terms are used, *momentary executive processing load* and *maximum executive processing load*. Momentary executive processing load (momentary EPL) is defined as the number of schemes a subject must activate in order to complete one particular step in an executive sequence. Maximum executive processing load is defined as the maximum value reached by the momentary EPL function, in the course of an entire executive sequence.

Note that the definitions of operating space and storage space do not imply two different capacities, each with their own limit. Rather, they imply one capacity that can be flexibly allocated to either of two functions. Note further that these definitions do not imply that scheme maintenance is carried out by some sort of passive mechanism, such as dumping schemes in a storage bin with a certain number of slots. Maintenance and re-accessing of schemes is seen as a highly active process, which has the same properties as the original activation and transformation of schemes, and which draws on the same resources.

With these definitions in mind, let us turn to a consideration of the demands which are placed on a subject's executive processing space, in the course of assembling and applying the various executive control structures that were described in Chapters 6 through 10.

THE MAXIMUM EPL OF STRUCTURES AT DIFFERENT STAGES

The Maximum EPL of Sensorimotor Control Structures

Substage 0: Operational Consolidation

Consider first the developmental tasks that children master during infancy, and the control structures on whose presence this mastery depends. In the preliminary substage of the period (1 to 4 months), children consolidate the basic sensorimotor control structures that are responsible for producing voluntary movement. As the reader will no doubt remember, these control structures include procedures for getting the hand from one position to another, and procedures for tracking moving objects with the eyes. The executive control structure for regulating visual tracking was represented in Chapter 4 as follows:

PROBLEM SITUATION   OBJECTIVE
- Interesting object disappears,   - Re-locate the moving object, in
  while moving downwards.   the center of one's visual field.

STRATEGY
1. Move eyes in downward direction
   until object comes into view.

What would the maximum executive processing load (EPL) of such a structure be? In order to answer this question, it is first necessary to specify the order in which each component of the structure would be activated. This is done graphically in Figure 13.3. As may be seen, the assumption is that infants first record the existence of an object moving slowly through their focal field of vision, in a downward direction. Next, as the object disappears from focal view, they record the existence of a blank field, or more accurately, a blank central field. Next they set up the goal of relocating the object, that is, of returning the object to the center of their field of vision. Finally, in order to accomplish this goal, they select and execute a particular motion with their eyes, perhaps using peripheral input as an access cue. Then, either as this motor operation is executed, or immediately afterwards, they note the new state of their perceptual field and decide whether or not their original goal has been attained.

The momentary EPL at each point in this operational sequence is shown in Table 13.1. As may be seen, this load builds up gradually, and reaches its maximum at the point when the infants note the correspondence or lack of correspondence between the current perceptual state, and the goal state they are trying to achieve. At this point, the load is equal to

$$OP_{motor} + OP_{comparison} + OP_{sensory} + S,$$

where OP_{motor} represents the space required for executing the ongoing motor movement,

$OP_{comparison}$ represents the space required for making a mental comparison between a current perceptual state and a desired perceptual state,

$OP_{sensory}$ represents the space required for registering the current perceptual state,

and S represents the space required for storing some record of the desired perceptual state

If one assumes that the comparison operation does not take place in perfect parallel with the ongoing perceptual and motor activity, but rather in the intervals that exist between motor and perceptual operations, this expression may be rewritten more simply as $OP_{comparison} + 3S$. The specific schemes in the subject's

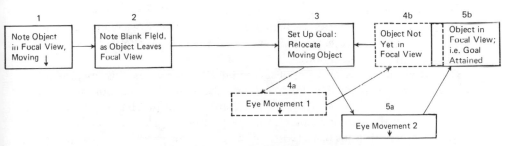

Fig. 13.3. Perceptual and cognitive steps in tracking slowly moving objects.

TABLE 13.1

Executive Processing Load (EPL) for Tracking Slowly Moving Object

Step	Operation	Schemes in executive processing space (EPS)	Momentary EPL
0	Note object in focal view, moving downward.	(i) Sensory scheme recording movement.	$OP_{sensory}$
1	Note blank field as object leaves focal view.	(i) Sensory scheme recording blank field. (ii) Stored sensory scheme, recording previous view.	$OP_{sensory} + S$
2	Set up previous sensory state as goal.	(i) Mental operation tagging previous scheme as goal. (ii) Sensory scheme recording blank field. (iii) Stored sensory scheme, recording previous view.	$OP_{goal\ set} + OP_{sensory} + S$
2a	Move eye downward.	(i) Motor scheme directing eye movement. (ii) Sensory scheme recording (changing) perceptual field. (iii) Stored sensory scheme recording goal.	$OP_{motor} + OP_{sensory} + S$
2b	Compare current view to desired view: note that object is not yet in center of field.	(i) Motor scheme directing ongoing eye movement. (ii) Mental operation comparing current view to desired view. (iii) Sensory scheme recording current view. (iv) Sensory scheme storing desired view.	$OP_{motor} + OP_{comparison}$ $+ OP_{sensory} + S$
3	Move eye downward.	As in 2a.	As in 2a.
4	Compare current view to desired view: note that goal has been attained.	As in 2b.	As in 2b.

executive processing space remain the same. It is just that two of the schemes (i.e., the motor and perceptual schemes) are presumed to be in a temporary state of storage. As a consequence, they are denoted by the symbol S (for storage), rather than OP (for operation).

Although the above estimate of maximum EPL is a reasonable one, for the balance of the chapter this estimate will be rescaled and labelled more simply as $OP_{sensorimotor}$. The reason for this rescaling is the same as in Chapters 6–10. The major focus of the present chapter is not on the processing load entailed by basic sensorimotor operations of this sort; rather, it is on the processing load entailed by the more complex structures of which such operations constitute components. For this purpose, it is convenient to have a single symbol to denote the maximum EPL which such an operation entails, while recognizing that the single symbol may denote an activity which is itself quite complex.

Substage 1: Operational Coordination (4–8 Months)

As the reader may remember, the first type of structure which emerges during the substage of operational coordination is the secondary circular reaction. In this reaction, one sensorimotor scheme is set up as a goal, and another sensorimotor scheme is used as a means towards achieving it. One structure used as an illustration in Chapter 7 was the structure for setting a mobile in motion with the hand, which may be modelled as follows:

PROBLEM SITUATION   OBJECTIVES
- Mobile at Y   ⟶ • Move mobile
- Hand at X   • Move hand to mobile

STRATEGY
1. Move arm from X to Y.
2a. Strike or touch mobile with hand.
2b. Monitor reaction of mobile.

If one is to determine the maximum EPL of assembling such a structure—as opposed merely to executing it—one must first consider the various ways in which the structure might be assembled. Consider, therefore, the requirements which would be entailed if the structure were assembled in the course of exploration.

Figure 13.4 illustrates a series of exploratory acts that infants might go through in the course of their everyday interaction with the world, which would lead them to assemble such a structure. As may be seen, the infants first reach out to touch the mobile, not with the intention of moving it, but simply with the intention of feeling the sensation which the mobile will generate in their finger. In doing so, the infants go through a series of operations that are formally identical to those for tracking the movement of an object, but which involve a different set of specific figurative and operative schemes. As soon as the infants succeed in touching the mobile, their visual field immediately changes. Now they are faced with a small, brightly coloured object, which moves through their field in an interesting fashion. As this object starts to disappear from their field of view in some particular direction, they quite naturally set themselves the goal of relocating it, and go through the second sequence of steps indicated in the figure. Finally, as the mobile gradually stops, the infants find themselves back in the

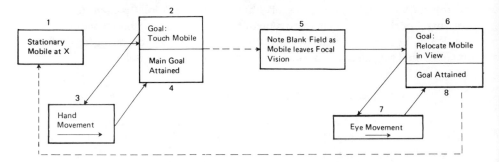

Fig. 13.4. Steps in discovering the connection between arm movement and mobile movement via exploration.

original situation. Assuming that nothing of greater interest has entered their visual field in the interim, they re-enter the first loop at step 2, and repeat the entire sequence.

If one actually observes 4-month-old infants as they explore a novel object which is moveable, one finds that they become totally absorbed by their manual and visual activity. It is not at all unusual to see them go through an exploratory sequence such as that which has been described some six or seven times in a row. As they do so, they may become more and more excited. In fact, some infants become so excited that their motor performance decays, and they begin to cry in frustration (White, 1975). Before they reach this point, however, a very interesting change takes place. This is that they begin to reach back to the mobile before it has fully stopped moving, and do so with greater force than on the first trial. What these two changes appear to imply is that the infants have discovered the connection between the two schemes (Watson, 1966). No longer are they returning to the first scheme because there is nothing else to do. Rather, they are returning to it because they want to produce the movement which they observed on the first trial. Given that this is what takes place internally, one would expect that the first structure would be retagged as one whose application could lead to the application of the second structure, and that the practice trials would rapidly consolidate the appropriate superordinate structure. In order to determine the maximum EPL for assembling such an executive structure via exploration, then, one need only determine the EPL which this initial discovery or connection entails.

What exactly is this EPL? As is shown in Table 13.2, the only real requirement for discovering the connection between the application of one scheme and another is that some trace of the first scheme's activation still be present while the second scheme is being applied. Whether this is a trace of the operation executed or the terminal state produced does not much matter, since the scheme already exists in the child's repertoire as a coherent whole, with each of the com-

TABLE 13.2

Executive Processing Load (EPL) for Discovering Arm-Movement–Mobile-Movement Connection via Exploration

Steps	Operation	Schemes in executive processing space	Momentary EPL
1–4	Reach out arm to mobile.	(i) Sensorimotor scheme for touching.	$OP_{sensorimotor}$
5–8	Track mobile.	(i) Sensorimotor scheme for tracking. (ii) Stored sensorimotor scheme for touching.	$OP_{sensorimotor} + S$

ponents linked to each other component. Accordingly, the maximum EPL should be $OP_{sensorimotor} + S$, where $OP_{sensorimotor}$ stands for the EPL required for executing the tracking scheme, and S stands for the space required for storing some trace of the activation of the arm-movement scheme whose activation precedes it.

Although exploration is the most likely process by which an infant would acquire a secondary circular response of the sort indicated, it is by no means the only one possible. Another possibility is that the structure might be acquired via imitation.

Suppose that a baby girl had an older brother who came over to her crib and became interested in the mobile which was hanging there. Suppose further that he struck it several times, and observed the consequences. The movement of the mobile would very probably elicit a tracking response in the infant, of the sort illustrated in Figures 13.3 and 13.4. While this would not necessarily lead to the assembly of the new executive structure, it could well do so, providing the following conditions were met: (1) The infant would have to watch her sibling at the moment when he struck the mobile, (2) The infant would have to have a scheme in her repertoire which permitted her to "encode" this action, that is, to differentiate it from other actions, (3) The infant would have to have a corresponding action scheme in her own repertoire, a "pointer" to which was activated during the encoding act. (4) The infant would have to be close enough to the mobile so that she could "try out" the effect of this scheme for herself.

If all of these conditions were met, there is a chance that the infant might imitate her brother, once he stopped playing with the mobile and wandered off elsewhere. As a consequence, the infant might acquire the mobile-hitting response without having to engage in much exploratory activity of her own. While this might decrease the time it would take the infant to acquire the reaction in comparison with exploration, it is important to realize it would not eliminate one very important requirement. In order to assemble the appropriate structure, the infant would still have to make the psychological connection between the two schemes of which it was comprised. This connection is not one that a sibling could make for her. All the sibling could do would be to increase the probability that the infant would make it, by increasing the probability that she would activate the appropriate schemes, in the appropriate sequence. Thus, the EPL for assembling the structure via imitation, would not be different from the EPL for assembling the structure via exploration. It would remain at $OP_{sensorimotor}$ (the space required for tracking the moving mobile) + S (the space required for storing a pointer to the immediately prior activity, namely, hitting).

The same point can be made with regard to *mutual regulation*. Because the secondary circular reaction under consideration is not a social one, it is unlikely that it would be acquired in the course of any kind of mutual regulation other than direct instruction. However, it could conceivably be acquired in this fashion. Suppose, for example, that a mother had just provided her child with a mobile toy. Suppose further that she wanted the pleasure of seeing the child use it, and that she knew (albeit intuitively) that it had the prerequisite capabilities for doing so. Under these conditions, the mother might well set about to teach her child how the new mobile worked. For example, she might first insure that she had her infant's attention by eliminating all potentially distracting stimuli and waiting until its gaze was focused on her face. She might then raise her hand in front of her face, and monitor the infant's gaze until it fell on her hand. She might then strike the mobile, accentuating the movement which was involved, and performing it in a slow enough fashion that the child could track it easily. As the mobile began to move, she might make an interesting noise to highlight the event of interest and to increase the probability that the infant would take an interest in producing the movement itself. Finally, when the child did initiate a movement, she might re-position the mobile slightly, so that whatever action the child generated would be more likely to yield success.

The above sort of instruction might conceivably enable infants to acquire the relevant control structure more quickly than they would via exploration or simple imitation. However, the increased speed of learning would once again come about as a result of an increased probability that they would activate the appropriate schemes in the appropriate order themselves. It would not come about by eliminating of the requirement for them to connect these schemes on their own, once they had done so. Consequently, the EPL for the assembly process would remain the same, namely $OP_{sensorimotor}$ (the space required for tracking the mobile) + S (the space required for storing a pointer to the prior motor movement).

Of the various possible processes by which a child might acquire a secondary circular reaction of this sort, those already considered are the ones which would be most likely to occur in most environments. Nevertheless, under certain circumstances, such a structure might also be acquired via problem solving. I once observed my son Jonathan in such a situation. He was about 4 months of age at the time, and had already acquired one or two secondary circular reactions for making objects move. One afternoon, as I was putting him down in his crib, I added a long piece of cardboard to the mobile that normally hung over his crib, so that the end of the cardboard hung down to within an inch of his waist. His reaction when I did so was very interesting. He looked at the cardboard with excitement, and thrust his arms out towards it as though trying to move it. Unfortunately, the piece of cardboard lay just beyond the reach of his hands. However, he kept swinging at it and bicycling with his legs as he did. Eventually, he happened to kick one of his legs high enough that it struck the cardboard and the mobile began to move. At that point he uttered a squeal of delight, and increased the energy of his kicking until he was striking the mobile on about every second try.

Whether or not Jonathan actually intended to move the mobile from the start can of course not be proven. All one can say is that his action did appear to have an intentional quality. The important point, however, is that as long as an infant could formulate this sort of goal (i.e., to move something) but was not quite sure how to achieve it, then it is possible that he might acquire new circular responses via problem solving. He might try a varied sequence of operations, until he finally succeeded in producing the event in which he was interested. And he might then repeat the operation that was successful. This being the case, the maximum EPL of acquiring a structure via problem solving must also be examined.

Figure 13.5 presents an account of the mental acts through which an infant

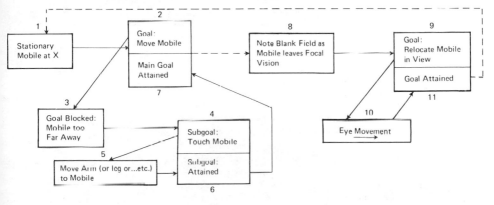

Fig. 13.5. Steps in discovering the connection between arm movement and mobile movement via problem solving.

would have to pass in order to succeed in such a problem solving process. As may be seen, the various operations are formally identical to those involved in exploration. The only real difference lies in the intentionality with which they are executed. In exploration, one acts on an object in a particular way "because it is there". One then notices the result which is produced, and infers that one's own action produced it. By contrast, in problem solving, one sets about to produce a particular result, and tries a number of possible actions. Having finally succeeded, one then infers that the most recent action was the one which was responsible for the success.

The momentary EPL at each step in the problem-solving process is presented in Table 13.3. As may be seen, the EPL reaches its maximum at a slightly earlier point in time than it does in the course of exploration, namely at the point when the child first reaches out toward the mobile in order to make it move. However, the maximum EPL remains the same in absolute magnitude, $OP_{sensorimotor} + S$. The reason for this is that in exploration one must execute a particular operation (OP_x) while one stores a pointer to a previous operation (S). In problem solving, one must execute a particular operation (OP_x), while one stores a pointer to an *intended* operation (S). The total number of schemes that must be dealt with in each case thus remains the same, as does the maximum EPL for doing so ($OP_x + S$).

This point is important. As we have already seen, the maximum EPL for acquiring a structure via exploration, imitation, and mutual regulation is identical. Now it has been suggested that the EPL for acquiring a structure via problem solving is also identical, or at least very nearly so. The conclusion that follows is

TABLE 13.3

Executive Processing Load (EPL) for Discovering Arm-Movement–Mobile-Movement
Connection via Problem Solving

Steps	Operation	Schemes in executive processing space	Momentary EPL
1–2	Set moving mobile as goal.	(i) Goal representing sensory image of movement.	S
3–7	Reach out arm (or leg) to mobile.	(i) Sensorimotor scheme for reaching (or kicking, etc.). (ii) Stored sensory scheme representing goal of movement.	$OP_{sensorimotor} + S$
9–12	Track mobile.	(i) Sensorimotor scheme for tracking movement. (ii) Stored scheme representing previous movement (kick).	$OP_{sensorimotor} + S$

that one does not really need to consider all possible processes by which a particular structure might be acquired after all, in order to determine the maximum EPL it would entail. At least at this level, one can simply select a process that has a reasonable degree of ecological probability, and model the operations it entails.

Substage 2: Bifocal Coordination (8–12 Months)

During the second substage of the sensorimotor period, infants coordinate two pairs of nested sensorimotor executives into a superordinate structure of greater complexity still. Because each of these nested executive structures has its own external focus, children's operative activity for the first time becomes bifocal rather than unifocal. One example of a bifocal structure that was presented in Chapters 5 and 7 was the one for removing a barrier. Here the two foci were the barrier and the toy behind it, and the executive control structure was as follows:

PROBLEM SITUATION	OBJECTIVES
• Stationary toy at Y.	• Produce movement in toy.
• Barrier blocks access.	• Produce movement of barrier.
• Barrier at Z.	• Move hand to Z.

STRATEGY

1. Move arm in direction Y.
2. Push object at Y with hand, until it moves.
3a. Check availability of object at X. If available, go to 2a, otherwise, return to step 1b.
3b. Move hand toward object at X.
4. When hand touches toy at X, pick it up and begin to play with it.

Of the various possible ways in which infants might acquire such a structure, the most likely would be via problem solving. In the course of their everyday interaction with the world, it would be quite likely that their access to an interesting toy would be blocked by some other object, and that they would have to set themselves the goal of removing this obstacle before they could play with the toy in which they were interested. The steps that would be entailed by this process are shown in Figure 13.6. The EPL at each step is listed in Table 13.4. As may be seen, the maximum EPL comes at the point when the infants first move their arm toward the barrier, with the intention of pushing it to the side. At this point

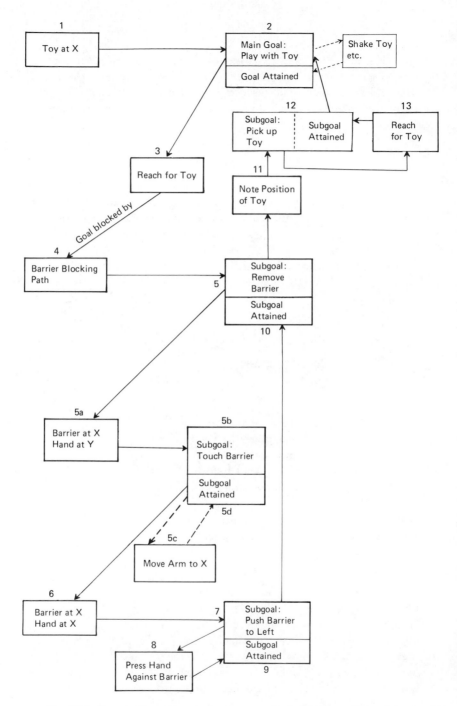

Fig. 13.6. Steps in discovering the barrier-removal principle via problem solving.

TABLE 13.4

Executive Processing Load (EPL) for Assembling the Barrier-Removal Executive via Problem Solving

Steps	Operation	Schemes in executive processing space	Momentary EPL
1	Note toy at X.	(i) Sensory scheme representing presence of toy.	$OP_{sensory}$
2a	Activate scheme representing toy play.	(i) Scheme representing stored image of toy play. (ii) Sensory scheme representing presence of toy.	$OP_{sensory} + S$
2	Set toy play as goal.	(i) Operation tagging play as goal. (ii) Scheme representing stored image of play. (iii) Sensory scheme representing presence of toy.	$OP_{goal\ set} +$ $OP_{sensory} + S$
3	Activate reaching scheme.	(i) Sensorimotor scheme representing subgoal of reaching for toy. (ii) Scheme representing main goal of playing with toy.	$OP_{sensorimotor} + S$
4	Note barrier blocking reach.	(i) Sensory scheme representing barrier. (ii) Scheme representing stored main goal (play).	$OP_{sensory} + S$
5	Activate scheme representing barrier removal and tag as subgoal.	(i) Operation setting barrier removal as goal. (ii) Scheme representing barrier removal. (iii) Main goal (play with object).	$OP_{goal\ set} + 2S$
5a–5e	Activate first sensorimotor scheme in attempt to remove barrier.	(i) Sensorimotor scheme representing subgoal + reaching and touching barrier. (ii) Scheme representing subgoal of barrier removal. (iii) Scheme representing main goal (play with toy).	$OP_{sensorimotor} + 2S$
6–9	Remove barrier.	(i) Sensorimotor scheme representing position of barrier, subgoal of lateral movement + lateral motor movement. (ii) Scheme representing subgoal of barrier removal. (iii) Scheme representing main goal (play with toy).	$OP_{sensorimotor} + 2S$

(Continued)

TABLE 13.4 (*Continued*)

Steps	Operation	Schemes in executive processing space	Momentary EPL
10	Note removal of barrier.	(i) Sensory scheme representing movement of barrier. (ii) Scheme representing main goal (play with toy).	$OP_{sensory} + S$
11	Activate sensori-motor scheme for picking up toy.	(i) Sensorimotor scheme controlling reach. (ii) Scheme representing main goal (play with toy).	$OP_{sensorimotor} + S$
12	Play with toy.		

the EPL is $OP_{sensorimotor} + 2S$, where $OP_{sensorimotor}$ represents the space required for the directed manual movement, S_1 represents the intention of monitoring the movement of the barrier until some sideways displacement has been produced, and S_2 represents the intention of switching the focus of attention back to the toy, once this first goal has been achieved.

An important assumption which underlies the analysis in Table 13.4 is that infants can deal with the intention of playing with a toy as one chunk, while they are trying to remove a barrier. That is, the assumption is that they do not need to store a pointer both to the action they intend to execute on the toy, and the effect they intend to produce. Any scheme that represents the toy will function as a pointer, and permit a regeneration of the whole structure, once the barrier is removed. It is for this reason that the maximum EPL goes up by only one unit as the infant progresses from substage to substage, rather than doubling. It is also for this reason that the number of objectives in the goal stack increases arithmetically as one goes from one substage to the next, rather than increasing geometrically.

If the goal of playing with the toy can be stored as one chunk, the question might be raised as to why the act of removing the barrier cannot also be dealt with as one chunk as well. Were this the case, then the EPL of the barrier removal task would be the same as that of the secondary circular reaction, $OP_{sensorimotor} + S$. The reason that the barrier removal cannot be dealt with as one chunk, and the reason that the maximum EPL of the task must be at least $OP_{sensorimotor} + 2S$ is that the act of removing a barrier requires the temporary storage of a parameter which would be unlikely to be known in advance, and which would therefore be unlikely to be prepackaged. This parameter is the specific purpose of hitting or pulling the barrier on this specific trial. Note that this purpose is not simply to observe what happens, as it might be in many secondary circular responses. Nor is it simply to produce movement. It is to produce a lateral movement which will free up access to the goal object. It is the set-ting of this objective which initiates the motor movement in the first place. Hence, a scheme representing this purpose must be active when the first motor movement is initiated. Moreover, it is the attainment of this objective which serves as the cue for switching the focus back to the desired toy. Hence, the scheme must remain active while the movement is being executed. The only condition under which the maximum EPL would not be $OP_{sensorimotor} + 2S$ would be if the child's environment had been carefully arranged so that he had a good deal of prior experience in moving objects just like the barrier, in just the way which was necessary for them to free up access to something behind them. While this is certainly possible, it is likely to be characteristic of the sort of carefully arranged environment children encounter in formal school curricula, not the sort of environment they encounter in the course of their normal ex-ploration, or in the course of the informal instruction that is provided by their parents.

Nevertheless, the above analysis does suggest an important caveat. Although the maximum EPL of all processes is equivalent at the second substage, begin-ning at the third substage the possibility of EPL reduction via direct and sus-tained instruction does exist.

Substage 3: Elaborated Coordination (12–18 Months)

During the final substage of the sensorimotor period, children become capable of effecting some additional elaboration to the structure of Substage 2. An ex-ample that was presented in Chapter 5 was for the napkin and keys task, which was represented as follows:

PROBLEM SITUATION   OBJECTIVES

- Interesting object (e.g., keys) at Y. ⟶ • Play with object.
- Object just out of reach.   • Bring object within reach.
- Object on napkin, which is   • Move napkin.
  within reach.
- Napkin at Z.   • Move hand to Z.

STRATEGY

1. Move arm from X to Z.
2. Pull object at Z.
3. Monitor new position of keys. If
   not within reach, repeat
   2 + 3 with more vigor. If
   within reach go to 4.
4. Repeat 1 + 2 for keys, instead
   of napkin.

Once again, the most likely way in which infants would assemble such a structure would be via problem solving. At some point, they would be likely to be confronted with a toy that was just beyond their grasp. After trying unsuccessfully to stretch out their hands and reach it, they would sit back and look for some other way to bring the object within reach. At that point, their eyes would fall on the napkin, and they would set themselves the goal of moving it toward them. Because this goal would be attainable by simply reaching out and pulling, they would embark on it directly. The steps that would be involved in encoding and solving the problem in this fashion are similar to those for the barrier removal problem, with the exception that the children would have to notice an additional feature in the problem (the keys on the napkin), set themselves an extra subgoal (moving the toy), and keep this subgoal active while they reached out to the napkin. The EPL at this point would therefore be one unit higher, namely $OP_{sensorimotor} + 3S$.

This completes my analysis of the maximum EPL which Piaget's mean-ends control structures entail. Although the models that I have presented have been quite detailed, the details will hopefully not have obscured the following general points.

1. The first is that, at each successive stage of development, the maximum EPL of the infant's control structures increases by one unit. The values which were suggested were $OP_{sensorimotor}$ for primary circular reactions, $OP_{sensorimotor} + S$ for secondary circular reactions, $OP_{sensorimotor} + 2S$ for bifocal reactions, and $OP_{sensorimotor} + 3S$ for elaborated bifocal reactions.

2. The second general point is that the maximum EPL for these various structures is relatively independent of the process by which they are acquired. Regardless of whether a given structure is assembled by exploration, problem solving, imitation, or short-term instruction, the maximum EPL that it entails remains the same. The only possible exception to this rule is for structures which are assembled in the course of some carefully planned sequence of instruction. Even then, the exception emerges only at Substage 2 and 3.

3. The third general point is that there is a direct relationship between the number of entries in an executive structure's list of objectives, and the maximum EPL which the structure entails. This point may be less obvious than the first two. However, it is equally important. Primary circular reactions such as visual tracking have one entry in their objective list, for example, relocating an object. Their maximum EPL is $OP_{sensorimotor}$. Secondary circular reactions have two entries in their objective list: e.g., moving the hand to a given location, and visually monitoring the result. Their maximum EPL is $OP_{sensorimotor} + S$. Bifocal reactions have three entries in their objective lists (e.g., moving the hand to a location, monitoring the result, and then refocusing on a second object). Their maximum EPL is $OP_{sensorimotor} + 2S$. Finally, elaborated bifocal structures have

four entries in their objective list. Their maximum EPL is $OP_{sensorimotor}$ + 3S. In each case, then, the maximum EPL is equal to the operating space required to reach the lowest-level entry in the objective list, plus one unit of storage space for each of the higher-order entries. Stated in symbolic form, the maximum EPL is equal to OP_x + $(n-1)$ S, where x equals the level of operation entailed by the structure (in this case, sensorimotor), and where n equals the total number of entries in the objective list.

Once the generality of the preceding formula is appreciated, it becomes unnecessary to work out a separate analysis to determine the maximum EPL of each separate sensorimotor structure that was described in the chapter on infancy. One can simply count the number of entries in the objective list of each structure, note the type of operation entailed, and use the above formula as a guide to computing the maximum EPL. As the reader may remember, all the sensorimotor structures that were described at any substage had the same number of entries in their objective list as those that were used as illustrations above. They also entailed the same basic type of operation. It can therefore be asserted that they also have the same maximum EPL, and that the values derived above apply to any of the other structures at each sensorimotor substage as well. In short, it can be asserted as a general rule that the maximum EPL associated with each sensorimotor structures is as follows:

Substage	Label	Age of acquisition (months)	Maximum EPL
0	Operational consolidation	1–4	$OP_{sensorimotor}$
1	Operational coordination	4–8	$OP_{sensorimotor}$ + S
2	Bifocal coordination	8–12	$OP_{sensorimotor}$ + 2S
3	Elaborated coordination	12–18	$OP_{sensorimotor}$ + 3S

The Maximum EPL of Relational Control Structures

Because the structural progression that takes place during the relational stage is formally identical to that which takes place during the sensorimotor stage, one might expect that the maximum EPL that is entailed by the structures at each substage would be formally identical as well. In fact, this is the case. If one rescales the maximum EPL of elaborated sensorimotor control structures as $OP_{relational}$ instead of $OP_{sensorimotor}$ + 3S, one can show that the maximum EPL's of the control structures that are observed during the relational stage are as follows:

Substage	Label	Age of acquisition (years)	Maximum EPL
0	Operational consolidation	$1-1\frac{1}{2}$	$OP_{relational}$
1	Operational coordination	$1\frac{1}{2}-2$	$OP_{relational} + S$
2	Bifocal coordination	$2-3\frac{1}{2}$	$OP_{relational} + 2S$
3	Elaborated coordination	$3\frac{1}{2}-5$	$OP_{relational} + 3S$

One can also show that the preceding values are independent of the process by which the structures in question are assembled.[2]

The Maximum EPL of Dimensional and Vectorial Structures

The same sort of analysis may also be applied to the structures that emerge during the dimensional and the vectorial stages. The demand that is inherent in operations such as weight or number extraction may be rescaled from $OP_{relational} + 3S$ to $OP_{dimensional}$. When this is done, the values of EPL that are associated with each substage may be shown to be as follows:[3]

Substage	Label	Age of acquisition (years)	Maximum EPL
0	Operational consolidation	$3\frac{1}{2}-5$	$OP_{dimensional}$
1	Operational coordination	5–7	$OP_{dimensional} + S$
2	Bifocal coordination	7–9	$OP_{dimensional} + 2S$
3	Elaborated coordination	9–11	$OP_{dimensional} + 3S$

Similar analyses for the vectorial period lead to the conclusion that the following values are appropriate for that stage:

Substage	Label	Age of acquisition (years)	Maximum EPL
0	Operational consolidation	9–10	$OP_{vectorial}$
1	Operational coordination	11–12	$OP_{vectorial} + S$
2	Bifocal coordination	13–14	$OP_{vectorial} + 2S$
3	Elaborated coordination	15–18	$OP_{vectorial} + 3S$

[2]The set of analyses that support these assertions are available on request.
[3]Again, the analyses to support these conclusions are available on request.

THE THEORETICAL PROBLEMS REVISITED

At the beginning of the chapter, it was suggested that—if the maturation hypothesis is to be treated as more than a default option—it will be necessary to specify (1) what aspect of the psychological system is subject to maturational influence, and (2) how this aspect sets an upper bound on the executive control structures that children can assemble at any given stage of development. With the foregoing analysis as a guide, it is now possible to attempt such a specification. The answers that the analyses suggest are (1) that the aspect of children's system which is subject to maturational influence is their short-term storage space, and (2) that the size of this space sets a limit on the new executive control structures children can assemble, by limiting the complexity of the patterns they can detect in the course of applying their existing executive structures. These hypotheses may be put in a more explicit and testable form. (1) For most children, short-term storage space grows at the rate indicated by the EPL analyses, in response to very general maturational influences. (2) Until children acquire a short-term storage space of the size which is appropriate for any substage, they will not be able to assemble the structures of that substage without a great deal of instructional assistance, because they will not be able to focus on, and to interrelate, the subordinate structures.

Finally, with these two suggestions as a guide, it becomes possible to suggest an explanation for each of the five sets of data that were listed as problematic at the beginning of the chapter.

1. The first datum was that the process of spontaneous intellectual development takes a good deal longer to complete than one might expect if hierarchical integration were the only process at work. The explanation for this datum is quite simple. Hierarchical integration is not the only process at work. Development also depends on the growth of short-term storage space. This growth takes place at a very slow rate, since it is produced by slowly occurring maturational changes in the psychological system as a whole.

2. The second troublesome piece of data was that domain-independent development appears to stop at about 15 to 18 years of age. The explanation for this datum is equally simple. The growth of short-term space also stops at this age because it is under the control of maturational influences, and because this is the age of biological maturity. Further intellectual development may still occur. However, it will occur only as a result of domain-specific reorganizations in the subjects' existing repertoire of structures, not as a result of a domain-independent increase in the amount of short-term storage space which they have available for coordinating these structures.

3. The third troublesome piece of data was that intellectual development appears to decelerate between the ages of 1 month and 18 years, at approximately the same rate as physical development. Once again, the explanation for this

datum is simple. Because the growth of short-term storage space is under the control of the same sort of maturational factors as is physical development, it naturally follows a similar growth curve.

4. The fourth troublesome piece of data was that intellectual development takes place at approximately the same rate across a broad range of content domains. The explanation here is that children's ability to detect a corelational pattern in their existing executive structures is limited by the same parameter in any domain, regardless of the process by which the pattern is detected. Other things being equal, therefore, they will reach the same ceiling level of performance in each domain at approximately the same time.

5. The final troublesome piece of data was that children can be extremely resistant to instruction on developmental tasks, even though they may have all the prerequisite component structures in their repertoire. The explanation for this datum is that the integration of component structures—even in an instructional setting—is still dependent on the child's short-term storage space (STSS). It is just that the absolute size of STSS that is required may be reduced, if some sort of chunking or reorganization of the child's existing structures can be effected. In fact, the performance of the lowest developmental group in Figure 13.2 (i.e., their failure to profit from instruction) was actually predicted by analyzing the maximum EPL of the instructional sequence, and by measuring the STSS that the different groups had available (Case, 1977b).

To say that the STSS hypothesis flows directly from the set of executive models that were presented in previous chapters, together with the specific analysis of these models which was presented in the present one, is not to say that it is correct. The details of any one of the specific analyses might be in error, as might be the models on which they were based. To say that the STSS hypothesis suggests a simple and parsimonious explanation for five problematic pieces of data is also not to say that it is correct. A different theoretical model might be able to suggest an equally parsimonious set of explanations that would be quite different. On the other hand, to say that the hypothesis meets these requirements is to say that it must at least be taken seriously. When a hypothesis attains this status—that is, when it is consistent with a more general theory, and appears capable of explaining a variety of otherwise anomalous data—the normal procedure is to subject it to empirical investigation, and to see if the new body of data that emerges provides it with any further support.

In the next two chapters, two sets of studies are reported that were designed to accomplish this objective.

CHAPTER 14

Short-Term Storage Space and Its Development

Of the various propositions that were advanced in the previous chapter, two of the most basic were (1) that children's short-term storage space (STSS) increases during each stage, and (2) that the values of STSS at Substages 1, 2, and 3 are S_x, $2S_x$, and $3S_x$ (where x refers to the level of operation that is characteristic of the stage in question, and S refers to the space required to store a pointer to such an operation). In the present chapter, a number of studies are reported which were designed to test these two propositions. Before the studies are presented, however, a word must be said about the conceptual requirements which any psychological test must meet, in order to be considered a valid indicator of a subject's STSS.

Within the context of the present theory, a test must meet the following four requirements if it is to qualify as an STSS measure.

1. It must require the subject to execute a series of formally identical operations (OP1, OP2, OP3, etc.).
2. It must permit the developmental level of these operations to be clearly specified (sensorimotor, relational, dimensional, etc.).
3. It must require that a pointer to each prior operation be stored, while each subsequent operation is executed, thus producing an increasing executive processing load at each step (i.e., Step 1: EPL = OP_x, Step 2: EPL = OP_x + S, Step 3: EPL = OP_x + 2S, etc.).
4. It must permit the experimenter to determine the number of such steps which subjects can execute—and hence the number of pointers they can store—before their executive processing space becomes overloaded.

If a test meets the requirements, it may be said to possess the basic conceptual structure of an STSS measure. Both OP_x and k may be estimated, where OP_x represents the type of operation in question, and k represents the maximum number of pointers to such operations which can be stored. Note that the difference between a test of STSS and other developmental tests is a simple one: higher-level items differ from lower-level items only in the quantitative load that they place on the subject's system. There is no concomitant demand for a more complex problem representation, goal stack, or strategy.

Although the conceptual structure of an STSS measure is quite simple, in practice such measures are rather difficult to design. This is because a number of stringent technical requirements must also be met, in order to insure that the estimates of STSS generated by the measure are not confounded by other factors. The following technical requirements are particularly important.

1. The test must engage subjects' motivation sufficiently that they actually do execute the required operations, and attempt to store the products. Otherwise, the test will underestimate the true size of their STSS.
2. The test must provide sufficient pretraining that both the general objective of the test and the required operations are thoroughly familiar. Otherwise subjects will have to devote extra processing space to dealing with these unfamiliar aspects of the situation, and once again the test will underestimate their true STSS.
3. The test must preclude the possibility of solution by means of some mnemonic or space-saving device (e.g., the use of one's fingers to remember numbers). Otherwise, the test will overestimate the size of subjects' STSS.
4. Finally, the test must preclude the possibility of chunking, that is, of storing several operational products as one unit. If subjects are able to chunk several operational products as one unit, then the test will once again overestimate the true size of their STSS.

The above technical requirements are easier to state in theory than they are to realize in practice. Nevertheless, we have made at least some progress in developing measures which meet them, for each of the four major stages of development.

THE GROWTH OF SHORT-TERM STORAGE SPACE (STSS) DURING INFANCY[1]

The basic structure of our infant STSS measure is a simple one. The infant is seated in front of the apparatus that is indicated in Figure 14.1. The experimenter then reaches out and demonstrates how the apparatus works. Start-

[1]The work reported in this section was conducted in collaboration with Debra Sandlos. Valuable assistance was also provided by Mari Peterson.

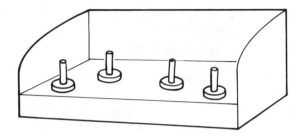

Fig. 14.1. Apparatus for assessing sensorimotor STSS.

ing with the peg on the left, the experimenter pulls each one of the pegs in sequence. As each peg is pulled, a chime sounds, so that the infant's attention is secured. After each of the pegs has been pulled, the experimenter re-sets the apparatus, and invites the infant to follow.

Following the analysis that was outlined in the previous chapter, it may be assumed that the EPL required to monitor the experimenter's demonstration and to imitate it should be $OP_{sensorimotor} + S$ for each one of the pegs. Because the pegs are set far enough apart so that no two pegs can be viewed at the same time, it may further be assumed that the intention to deal with some other peg, while the infant is actually focusing on the first peg, entails a further storage requirement: namely the requirement for storing a pointer to that peg's existence. Accordingly, it may be assumed that the EPL for imitating the entire sequence of operations is a direct function of the number of pegs in the sequence. In order to ring one bell, the infant needs an executive processing space of $OP_{sensorimotor} + S$. In order to ring two bells, the infant needs a space of $OP_{sensorimotor} + 2S$. In order to ring three bells, a space of $OP_{sensorimotor} + 3S$ is needed, and so on.

On the basis of the preceding analysis, it may be concluded that the bell-ringing game meets all four of the conceptual requirements for a test of STSS. First, infants are required to execute a set of formally identical operations. Second, the developmental level of these operations may be specified ($OP_{sensorimotor} + S$). Third, some pointer to each operation must be stored, while each other operation is executed. Fourth, the experimenter can determine how many of these pointers children can store, by noting how many of the operations they complete successfully.

While the preceding description captures the general structure of the bell-ringing game, it says nothing about the details of its administration. These details were worked out in pilot studies, with a view to meeting the four technical requirements listed at the beginning of the chapter.

1. **Motivation.** To minimize general motivational difficulties, the experimenter visited the infant center where the study was conducted several times prior to the day of testing, and did not withdraw any infant from its usual room

until it appeared to have adjusted well to her presence, and to be relatively alert. The experimenter also asked one of the daycare workers to accompany any infant to the testing room who appeared to evidence any anxiety at going off alone.

A motivational difficulty of a more specific sort was also of concern. This was that the infants might become so interested in the first peg that they would ignore the others—not because they had forgotten them—but because playing with the first one was so pleasurable. In order to guard against this possibility, the apparatus was designed so that (a) each chime would only ring once when its peg was pulled, and (b) each of the chimes would have its own distinctive sound. The hope was that the first of these two features would prevent the infants from becoming too interested in pulling the first peg, while the second would give them the added incentive to move on and pull the other pegs.

2. **Task familiarity.** In order to insure that the infants were familiar with the general task situation, they were presented with a total of three practice trials, and tested on two successive days. Their final score was the highest score they achieved on any one of the six trials.

3. **Space-saving strategies.** Although the pegs were placed far enough apart that the infants would not notice two of them in one glance, it seemed possible that they might discover a peg about which they had forgotten, simply by scanning their environment. In this case the measure might overestimate their true STSS. In order to guard against this possibility, each session was videotaped, and any trial was eliminated in which an infant pulled a second or third peg after letting its eyes wander aimlessly about the room, or after letting its eyes explore the rest of the apparatus.

4. **Chunking.** The final problem to guard against was higher-order chunking. While the literature contains no record of this sort of activity in infants, it seemed possible that if the pegs were arranged in a straight line, some sort of visual chunk might be formed. Rather than storing a record of each peg's existence individually, an infant might simply store a record of the whole group as a single unit (e.g., a line). Were this to happen, only one pointer would need to be stored. In effect, the infant could simply remember to scan right after each peg had been pulled. To guard against this possibility, the pegs were arranged in an irregular semicircle rather than in a line. Although the same argument could conceivably be raised with regard to this sort of arrangement, it should be noted that—as a minimum—the infants would have to record the existence of three separate pegs as units before they could detect the pattern of the whole group. Because this would itself entail an EPL of at least $OP_{sensorimotor} + 3S$, we decided that the semicircular pattern would be adequate for our purposes.

Having satisfied ourselves that the measure met the basic conceptual and technical requirements for a measure of STSS, we conducted a formal experiment.

Study Number 1

Subjects

A total of 17 male and 15 female infants ranging from 4 to 18 months of age were tested. All infants were enrolled in metropolitan Toronto daycare centres, and were tested on the premises.

Apparatus

The apparatus that was used was the one illustrated in the Figure 14.1. Each of the pegs was brightly colored, and of a size that would fit easily into an infant's hand. The pegs were placed in the pattern indicated, at a distance of about 7 inches from each other. In order to produce the chiming sounds, bells were mounted on the underside of the box, directly under each peg. A hole was then drilled in the box at each point. Finally, a string with a clapper at the end was led through the hole, and attached to the bottom of the appropriate peg. The result was that when each peg was pulled, a distinctive chiming sound resulted. However, this sound could only be produced once because the clapper came to rest against the bell, and had to be pulled away from it by the experimenter before the bell could ring again. The back of the box was left open so that the experimenter could reset each clapper unobtrusively.

Procedure

Infants were tested individually in a quiet room. The experimenter sat the infants in front of the apparatus, in a position where they could reach each peg with ease. As soon as they directed their gaze in the appropriate direction, the experimenter demonstated the peg game to them. Beginning with the peg on the infants' left, the experimenter pulled each peg in turn, thus causing it to emit its distinctive chime. She then reset each peg on the board and re-set the clappers, encouraging the infants to try the game themselves as she did so. As soon as the infants did try the game, she repeated the procedure for a total of three trials. The infants' score was the greatest number of pegs which they pulled on any trial, on either of the two days on which they were tested.

Results

The results are shown in Table 14.1. As may be seen, the majority of infants in each age range performed as predicted. Those subjects who did not perform at the mean level were not evenly distributed: they tended to perform one level above rather than one level below the predicted value. Thus, the overall means were a few tenths of a point higher than the hypothesized values. The serial position curve for all subjects combined was also determined. As was expected, this

TABLE 14.1

Performance of Infants on the Sensorimotor Span Test

Substage	Hypothesized age range (months)	Mean age of test population in months (number of subjects)	Hypothesized STSS	Expected mean score	Actual mean score (SD)	Percentage of subjects performing at predicted level
1	4–8	6 (n = 7)	S	1	1.33 (.51)	66
2	8–12	10 (n = 6)	2S	2	2.29 (.95)	57
3	12–18	15 (n = 11)	3S	3	3.27 (1.0)	63

curve had the same basic shape as memory-span curves at higher age levels. That is, it showed an elevation in both the initial and the terminal positions.

Discussion

The results from this study were only preliminary. They need to be replicated with a greater number of subjects, and with variations in the testing parameters. In spite of the preliminary nature of the results, however, their conformity with the predictions is encouraging. It seems possible (1) that STSS does grow during the age range tested, and (2) that its absolute values at each substage are those that were suggested in the previous chapter.

THE GROWTH OF STSS DURING EARLY CHILDHOOD[2]

Test 1: Word Span

There is an STSS measure already in existence that meets the basic conceptual criteria for the relational period. In this test, children are presented with a series of words at 1-second intervals, and are asked to repeat them. The experimenter begins by presenting a short series of words, and gradually works up to series that are longer, until the subject can no longer repeat the whole series without error.

From the present perspective, there are four important characteristics of this test. (1) Children are asked to execute a series of intellectual operations that are formally identical; that is, encoding and repeating each word. (2) The developmental level of this operation can be specified; the operation is a relational one of the sort which was described in Chapter 7 and which emerges at the age of 1 to $1\frac{1}{2}$ years. (3) The product of each encoding operation must be stored while each subsequent operation is executed; otherwise recall of all the words at the end of the sequence becomes impossible. (4) The point at which the subjects' STSS becomes overloaded can be determined, by varying the length of the word list they are asked to repeat, and noting the point at which they can no longer do so successfully.

Although the word-span test has the basic structure of an STSS measure, considerable care must be taken in designing the details of its administration in order to insure that it also meets the four technical requirements.

1. **Motivation.** In order to ensure that children's motivation remains high, considerable effort must be invested in putting them at ease. In general, it is desirable for the experimenter to meet the children on several occasions prior to testing, and to play a few games with them. It is also desirable for the ex-

---

[2]The work reported in this section was conducted in collaboration with Peter Liu.

perimenter to praise them repeatedly in the course of the testing, and to eliminate any trials where they become distracted by some irrelevant object or event in the testing environment.

2. **Item familiarity.** In order to ensure item familiarity, simple concrete nouns should be used, which are known to be within the children's active vocabulary. Care should also be taken to make sure that each individual child knows each word prior to the testing.

3. **Space-saving strategies.** A common space-saving strategy on tests such as word span is verbal rehearsal. It has generally been noted, however, that children rarely utilize this strategy prior to the age of 5 years (Flavell *et al.*, 1966). As long as the test is only intended for use in the preschool period, then, this strategy is unlikely to constitute a problem.

4. **Chunking.** Another potential problem with word-span tests is that children may group individual words into higher-order patterns. Once again, however, this is unlikely to be a problem during the preschool period. Jensen and Rohwer (1970) have shown that preschoolers' span on tests of free recall is not greater for sets of categorically related words than it is for words which are unrelated—in contrast to the span of elementary school children which is higher on the former type of list. Rohwer (1970) has also shown that preschoolers do not generate imaginal pairings of items. That is, they do not form idiosyncratic chunks based on any sort of visual imagery. Thus, the only real source of concern is that the children might have some previously learned association between two of the words already, which might help them if these two words appeared in contiguous positions (e.g., star fish). Each set of words at each level should therefore be examined with considerable care, in order to rule out this possibility.

Test 2: Action Span

In order to assess children's STSS in a nonverbal as well as a verbal fashion we decided to develop a second test as well. In our new test, children were seated facing a box with a number of different objects protruding from it. The five different types of objects are illustrated in Figure 14.2. The first object on the left is a small lever, which can either be swung up against the box on which it is mounted (revealing an arrow pointing up), or down against the box (revealing nothing). The second object is a small dowel, which fits snugly into the box and which may be pushed (thus dropping with a clatter), or else pulled out of the box and held in the hand. The third object is a dial with a flag on it. The flag may either be twisted to the right (toward a frowning face) or to the left (toward a smiling face). The fourth object is a small door, which can either be opened (revealing a set of bright polka dots), or closed (revealing nothing). The fifth object is a small picture of a bunny, formed by pasting a picture of a bunny's head

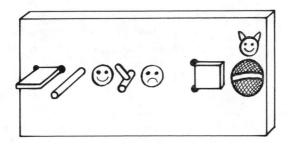

Fig. 14.2. Apparatus for assessing relational STSS.

over a one inch hold stuffed with cotton batton, and stretching an elastic band across the hole. The bunny may either be stroked with the hand, or else made to squeak by pulling and releasing the rubber band.

The five gadgets were arranged in sets of increasing magnitude, in the same fashion as the words in the word-span test. For each word-span trial, an analogous *action-span trial* was constructed, by building a box with the same number of gadgets on it, and randomly assigning one of the two possible actions to each gadget. This meant that the action-span test met the same basic conceptual requirements as the word-span test. First, the test required the subject to execute a series of formally identical intellectual operations, namely encoding the relationship which the experimenter produced between each object and the box. Second, the level of this operation could be clearly specified (relational), as could its age of emergence (1 to $1\frac{1}{2}$ years). Third, as any current operation was observed, a pointer had to be stored to each of the previous operations. Otherwise the subject would not remember which particular action had been executed on that particular trial. Finally, the number of such pointers which a child was capable of storing could be determined quite easily, by systematically increasing the number of actions that had to be imitated.

The four technical requirements were met as follows:

1. **Motivation.** Pilot testing revealed that the test was highly motivating. Thus, no special efforts were necessary to insure attention, other than monitoring children's gaze as each operation was executed, to make sure that their eyes were following the demonstration.

2. **Task familiarity.** Children were introduced to all five of the gadgets, and to each pair of operations which could be executed on them, prior to the actual testing. This insured at least some familiarity with each operation, as well with the overall context of the game.

3. **Space-saving strategies.** One possible space-saving strategy on this sort of task would be to think of a name for each operation, and to rehearse the name as further operations were demonstrated. As was mentioned above, however, neither naming nor rehearsal are strategies that appear on memory tasks during

the preschool period. Another possibility was that children would use their hands or body parts as an external memory, to store some information about one operation or another. Again, however, this sort of strategy is not normally observed during this age range, and was not observed in the pilot testing.

4. **Chunking.** The only possible source of chunking we could think of was that between the two gadgets that were hinged. It seemed possible that both the vertical lever and the horizontal door might be encoded as open or shut, and that—if both were put in the same position in immediate succession—the child might code them as one unit (e.g., doors shut). Trials where this might be a possibility were therefore eliminated.

Having satisfied ourselves that our measures met the basic requirements for assessing children's STSS, we conducted a second experiment.

Study Number 2[3]

Subjects

Twenty preschool children were selected at each of the four different age levels specified by the theory, from daycare centers serving upper middle-class neighbourhoods. All children had IQ scores between 100 and 120, as measured by the Catell and the Stanford Binet.

Procedure

Children were withdrawn from their regular daycare center and were administered each measure on an individual basis. The word-span test was always administered first, followed by the action-span test. For each test, the same basic procedure was followed. The experimenter began by presenting the Level 1 items, then worked up to the higher-level items, warning the subject each time that a more difficult level was reached. Testing was terminated when a subject failed all five of the trials at any one level. A score of 1 was assigned for passing three of the five trials at any level correctly. An additional score of .2 was added for any additional item that was passed at levels where the criterion of 3/5 was not attained.

Results

The results are shown in Table 14.2. As may be seen, the majority of children in each age range performed as predicted. Those subjects who did not perform at the mean level tended to perform one level below the predicted value, although they typically got at least one or two items correct at the predicted level as well.

---

[3]This study was conducted by Peter Liu, as a part of his doctoral dissertation.

TABLE 14.2

Performance of Preschoolers on Relational Span Tests

Substage	Hypothesized Age range (years)	Mean age of test population	Hypothesized relational STSS	Expected mean score	Obtained mean score (and SD)		Percentage of subjects receiving predicted score	
					Word span	Action span	Word span	Action span
0	$1-1\frac{1}{2}$	1 yr, 5 months (n = 20)	0	1[a]	1.0 (.44)	1.03 (.07)	70	100
1	$1\frac{1}{2}-2$	1 yr, 11 months (n = 20)	S	2	2.37 (.34)	2.17 (.33)	85	70
2	$2-3\frac{1}{2}$	3 yrs, 1 month (n = 20)	2S	3	3.10 (.32)	3.28 (.29)	75	60
3	$3\frac{1}{2}-5$	4 yrs, 5 months (n = 20)	3S	4	4.0 (.21)	4.11 (.25)	85	70

[a]Because each individual operation entails an EPL of $OP_{relational}$, a child with an STSS of 0 should still imitate one action successfully, providing he or she has reached the preliminary substage of the period.

Discussion

Once again, the results support the general analysis of the previous chapter. They suggest that children's STSS for relational operations increases at the rate indicated, regardless of the task that is used to assess this increase.

THE GROWTH OF STSS DURING MIDDLE CHILDHOOD[4]

The growth of STSS during middle childhood has already been researched by Pascual-Leone and his colleagues (see Burtis, 1974; Case, 1970, 1972b; DeAvila, 1974; Diaz, 1974; Parkinson, 1976; Pascual-Leone, 1970; Pascual-Leone & Smith, 1969; Pulos, 1979). Moreover, the results of this work have already provided substantial support for the notion that STSS increases during this age range at the rate hypothesized. From the present point of view, however, there is one problem with the measures which have been designed to date. This is that the operations which they entail are not always easy to specify. In fact, they have been the object of a good deal of controversy (see Case & Serlin, 1979; Pascual-Leone & Logan, 1978; Trabasso & Foellinger, 1978). In order to circumvent this difficulty, Kurland and I decided to devise a new measure. The operation that we chose to embed in our new test was counting, because counting is the fundamental component of so many executive control structures during this age range. The basic idea was to have children count a set of objects, and to recall the number of objects in each set after it was removed, then to increase the number of sets they were asked to count until the point was reached where they could no longer keep track of all the totals. Our assumption was that 4-year-olds would only be able to do this for one set ($OP_{dimensional}$), that 5- and 6-year-olds would be able to do it for two ($OP_{dimensional} + S$), and so on.

Note that the above procedure meets all the conceptual requirements for a valid STSS measure. First, the subject must execute a particular operation a number of times in a row. Second, the developmental level of the operation (dimensional) can be clearly specified. Third, the product of each operation must be stored. Finally, the number of products that must be stored can be varied by the experimenter, so that the subjects' overload point can be determined.

In addition to meeting all the conceptual requirements for a test of STSS, the test was designed to meet all the technical requirements as well.

1. **Motivation.** In order to ensure that motivation remained high, pacing was kept flexible and feedback was tailored to each subject individually. A

[4] The work reported in this section was conducted in collaboration with Midian Kurland (Case & Kurland, 1978).

ceiling-basal method of assessment was also used, in order to minimize the number of trials presented.

2. **Task familiarity.** In order to insure that subjects were familiar with the objectives and operations of the test, a period of pretraining was included prior to testing.

3. **Space-saving strategies.** In order to decrease the likelihood that subjects might employ some space-saving strategy, three separate controls were introduced.

   a. First, to eliminate verbal rehearsal, subjects were instructed not to rehearse, and were presented each array without any interarray interval. In addition, any trial on which the subject was seen to pause before counting one of the sets was eliminated. It is, of course, conceivable that a subject might rehearse while in the middle of counting a set. However, as the reader may verify, this is rendered difficult by the fact that the items one might like to rehearse are numbers, and the activity in which one is engaged (i.e., counting) severely interferes with number rehearsal. Thus, unless one pauses in the middle of counting, rehearsal is extremely difficult.

   b. Rehearsal is not the only space-saving strategy that might be possible in a test such as this. One might also subitize; that is, one might draw on the capacity of the perceptual system to detect the quantity of small groups of objects. Because this could reduce the executive processing load, we wanted to prevent its occurrence. To do so, we embedded the objects to be counted in an array of distractor objects, which had the effect of breaking up the perceptual gestalt.

   c. Finally, to prevent subjects counting by two's or adapting some other simplified counting procedure, we required all subjects to count aloud, and to touch each object which they counted with their fingers.

4. **Chunking.** In order to prevent higher-order organization or chunking of the arrays totals, sequences were eliminated that showed any recognizable pattern (e.g., 1 2 3; 2 4 6; 1 3 5; 7 6 5).

Although the counting-span test meets all of the necessary requirements for a test of STSS, it is clearly dependent on an important class of verbal skills; that is, those involved in counting. In order to assess children's STSS nonverbally as well, we turned to a measure that had been developed by Pascual-Leone's research group. The test which we used was the CUCUI, a measure developed for Mexican American children by DeAvila (Diaz, 1974). In this test, children are presented with a clown figure with one of its body parts painted a bright colour. The picture is then removed, and replaced with an exact replica with no parts painted. The children's task is to point to the part that was painted in the previous picture. Once they have grasped this basic notion, the number of coloured parts is increased in a systematic fashion, until they reach the point where they can no longer recall all of them correctly.

The operation on which this task depends is spatial localization; more particularly, spatial localization in a familiar, symmetrical array. At the time the task was developed, it was not clear how best to classify this operation. However, as a result of pilot work that we conducted in our research group[5], we decided that the operation could best be classified as dimensional. It first emerges at the age of about 4 years, and is assembled out of a set of more primitive relational-components. These components, in turn, first emerge at about the age of $1\frac{1}{2}$ years.

Once the nature of the operation that the task entails is specified, it becomes clear that it meets all the basic requirements for a nonverbal STSS measure. First, children are asked to execute a series of operations which are formally identical. Second, the developmental level of each operation can be identified (dimensional). Third, while the children are executing any one operation, they must store a pointer to indicate the product of each previous operation. Finally, the point at which overload occurs can be determined by systematically increasing the number of parts which are coloured, and noting the point at which the subject's performance begins to break down.

In addition to meeting the basic conceptual requirements for a test of STSS, the test meets most of the technical requirements as well.

1. **Motivation.** The test is highly motivating. In fact, children are willing to persist at it for much longer than they are at the other tasks.
2. **Task familiarity.** The test can be preceded by sufficient practice that both the general objective and the specific operations are familiar.
3. **Space-saving strategies.** Most of the space-saving strategies can be detected and eliminated, since they require moving some external body part as a retrieval aid. To prevent any sort of *iconic* storage, we asked subjects to look at a grid for 2 seconds before we showed them the blank picture.
4. **Chunking.** Finally, higher-order storage can be minimized by careful selection of the items presented, at least at lower age levels. In our pilot work we discovered two kinds of chunkable items: items where some sort of symmetry was involved (e.g., both eyes colored) and items where all the body parts in a particular spatial location (e.g., top right) had spots on them. (Bödy, 1977). We therefore eliminated such items from the task.

---

[5]This work was conducted in collaboration with Peter Liu.

Study Number 3[6]

Subjects

Six boys and six girls at each of four different age levels were tested. The age levels were 4, 6, 8, and 10 years. The children were selected from a university laboratory school. As a consequence, they were quite homogeneous with regard to IQ, quite high in SES, and quite test wise. Although for many purposes this sort of population might have been less than ideal, for the purpose of our study it was acceptable, because the objective was to estimate optimum performance at each age level.

Procedure

Each subject was removed from his or her regular classroom individually, and tested in a small room made available by the school for this purpose. After the subject had been put at ease, he or she was presented with the counting-span test, followed by the CUCUI. For each test, five trials were presented at each level. However, unlike the previous tests, trials at different levels were intermixed, so that the subject was never sure how many items would be presented. If a subject got three items correct at any level one point was awarded. If a subject got less than three items correct no score was awarded for that level.

Results

The results are presented in Table 14.3. As may be seen, the scores at each age level were quite close to each other, with the grand means differing by only $\frac{2}{100}$ of a point. The absolute values at each age level were also approximately as predicted although the proportion of 10-year-olds passing the most difficult items did not quite reach 50%.

Discussion

Older children still appeared to be chunking some items on the CUCUI. Thus, we have utilized the more complex figure that is illustrated in Figure 14.3 in our subsequent studies. There also seemed to be some chunking of certain numbers on the counting-span test, and children appeared to lose their motivation as the test proceeded. Accordingly, we have modified the items that we have presented in subsequent studies, and included only three trials at each level. These minor difficulties aside, however, the main points of the data will no doubt be apparent. They show that children's STSS does grow on each measure

---

[6]This study was conducted in collaboration with Midian Kurland.

TABLE 14.3

Performance of School-Age Children on the Dimensional Span Test

Substage	Theoretical age range (years)	Mean age of population tested (years)	Hypothesized STSS[a]	Expected mean score	Actual mean score (SD)		Percentage of subjects performing as predicted	
					Counting span	Cucui	Counting span	Cucui
0	$3\frac{1}{2}$–5	4.0	0	1[b]	1.1 (.13)	1.4 (.41)	100	91
1	5–7	6.0	S	2	2.5 (.50)	2.2 (.44)	63	73
2	7–9	8.0	2S	3	3.3 (.69)	3.2 (.57)	58	66
3	9–11	10.0	3S	4	3.8 (.72)	3.7 (.30)[c]	41	41

[a]STSS refers to storage space over and above that entailed in executing one operation.
[b]In both tests a score of 1 is the automatic result of executing one such operation correctly.
[c]This value may be an underestimate due to presence of a ceiling effect.

Fig. 14.3. Revised figure used in assessment of dimensional STSS (Mr. Cucumber).

at the approximate rate predicted by the theory, but that the rate of growth may decelerate somewhat more quickly than specified at the end of the stage.

THE GROWTH OF STSS DURING ADOLESCENCE[7]

Unfortunately, we have not yet completed our study of children's STSS during the vectorial period. However, such preliminary work as we have attempted has been encouraging. The measure we have developed is called the ratio-span test. On this test, children are presented with cards with yellow and green dots on them. They are then asked to determine how many groups of green dots there are for each yellow dot on each page (i.e., the ratio of yellow to green dots). All of the other procedural details are identical to the counting-span test. Testing begins with a 1-item trial, moves on to 2-item trials, and so on, until a level is reached where the subjects can no longer recall all the answers.

Because the only difference between the ratio-span test and the counting-span

---

[7]The work in this section was conducted in collaboration with Bob Sandieson, Midian Kurland, and Debra Sandlos.

test is that the latter requires a vectorial rather than a dimensional operation, it follows that the new measure should meet all the basic conceptual and technical requirements for an STSS test for the vectorial period. On this assumption, we decided to administer it to a group of subjects aged 9 years to adult.

Study Number 4

Subjects

The 9- to 10-year-old sample was obtained by testing all 37 children in Grades 3 and 4 in the university's laboratory school. The 11- to 12-year-old sample was obtained by testing all children in Grades 5 and 6 in the same school. Unfortunately the children whom we arranged to test at the next two age levels were not actually available when it came time for the actual test administration. Accordingly, we decided to test an adult sample instead. This sample comprised graduate students at the Ontario Institute for Study in Education.

Procedure

Most of the procedural details were the same as for the counting-span test, except that a ceiling-basal method was not deemed necessary, and only three trials were presented at each level. Subjects were given one point for any level where they scored 2 or 3 out of three, and one third of a point for any level at which they scored one out of three.

Results

The results are presented in Table 14.4. As may be seen, the norms at each age level were reasonably close to those that had been predicted. There was a good deal of variance as well, however, with a substantial number of subjects performing above and below the predicted level.

Discussion

The data in Table 14.4 are only preliminary. Further data need to be gathered for Substage 2. In addition, further data on some other measure would be desirable (for work in this direction, see Biemiller, 1981). Nevertheless, for a first study, the data are once again encouraging. STSS growth during the vectorial period does appear to take place at approximately the same rate as during the other periods. Moreover, this rate appears to correspond quite closely to that predicted by the theory.

TABLE 14.4

Performance of Children on the Vectorial Span Test

Substage	Hypothesized age range (years)	Mean age of population tested (years)	Hypothesized STSS	Expected mean score	Actual mean score (SD)	Percentage of subjects performing at predicted level or higher
0	9–11	10.3	0	1	1.25 (.80)	77
1	11–13	12.3	S	2	2.06 (1.08)	72
2	13–15	–	2S	3		
3	15+	25	3S	4	4.0	80

INTERCORRELATIONS AMONG STSS MEASURES

The most obvious data of relevance to the STSS hypothesis are those that have already been reported. There is a second sort of data, however, that deserve at least some consideration. These are data indicating the rank order correlations among different STSS measures. As was mentioned in Chapter 3, it is possible for two tests to yield identical mean scores at any given age level, and still not correlate significantly. Tests of conservation and seriation, for example, yield approximately the same mean scores when administered to 7-year-olds. Although the same proportion of children pass each measure, however, the children who pass conservation are not necessarily the same ones as those who pass seriation. Hence, the tests show rank order correlations that are weak or insignificant.

What sort of correlations would one expect among different STSS measures? If the analyses in the previous chapter are correct, one would certainly not expect the correlations to be zero. Children who have a very large executive processing space should tend to have an advantage over those who have a very low executive processing space on any test of STSS, regardless of the specific operations that the test entails. Hence, they should tend to preserve their rank order with respect to the other children across tests.

On the other hand, however, one would not necessarily expect the correlations among STSS measures to be high. This is because one never measures total processing capacity in a content-free manner. One measures STSS for a particular type of operation. If child A and child B have approximately the same total processing capacity, they might still perform quite differently on two different STSS measures, as a function of differential facility with the operations in question. For example, child A might find spatial operations easier to execute than child B. Consequently, he might do better than child B on the CUCUI. On the other hand, child B might find numerical operations easier to execute than child A. Consequently, child B might do better than child A on the test of counting span. This would result in a failure to preserve a constant rank ordering across tests, which would attenuate the correlation among them.

In general, therefore, it may be said that STSS measures should show a significant intercorrelation due to the fact they all tap the same underlying executive processing capacity. On the other hand, they should not show a high intercorrelation because each test also assesses a subject's proficiency for a particular class of operations.

What about the pattern of correlations among measures? If STSS test A correlates highly with some other mental test X, insignificantly with test Y, and negatively with test Z, should STSS test B show the same pattern? As long as neither STSS test shares any specific operation with tests X, Y, and Z, the answer to this question is yes. Under these circumstances, the correlations between the STSS measure and the other measures should be a function of whether or not they tap the same underlying quantitative capacity. Hence, the pattern of the correlations should be the same. From a statistical point of view, this means that tests of STSS should all load on the same factor, when the correlation matrix is factor-analyzed.

Consider now the results from two empirical investigations. One of the first studies to assess the correlations among STSS measures was conducted by Case & Globerson (1974). In this study, 43 children aged $7\frac{1}{2}$ to $8\frac{1}{2}$ years served as the subjects. The children were drawn from an upper middle-class school in a suburb of San Francisco, and were administered three of the earliest STSS measures to be developed: the Compound Stimulus Visual Information Task (Pascual-Leone, 1970), the Digit Placement Task (Case, 1972b) and the Backward Digit Span Test (Jensen, 1964). The details of these measures are not important. What is important is that they yield the same mean scores at this age level, but involve different types of basic operation. The Backward Digit Span Task requires the reordering of verbal input, without regard to magnitude. The CSVI requires a sequence of manual responses to a set of embedded visual forms. The Digit Placement Test requires the placement of a digit with respect to a visually presented numerical series.

Table 14.5 shows the correlations of the three measures, both with each other

TABLE 14.5

Pearson Correlation Coefficients for Tests Administered in Case and Globerson Study
(values in parentheses are corrected for attenuation)

Test (reliability)	Backward digit	Digit placement	CSVI	Raven	Block design	Embedded figures	Rod and frame
Backward digit span	1						
Digit placement	.51**	1					
	(.70)						
CSVI	.43**	.53**	1				
	(.49)	(.70)					
Raven matrices	.32*	.35**	.38**	1			
	(.37)	(.49)	(.41)				
Block design	.44**	.22	.28*	.58**	1		
	(.53)	(.31)	(.31)	(.67)			
Embedded figures	.20	.25*	.28*	.40**	.41**	1	
	(.28)	(.40)	(.36)	(.53)	(.56)		
Rod and frame	.29*	.28*	.30*	.64**	.68**	.33*	1
	(.33)	(.37)	(.31)	(.69)	(.76)	(.47)	

* $p < .05$.
** $p < .01$.

and with four other measures: the Raven Progressive Matrices, the Block Design Subtest of the WISC, the Children's Embedded Figures Test, and the Rod and Frame test. As may be seen, the correlations among the STSS measures are all significant, and range in magnitude from .4 to .5. The STSS measures also show the same pattern of correlations with the other measures. The result is that, when the matrix is factor analyzed, two distinct but correlated factors emerge. The STSS measures all load exclusively on the second factor, while the other measures all load exclusively on the first (Case & Globerson, 1974).

In a recent study conducted by Collis and Romberg (1979) a similar pattern was observed. Four different STSS measures were used, the Counting Span Test, the CUCUI, the Digit Placement Test, and the Backward Digit Span Test. The subjects were 139 children aged 5 to 8 years, who were attending a middle-class primary school in Australia. The correlations among the measures were all significant and ranged in magnitude from .43 to .66. Collis and Romberg scored the measures in a variety of manners, and conducted a variety of factor analyses. However, in all of these analyses only one factor emerged with an eigenvalue greater than 1. All of the STSS measures showed substantial loadings on it.

CONCLUSION

The tests that were described in the present chapter were designed to involve a variety of operations, and to be appropriate for children at a variety of age levels. However, they all met the same conceptual and technical requirements, and they all showed the same basic pattern. First, they all revealed a regular pattern of growth within each stage. Second, the rate of growth was constant across tasks. Third, the rate of growth was in reasonable conformity with the rate that had been predicted. Finally, at least for the dimensional stage, the tasks showed a pattern of intercorrelations that indicate the presence of a good deal of operationally specific variance for each test, but a common underlying factor for all the tests as well, Again, this is in accord with the general theory.

On the basis of these four types of data, it seems reasonable to conclude that the hypotheses that were stated at the outset of the chapter are correct. That is, it seems reasonable to conclude (1) that STSS does increase during each major stage of development, and (2) that the values of STSS at each substage of each major stage are S_x, $2S_x$, and $3S_x$.

CHAPTER 15

The Role of Short-Term Storage Space in the Executive Assembly Process

INTRODUCTION

Given that children's short-term storage space (STSS) grows at the rate that was hypothesized, the next question is whether it also plays the developmental role that was hypothesized. That is, the next question is whether the size of children's STSS sets a limit on the complexity of the executive control structures they can assemble, when exposed to the appropriate opportunities for learning. In the present chapter, a series of studies are reported that were designed to address this question.

DATA ON CHILDREN'S READINESS FOR LEARNING

Study 1[1]

The first study focused on the executive control structure for manipulating variables in a scientific experiment. In its normal form, this is a structure that is not acquired until the age of 15 or 16 years; that is, until the end of the vectorial period (Inhelder & Piaget, 1958). In a simplified form, however, one can see that

---

[1]This study was conducted with the assistance of Tamar Globerson, Bart Bödy, Bob Kahn, and Meg Korpi.

it could conceivably be acquired much earlier. The basic insight on which the structure depends is that quantitative variation along one dimension (e.g., weight) cannot be singled out as the cause of a particular event (e.g., beam tilting), if quantitative variation along some second dimension (e.g., distance from the fulcrum) is also present. This basic insight should be accessible to children as young as 7 or 8 years of age, because this is the age at which they can handle other bidimensional control structures.

Of course, 8-year-olds are rarely exposed to such carefully controlled, two-variable situations in their everyday life. Thus, they are unlikely to develop even a simplified form of the control-of-variables structure spontaneously. On the other hand, there should be no difficulty in providing them with this sort of opportunity, by designing an appropriate unit of instruction. Thus, they should be enabled to acquire a simplified form of the structure, providing that they have the requisite STSS.

This sort of situation provides an ideal opportunity for determining whether STSS does, in fact, play the limiting role in development which has been hypothesized. One has only to select two different groups of children, one with an STSS of OP $_{dimensional}$ + 2S, and one with an STSS of OP $_{dimensional}$ + S, and then expose each group to the same opportunity for learning. If the hypothesis is correct, the former group should acquire the structure quite easily, whereas the latter group should experience a great deal of difficulty.

The first study was designed to test this prediction. A series of instructional activities was devised to teach children the control-of-variables principle in a two-variable context. Then, a series of activities was designed to teach children how to consider a number of other variables at the same time, without overloading their processing capacity. Then children at two different STSS levels— OP $_{dimensional}$ + 2S and OP $_{dimensional}$ + S—were selected. Finally, these subjects were assigned either to a treatment group or to a control group. The treatment group received four 20-minute instructional sessions spread across ten days. The control group received their regular classroom instruction. At the end of the treatment period, all subjects were tested on two novel Piagetian problems. One problem required the isolation and manipulation of five variables which affect the length of time a marble will stay on a spinning wheel (Inhelder & Piaget, 1958, p. 210); the other problem required the isolation and manipulation of four variables that affect the flexibility of a rod (Inhelder & Piaget, 1958, p. 46). It was predicted that the only subjects who would pass either of these posttests were those who had been exposed to an appropriate opportunity for assembling the control-of-variables structure, and who also had an STSS of the required magnitude.

The details of the study have been reported elsewhere (Case, 1974). For the moment, what is important is the results. These are presented in Table 15.1. As may be seen, the basic prediction was confirmed. The majority of subjects in the

TABLE 15.1

Percentage of Children Passing Control of Variables Task in Study 1

Condition	STSS level for dimensional operations	Mean age	Bending rods (%)	n	Spinning wheels (%)
Treatment	2S	8.1	80	10	80
	S	6.0	20	10	40
Control	2S	8.1	0	10	0
	S	5.9	0	6	0

target group did pass both posttests, while the majority of subjects in the other groups did not.

Study 2[2]

The results of the first study could be criticized on two grounds. First, it could be suggested that the conditions of structural acquisition were rather artificial, as was the underlying structure that was produced. Showing that subjects' STSS limits their ability to acquire a simplified control-of-variables algorithm as a result of direct instruction is not the same as showing that it limits their ability to acquire a full control-of-variables structure, as a result of their own equilibrative activity. If the latter sort of claim is to be made, it must be tested more directly. Second, it could be suggested that childrens' STSS was not properly assessed. Previous studies had shown that the majority of 6-year-olds have an STSS of $OP_{dimensional} + S$, and that the majority of 8-year-olds have an STSS of $OP_{dimensional} + 2S$. However, if one is to demonstrate that an STSS of the latter magnitude is necessary for acquiring a bivariate structure, one must also assess the particular children who are being exposed to the learning opportunity and show that they do, in fact, have the STSS hypothesized.

In order to counter these two criticisms, a second study was conducted. In this study, children's STSS was measured with two tests: the CUCUI and the Backward Digit Span Task. In addition, a different control structure was investigated, one that emerges spontaneously in the 6- to 8-year-old age range. Finally, a treatment was devised which would provide children with some indication that their current control structure was inadequate (thus inducing disequilibrium) but which would offer no direct instruction on how to assemble a more adequate one.

The control structure that was investigated was the one for assessing liquid

---

[2]The second study was conducted with the assistance of Libby Wyatt and Meg Korpi.

quantity. As the reader may remember, 6-year-olds normally assess liquid quantity on the basis of height, whereas 8-year-olds normally take account of both height and width. It was reasoned that if a group of children could be found who had not yet acquired the bidimensional control structure, but who had an 8-year-old STSS (i.e., OP $_{dimensional}$ + 2S), then they should acquire the structure spontaneously when exposed to some disequilibrating experience. By contrast, if a similar group were found who had a 6-year-old STSS (i.e., OP $_{dimensional}$ + S), they should not acquire the structure spontaneously, under the same acquisition conditions.

To test this hypothesis, it was of course necessary to expose children to a situation where they would have to make quantity judgments. The apparatus that was used for this purpose is illustrated in Figure 15.1. Two standard jars were placed on the balance arms of the apparatus throughout the experiment. The children were then presented with pairs of beakers differing in diameter and

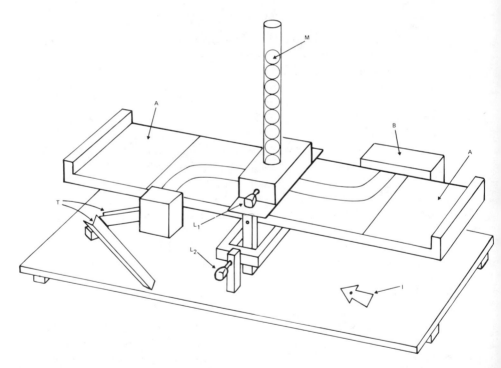

Fig. 15.1. Apparatus for training children on quantity comparison. A = balance arms; B = box into which marbles roll, if right hand side of beam goes down; L$_1$ = lever for releasing marble into chute; L$_2$ = lever for freeing balance arm; M = marbles; T = track down which marble rolls if left hand side of beam goes down; 1 = indicator pointing to side of beam which subject predicts will go down.

height, and filled with different quantities of water. For each pair of beakers they were asked to judge which had more, and to pour the contents of this beaker into the standard jar on the left side of the balance arm. They were then asked to pour the contents of the other beaker into the standard jar on the right hand side, and to observe what happened when the balance arm was released.

No other feedback was presented. The beaker comparisons were arranged so that a height-only strategy would yield success on three quarters of the trials, and failure on the remaining quarter. The subjects were drawn from a school in a lower middle-class area and were screened with the Raven Progressive Matrices to ensure that they were of average or above average intelligence. Two tests of conservation were also administered: liquid substance, and liquid weight. In order to be included in the study, children had to have a dimensional STSS of either S or 2S, show no evidence of conservation, and justify their conservation response exclusively in terms of the height of the liquid columns.

After children who met these criteria had been selected, they were randomly assigned to one of two conditions: treatment or control. The treatment subjects received 60 trials on the apparatus at the rate of 12 trials per session, twice a week. Each session was conducted individually, and lasted about 10 minutes. The control group received nothing. One week after the treatment, the children were posttested using the quantity assessment scale which was described in Chapter 8.

The details of the assessment procedure are presented in Case (1977b). The results are presented in Table 15.2. As may be seen, the predictions were once again confirmed. The only group for which the majority of subjects passed the posttest was the group who received the appropriate treatment, and who had the prerequisite STSS.

Studies 3 and 4[3]

The sort of study that has been reported so far could still be criticized, on the grounds that changes in STSS were confounded with changes in age. While the size of children's STSS may very well be the factor producing the observed developmental limitation, it could be argued that some other age-related factor might equally well be responsible, because the two groups in both studies differed in chronological age as well as STSS.

Exactly what this other factor might be is not clear. Nevertheless, from a purely logical point of view, the criticism is clearly a valid one. We therefore decided to replicate each of the studies that had already been conducted, using children of the same age but different STSS.

---

[3] These studies were conducted in collaboration with Meg Korpi, and with the assistance of Irene Furman, Andrea Morrison, and Veronica Fabian.

TABLE   15.2

Percentage of Children Showing Bidimensional Quantification in Study 2

Condition	Measured STSS		Mean age	n	Posttest
	Cucui	BDS			
Treatment	3.4	3.0	8.1	9	100%
	2.4	2.2	6.3	12	41%
Control	2.8	2.9	7.11	9	44%
	2.2	2.2	6.3	12	25%

The first experiment that was replicated was the one involving the control of variables. The treatment was kept the same, but the subjects were selected on the basis of their measured STSS. The children who were pretested were all in the age range from $6\frac{1}{2}$ to $7\frac{1}{2}$ years. The STSS measures that were used were the CUCUI and the Backward Digit Span. Children's understanding of the concept to be taught was also assessed at the outset, in order to check on the possibility that their knowledge of the control-of-variables structure might already be different. The test that was used for the pretest was the spinning wheels problem. The test that was used for the posttest was the bending rods problem.

The results are reported in Table 15.3. As may be seen, the pattern was identical to that in the first study. To eliminate any remaining effects of age, the residual effects of this variable were partialled out statistically. Under these conditions, it was found that STSS still accounted for a significant proportion of the variance in postest scores (20%). The converse, however, was not true. When STSS was removed first in the regression analysis, age no longer accounted for a significant proportion of the remaining variance (STSS: 34% Age: 1%).

TABLE   15.3

Percentage of Children Passing Control-of Variables Task in Study 3

Condition	Measured STSS		Mean age	Pretest (%)		Posttest (%)
	CUCUI	BDS				
Treatment	3.2[a]	3.0	7.6	18	(n = 11)	63
	1.9	2.1	7.0	0	(n = 9)	0
Control	3.0	2.9	7.5	0	(n = 12)	17
	2.0	2.5	7.1	0	(n = 5)	0

[a]Score of 3 = $OP_{dimensional}$ + 2 S score of 2 = $OP_{dimensional}$ + S.

The next experiment that was replicated was the quantity assessment study. Once again, the treatment was kept the same, but the subjects were selected differently. The children who were selected were all between the age of $5\frac{1}{2}$ and 7 years, and had scores on the CUCUI and Backward Digit Span of either 2 or 3 (OP $_{\text{dimensional}}$ + S, or OP $_{\text{dimensional}}$ + 2S).

The results are summarized in Table 15.4. As may be seen, the pattern was once again identical to that in the previous study. All groups showed some progress. However, the only group in which a clear majority showed evidence of bidimensional quantification was the one which had been exposed to the required experience, and which also had the required STSS.

Study 5[4]

While the pattern of data in Tables 15.3 and 15.4 is strong, one criticism might still be made of it. This is that the pattern emerges at only one point in development, namely the transition from OP $_{\text{dimensional}}$ + S to OP $_{\text{dimensional}}$ + 2S. It could be argued that there is something else about this point which is critical, and that the STSS measures merely serve as an index of it. Partly to counter this criticism, and partly to make contact the Siegler's work on the balance beam, we decided to do a fifth training study. This study was again designed to teach children how to cope with a bidimensional problem. However, the control structure which was taught was designed to require a dimensional STSS of S, rather than 2S. The particular structure whose acquisition was studied was the one for bidimensional compensation on the balance. As the reader may remember, children's executive control structures for dealing with balance scale problems pass through four substages during the period of dimensional operations. During the preliminary substage ($3\frac{1}{2}$–5 years), children learn to pick the side with the larger or heavier of two weights. During Substage 1 (5–7 years), they learn to pick the

TABLE 15.4
Percentage of Children Showing Bidimensional Quantification in Study 4

Condition	Measured STSS				Percentage showing bidimensional quantification
	CUCUI	BDS	Mean age	n	
Treatment	3.2	3.3	6.8	8	100
	2.2	2.2	6.6	8	38
Control	3.6	2.9	6.9	3	33
	2.2	2.2	5.10	5	20

[4]The study reported in this section was conducted in collaboration with Rita Watson, and with the assistance of Debra Sandlos.

side with the greater number of weights. During Substage 2 (7–9 years), they learn to pick the side whose weights are at a greater distance from the fulcrum, when the number of weights on each side is the same. Finally, during Substage 3 (9–11 years), they learn to come to some sort of compensation between weight and distance, in situations where the two factors suggest opposite answers.

The object of the fifth study was to foster the development of an executive control structure that would have the same power as the compensation struc-ture used by 9- and 10-year-olds, but which would require a lower STSS. Note that, according to the theory, it is not the fact of having to focus on two dimen-sions, per se, which delays the acquisition of the control structures of Substages 3 and 4. It is the fact of having to focus on them simultaneously and as indepen-dent entities. The specific objective of the training program, therefore, was to eliminate this requirement. The structure we hoped to develop may be represented as follows:

PROBLEM SOLVING   OBJECTIVES
• Balance beam with weights.   ⟶   • Predict which side will go down.
• Particular number of elements   • Determine side with greater
  (weights and distance pegs) on   number of elements (weights
  each side   and distance pegs).

STRATEGY
1. Count the total number of
   elements (weights and distance
   pegs) on each side.
2. Pick side for which this number is
   greater.

Note that the above structure has the effect of chunking a consideration of both dimensions as one unit during each phase of the problem. Although it should have the same power as a Level 3 structure, therefore, it should be able to be assembled and executed with a lower STSS. In fact, because it effectively reduces the task to a one-dimensional problem, the structure should be able to be assembled and executed with the same STSS as any other one-dimensional problem, namely $OP_{dimensional} + S$.

Subjects

Three classes of grade one children were pretested with the Cucumber and the Counting-span tests, in the modified form mentioned in the previous chapters.[5]

---

[5] The Cucumber is the name given to the clown figure in the revised version of DeAvila's Cucui test (see Figure 14.3).

They were also given the balance beam strategy assessment test devised by Siegler (1976). In order to be included in the study, children had to show no evidence of paying systematic attention to distance from the fulcrum, and to show a score of either 1 or 2 (i.e., OP $_{dimensional}$ or OP $_{dimensional}$ + S) on both the STSS measures.

Treatment

At the beginning of the instructional session, children were presented with several balance beam problems where the distance from the fulcrum was the same on each side. They were asked to predict which side would go down, and were allowed to test their prediction to see if it was correct. Since subjects had been selected for their use of a weight-only strategy, their predictions were always correct. They were therefore congratulated, and asked to explain how they had managed to predict the result successfully. The object of this preliminary period was simply to familiarize the children with the apparatus, and to make them aware of the strategy they were currently using.

After several problems of this sort had been presented, children were presented with a problem where the weights were equal, but the distance from the fulcrum was not. When their prediction was disconfirmed, they were asked how they had been fooled. Many children spontaneously focused on the distance variable at this point. However, those who did not were told that the weights were the same, and were asked to look for something that was different between the two sides. If children still did not notice the distance difference, it was pointed out to them. Once children had focused on distance—regardless of how strong a prompt had been necessary to get them to do so—they were asked to manipulate the distance of the weights on each side, to see for themselves if that was what had fooled them.

Once the children had manipulated the distance variable, and decided that it did make a difference, they were given an additional demonstration to make the effect of distance even more salient. They were told to pretend that they were a balance beam, and to hold a heavy object in close to the centre of their body, and then far out from the centre of their body. The farther out the subjects held the object, of course, the more difficult it was for them to support it. The experimenter then gave them a verbal rule to summarize what they had learned, "the farther out a weight is, the harder it pulls down."

In the next phase of the instruction, the experimenter presented a variety of equal weight and equal distance problems, oscillating between the two types until the child was performing without error. Several problems were then presented where both weight and distance varied and where the two dimensions were in conflict. As soon as children made an error, the experimenter asked them why they thought they had been fooled this time, and encouraged them to develop a strategy for taking both weight and distance into consideration simultaneously. Many children did so spontaneously. However, for those who did not, the experimenter showed them how to count the number of weight and the number of distance pegs on each side all at once. A large number of new trials was then presented, in order to let the subjects consolidate their new strategy.

Procedure

A total of 41 subjects were identified who did not focus on distance during the pretest, and who had an STSS of $OP_{dimensional}$ + S. Twenty-two of these were assigned to the treatment condition. Nineteen were assigned to the control condition. Unfortunately, only seven subjects were identified who had an STSS of $OP_{dimensional}$ + 0, and whose initial strategy on the task could be clearly identified. All these subjects were assigned to the treatment condition, in order to maximize the reliability of the inference which could be drawn about its effect.

After the children had been selected for participation in the study, those who were assigned to the treatment condition received two instructional sessions lasting from 10 to 20 minutes. The amount of time was geared to the needs of the student. Thus, those who were the slowest learners received the most attention.

One week after the instruction, the children were again administered the strategy assessment measure, by a tester who was unaware of their treatment group.

Results

The results are presented in Table 15.5. As may be seen, the prediction was confirmed. The only group who showed evidence of acquiring a new control structure was the group who had an STSS of $OP_{dimensional}$ + S, and who had been exposed to the instruction. In spite of the small number of subjects in the low STSS group, an analysis of variance revealed that the STSS effect was significant. A regression analysis also revealed that the effect remained significant, even after the residual effects due to age had been eliminated. The residual amount of variance accounted for by the STSS factor was 25%.

TABLE 15.5

Percentage of Children Passing Weight-Distance Conflict Problems on Posttest

Condition	Dimensional STSS Level	Percentage passing
Treatment	S	74 (n = 22)
	0	0 (n = 7)
Control	S	0 (n = 19)
	0	—

Discussion

The fifth study demonstrated that the same kind of prediction can be made for the balance beam task as was made for the control of variables task and the task of liquid quantification. It also demonstrated that the same kind of prediction can be made with regard to the transition from a dimensional STSS of 0 to S as was made for the transition from a dimensional STSS of S to 2S. As such, it established the generality of the phenomenon of developmental readiness, and of the present theory and measures in predicting it. There is one final criticism which could still be made of the fifth study, however, or indeed of any study which employed a similar experimental methodology. This is that, because the measured differences in STSS are naturally occurring ones, they might be correlated with some other naturally occurring difference, which might be the real source of the readiness effect.

Of course, to be taken seriously, any counterinterpretation of this sort would have to specify just what this other factor might be. Moreover, it would have to provide a reasonable account of why this other factor was important for hierarchical integration, and why certain levels of this factor were necessary for some types of integration, while other levels were necessary for others. As yet, no counterexplanation has been proposed which meets these criteria. Nevertheless, to increase our confidence that our inference about the developmental importance of STSS was justified, we decided to do one final study.

READINESS FOR LEARNING IN ADULTS: A NEW EXPERIMENTAL PARADIGM

The objective of the final study was to produce a difference in STSS experimentally, and to determine whether subjects' learning potential would still be affected. The reasoning was that—if subjects' learning potential were still affected—no counterexplanation for this fact would be possible, since no other differences would be present between the two experimental groups. In order to accomplish this objective, we decided to work with adults.

Study 6[6]

The basic design of the study was a simple one. First, a large number of adults was recruited for participation in a learning experiment. Next, the subjects were randomly divided into two groups. Next, each group was exposed to a different

---

[6] This study was conducted in collaboration with Jill Goldberg.

condition. Both groups learned a new operation. However, one group was provided with massive training in the operation, with the result that the operation became so automatic that they had a good deal of processing space left over for storage. The other group was provided with very little practice in the operation, with the result that the operation consumed most of their processing space, and they had very little space left over for storage. Finally, the two groups were exposed to an identical opportunity for learning. In particular, they were exposed to an identical opportunity for assembling a new executive control structure, which entailed the new operation as a component. It was predicted that the group with the high STSS would profit from this opportunity, whereas the group with the low STSS would not. As usual, a prediction was also made about the absolute level of STSS that would be required for reaching various absolute levels of executive functioning.

Subjects

The subjects in the study ranged in age from 20 to 30 years, and were recruited by placing advertisements on a university bulletin board. The advertisements offered money for participation in a study involving learning and memory. After a pool of 30 subjects had been obtained in this fashion, they were randomly divided into two groups, which were labeled the high STSS group and the low STSS group.

Experimental Manipulation

The operation that the subjects were taught was an artificial procedure for counting. Subjects were first taught to repeat the following ten words in order: piff, pinkle, pinatoo, naff, napple, napatoo, oligofloff, doff, dopple, dopatoo. They were then asked to use the words to count various sets of objects, until they could do so without error. In the low-STSS group, subjects were then presented with the counting-span test, and asked to try it using their new counting language. The mean number of cards recalled under these conditions was two. Accordingly, it was assumed that this group could handle an executive processing load of $OP_{counting} + S$.

In the high-STSS group, subjects were asked to go away and practice their new counting language everyday, until they felt that they could count and remember four sets of objects. At this point, they were asked to return to the laboratory for further testing. On the average, it was several weeks before any subject felt that he or she had reached this level of proficiency. When all the subjects in this group had returned, their mean recall on the counting-span test was, in fact, four cards. Accordingly, it was assumed that they could handle an executive processing load of $OP_{counting} + 3S$.

Learning Task

In order to permit the formation of a new executive control structure in each group, an apparatus was designed that was formally identical to the balance scale task, but which was completely novel. The apparatus was called the marble chute task. In this task, the subject is seated facing two white cards. These cards are placed side by side, as is illustrated in Figure 15.2. Each card contains a number of bright green spots, which function as the foreground of the display. Each card also contains a number of pale yellow spots, which function as the background. Subjects are told that the number of spots on the cards determines which of three chutes a marble will come down. The first chute is on the left. The second chute is in the middle. The third chute is on the right. The subjects' task is to count the dots on each trial, and to figure out which chute the marble will come down.

Although it may not be evident at first glance, the marble chute task places subjects in a situation which is formally identical to the one they would experience if they did not know how a balance beam worked, and were asked to figure this out by observing its operation across trials. The number of green spots on each card plays the role of the number of weights on each side of the balance arm. The number of yellow spots plays the role of the number of distance pegs from the fulcrum. Finally, the behaviour of the marble plays the role of the balance arm itself. Coming down the right chute is formally equivalent to

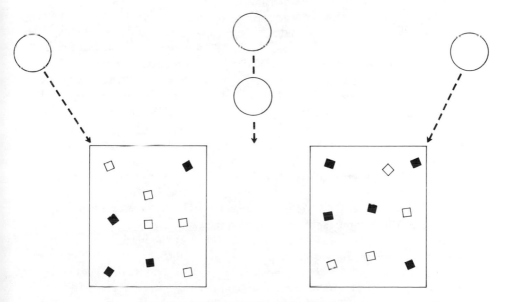

Fig. 15.2. Visual display for marble chute task.

tilting to the right. Coming down the left chute is formally equivalent to tilting to the left. Coming down the centre chute is formally equivalent to balancing.

Of course, the operation of the balance beam conforms to natural laws, while the operation of the marble chute apparatus need not. This is an advantage, since it means that the apparatus can be made to function according to a principle which is formally identical to that governing the operation of a balance beam, without the subject guessing in advance that this is the case, or having any cue other than the behaviour of the marble on each trial that this is so. For the present study, we decided to facilitate subjects' induction of the underlying principle by introducing them to easy problems first, and gradually working up to more difficult ones. The problems we constructed were analogous to those solved by children on the balance beam between the ages of 3 and 10 years.

At Level 0, the problems were extremely simple. All of the card pairs were constructed so that (1) one card had green dots on it, while the other did not, and (2) the number of yellow dots on each card was equal. On these problems, the marble always came down the chute on the side that had the green dots. To develop a control structure for dealing with this kind of problem, we reasoned, would be like developing a control structure for solving balance problems where a weight is placed on one arm, and nothing is placed on the other. These problems are normally solved by 3-year-olds, and present no difficulty whatever for 4-year-olds, who can handle an executive processing load of $OP_{dimensional}$. Accordingly, we predicted that both the high and the low STSS groups (STSS = $OP_{counting}$ + S and + 3S) would be able to solve them.

At Level 1, the problems were slightly more complex. Now all the card pairs were constructed so that both sides had green dots on them. The number of yellow dots each side still remained the same. However, the number of green dots varied and the marble always came down the side with the greater number. If the number was equal, then the marble came down the centre chute. To develop a control structure for dealing with this class of problems, we reasoned, would be like developing a structure for solving balance beam problems where several weights are placed on each arm of the balance, but at the same distance from the fulcrum. Because these problems are normally solved by 6-year-olds, who can handle an EPL of $OP_{dimensional}$ + S, we predicted that these problems, too, would be solved by both the low-STSS ($OP_{counting}$ + S) and the high-STSS ($OP_{counting}$ + 3S) groups.

At Level 2, the problems were more complex still. Now the cards were constructed so that the number of green dots on each side was always equal, but the number of yellow dots was not. On these problems, the marble always came down the side with the greater number of yellow dots. To develop a control structure for dealing with these kinds of problems, we reasoned, would be like developing a control structure for dealing with balance problems where the distance of each set of weights from the fulcrum varies, but the number of weights in each set does not. Because children normally solve these problems by the age of 8 years, at which time they can handle an EPL of $OP_{dimensional} + S$, we predicted that the subjects in the high-STSS group (STSS = $OP_{counting} + 3S$), would solve them, but that those in the low-STSS group (STSS = $OP_{counting} + S$) would not.

At Level 3, the problems increased in complexity once again. This time, the number of green dots on each side was unequal, and the number of yellow dots on each side was unequal as well. Moreover, the relative number of green dots suggested that the marble would go one way, while the relative number of yellow dots suggested that it would go the other. In fact, the marble always came down the side with the greater number of dots along the dimension of greatest difference. For example, if the right side had two more yellow dots than the left, while the left side had one more green dot than the right, then the marble would come down the right side. To develop a control structure for dealing with this kind of problem, we reasoned, would be like developing a control structure for solving balance problems where weight and distance are in conflict. Since these problems are normally solved at the age of 9 or 10 years, by which time children can handle an EPL of $OP_{dimensional} + 3S$, we once again reasoned that the subjects in the high-STSS group would learn how to solve them, but those in the low-STSS group would not.

Control for Space-Saving Strategies

The rationale for all the preceding predictions was dependent on one critical assumption: that subjects could not induce the underlying principle which was at work in any of the marble chute problems unless they used the artificial language they had just been taught. While it is easy to ensure that subjects use a new language externally, however, it is quite another matter to ensure that they use it internally. As anyone who has learned a new language in adulthood can testify, counting in that language does indeed impose a severe mental burden; however, it is one which can be overcome quite easily, be covertly counting in one's native tongue, and making all one's calculations using this more familiar set of numbers. Another space-saving strategy in the present case would be to estimate the number of dots in each array visually, and to use this information as a basis for figuring out how each problem works. If our study was to have any chance of success, we reasoned that we would have to find some procedure for eliminating the use of either sort of space saving strategy: some procedure for ensuring that subjects could only solve each problem by using the new language.

The procedure we decided upon was somewhat unusual. We invented an artificial system for determining a number's cardinality. In our system, the magnitude of a number was not determined by its ordinal position in the number string. The number doff, for example, was not necessarily of greater magnitude than the number piff, simply because it came later in the number series. Instead, the magnitude of a number corresponded to the number of syllables it contained. Hence, piff, doff and naff were all considered equal and of small magnitude. Pinkle, napple and dopple were all considered equal and of greater magnitude. Pinatoo, napatoo, and dopatoo were all conssidered equal and of greater magnitude still. Finally, oligofloff had the greatest magnitude of all. While this system was arbitrary, it had the advantage of ensuring that there would be no one-to-one correspondence between the results achieved by quantifying via visual estimation or counting in English, and the results obtained by quantifying in the new language.

Procedure

Subjects were administered the counting-span test immediately prior to starting the marble game, and immediately after they had completed it. Subjects were introduced to the marble game by being told that the objective was to figure out which of the three chutes a marble would come down on each trial. They were also told that this could be done only if they used the new counting system they had learned. They were asked to count aloud, so that the experimenter would be sure they were using this system, and to touch each dot as they did so. As soon as a subject solved six problems correctly at any one level, the problems at the next level were introduced. Subjects were told that the game was over after one of two criteria had been met (1) the subject had solved all four classes of problems or (2) the subject had completed four 20-minute sessions, in each of which he had been presented with sixty problems.

Results

What was of interest was the highest level of problem the subjects would learn to solve. Table 15.6 presents the percentage of subjects in each group who attained the criterion on the most difficult problem class. As may be seen, the

TABLE 15.6

Percentage of Subject's Using a Sophisticated Bidimensional Rule in Study 6

Condition	Measured STSS	% Passing
Practice	$OP_{dimensional} + 3S$ (Mean score = 4.2)	86 ($n = 15$)
No practice	$OP_{dimensional} + S$ (Mean score = 2.2)	14 ($n = 14$)

prediction was confirmed. The majority of subjects in the high-STSS group solved the problem, while the majority of subjects in the low-STSS group did not. Figure 15.3 presents the mean scores of each group, on both the counting-span and rule-acquisition test. As may be seen, in both groups the average rule level was just slightly below the average STSS level, on both testing days.

Discussion

Clearly, the period of counting practice had an effect on subjects' ability to develop a complex executive control structure which utilized the counting system as its basic operation. The obvious interpretation is that subjects in the

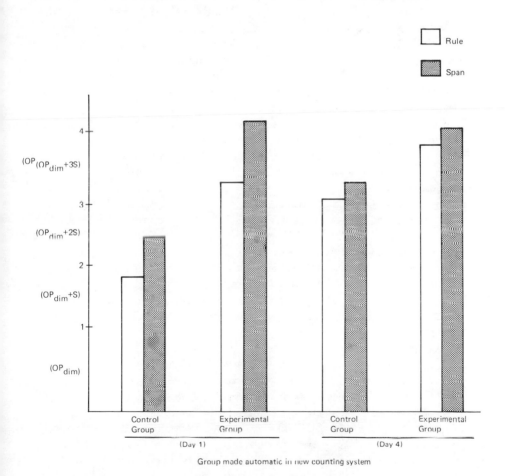

Fig. 15.3. Mean score of each group on marble chute and span tests, at the outset and completion of the study.

no-practice condition, because they could only handle an EPL of OP $_{counting}$ + S, were unable to develop a bidimensional control structure. By contrast, subjects in the practice condition, because they could handle an EPL of OP $_{counting}$ + 3S, were able to develop such a structure.

CONCLUSION

All the studies which have been reported in the present chapter required some sort of dimensional thought. It is therefore possible that the hypothesized relationship holds only for the dimension period, and not for earlier or later periods. On several grounds, however, this seems quite unlikely. It seems unlikely on theoretical grounds, since the type of analysis one can conduct for the other periods is identical to the ones which were conducted for the dimensional period. And it seems unlikely on empirical grounds, since such evidence as exists at other periods is identical in form to that which has been summarized in the present chapter. In fact, if anything, the evidence for earlier periods is somewhat stronger. We have recently completed two studies with preschoolers, for example, which presented them with the opportunity to assemble a relational control structure, and which assessed their relational STSS. One structure was linguistic in nature (Daneman & Case, 1981). The other was nonlinguistic (Liu, 1981). In both studies, the correlation between subjects' STSS and their learning potential was very high (.75 and .95, respectively). In fact, the correlations were a good deal higher in these studies than in those which have been reported in the present chapter. In the studies which were reported, the correlations of STSS with learning ranged in magnitude from .5 to .7. Thus, if anything, it would appear that the growth of STSS exerts a more powerful influence during the early stages of development than it does during the later stages. Although this raises some doubt about the influence of STSS on executive development during the vectorial stage, it provides no challenge to the assumption that STSS growth plays a major role during the earlier stages.

The correlational data do suggest one important caveat, however, which must be considered before concluding. This is that while children's STSS exerts an important influence on the level of control structure they can assemble, it is by no means the only factor which exerts such an influence. As is apparent in every table in the present chapter, some children within a given STSS level always manage to perform at a higher level than one would predict, given only a knowledge of their STSS scores. Similarly, some children always perform at a lower level than one would predict, given the same knowledge. While these deviations might possibly be due to measurement error, it seems more likely that there are important sources of variation in learning potential other than those created by variation in STSS. The present theory allows for at least two such factors, (1) variation in the efficiency of the subjects' general regulatory processes or subprocesses, and (2) variation in the subjects' repertoire of domain-specific schemes. Both of these factors will be considered briefly in subsequent chapters. First, however, the growth of STSS must be examined in greater detail.

CHAPTER 16

Operational Efficiency and the Growth of Short-Term Storage Space

TWO MODELS OF STSS GROWTH

Given that the growth of STSS plays an important role in regulating the development of children's executive structures, a question that naturally arises is what produces the growth of STSS itself. In the 1970s, as models of human information processing became more sophisticated, two of the most common answers to this question were that the growth of STSS was produced by the development of mnemonic strategies, or by the development of higher order informational chunks (Chi, 1976). Experiments that examined the role of these factors showed that both factors were, indeed, potent sources of variance on certain short-term memory tasks. They also showed that both factors did, in fact, account for an important component of the measured growth on such tasks—at least when the tasks were administered under relatively unconstrained conditions (see Belmont & Butterfield, 1971; Case, 1974; Dempster, 1978; Flavell, 1971).

As the decade wore on, however, considerable evidence was also gathered that these factors were not the whole story, and that sizeable developmental differences remained when these factors were controlled (see Burtis, 1982; Dempster, 1981; Huttenlocher & Burke, 1976). The data which were presented in Chapter 14 provide further support for this conclusion, in that they show a clear growth of STSS from 1 to 3 units within each major stage, even when every obvious source of strategies or chunking is controlled.

If the growth of STSS within each stage cannot be explained in terms of chunking or mnemonic strategies, how can it be explained? At least two different explanations would appear to be possible. The first is that the growth is due to a maturationally based increase in the size of the child's total processing space. The second is that the growth is due to a decrease in the space that is required for executing the basic operations that are characteristic of each stage.

These two possibilities are illustrated graphically in Figures 16.1 and 16.2. As may be seen, both models are based on the same underlying assumption, namely that a subject's total executive processing resources can be flexibly allocated to either of two functions (1) executing current intellectual operations (encoding, transformation, retrieval, etc.) and (2) maintaining the products of previous operations in short term storage. Stated differently, both models assume that subjects' total processing space at any point in time must be equal to the sum of the space that they are currently devoting to operating, plus the space which they have left over for short-term storage. In symbolic terms, this assumption may be stated as follows:

$$TPS = OS + STSS$$

where TPS is the total processing space, OS the operating space,
and STSS the short term storage space.

The essential difference between the two models is that, in the first, TPS is presumed to increase while OS remains constant. By contrast, in the second, OS is presumed to decrease while TPS remains constant. For this reason, the two models are referred to as the *TPS-increase* and the *OS-decrease* models, respectively.

EXISTING DATA OF RELEVANCE TO THE TWO MODELS

At first glance, it might appear that the TPS-increase model is preferable. It is this model that most clearly involves a maturational change. And, as will be remembered from Chapter 13, it was to accommodate a variety of maturational data that the notion of STSS was introduced into the theory in the first place. On the other hand, it must also be remembered that the assumption on which the TPS-increase model is based—namely that OS remains constant after overlearning—has been seriously challenged. The data that most directly challenge this assumption were gathered by Chi (1975). What Chi showed was that—even though children were prefamiliarized with a set of photographs, and even though these photographs were of their friends, and even though they could label these photographs with the same degree of accuracy as could adults (namely, 100%)—they still could not do so as quickly or as easily as could adults. Not only did Chi's study challenge a basic assumption on which the TPS-increase model is based, therefore, they also provided evidence in support of a

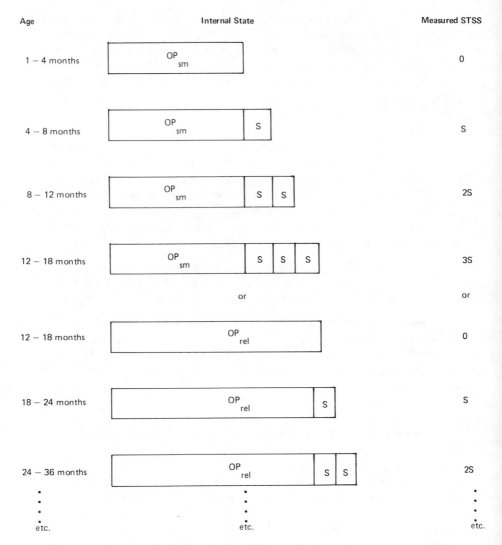

Fig. 16.1. Schematic illustration of the model that holds that total processing space increases with age (the TPS-increase model).

basic assumption on which the OS-decrease model is based, that the difficulty of executing basic intellectual operations decreases with age.

There was a second datum that was gathered in the 1970s which also challenged the TPS increase model but left the OS-decrease model unscathed. This was the datum which indicated that children's span on certain STSS measures begins to asymptote at the age of 5 years instead of 16 years (see Chapter 4). For

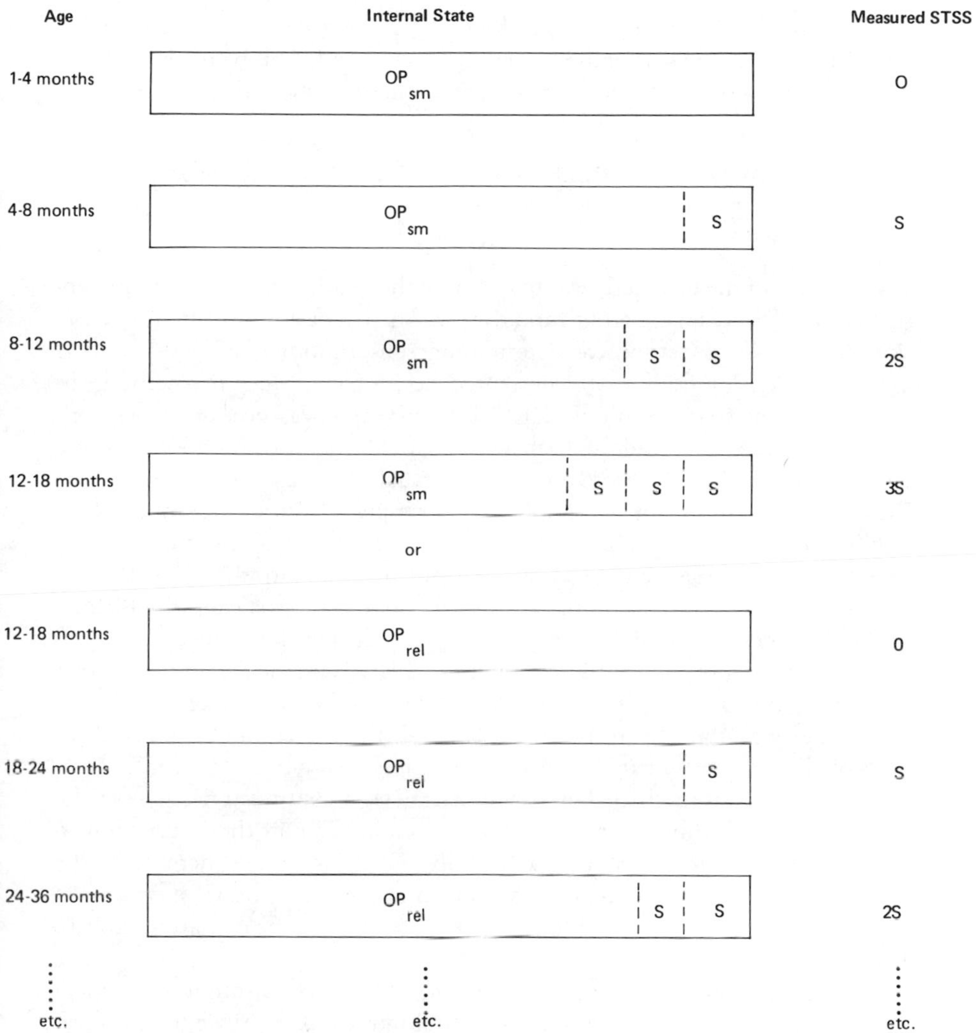

Age	Internal State	Measured STSS

Fig. 16.2. Schematic illustration of the model that holds that the required operating space shrinks with age (the OS decrease model).

the TPS-increase model, this is a serious problem. If TPS continues to grow from 5 to 16 years, why should STSS asymptote on any test? For the OS decrease model, however, this datum presents no problem. It can be explained by suggesting that, towards the end of a stage, children's operations become about as efficient as they are ever going to be. As a consequence, any further saving in TPS is likely to be minimal, and any further growth in STSS is likely to be minimal as well. By the mid-1970s, therefore, it seemed that the OS-decrease model was the more likely of the two models to be valid. This being the case, we decided to do a series of studies to test the model in a more direct fashion.

NEW DATA OF RELEVANCE TO THE TWO MODELS

Study 1[1]

The object of the first study was to examine the relationship between the sensorimotor STSS of an age group, and the OS which a basic sensorimotor operation entails. As a method for determining sensorimotor STSS was already available, assessing this variable presented no problem. Since no method was available for assessing sensorimotor OS, however, it was necessary to invent one. The general procedure that was adapted for this purpose was the chronometric technique. From both a conceptual and a technical point of view, this technique is extremely simple. One simply measures the number of milliseconds it takes for subjects to execute an operation. Then, if it takes less time for them to execute the operation at one age than another, one assumes that it also requires less operating space. A theoretical rationale for this assumption will be presented at the end of the next chapter. For the moment, it is sufficient to note that the assumption has been validated empirically, in the context of automization studies with adults. What these studies have shown is that, if one provides a subject with massive practice in the use of an operation, three sorts of change continue to take place, well after the criterion of error free performance has been reached. These changes are (1) a continued decrease in the amount of mental effort or attention that the subjects report they must apply in order to execute the operation successfully, (2) a continued increase in the number of other things that they can do simultaneously and (3) a continued decrease in the amount of time that they take to execute the operation (Logan, 1976).

Because the above three measures are highly correlated, any one of them could potentially be used as a developmental index of OS. Since the first two measures would obviously be inappropriate for infants, however, we decided to opt for the third one. The particular operation whose speed we decided to measure was reaching, because reaching is the major operation which is involved in the sensorimotor span test which had been developed earlier, the peg-pulling task.

Apparatus

The apparatus for assessing speed of reaching consisted of a box which was open at the top and one side, and which had a hinged lid. Objects were popped

---

[1] This study was conducted in collaboration with Debra Sandlos.

up from inside the box, and the child was allowed to reach for them. Inside the box, just below the lid, was a bell which emitted a distinctive sound as the objects brushed by it. This sound served to warn the infant of the impending opening of the lid, and the arrival of the object. The apparatus is illustrated in Figure 16.3.

Scoring

The children were seated on the opposite side of the box from the experimenter, and in such a way that they could not see inside the box. Their behaviour as they reached for the object was then videotaped. The time in tenths of a second was spliced onto the videotape in the upper right-hand corner of the viewing field. Two times were recorded, (1) the time from the point when the lid opened until the children's hands began to move (decision time), and (2) the time from the point where their hands began to move, until they made contact with the disc (motor time).

Training Procedure

The infants were first introduced to the game of putting a metal disc in a piggy bank. This was an activity which most of the infants found highly motivating, and which made them eager to reach for new metal discs. After the infants had been introduced to the piggy bank game, a new group of metal discs was placed inside the box, and the infants were seated so that they were facing it. Some of the younger infants were placed in the experimenter's lap to insure that they were facing in the correct direction, and felt secure. The lid of the box was then closed, and the box was reoriented so that they could not see inside it.

Once the child was facing the box, the experimenter put her hand into the open side (which the child could not see) and picked up one of the metal discs.

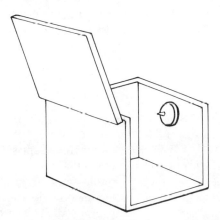

Fig. 16.3. Diagram of apparatus for measuring speed of reaching.

After tapping it against the front of the box to insure that the infant's eyes were oriented in the correct direction, she then popped the disc out of the box at the top, and while bringing the disc up against the underside of the lid, brushed it against the bell, thus providing another cue to orient the infants' eyes in the right direction. Because the lid was hinged, the effect of the procedure was rather like that of a jack-in-the-box. A total of 24 trials was presented, spread across two testing sessions. Each trial began when the disc popped up, and ended when the child had reached out and grabbed it.

Subjects

Subjects were attained from daycare centers in downtown Toronto. They were first tested on the sensorimotor STSS test (i.e., the peg-pulling task). They were then tested on the reaching task. A total of 26 male and 24 female infants participated, ranging in age from 4 months to 26 months.

Predictions

On the assumption that increases in STSS are caused by decreases in OS, it was predicted that there would be an inverse monotonic relationship between the span of an age group and the time on our two measures. Note that—with regard to motor time—the procedure of putting the infant at arm's length from the disc acted against the hypothesis being tested, since it meant that the children with the higher span (i.e., the older subjects) actually had to move their arms farther in order to reach the disc.

Results

The results are shown in Figure 16.4. As may be seen, the relationship was as predicted. In fact, it appears that the speed-span function was linear. For every increase in span there was a decrease in reaching time of approximately the same magnitude. Essentially the same results were achieved when decision time was analyzed. The correlation of span with decision time was .56 ($p > .001$), and with motor time was .57 ($p > .001$).

Discussion

The OS model may be thought of as comprising two postulates: (1) that OS decreases within each stage, and (2) that this decrease produces a corresponding increase in STSS. The data in Figure 16.4 provide strong support for the first of these two postulates. As long as one accepts the measurement assumption on which the chronometric technique is premised—namely, that operating time provides a good index of OS—it is hard to see how else the data could be interpreted. What they indicate is a steady decrease in OS throughout the sensorimotor period.

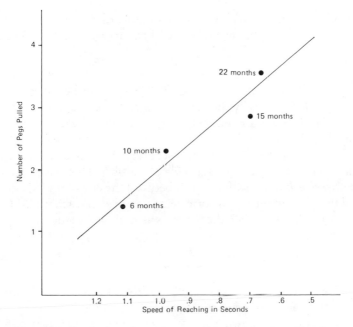

Fig. 16.4. Results from the study on reaching speed and reaching span.

The implications of the data for the second postulate are less clear. In and of itself, an inverse relationship between two developmental variables does not necessarily indicate the presence of a causal connection, since almost any two developmental variables will show some degree of correlation, due to their common association with age. On the other hand, very few developmental variables show the sort of linear relationship which is illustrated in the figure. This sort of relationship can only be obtained if the two variables in question both show a steady change throughout the age range under investigation, and both change at approximately the same rate as well.

On balance, therefore, it seems fair to conclude that the data provide strong support for the first postulate of the OS model, and at least some degree of support for the second postulate as well.

Study 2[2]

The object of the second study was to determine whether a parallel set of changes in OS and STSS take place during the relational period. In order to accomplish this objective, it was necessary to select a particular relational operation, and to measure the speed with which different age groups could execute it.

[2] This study was conducted in collaboration with Jill Goldberg and Midian Kurland.

The particular operation which we selected was word repetition, since this was the operation entailed by our first relational STSS measure, namely Word Span.

Procedure

The details of the procedure have been spelled out elsewhere (Case, Kurland, & Goldberg, 1982). Basically, however, each child was administered two different tests. The first was a standard test of word span, which was administered as described in Chapter 13. The second was a test of word repetition speed. In this test, subjects were familiarized with a set of seven words, and given one practical trial in repeating each one as quickly as possible. They were then given a large number of test trials, with the time between the end of the experimenter's voice and the onset of their own voice being recorded on each trial. Their final score was the median of all the times which they recorded, expressed in milliseconds.

Subjects

Forty subjects were tested, ranging in age from 3 to 6 years. A total of 12 3-year-olds, 10 4-year-olds, 9 5-year-olds, and 9 6-year-olds participated. The two younger age groups were drawn from a daycare center that serves the university community. The two older groups were drawn from the university-affiliated laboratory school.

Predictions

Three predictions were made: (1) that there would be steady decrease with age in the time required for word repetition, (2) that there would be an inverse monotonic relationship between this decrease and increases in STSS, and (3) that there would be a significant correlation between word repetition time and word span, when the effects of age were removed statistically.

Results

All three predictions were confirmed. The means scores for each measure are presented in Figure 16.5. As may be seen, the relationship between speed and span was monotonic, and approximately linear. The correlation between the two measures was also significant ($r = .74, p. < .001$) and remained so when age was partialled out statistically ($r = .35, p < .02$).

Discussion

Because the form of the data in the second study was the same as in the first, the same two conclusions were drawn. It was concluded (1) that the data provide direct support for the first postulate of the OS model, namely, that OS decreases

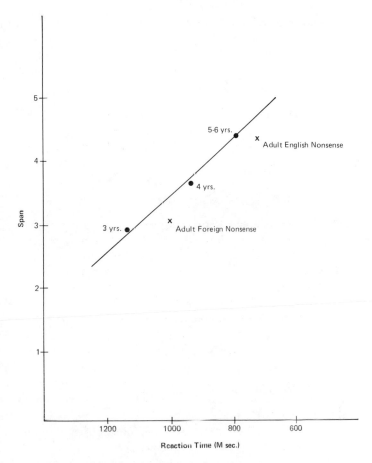

Fig. 16.5. Results from the studies on word speed and word span (Studies 2 and 4).

systematically throughout the relational period, and (2) that the data provide at least indirect support for the second postulate of the model as well.

Study 3[3]

The object of the third study was to determine whether a parallel set of changes in OS and STSS take place during the dimensional period. In order to accomplish this objective, it was necessary to select a particular dimensional operation, and to measure the speed with which different age groups could ex-

[3]This study was conducted by Midian Kurland, as part of his doctoral dissertation (Kurland, 1981).

ecute it. The particular operation which we selected was counting, since this was the operation entailed by our first dimensional STSS measure (i.e., the counting-span test).

Materials

The materials for assessing subjects' speed of counting consisted of a set of eight cards like those used in the counting-span test. On each card were a number of green dots which were to be counted, and a number of yellow dots which were to be ignored.

Procedure

Using a practice card, subjects were taught to count only the green dots, while ignoring the yellow distractors. Subjects were instructed to touch each dot with their finger as they counted, and to count out loud. Even the youngest subjects had no trouble in learning to follow this procedure. Once the subjects had demonstrated that they were able to count a practice card correctly, the tester put eight cards face down directly in front of them and said, "Now, when I turn these over, I want you to count the green dots as fast as you can without making mistakes". The tester then turned over the first card while simultaneously starting a stop watch. As soon as the subject had counted the last dot on the card, the tester stopped the watch. This cycle was repeated for each of the remaining seven cards. The tester noted any miscountings. The subject's total time to count the eight cards was then recorded, along with the total number of dots actually counted (50 dots plus or minus any dot counted twice or missed). The subjects' total time was then divided by the number of dots counted, so that their score would reflect their counting time per dot.

Immediately following the counting-speed test, the modified counting-span test was administered. Subjects were informed that they would have to count some more cards, but now they would need to remember how many dots they counted instead of trying to do the test quickly. After the counting-span test had been administered, the counting-speed test was readministered, using the same eight cards. In assigning speed scores, the mean of the two counting-speed tests was used.

Subjects

Eighty-four subjects were drawn from a predominantly middle- to lower-class school population in a small city in rural Ontario. Six boys and six girls from each of grades K–6 were selected. Subjects selected in each grade were those whose birthdates fell closest to the date of testing.

Predictions and Results

The same predictions were advanced as for the previous study.

Once again, all three predictions were confirmed. It was found that there was (1) a steady decrease in the time required to count an individual dot throughout the dimensional period, (2) an inverse relationship between this decrease and the increase in counting span, (see Figure 16.6), and (3) a strong correlation between the two variables ($r = .71$, $p < .001$) which remained significant when the effects of age were partialled out statistically ($r = .35$, $p < .001$).

Discussion

Once again, the data provide strong support for the notion that there is a steady decrease in OS throughout the dimensional period, and at least some

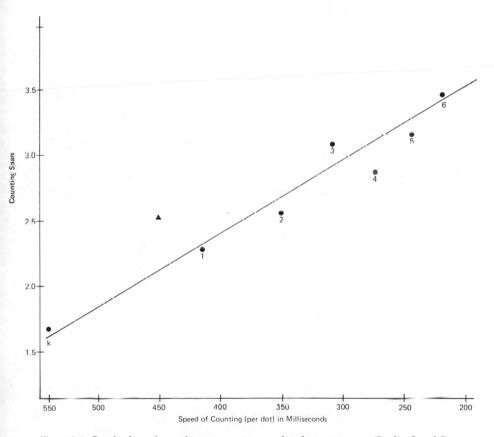

Fig. 16.6. Results from the studies on counting speed and counting span (Studies 3 and 5).

support for the notion that this decrease produces a corresponding increase in STSS.

Study 4[4]

The fourth study was designed to provide stronger support for the second postulate. That is, it was designed to provide a stronger test of the notion that the measured decreases in OS and the measured increases in STSS are causally linked. The technique which was used for this demonstration was to manipulate OS experimentally. A group of adults were taught a novel operation, and the increased operating time which the new operation entailed was then measured. Next their STSS was measured, to see if it had been reduced by a comparable amount. The particular operation which was used in the study was nonsense syllable repetition. The STSS measure was a nonsense word-span test.

Materials

Two different groups of nonsense syllables were used. The first group had a close approximation to English, and was referred to as the English Nonsense List. The second group had a more remote approximation to English, and was referred to as the Foreign Nonsense List. The words on the English nonsense list were loats, thaid, flim, brup, meeth, zarch, and dast. The words on the foreign nonsense list were tsitk, lloach, chatz, lleemph, pfluch, mfaffl, and tkipf. The double "l" was pronounced as in Spanish. The "ch" was pronounced as in the Scottish loch. The "ts" was pronounced as in the English "boats". The "pf" was pronounced as in the German "pfeiffer". The "tk" was prounounced as in the English phrase "that-kid".

Subjects

Two groups of subjects were used, both of which were university educated. The group that received the English nonsense list comprised five males and four females. The group that received the Foreign nonesense list comprised five males and five females.

Procedure

Subjects were provided with practice in repeating each word until they reached a criterion of three successes in a row. The testing procedure was then introduced in the same fashion as for Study 2, with the following two exceptions. The first exception was that the words on the Word Span tests were

---

[4]This study was conducted in collaboration with Midian Kurland and Jill Goldberg.

presented via tape recorder rather than orally. The reason this change was introduced was to standardize the pronounciation of the foreign nonsense words.

The second change was that the time interval was measured from the beginning of the experimenter's voice to the beginning of the subject's voice. The reason for this change was that adults can often recognize words before the word has been fully uttered. Thus, when the words are familiar, they can often beat the clock. In order to insure that all trials would be usable, it was decided to measure from the beginning rather than the end of the experimenter's voice. In order to equate the adults and children with regard to the interval being assessed, the average length of the words heard by the children was computed in milliseconds (273) and added to their scores. This meant that, for each group, the time interval that was used as the dependent variable was from the beginning of the word to the onset of the subject's repetition of it.

Predictions

On the assumption that a decrease in OS causes the measured increase in STSS, it was predicted that the adults' word span would be closest to that of the age group for which their speed of word repetition was most similar. That is, it was predicted that the adult speed-span point would lie on the regression line through the children's speed-span points.

Results

As may be seen from Figure 16.5, both points fell close to the regression line, though slightly below it. A statistical test revealed that neither point lay outside the confidence interval for the line; that is, that neither point deviated significantly from what had been predicted.

Discussion

As long as the changes in STSS and OS were ones which took place spontaneously, one could always have argued that the obtained correlation was an artifact, which emerged due to the concurrent action of some third factor. This argument cannot be applied to the experimentally produced changes. The adults in the fourth study experienced only one change: a change in the operating space that they had to devote to word repetition. Nevertheless, when OS was varied in this fashion, the results were exactly the same as when it had been allowed to vary naturally. Not only were they qualitatively the same, they were quantitatively the same. That is, the adults had a measured STSS which was not significantly different from that of young children with the same functional OS. This finding is an important one, for it permits a clear choice to be made between the OS and TPS models. Were there any increase in TPS with development, one would expect adults to have a higher STSS than children, when equated for OS. That they do not suggests that developmental increases in STSS are exclusively a function of developmental decreases in OS.

Study 5[5]

The object of the fifth study was to replicate the results of the fourth study, with a dimensional operation and STSS measure. The operation that was selected was counting. The STSS measure was the Counting Span test. A group of adults were taught to count in a new language. Their performance on the Counting Speed test and Counting Span test was then compared with that of 6-year-old children.

Materials

The physical materials were the same as those in Study 3. The new counting language was as follows: rab, sliff, dak, leet, raok, taid, fap, flim, moof, zeer.

Subjects

Sixteen adults ranging in age from 20 to 60 years were recruited from a university community. They were each paid 2 dollars.

Procedure

To learn the nonsense numbers, subjects repeated the list until they could do so without error, then used them to count a series of practice arrays. Subjects were practiced on these arrays until they were able to count without error at the rate of two dots per second. This rate was selected as it was the rate at which the youngest group was found to count in study three.

Predictions

On the assumption that developmental differences in STSS are caused by developmental differences in OS, it was again predicted that the adult speed-span point would lie on the regression line through the children's speed-span points.

Results

The adult speed-span point is indicated with a triangle in Figure 16.6. As may be seen, the point fell close to the regression line. Once again, statistical tests revealed that the point did not differ sufficiently from it.

[5]This study was conducted in collaboration with Midian Kurland, and with the assistance of Debra Sandlos.

Discussion

The same logic may be applied to the data from this study as the previous one. When 6-year-olds and adults were equated as to their speed of executing a basic operation, their spans were also equated. The only obvious way in which such results could be obtained is if a direct tradeoff exists between OS and STSS, and if the total processing space available to 6-year-olds and adults is equivalent. If the total processing space were not equivalent, one would have expected the adults to have a higher STSS than the children, even though their counting rate (and hence OS) was equivalent.

SUMMARY AND CONCLUSION

Five studies were reported in the present chapter, each bearing on the question of what produces the observed developmental increase in STSS. The first three studies demonstrated a monotonic relationship between naturally occurring increases in STSS and naturally occurring increases in operational speed. Because operational speed is normally taken as an index of operational efficiency, these studies were taken as preliminary evidence in favor of the OS decrease model of STSS growth; i.e., the model which postulates that operational efficiency increases with development, and that STSS growth results from the additional resources that become available, as operational execution begins to take less effort.

Stronger evidence in favor of this model was gathered in the second two studies. In each of these studies, adults' operational efficiency was manipulated directly, by requiring them to execute an unfamiliar operation. Moreover, in each case, the results of this manipulation were the same. The adults' operational speed was significantly decreased, and their STSS was reduced to the level of children who normally function at a comparable level of efficiency. If the growth of STSS was even partially due to some increase in the total attentional capacity of the system, it was reasoned that adults' performance on the STSS measure would have remained superior to that of young children, even though it might have been somewhat reduced in its absolute value. That the two groups' performance was equivalent, then, may be taken as strong evidence against the TPS-increase model of STSS growth, and in favor of the OS-decrease model.

CHAPTER 17

The Role of Experience and Maturation in the Growth of Operational Efficiency

INTRODUCTION

Given that STSS growth plays the role in children's development that was originally hypothesized, and given that STSS growth is a direct function of increases in operational efficiency, a further question that arises is what produces the increase in operational efficiency.

A number of the results that were reported in the past two chapters point to practice as an important but hidden source of this increase. The most telling results are the ones that show (1) that adults who are unpracticed in a particular operation cannot execute that operation any faster than young children (Chapter 16), (2) that their measured STSS under these circumstances is equivalent to that of young children (Chapter 16), (3) that their capacity for assembling new control structures under these conditions is also equivalent to that of young children (Chapter 14), and (4) that when they are provided with massive practice, their OS, STSS, and executive capabilities all gradually return to normal (Chapter 14).

Given that young children are less practiced than adults in virtually all basic operations, and given that their operational capabilities bear such a close resemblance to those of adults when these differences in practice are eliminated, it seems only reasonable to assume that practice is the underlying factor which is responsible for producing the gradual change in children's operational capabilities to begin with. This conclusion gains added credibility in the light of a recent paper of Newell and Rosenbloom (1981). What these authors provide is a model for the way in which practice might have the effects that are observed. Their model shows how local changes in the organization of specific operations (i.e., *chunking*) could generate the sort of growth curve that is observed in most studies of adults' or children's learning.

There is a paradox in attributing children's OS and STSS growth to practice, however, which was alluded to at the beginning of the previous chapter. This is that the reason for focusing on such factors to begin with was to explain a set of developmental data which did not appear to be explicable in terms of practice, but which pointed to the role of maturation. These data included (1) the fact that development takes place across so many domains at the same rate, and (2) the fact that this rate bears such a close resemblance to that of maturationally controlled variables, such as physical stature. While the first of these facts might possibly be explained by means of some sort of practice model, it is hard to see how the second could be, at least without making several additional and highly questionable assumptions (see Chapter 13).

The problem one is left with, therefore, is a puzzling one. While the data on adults' functioning appear to implicate practice as the factor that produces the changes in children's basic operative capabilities, the data on children's functioning appear to implicate maturation. Yet both sorts of data involve similar changes in speed of processing, in short-term storage space, and in the capacity for assembling new executive structures.

As with any paradox, there would appear to be more than one solution to the above dilemma. The most obvious solution would be to find a way to explain the time-course and breadth of children's operative development via practice, in a fashion that did not make any unreasonable assumptions. This would permit one to preserve a one-factor (i.e., practice-only) model, and thus to satisfy the demands of parsimony. On the other hand, Occam's Razor of Parsimony is a two-edged sword. Thus, if the assumptions one had to make—even though they were in and of themselves quite reasonable—began to multiply as one moved from one general class of data to the next, or from one particular datum to the next within any given class, then the same criterion would demand that the one-factor model be rejected. Assuming that this sort of proliferation of assumptions did not take place, however, the one-factor approach would appear to be preferable.

The other approach would be to assume that a two-factor model was necessary (i.e., that neither practice nor maturation is sufficient to explain the overall pattern of data by themselves, but that, taken together, they could do so). The most obvious two factor explanation would run as follows (1) whenever anyone receives practice in a novel operation, operational efficiency and speed increase, up to some asymptotal value which is set by the efficiency of their psychological system and (2) as children mature, these physiological limits change, at a rate and in a fashion which is set by maturation.

Taken together, these two assumptions could be used to explain the data on children's and adults' functioning in a simple and coherent fashion. Consider first the data on children's functioning. The cross-domain parallels in the rate of development could be explained by invoking the notion of a common ceiling. Given that children receive a certain reasonable amount of practice across domains, the two-factor model predicts that a common asymptotal value of OS should be reached, and that this should lead to common values of STSS, as well as common capabilities for executive assembly, across a wide variety of domains. By the same token, the model predicts that the time course of this growth should be linked to the time course of physiological maturation, and that some sort of parallel with other maturational variables should therefore be present.

Consider next the data on adults' functioning. Given that adults are as unpracticed as children in a particular operation, the model predicts that they should function in a very similar fashion on all three sorts of test, i.e., on tests of OS, STSS and executive capability. However, given that both children and adults are provided with massive practice in the operation in question, the model predicts that this equivalence should disappear, and that both groups should return to their maturationally determined levels of functioning.

PROBLEMS WITH CURRENT MODELS

As will no doubt be apparent, both the one-factor and the two-factor models have their drawbacks, at least in their present state of development. The drawback of the one-factor (practice-only) model is that, as yet, it can provide no explanation for the fact that OS and STSS develop at the same rate across different domains, or at a rate which is similar to that observed for variables with a clear maturational component. The drawback of the two-factor (practice-plus-maturation) model is that, as yet, it can provide no explanation for how maturation has the particular effects which it does.

To say that each of the two models has its drawbacks, of course, is not to say that no work of an empirical nature can be conducted, in order to determine which of the two models is more plausible. To the contrary, because the two models make different predictions about a variety of phenomena, it should be possible to test their relative plausibility quite directly. Then, once this is done, it should be possible to focus on the model which appears to have the greater promise, and to work on eliminating the drawbacks it possesses in its current state.

In the present chapter, both of these tasks are attempted. First, a series of studies is reported which was intended to permit a more informed choice to be made between the two models. Then, one of the two models is developed further, in the hopes of eliminating some of its current drawbacks, and stimulating further work of an empirical nature.

NEW DATA OF RELEVANCE TO THE MODELS

Study 1[1]

Assuming that different children receive different amounts of practice in different specific operations, and assuming further that the one factor (practice only) model is valid, it follows that any given child should have an irregular profile of scores on a battery of OS and STSS measures whose development depends on different sorts of experience. Conversely, it follows that he or she should have a more regular profile of scores on measures which depend on similar sorts of experience. This being the case, it follows further that the correlations among the measures which depend on different experience should be relatively low, while the correlations among measures which depend on similar experience should be relatively high.

Quite a different pattern of data should be expected if the two factor model is correct. According to the two factor model, children might still have a regular pattern of scores across STSS and OS measures that depend on different sorts of experience, providing that they have had sufficient experience of relevance to each to bring them to a common asymptotal level. Thus, if the two-factor model is correct, one would not necessarily expect a large difference in the magnitude of correlations among tasks that did and did not share common experiential requirements.

How might one set up a situation where one set of measures shared a common set of experiential requirements, whereas another group did not? A number of different procedures might be adopted. However, one of the simplest would be to create one group of measures which shared a common set of operational requirements (e.g., counting), and to contrast them with another group which shared a different set of operational requirements (e.g., counting versus naming pictures). It was this procedure which was followed in the first study. An OS and STSS measure were administered which both entailed the same basic operation (counting). Next, two additional measures of OS and STSS were administered which involved different operational requirements (spatial localization and picture naming). Finally, the correlations among all four tests were computed, and compared.

---

[1]This study was conducted in collaboration with Midian Kurland.

Measures

The two measures that entailed a common operational component were the counting-span test and counting-speed test. The measure that entailed spatial localization was the CUCUI. Finally, the measure that involved verbal labelling was Biemiller's picture labeling test (Biemiller & Bowden, 1980). In this test, children are presented with 25 line drawings of familiar objects, depicted in characteristic-view renderings. The children's task is to label each of the pictures as quickly as possible. Their score is the total time it takes them to label all the pictures on the card, divided by 25.

Subjects

The first study in this series was conducted in conjunction with study number three in the previous chapter, and used the same subjects. Twelve children at each of five age levels (4, 6, 8, 10, and 12 years) were tested. There were six boys and six girls in each group.

Procedure

All four tests were administered in one sitting. The picture labeling test was administered last.

Results

The intercorrelations among the four measures are presented in Table 17.1. The values with age partialled out are shown below the diagonal. As may be seen, the values with age partialled out were considerably lower than the values with age included. However, (1) all the correlations remained significant, and (2) the basic pattern remained unchanged: the measures of OS and STSS that shared a common operation correlated no more highly than those which did not.

TABLE 17.1

Intercorrelation of Four Speed and Span Measures

	Counting span	CUCUI	Counting speed	Picture naming speed
Counting span		.83**	.79**	.69**
CUCUI	.34**		.83**	.70**
Counting speed	.33**	.30**		.72**
Picture naming speed	.37**	.38**	.46**	

*$p < .01$.
**$p < .001$.

Discussion

The data from this study do not constitute a critical refutation of the notion that practice is the only factor that is responsible for the developmental decrement in OS. Nevertheless, they do suggest that the factor which ties together tests of OS and STSS is not a highly specific one. Thus, if practice is the only mechanism which is responsible for the developmental relationship between OS and STSS it is likely to be a practice of a very general sort. Either that, or individual children must receive approximately the same amount of practice across different operational domains.

Study 2[2]

The objective of the second study was to determine the rate of OS decrement in two populations whose physical and cultural environments were radically different, and whose general opportunities for practice were therefore also very different. It was reasoned that—if the one factor (practice-only) model were correct—then the two populations should show different rates of OS growth. By contrast, if the two-factor (practice + maturation) model were correct, the OS curves for the two populations should be quite similar. Assuming that both groups receive whatever minimal practice is necessary in order to reach their asymptotal level of functioning, their OS should be largely a function of maturation, and both groups should progress at the same approximate rate. Both groups should also asymptote at the same level, and should reach this level at the same age.

Subjects

The first population of subjects lived in a small city (population 30,000) in Eastern Ontario, about 100 miles from Toronto. They were drawn from a school which served a lower middle-class area, and which had a precision teaching curriculum in place. Precision teaching is an approach to instruction which places great emphasis on the isolation and drill of specific skills, and which provides a good deal of occasion for children to engage in speeded practice.

The second population of subjects lived in isolated rural villages in the Eastern region of Ghana, West Africa. They were all attending small Western-oriented primary schools. However, they were not being provided with any particular practice in counting, and lived in a culture which did not put a premium on this skill. Even in cooking and barter, multiple units of the same size are rarely used in village life in Ghana. Hence, there are relatively few occasions for subjects to

---

[2] This study was conducted in collaboration with Midian Kurland, and with the assistance of Thomas Fiati, and S. E. A. Williams.

practice their counting skills. Such occasions as do occur are primarily in children's rhymes and games.

Measures

Several measures were administered. However, for the present purpose, the important measure was the test of counting speed. This was administered in the standard fashion, as was described in the previous chapter. The North American group was tested in English; the West African group was tested in Ewe.

Results

The results are shown in Figure 17.1. As may be seen, there appeared to be a slight difference in OS favoring the North American group at the youngest age level. This difference presumably reflected the different opportunities for practice which are available in the two cultures. By and large, however, the two curves were far more alike than they were different. Of particular interest was the finding that the two groups reached the same asymptotal level of performance, and did so at the same age.

Discussion

If one accepts that the two populations in question had different opportunities to practice dimensional operations such as counting, then the results from the second study constitute compelling evidence against the one factor (practice only) model. On the other hand, if one does not accept this assumption, the results are of little significance. While the results are congruent with the two factor model, then, they do not rule out the one factor model conclusively.

Study 3[3]

The object of the third study was to examine the effects of massive practice on OS, using an experimental rather than a naturalistic paradigm. Children were given 3 months of intensive daily practice in counting. Their speed of counting was then compared with that of children who had not had this sort of massive practice. It was reasoned that if the one factor (practice-only) model of OS decrement were valid, then the children in the treatment group should show a substantial superiority over the children in the control group, both in OS and in STSS. By contrast, if the two factor (practice plus maturation) model were valid, the degree of superiority should be modest or negligible. Because children

[3] The third study was conducted by Midian Kurland, as part of his doctoral dissertation (Kurland, 1981).

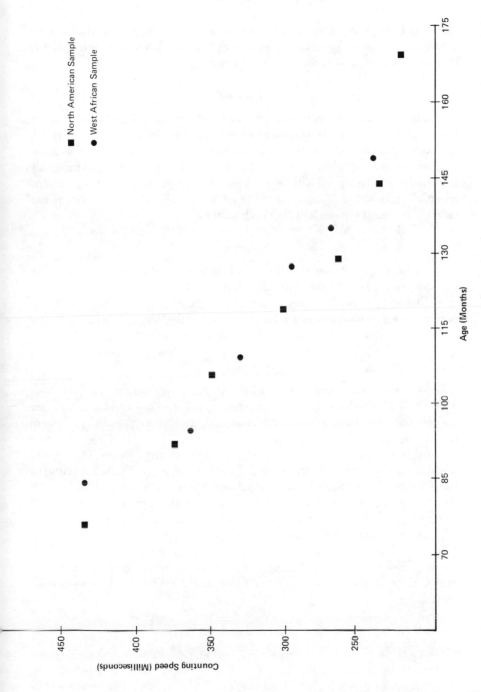

Fig. 17.1. Results of studies on counting speed conducted in North America (Ontario) and West Africa (Ghana).

receive at least some practice as a matter of course, the efficiency of their counting should to a large degree be determined by their level of maturation, and further practice should have relatively little impact.

Materials

Two sets of materials were prepared, one for the treatment group and one for the control group. The treatment materials consisted of large sheets of paper that were subdivided into sections. In each section was a set of dots such as those used on the tests of counting speed and counting span. The control materials consisted of similar sheets, with sets of letters in each section. For the treatment group, the task was to count the dots in each section. For the control group, the task was to sound out the letters in each section.

Subjects

The subjects were drawn from the same Ontario school system as those in the previous study. That is, they were drawn from a lower middle-class group in a small Ontario city, where a precision teaching program was in place. Counting dots was not a focus of this program. However, for the purpose of the study, the school agreed to make it a focus for the experimental subjects.

Design

The experimental subjects were all drawn from the same grade one class, which had 18 children in it. The teacher was first asked to rank order her children from 1 to 18 in terms of their general ability. Nine equivalent pairs were then formed from adjacent rankings. Within each pair, one child was randomly assigned to the treatment group, the other to the control group. Three additional control groups were also studied. The first consisted of all the children in the other grade one class in the same school. The second consisted of half the children from each of the two grade two classes in the same school. The third consisted of a small group of adults, who were friends of the experimenter. None of these latter three groups was given any special training.

Each child was tested three times in the course of the experiment, once three months before the treatment began, once at the outset of the treatment, and once at the end. Each adult was tested twice, at either end of a three month interval.

Procedure

During the first week of the treatment period, the children in the treatment class were presented with stop watches and were instructed in the mechanics of using the practice sheets. Every time they finished a section, they were asked to note the time it took them to do so. The treatment itself then lasted for 15 to 25 minutes a day, for a total of 3 months. During this time, the children in the experimental group counted more than 5000 arrays of dots. The children in the matched control group sounded out letters for a corresponding time period.

It is hard to judge how much practice 5000 trials might be, relative to that which children receive normally in their everyday life. However, it seems reasonable to assume that a normal grade one child would not have the occasion to count an array of objects more than five times per day. In fact, it seems reasonable to assume that he or she would not have the occasion to count more than two or three sets of objects per day. Under these assumptions, then, it may be said that the counting group received the equivalent of somewhere between $2\frac{1}{2}$ and 5 years of practice in counting, concentrated within a 3-month period.

Results

The procedure of giving the children stop watches and having them time their performance turned out to be remarkably motivating. The children remained eager to engage in the activity throughout the 3-month period, and expressed regret when the study was over. In part, this may have been due to the continued enthusiasm of the teacher, who was a devotee of precision-teaching methods, and interested in the effects of massive practice.

The performance of each group on the counting-speed test is illustrated in Figure 17.2. As may be seen, the counting group made remarkably little progress in comparison to any of the other groups. In fact, by the end of the study, they had not exceeded the level of performance of any of the groups whose performance at the outset had been superior to their own. Moreover, what small gain they did show appeared largely attributable to a warm-up effect. Children in the various control groups tended to reach their ceiling counting speed quite slowly. Their performance on the second half of the trials was thus clearly superior to their performance on the first half of the trials. By contrast, children in the treatment group tended to reach their ceiling counting speed very rapidly. Thus, their performance on the second half of the trials was only marginally better than their performance on the first half. With this warm-up effect partialled out, the improvement of the experimental group was even smaller than that indicated in the figure.

Discussion

The data from the third study provide little support for the one-factor (practice-only) model of OS decrement. Nor are they the only data of their sort. The effect of practice on basic skills was a topic that received a good deal of scrutiny at the turn of the century. While the studies were not always designed in a carefully controlled fashion, by and large they revealed a similar pattern: as long

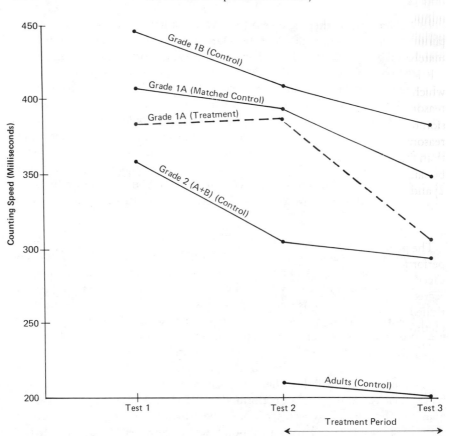

Fig. 17.2. Results from study on effects of massive practice (Kurland, 1981).

as children were reasonably familiar with a basic skill, further practice produced a relatively small increment in performance, compared to that which occurred spontaneously in the course of development (see Kurland, 1981, for a review).

Of course, one could always argue that the sorts of practice that have been provided in the past have not been the right sort, and that—were a different sort of practice provided—the results would be considerably different. Even allowing for the possibility that more sizeable experiential effects may be found if different forms of practice are provided, however, it seems unlikely that they will be of sufficient magnitude to completely account for the developmental changes in OS that are observed, given the overall pattern of the data. In previous chapters, it will be remembered, it was shown that the rate of STSS growth is very similar across widely different domains. In addition, it was shown that children's executive development also takes place at the same rate across domains, and that these data are quite similar to the rate of growth in physical stature. Now, in the present chapter, three additional pieces of data have been added. Study 1 showed that tests of OS and STSS that share a common specific operation correlate no more highly than those that do not. Study 2 showed that populations with a great deal of opportunity for practicing basic operations show the same general growth curve with regard to OS as those which do not. Finally, Study 3 showed that massive practice in basic operations produces relatively little impact on OS, at least when the operation in question is one with which subjects are relatively familiar. In each case, the one-factor model would have predicted results that were different from those which were actually obtained. Even allowing for the fact that more sizeable practice effects may possibly be found with some different treatment in the future, then, it seems fair to say that the overall pattern of data is still likely to favor the two-factor model.

Of course, to say that the two-factor model appears more promising than the one-factor model is not to say that it is adequate either. As was mentioned at the outset, the two-factor model in its present form also has a very serious drawback, because it does not specify what sort of maturational changes are of relevance to children's intellectual development, nor how these might exert an impact on OS and STSS.

In the interest of reducing these difficulties, therefore, and of stimulating further empirical work on the problem of OS and STSS growth, I would like to conclude by developing the two-factor model a bit further, and introducing a more explicit physiological component.

TOWARD A NEUROPHYSIOLOGICAL MODEL OF EXPERIENTIAL AND MATURATIONAL CHANGE

Contemporary research in neuropsychology has been strongly influenced by the pioneering work of Hebb (1949). One postulate of Hebb's theory, in particular, has received a great deal of empirical support. This is that—when learning takes place—a chemical change occurs in the synapses between neurons, such that the assembly of cells representing one event (e.g., a stimulus) is more likely to trigger the activation of the cells representing other events (e.g., correct responses). In fact, with the advent of modern assessment techniques, it has even become possible to observe this sort of change taking place experimentally and to specify many of the chemical changes that are involved (Kandel, 1979).

Given that Hebb's model constitutes a reasonable approximation to the sorts of changes that take place with practice at the neurological level, Figure 17.3 might be said to constitute a reasonable approximation of the state of affairs in the cortex, before and after the learning of a new operation is practiced. Before practice (Figure 17.3a) the activation of cell-assembly number 1 (e.g., the word

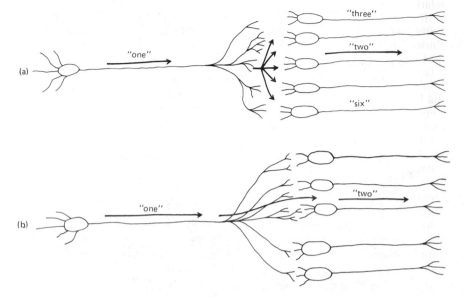

Fig. 17.3. Hypothetical connections between two neurons (a) when very little learning has taken place and (b) when extensive learning has taken place.

"one") does not automatically trigger the activation of cell-assembly 2 (e.g., the word "two"). Cell-assembly number 2 is activated only after a certain level of activation has gradually built up in the alternative cell assemblies as well (e.g., six, three, nine, etc.), and some additional process corresponding to a decision has favored the activation of the assembly representing the number two over these other possibilities.

The situation after practice is presented in Figure 17.3 (b). Note that sufficient positive connections now exist between two of the assemblies (e.g., those representing one and two), and sufficient inhibitory connections now exist between the first assembly and the other possible alternatives, that the activation of the first assembly (e.g., one) triggers the activation of the second (e.g., two) rapidly and automatically, with no spread of lateral activity whatever.

Although the above models are no doubt oversimplified, they are nevertheless sufficient to explain the data which our adult training studies have revealed. The first datum is that, with practice, adults' speed of counting in a new language improves dramatically. This datum may be explained by postulating that—with the transition from the state of affairs in Figure 17.3 (a) to that in Figure 17.3 (b)—the interneuronal activation process itself becomes more rapid. The second datum is that the increase in counting speed is accompanied by an increase in the STSS for numbers in the new language. This may be explained by suggesting that with the decrease in lateral activation comes a decrease in the interference with activity in adjacent neural tissue, such as the stored record of previous operations. And with this decreased interference comes an increase in measured STSS.

If this sort of model accurately reflects what takes place as a result of learning, what sort of model might explain the change that takes place as a result of maturation? The sort of change one would hope to find would be one which also produces its effect by influencing the degree of lateral transmission (or interference) and the speed of linear transmission. However, it would have to do so in a fashion that is not specific to any one particular set of cell assemblies, and which takes place very gradually. A number of possibilities might be suggested, such as a change in the chemical properties of whole areas of the brain, or in the number of potential dendritic connections. A particularly attractive possibility, however, would be a change in the degree of neuronal myelinization.

Myelin is a fatty substance that surrounds certain classes of neurons. And, as Tasaki (1953) has shown, one of the primary functions of myelin is to speed up neuronal transmission. Rather than propogating themselves slowly, action potentials jump along the length of a neuron, moving directly from one gap in the myelin sheath to the next. Another function of myelin is to act as an insulator. In effect, the build-up of myelin also prevents leakage across nerve pathways, thus decreasing the amount of lateral transmission, and the amount of interference that results.

This is a second factor that would produce a change in the speed of operating and in the size of STSS, but for maturational or general experiential rather than specific experiential reasons. Before myelinization, linear transmission would be slow due to the absence of a myelin sheath. Similarly, lateral transmission would be high, due to the absence of insulation. As a consequence, speed of operating would be slow, and STSS would be low, regardless of how much practice was presented. This state of affairs is illustrated in Figure 17.4 (a).

By contrast, after myelinization, linear transmission would be rapid and lateral transmission would be negligible, with the result that operational speed and STSS would be high—provided, that is, that some practice in the operation in question had also been presented. If no practice had been presented, then the slowdown and leakage at the nerve junctions would mask the improvements that had been effected within the nerves themselves, and hence prevent the child's increased level of functioning from being detected.

Given that myelinization could play this sort of facilitative role in human development, it becomes of considerable importance to ask whether there is any evidence that it actually does. In fact, while the evidence is by no means conclusive, it is certainly suggestive. Of all the physiological changes that take place with the development, myelinization is perhaps the most salient. Although it was once believed that the process of myelinization was complete by an early age, it has since been shown that this is not the case. The process continues well

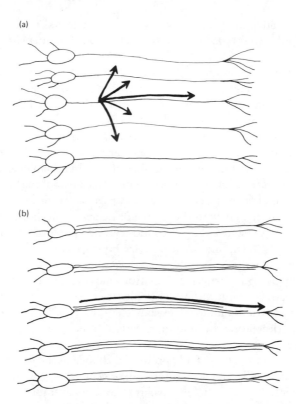

Fig. 17.4. Hypothetical nerve impulses (a) before much mylenization has taken place and (b) after extensive myelinization.

into adolescence, and does not taper off until the age when physical growth also tapers off, namely 16 to 25 years (Yakovlev & Lecours, 1967). It has also been shown that the process does not occur evenly, but rather in cycles. Major *waves of myelinization* take place, which begin or end at 1 month, 4 months, 1 to 2 years, 3 to 4 years, 10 years, and 18 to 25 years of age. Moreover, these waves take place in neurological systems which serve different psychological functions. The systems that myelinate from 1 to 4 months are those for controlling isolated sensory and motor functions. The systems that myelinate from 4 months to $1\frac{1}{2}$ years are those for coordinating such sensory and motor functions. Finally, the systems that myelinate from $1\frac{1}{2}$ to 4, $1\frac{1}{2}$ to 10, and $1\frac{1}{2}$ to 18 years of age are those for operating on basic sensorimotor functions at higher and higher levels of abstraction and integration (Yakovlev & Lecours, 1967). While the cycles of myelinization cannot be mapped precisely onto the operational cycles that are described in the present volume, then, there does appear to be at least some correspondence between them. It therefore seems reasonable to suggest, at least as a working hypothesis, that successively higher levels of cognitive operation are controlled by successively higher systems in the brain. It also seems reasonable to suggest that each of these systems has its own characteristic period of myelinization, at least given normal experience. Finally, it seems reasonable to suggest that the degree of myelinization of any system will determine the maximum OS for the class of operations which it is responsible for controlling and that the maximum value of STSS that is possible when myelinization is complete will be approximately $OP_x + 3$ units.

In conclusion, it seems worthwhile to point out that the word maturation is used in more than one sense in the developmental literature. In the first sense, it is used to refer to age-related changes that are entirely biological; that is, to changes that would take place if a child were reared in a cupboard and provided with adequate biological nourishment. In the second sense, the term is used to refer to age-related changes that are biological, but which require a normal human environment if they are to emerge. Changes of this latter sort would not be affected by any specific experience, but might well be affected by the total pattern of experience to which a child was exposed. As a consequence, they would not emerge if the child were reared in a cupboard.

Although the data are not completely unequivocal, myelinization appears to involve change of the latter sort. Thus, while some change in myelinization may take place in response to purely biological factors, it appears that the rate and timing of myelinization is affected by the general pattern of experience to which an organism is exposed (Rosensweig & Bennell, 1976). Thus, while it is unlikely to make much difference how much counting children are exposed to in the course of their development, it very probably does make a difference how much relational activity they are exposed to in total. The general pattern of such experience may not only affect the rate of myelinization during the period from $1\frac{1}{2}$ to $4\frac{1}{2}$ years, it may also affect the terminal level that is reached in the corresponding neurological system, and the timing of the waves of higher-order myelinization that follow.

SUMMARY OF PART III AND CONCLUSION

At the end of the first section, a summary of the present theory of stages was presented in postulate form, and the relationship of each postulate to the postulates of previous theories was indicated. I would like to conclude the present section by summarizing the present theory of stage transition in the same fashion.

The following two postulates, both of which were implicit in Piaget's theory, have been preserved in the present account of stage transition.

1. Stage transition involves the hierarchical integration of two or more struc-

tures, each of which is already within the child's operative capability (see also Werner, 1948).

2. Two of the most important regulatory processes that produce this integration are *problem solving* (see Piaget's equilibration) and exploration (see Piaget's reflective abstraction).

The following three postulates, which formed the cornerstone of both Baldwin's and Pascual-Leone's theories, were also preserved.

1. Regardless of the process by which a given set of structures is activated, they cannot be integrated unless they are actively attended to.

2. As a consequence, children's capability for hierarchical integration is limited by the size of their attentional capacity.

3. Attentional capacity changes with age, due to the influence of biological and general experiential factors.

The following two postulates, both of which were proposed by Pascual-Leone, were preserved as well.

1. The critical capacity values at 4, 6, 8, and 10 years of age are 1 (or OP_{dim}), 2 (or $OP_{dim} + 1$), 3 (or $OP_{dim} + 2$), and 4 (or $OP_{dim} + 3$).

2. These critical values are the same, regardless of the general process by which a particular structural integration takes place. The only exception is if the integration takes place in the course of well-planned and sustained instruction—in which case the critical value may be lowered.

Finally, the following three postulates, all of which played a central role in the theories of Vygotsky and Bruner, were also preserved.

1. Social processes such as mutual regulation and imitation can play a role in children's development which is just as important as the role played by auto-regulative processes.

2. A structure that is constructed in the course of social interaction at one stage of development (e.g., counting, ratio-comparison) can become an instrument of auto-regulation at the next.

3. A form of mutual regulation that is of particular importance for children's intellectual development—especially at the higher stages—is instruction.

In addition to the postulates that were preserved from previous theories, the following five postulates were added.

1. Regardless of the general regulatory process by which hierarchical integration takes place, the same four subprocesses are entailed. These are (1) schematic search, (2) schematic evaluation, (3) schematic retagging, and (4) schematic consolidation.

2. A parallel growth of processing capacity to that observed during the dimensional stage takes place during all of the other major stages of development as well. During each major stage, capacity grows from OP_x to $OP_x + 3$, thus procuding a distinct sequence of substages.

3. This cyclic growth of processing capacity is the result of a cyclic growth in

the efficiency of successively higher classes of operations, not an increase in *total processing capacity*.

4. The cyclic growth in operational efficiency will not take place without specific practice in the various operations in question; however, it is unlikely to be completely dependent on specific practice either. Rather, it is likely to be dependent on general maturational changes, in successively higher systems of the brain.

5. One possible way in which maturation could produce such changes is via myelinization of neural tissue. Because unmyelinated neural tissue permits lateral as well as linear transmission, it might also permit interference between an ongoing operation and the stored products of previous operations. Conversely, since fully myelinated tissue reduces such lateral transmission, it might minimize such interference, and permit up to three or four products of previous operations to be stored, while an ongoing operation is executed.

The final two postulates in the above set (i.e., those having to do with recurrent cycles of maturation and myelinization) are highly speculative. All the other postulates, however, are grounded in a solid historical tradition, and supported by a substantial body of empirical data. With these fundamental postulates as a guide, therefore, it becomes possible to address the third general question with which the study of intellectual development has historically been concerned, namely how to optimize the developmental process.

PART IV

Applications and Extensions
of the Theory

CHAPTER 18

Intellectual Development and Education

INTRODUCTION

Education is a process in which both the young and the old have a vital stake. It serves many functions. One of the most important, however, is to enable the younger and less-experienced members of a culture to acquire the values, insights and skills which are their heritage. Another is to prepare these same individuals for taking an active role in extending that heritage, by developing their intellectual potential to its fullest. When viewed in this fashion, it may be seen that the process of education and the process of development bear a necessary relationship to each other. In fact, one of the ultimate aims of education *is* development, both of the individual and the culture. It is perhaps not surprising, therefore, that educators have often turned to developmental theory: either for a justification of an approach to which they were already committed, or for suggestions on how to implement that approach, in a specific educational context.

As was mentioned in Chapters 2–6, different theories of intellectual development have been based on quite different metaphors of the young child. In addition, they have offered quite different views of the developmental process. As a consequence, they have tended to attract educators with equally different educational perspectives, and to be put to an equally wide range of different uses. Before examining the educational implications of the present theory, it is worthwhile to re-examine these previous theories, and the various uses to which they have been put.

THE PIAGETIAN PERSPECTIVE

Piaget viewed the child as a young scientist: constructing ever more powerful theories of the world, by the application of a set of logicomathematical tools of ever increasing power. These tools were seen as being of the child's own making, yet at the same time following each other in a universal and logically necessary sequence. Although Piaget did not spell out the educational implications of this view in great detail, a considerable secondary literature grew up, which had this as its primary objective. A number of distinct yet interwoven themes may be detected in this literature.

1. The first is that education should be geared to children's current stage of development (i.e., to the way in which they interpret the world, and the way in which they operate on it) (Hunt, 1961; Ginsburg & Opper, 1969; Siegel, 1969).

2. A second theme is that education should be oriented toward the spontaneous processes of learning and development (i.e., toward such autonomous processes as differentiation, coordination, equilibration, and reflective abstraction).

3. A third theme is that education should seek to broaden the base of children's intellectual development. While Piaget believed that all normal children pass through all four stages of development, he acknowledged that a great many adults fail the particular tests of formal operations which he and Inhelder designed. His interpretation of this finding was that many adults have a relatively narrow focus of interest and competence, which excludes such important areas as mathematics and science (Piaget, 1972). Given that this is the case, it follows that educators should seek to broaden the focus of children's interest and experience, so that they will be able to apply their operational structures to such domains. In fact, they should seek to broaden this focus to as wide a range of domains as possible (Case, 1973; Wohlwil, 1970).

In addition to these suggestions as to what educators should do, a number of suggestions have been made as to what they should not do.

1. The first is that educators should not put a heavy emphasis on direct instruction, or any other activity that might interfere with—rather than channel—the child's own active attempts to extract meaning from the world. As Piaget said, "Every time we teach a child something, we prevent him from discovering it on his own" (Piaget, 1964).

2. A second enjoinder is that education should not aim at producing undue developmental acceleration, that is, unnaturally rapid progress in a vertical as opposed to a horizontal direction (Piaget, 1964; Wohlwil, 1970). There is more than one reason for this enjoinder. One is that such attempts are unlikely to be successful, within the context of Piaget's framework, because development is seen as being regulated by very general structures, which are slow to change and which are under the control of internal, autoregulative processes. Another is

that such attempts would be of questionable value, even if they were successful, since development through the highest stages is seen as being universal in any case (Piaget, 1972).

The above general notions have been drawn on by at least two different groups of educators, in formulating their educational objectives and in designing curricula. This first group are those whose interest is in early childhood education. A substantial segment of the early childhood community already had a strong commitment to child-centred education, well before Piaget's theory was developed. What they found in Piaget's theory, however, was a psychological framework which supported this commitment, and a source of ideas concerning activities that might be appropriate for young children, and contribute to their intellectual growth (see Kamii & Radin, 1967). A second group which drew quite heavily on Piaget were located within the science and mathematics community. For this group, the attraction of the theory was that it specified the intellectual operations towards which a process-oriented science and mathematics education might be directed, and that it provided a fertile source of ideas concerning activities that could be used for the development of these processes, as well as tasks which could be used for their assessment (Karplus, 1964; Nuffield, 1964; Ginsburg, 1977, Lawson & Wollman, 1977).

THE BRUNERIAN PERSPECTIVE

Given Bruner's view of the child as the inheritor of cultural tools, he of course assigned the process of education a more central role in the process of development that did Piaget, and wrote on the topic more extensively. Of the various educational suggestions that Bruner advanced, the four which were most closely tied to his theory of development were the following:

1. Western educators should focus on teaching the general forms of representation, as well as the discipline-specific forms of inquiry, which constitute the Western cultural heritage. Such teaching should look forward as well as backward, keeping in touch with the most recent discoveries in various fields, and ensuring that the school curriculum reflects the most recent conceptual structure of each discipline.

2. In designing curricula that are oriented towards such a goal, an effort should be made to proceed from enactive to iconic to symbolic forms of representation, thus laying the groundwork at lower levels for continued development at higher levels.

3. In order to ensure that children actually do master the various intellectual tools to which they are introduced, they should not simply be told about them, but should be engaged in activities for which the tools are indispensible aids. Because the utility of many high-level tools lies in their ability to facilitate the

discovery of new knowledge, children should be engaged in independent, discovery-oriented learning from an early age.

4. For students who come from minority cultures, an effort should be made to bridge the gap between the forms of representation and cognitive strategies that they acquire in their own culture, and those used by the dominant majority. Otherwise, these groups will have little chance of playing a productive role in the mainstream culture, should they choose to do so.

As had been the case with Piaget's ideas, Bruner's ideas were also drawn on by several different groups of educators, both to provide a more detailed rationale for beliefs to which they were already committed, and for ideas on how to translate these beliefs into action. One group which found his ideas useful were those with a commitment to what might be termed classical, or academically oriented education (cf. Eisner & Vallance, 1974). In keeping with Bruner's suggestions, a number of these individuals became involved in efforts to re-vamp subject-area curricula, so that they more accurately reflected the structure of the various disciplines as construed by those who were at their forefront. The result of these efforts was a variety of new curricula in "old" subject areas (such as the New Math, or PSSC Science), as well as at least one curriculum in a relatively new area, social science (see Bruner, 1965; Eisner, 1974). Among those educators with a political commitment to minorities there was a second group who found Bruner's ideas useful. These individuals drew on his writings—as well as those of other psychologists—in formulating the objectives for the American educational effort that became known as Project Headstart.[1] Finally, a third group whose educational efforts were at least allied with Bruner's, even when they were not directly influenced by them, were those with an interest in breaking down traditional subject area barriers, and focusing on various modes of representation or strategies across disciplines. The movement for inquiry-oriented education and language across the curriculum constituted two such steps in this direction.

THE INFORMATION-PROCESSING PERSPECTIVE

Neither Newell nor Simon wrote extensively on the implications for education of their view of the young child as a manipulator of symbols, or as a processor of information. However, they both devoted at least some attention to the topic (cf. Newell & Rosenbloom, 1981; Simon, 1980), as did those who were interested in the application of their ideas to the problems of development (cf. Klahr, 1976; Seigler, 1977) or instruction (cf. Anderson, 1982; Greeno, 1978;

---

[1]For a personal account of Bruner's involvement in Project Headstart, as well as in the curriculum reform movement, see Bruner (1980).

Larkin, 1983). Moreover, many investigators who had grown up in the tradition of learning theory, and who had already devoted a good deal of effort to developing a technology of instruction, found it convenient to adopt the information processing metaphor, and to extend their efforts in directions suggested by it (cf. Anderson & Faust, 1973; Gagné & Briggs, 1979; Glaser, 1976; Resnick, 1976). Abstracting rather freely from the information-processing literature, and remembering that information processing theories do not in general attribute much importance either to stages or to endogenous factors in development, one may suggest the following general prescriptions as being congruent with the information processing approach:

1. Instruction should be preceded by a detailed mapping of the conceptual networks, and/or the conceptual strategies, which are used by experts in the domain of interest.
2. The next step should be a parallel mapping of the conceptual networks and/or the strategies of the children who are to be taught.
3. An instructional program should then be designed to lead the children from their current degree of cognitive incompetence to the desired state of competence, via a set of carefully arranged and sequenced activities, in which the children are encouraged to tackle increasingly complex problems, in an active fashion.

As might be expected, the above general prescriptions have been of greatest interest to educators whose subject matters lend themselves to precise task analysis, such as those in mathematical education (cf. Carpenter, Moser, & Romberg, 1982; Greeno, 1978). Information-processing methods are also being used, however, in subject areas where the underlying operations are less well understood, and where the methods offer the potential for clarifying their nature. One such area is English composition, where attempts are being made to understand the writing process, and to link this understanding to improved curricula (cf. Hayes & Flower, 1980; Scardamalia & Bereiter, 1984).

COMPARISON OF THE THREE PERSPECTIVES

The three theories that have been reviewed share a common concern with the process of intellectual development. As a consequence, the educational approaches with which they have been associated share a number of features in common as well, including (1) the view that fostering the development of high-level cognitive operations should be one of the major goals of education; (2) the view that any attempt to do so must meet children at their current cognitive level; and (3) the view that genuine progress will not take place unless children are involved in active cognitive processing of some sort.

Because the three theories differ widely in their interpretation of the nature of high-level cognitive operations, however, as well as the process by which these operations develop, the educational approaches with which they have been associated have often been quite different. For Piagetians—with their view of the child as a rational and autonomous young scientist—the perferred approach has most often been a child-centered one, in which children are encouraged to independently explore and reflect on as wide a variety of situations as possible. For Brunerians—with their view of the child as the inheritor of cultural tools—the preferred approach has most been one of cultural empowerment, in which children are exposed to the structure of contemporary academic disciplines, in the context of a discovery-oriented and age-appropriate curriculum. Finally, for information theorists—with their view of the child as a manipulator of symbols whose internal procedures for performing these manipulations are learned from experience—the commitment has most often been to a skill-teaching approach, in which both basic and high-level operations are taught directly, after careful task analysis.

THE PRESENT PERSPECTIVE

The view of the young child that has underpinned the present theory has been that of a problem solver; that is, an organism which is capable of representing the current situation in which it finds itself, as well as alternative situations with a higher affective value; then setting the attainment of some other situation as a goal, and developing a strategy for reaching it. This view has not been advanced so much as an alternative to the previous views, however, as a way of integrating them. Thus, the process by which children actually solve problems has been described in a fashion that is compatible with information-processing theory, and represented with an information-processing formalism. At the same time, the structures that result from children's problem solving have been construed as building on each other in the developmental fashion described by Piaget, and as being subject to the sort of biological constraints suggested by Baldwin and Pascual-Leone. Finally, in accord with the suggestions of Bruner and Vygotsky, the child's culture has been seen as contributing a vital set of intellectual tools to the child's repertoire, via processes such as imitation and mutual regulation. These tools are often the focus of the child's problem solving during one stage, and the instrument of his higher order problem solving during the next (See Chapter 12). In addition, they tend to become increasingly less universal and increasingly more difficult to master as the child approaches the vectorial stage (See Chapter 10).

What sort of approach to education would be most congruent with this overall view of the young child? Over the past 15 years, we have devoted a good deal of energy and experimentation to answering this question. The general goal we believe to be most compatible with this view is that of facilitating the development of the child's problem-solving capabilities—across as wide a range of culturally valued problem domains or subject areas as is possible. The general set of procedures we have evolved for reaching this goal are as follows:

1. *Specification of goals.* Our educational planning begins with an analysis of the values, insights, and skills that are the child's cultural heritage, and toward whose development the educational curriculum is to be devoted. This first step is of course premised on the assumption that such high-level insights and skills will not simply develop spontaneously, but must be actively facilitated.

2. *Analysis of adult control structures.* Our next step is to analyze the executive control structures used by adults who already embody these values, and who possess the relevant knowledge and skills. This step is based on the assumption that such structures do underlie all skilled problem solving, even when the problem solvers themselves are not aware of them.

3. *Analysis of developmental precursors.* Our third step is to analyze the developmental precursors of these structures: that is, the lower-level vectorial, dimensional, and relational structures that preceed them and on which their successful acquisition depends. This step is based on the assumption that all high-level structures do have such developmental precursors, an assumption that is fundamental to the present theory.

4. *Design of educational activities.* Our fourth step is to create a set of educational activities which will maximize the chance that each individual child will be able to engage in some task that is appropriate for his or her current structural level on one hand, and yet be able to progress toward higher levels on the other. Achieving this objective requires, first of all, that the top-level goal of any educational activity be clear to all the children who are going to participate in it. Otherwise they will not be able to access the most appropriate structures that are already in their repertoire. In addition, it requires that all children be able to make at least some degree of progress toward this goal from the outset. Otherwise they will have no motivation actually to apply these structures, and to think about the problems they encounter in an active fashion. Finally, achieving this objective requires that all children be able to genuinely understand the reason for any structural modification or elaboration that is required, and that they be provided with whatever degree of social faciliatation and practice is necessary, in order to complete the re-tagging and consolidation process. Otherwise, what will take place will not be a genuine structural progression, but rather the acquisition of isolated pieces of new knowledge.

5. *Implementation of the curriculum.* Our final step is to implement the resulting curriculum, in a context which permits the teacher to adapt to the needs of each individual learner, and to make decisions concerning such variables as (1) the child's original developmental level in the domain, (2) the balance of independent versus socially regulated activity that he or she feels most comfortable with, and (3) the amount of task simplification, prompting, and carefully monitored practice that he or she needs, in order to complete the

various subcomponents of the structural reorganization process (i.e., scheme-accessing, evaluation, re-tagging and consolidation).[2]

As will no doubt be apparent, the above educational approach contains a number of elements in common with all three of the previous educational approaches. The elements that are most closely related to the Piagetian approach are the notions (1) that a universal developmental sequence will be found to underlie the attainment of any adult structure, (2) that any attempt to bridge the gap between the adult and the child's structures must do so via a natural developmental route, and (3) that the rate at which children travels this route—at least in certain key respects—will be a function of internal changes in their cognitive system that can not be rushed, and to which the educator must therefore accommodate. The elements that are most clearly related to the Brunerian approach are the notions (1) that the structures which are the ultimate objectives of instruction are cultural inventions, (2) that one procedure for analyzing these structures is to work within the framework provided by conventional academic subject areas, and (3) that unless the educational environment is appropriately designed, students will be unlikely to actualize their full developmental potential. Finally, the elements that are most closely related to the information processing approach are the notions (1) that children's intellectual operations can be conceptualized as executive control structures, (2) that coaching and practice have a place in any well-balanced educational curriculum, and (3) that an educational curriculum can best be planned by analyzing both the child's and the adult's structures, and attempting to bridge the gap between them (Gagné, 1970; Glaser, 1976).

Although the above approach preserves many of the elements of previous educational approaches, it of course eliminates many features as well, and has a distinctive structure of its own. It therefore seems worthwhile to examine the nature of this structure in more detail, and to spell out the sorts of programmes and methods to which it is likely to lead, when it is applied in practice.

APPLICATIONS OF THE PRESENT PERSPECTIVE

The present approach has the potential to be applied to three closely related educational problems, namely (1) the problem of how to design new curricula so that they will provide a maximum opportunity for children to remain intellec-

---

[2] From a theoretical standpoint, one would expect that the amount of task simplification necessary would be a function of the size of children's STSS relative to that required by the task, while the amount of coaching and practice necessary would be a function of the efficiency of children's basic information processes (schematic accessing, re-tagging, etc.). Note that there is no need to assess these variables formally, however, since what is important is their combined action, and this can be inferred directly by observing children's performance on the task in which they are currently engaged.

tually active and to develop, without abandoning the goals of teaching them basic cognitive skills. (2) the problem of how to re-design existing curricula so that they will do a better job of enabling children to master the particular concepts and skills which they currently find most difficult, and (3) the problem of how to design better curricula for special students (i.e., for students who fail to show much profit from conventional approaches, due to some special handicap or disability).

Designing New Curricula

The most obvious application of the above five steps is in the design of new curricula: ones that effectively combine a concern for development with a concern for instruction in specific concepts and skills. As yet, we have not applied the approach to the task of designing an entire school curriculum in this fashion. The result we would hope for, however, would be that the approach would help curriculum designers to spell out the general sequence of attainments that could be expected in any given domain at different ages, as well as the hurdles that had to be overcome in passing from one of these levels to the next; also that the approach could help them to provide students with an opportunity for maximum horizontal enrichment within a level—thus leading to firm consolidation of existing structures and practice with basic operations—while at the same time aiding their gradual transition from one level to the next.

If such an approach were implemented, our expectation would be that the majority of children would reach a vectorial level of functioning in the majority of subject areas. Assuming that such an effort were accompanied by an appropriate program of professional development for teachers, an additional outcome might be that affective as well as cognitive benefits would accrue. As a result of understanding their students' reasoning more clearly, teachers might be better able not only to guide this reasoning but to identify with it, and to experience the excitement of helping youngsters to overcome the same set of hurdles that they once struggled with themselves. Similarly, as a result of receiving this sort of understanding and guidance, students might be better able not only to understand their teachers' instruction, but to identify with their long-term goals, and to see their teachers as models of an end state that was both desirable and attainable. Were affective changes of this sort to occur, it seems possible that the same powerful affective forces that contribute to children's development outside the classroom might be harnessed inside the classroom as well, and that the teacher-student relationship might begin to resemble that of mentor to mentee.

Redesigning Existing Curricula

A second task for which the above five-step approach could be useful—and one to which we have devoted a good deal of attention—is redesigning existing curricula, so that their most salient trouble spots are eliminated.

Even the best educational curricula have such trouble spots, that is, spots where a great number of students experience difficulty, and where a substantial proportion never really master the concepts or the skills that are taught. Moreover, it seems that the higher one proceeds in the school system, the more frequent these trouble spots become, as the world outside the classroom becomes a poorer and poorer substitute for the sort of activity that takes place within it. One of the the problems to which we have put the above general procedure, therefore, is that of diagnosing the reason for these problems, and of redesigning the curriculum so that—by remaining more closely in tune with students' level of development—it may do a better job of realizing the objectives to which its designers aspire.

Elsewhere, I have presented a detailed explication of the way in which the above five steps may be elaborated, in order to achieve this goal (Case, 1978c, in press). For the present purpose, however, it is probably best simply to provide an example. Consider, therefore, the problem of how to improve the teaching of a high-level cognitive operation in mathematices—namely ratio—to normal children who are just making the transition to the vectorial stage.

Phase 1: Specification of Goals

An objective that appears in most basic arithmetic curricula in that of enabling children to solve problems involving ratios or rates. These problems are of considerable importance in the everyday world outside the classroom, as well as in certain classroom subjects that are taught in secondary school such as physics and chemistry. As was indicated in Chapter 10, they are also an important subset of the tasks that are usually designated formal or vectorial. Accordingly, a method of solution is normally taught toward the end of primary school, i.e., at around the age 11 or 12 years.

The general form of the problems to which children are exposed is as follows: a verbal description of some situation is provided, in which two equivalent ratios are operative, but in which one of the quantities in one of the ratios is not known. The students' task is to represent the situation mathematically, and to determine the missing quantity. The following problem is a typical example:

John purchased 24 loaves of bread to sell in his grocery store last week, at a total price of 26 dollars. If he wishes to buy 30 loaves next week, how much will he have to spend?

Although such problems are normally introduced in the sixth or seventh grade, tests indicate that the majority of children do not master them, even by Grade 8 (Gajewski, 1980). In fact, the success rate reaches a value no higher than 50–60%, even in adulthood (Karplus et al., 1970). Given these statistics, it seemed likely to us that the procedure for solving these problems might require a higher level of intellectual functioning than many 11- and 12-year-olds are capable of—at least under current methods of instruction. It also seemed that the task of teaching students to solve these problems would serve as a good test case with which to assess the utility of our developmental approach. Accordingly, Alan Gold and I established the task of teaching children how to solve these problems as our goal.

Phase 2: Analysis of Adult Control Structures

As the reader will no doubt realize, the above sort of problems are quite straightforward. They may be solved by setting up an equation such as this:

$$\frac{24 \text{ dollars}}{26 \text{ dollars}} = \frac{30 \text{ loaves}}{D \text{ dollars}}$$

The equation may then be simplified and solved as follows:

$$24 \times D = 26 \times 30$$

$$\therefore D = \frac{30}{24} \times 36 \text{ (dollars)}$$

The answer is that John will have to pay $32.50 for the bread.

Although the above procedure for solving the problems is straightforward, and although children can be instructed in the various steps that it entails with relative ease, their poor performance on transfer and retention tests suggests that they do not fully understand it. Accordingly, it becomes of interest to know how they do understand the problems, and what sorts of structures they assemble spontaneously for dealing with them. In short, it becomes of interest to know what the natural developmental precursors of this procedure are.

Phase 3: Analysis of Developmental Precursors

Three different sorts of children must be studied, in order to determine the developmental precursors of the adult structure: (1) those who show no success on the problem, (2) those who show complete success, and (3) those who show some sort of intermediate level of performance.

1. *Analysis of early control structures that lead to failure.* A variety of unsuccessful control structures are used by 11- and 12-year-olds on ratio problems. These structures often involve an incorrect combination of multiplication and division. If one gets children to think their answers through, however, rather than to blindly apply some algorithm whose rationale they have not understood, it turns out that the most frequent incorrect structure is one which involves addition or substraction. Children reason that—because John paid $2.00 extra for the bread the first time, he will have to pay $2.00 extra the second time as well. The answer they give is therefore $32.00 (Inhedler & Piaget, 1958; Gold, 1978; Dennis, 1981).

2. *Analysis of early structures that lead to success.* Although the successful adult

strategy is one which involves setting up a formal equation and solving it via simplification or cross-multiplication, this method is rarely used by successful 11-or 12-year-olds, even if it is explicitly taught via a carefully constructed learning hierarchy (Anderson, 1976; Gold, 1978). The strategy that children use instead might best be called the *for every* strategy, or—somewhat more formally—the *unit method*. Children realize that the person in the problem has to pay a particular amount for every loaf of bread (i.e., for every single unit). Their first step is therefore to determine what this amount per unit is. Having determined this amount, they then determine what the total amount would be, if several units were purchased instead of one. Their reasoning therefore goes as follows:

> If John paid $26.00 for 24 loaves, this means that he must have been paying a little over $1.00 for every loaf. The exact amount is 26 divided by 24, or 1.083.
> If John wants to buy 30 loaves next week, that means he will have to pay 30 times 1.083, or $32.50.

In accordance with our general developmental approach, then, it was this strategy for solving the problems, not the adult strategy, which we set out to teach the children.

3. *Analysis of intermediate structures.* Interestingly enough, and in accordance with the trend that was described for the balance beam during this age range, even children who successfully apply the unit method often seem transitional, in the sense they use the method on some problems but not on others, falling back on the subtraction method instead. Although it is hard to say for sure, they appear to fall back in this fashion when the calculations get complex, or when they cannot see their way through the various semantic complexities that a problem entails. The easiest problems for them to solve are ones where one ratio is stated in unit form, and the other ratio is a simple multiple of it. Slightly harder problems are ones where the unit ratio must first be determined. And the hardest problems of all are ones where the unit ratio is not an even one, as in the example above.

Arranging these tasks in order of increasing complexity, a developmental hierarchy may be suggested (see Table 18.1). Given that the hierarchy in Table 18.1 is a valid one, the educational task becomes quite straightforward. It is to design a set of activities that will be appropriate for children who are functioning at levels 0 or 1—that is, at the levels which are typical for normal 11- and 12-year-olds—but which will enable them to move on to level 2 b, that is, to the simplest or easiest level at which all forms of the task may be solved.

Phase 4: Design of Curriculum

The job of designing such an instructional sequence involved three basic steps.

TABLE 18.1

Developmental Hierarchy for Arithmethic Word Problems

Level	Typical insight	Typical strategy	Typical type of problem solved
0	Same relationship holds each week between bread and dollars.	Addition or subtraction (i.e., find the extra number of dollars one week, then find dollar value for next week which will perserve this extra number).	$\frac{1}{3} = \frac{1}{D}$
1	Same relationship holds each week between one loaf of bread and dollars.	Multiplication (if dollar per loaf given for one week, multiply number of loaves next week by this value).	$\frac{1}{3} = \frac{4}{D}$
2a	Same relationship holds each week between one loaf of bread and dollars, and this can be computed via division, if it is not given.	Division, then multiplication (i.e., find dollar per loaf for one week, multiply number of loaves next week by this value).	$\frac{2}{8} = \frac{3}{D}$
2b	Same as 2a.	Same as 2a, except strategy can be applied to numbers which do not divide evenly.	$\frac{31}{26} = \frac{30}{D}$
3	Same ratio holds each week between bread and dollars.	Formation of equation (i.e., set up equation with D, then multiply and divide appropriately.	$\frac{31}{26} = \frac{30}{D}$

Creation of an Instructional Paradigm

Our first step was to create a developmentally appropriate instructional paradigm (i.e., one where the goal of the paradigm would be clear to all students, and where all students would also be able to achieve some degree of success at their current developmental level). An additional concern was that the task be one where students could determine the adequacy of their current approach on their own. The rationale here was to insure that children would genuinely understand the rationale for any change in their spontaneous procedure which they introduced and that, as a result, this change would be a permanent one with a broad range of applicability—not an isolated piece of rote knowledge.

The task that we devised to meet these criteria was introduced as follows (Figure 18.1): "The package on the left has two pieces of bubble gum in it. If the

Fig. 18.1. Materials for introducing the bubble-gum problem (Level 0).

packages on the right are the same, how many pieces of gum will we have on that side?

Note that this example does not require any but the simplest of arithmetic operations (i.e., addition), and that it uses very small numbers, so that the EPL of actually executing the addition operation will be minimal. Note further that the task draws on cultural knowledge available to American children, in combination with a clear visual display, to make it clear just how this operation is to be applied. Given the nature of the array, it would be very unlikely that any child would apply the Level 0 strategy, and suggest that three pieces of gum were necessary on the right. Note finally that—because concrete props are provided—children actually have the option of checking their answers to see if they are right. The children do not have to rely on the instructor to make this determination for them.

Progressive Elaboration

Having created a stripped down version of the task which we felt would be comprehensible to students at the beginning of the vectorial stage, our next step was to design a sequence of problems that would become progressively more complex, and that would give students the opportunity to elaborate their original insight in a fashion that would ultimately lead them to the creation of a higher order control structure. The basic problems that we created to bridge this gap were as shown in Figures 18.2–18.5.

Fig. 18.2. Materials for the first instructional problem in the bubble-gum sequence (Level 1a).

Note that the only feature that has changed in Figure 18.2 is the number of gum boxes on the right. The reason for increasing this number is to give the students a reason for using multiplication rather than successive addition, in coming up with an answer.

Note that the new feature in Figure 18.3 is that the number of pieces per box on the left is not given. Although the students can determine this number by visual inspection, they must nevertheless do so before they are able to apply the strategy of the previous level.

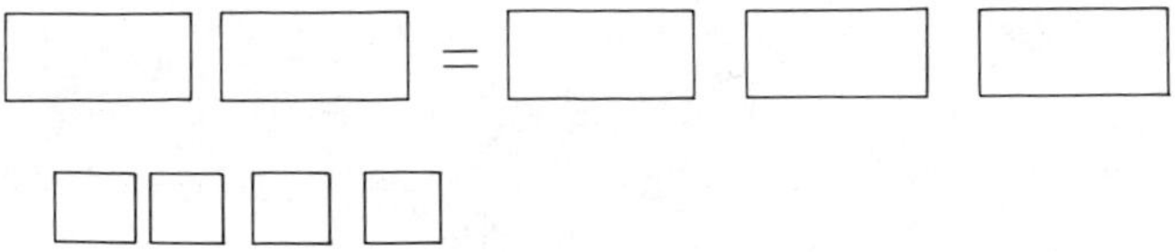

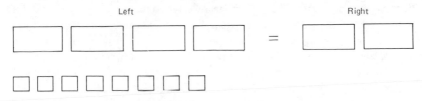

Fig. 18.3. Materials for the next set of instructional problems in the bubble-gum sequence (Level 1b).

Note that the altered feature in Figure 18.4 is once again the size of the set being used. The reason for changing the set size this time is to encourage the students to use division rather than visual inspection as a means of determining the number of pieces of gum per gum box on the left.

Left   Right

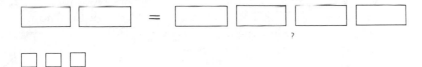

Fig. 18.4. Materials for the next set of instructional problems (Level 2a).

The new feature in the final example (Figure 18.5) is that the number of pieces of gum do not divide evenly into the number of gum boxes. To cope with this feature children can simply add a loop for computing the remainder or a decimal into the strategy which they have already developed.

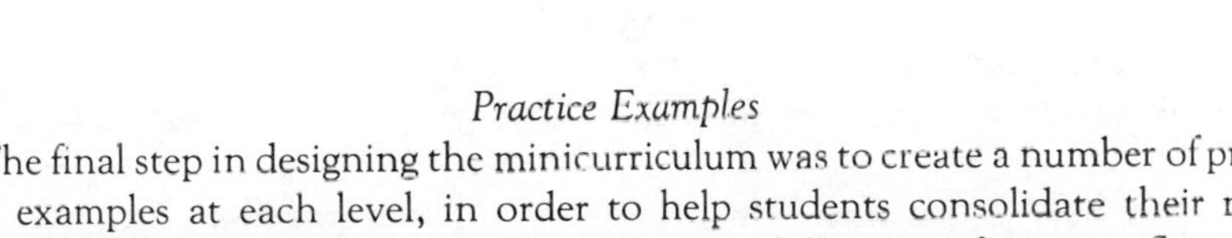

?

Fig. 18.5. Materials for the final set of instructional problems in the bubble-gum sequence (Level 2b).

Practice Examples

The final step in designing the minicurriculum was to create a number of practice examples at each level, in order to help students consolidate their new cognitive operations. Note that the inclusion of this sort of practice flows directly from the view of structual acquisition that was spelled out in Chapter 12. To insure that the new structures were generalizable, examples were also included at this point to where students had to determine the number of gum boxes rather than gum pieces, and to deal with situations that involved other materials entirely.

Phase Five: Implementation of the Curriculum.[3]

In the implementation phase, two different teachers took charge of the instruction, with each teacher teaching half the students in each of two different groups. One of these groups was composed of normal 10- and 11-year-olds. The other was composed of 12- and 13-year-olds who were normal in most respects, but who seemed to have particular difficulties with math. Both groups of children appeared to be at the same level in the developmental hierarchy at the outset. On problems using large or complex numbers, they would use the lowest-level strategy, namely addtion or subtraction. On problems using small numbers, and for which one ratio was unitary, they would use the Level 1 approach, with a strategy that employed either multiplication or successive addition.

Because the instructional paradigm was designed for children who were functioning precisely at this level, it proved to be quite effective, with the practice examples in effect serving as diagnostic probes to identify any residual problems. Virtually all the children succeeded on the first few examples, thus gaining confidence in their own ability to understand the task, and to devise a procedure for solving it. As the instruction moved on to Level 2 (i.e., to problems in which the unitary ratio first had to be computed) individual differences began to emerge. Some children understood that the problems were the same basic variety as they had just attempted, and that they simply had to calculate the number of gum pieces on the left-hand side first. Other students reverted to an addition or subtraction strategy. As specified by the general approach, the students who reverted were encouraged to actually place the pieces of gum in boxes, and to see what was wrong with their answer; then given prompts on succeeding problems until they were responding with insight and in an error-free fashion. A verbal rule was also provided to summarize what they had learned. By contrast, the students who used the reduce-to-unit strategy immediately were permitted to continue functioning in a more independent fashion. As practice was given, it became apparent that there were individual differences in the number of examples students needed before they could respond automatically, as well. No formal assessment was made along this dimension, and no formal practice criterion was established. However, the instruction was continued until all the students appeared at least reasonably automatic in their performance, a criterion which took about 40 minutes for average students to reach in both the normal and math-disabled groups.

The teachers' informal assessment of the instruction was that all the students enjoyed their experience, and appeared to benefit from it. In order to obtain a more rigorous asssessment, however, Gold designed a formal post-test, which he

---

[3]The details of the curriculum were developed, implemented, and evaluated by Alan Gold, as part of his doctoral dissertation (Gold, 1978).

administered both one week and one month after the instruction. The test in-cluded items for which the content and numerical values were different from those used in the curriculum, but the basic problem type was the same. However, it also included ones where the type of problem and specific procedure were different as well.

The results on the post-test—using 65% as a passing criterion—are presented in Table 18.2. As may be seen, very few children profited from the regular ap-proach. By contrast, the majority showed a clear benefit from the developmen-tal approach, and an intermediate number—depending on the particular group—profited from an approach which had been based on the view of development proposed by Gagné, namely that of cumulative learning.

One further word is perhaps in order, concerning the cumulative learning results. The cumulative learning curriculum was based on a learning hierarchy approach to the teaching of ratio which had been developed and validated by Anderson (1977), in a previous doctoral dissertation in our research group. The strategy which the children were taught was the adult one (i.e., the cross-multiplication strategy) and the method was to first teach all the prerequisite skills. As may be seen, the more talented students showed a clear benefit from this approach. Interestingly enough, however, when the performance of these students was examined in more detail, it was found that they were not suc-ceeding by using the approach which they had been taught. Rather, they were succeeding by using the more natural developmental precursor of this method (i.e., the unit-method). Evidentally, by breaking down the adult task into a number of subcomponents and by teaching those subcomponents which were not in the students' repertoire already, the learning hierarchy curriculum had enabled them to create their own understanding of the task, i.e., an understand-ing which was at their own level of development. That it did so is certainly to its credit. However, it seems clear (1) that it would have been a good deal easier for even the successful students had they been introduced to the more natural approach directly, and (2) that it was the failure to teach this sort of natural ap-proach which prevented the less-talented students from learning. This inter-

TABLE 18.2
Percentage of Children Passing Ratio Posttest

Task population	Developmental method (%)	Learning-hierarchy method (%)	Standard school curriculum (%)
Normal students	100	88	33
Math-disabled students	100	22	11

Criterion: 65% of items correct.
Number of children per cell = nine.

pretation gains further support from a follow-up study which was conducted by Dennis (1981). What Dennis showed was that—as long as the natural strategy was taught—it did not matter whether children were given concrete props to manipulate, and it did not matter whether the examples which they were given were familiar and concrete, or unfamiliar and abstract. Because these variations are the ones that are normally of significance in instructional research, it seems clear that the procedure of adapting the type of algorithm that is taught to children's natural way of looking at a problem is an important and potentially powerful one, in overcoming the trouble spots in existing curricula, and teaching high-level cognitive operations more effectively.[4]

Design of Remedial Instruction

A third educational task to which the five-step developmental approach can be applied is the design of remedial instruction; that is, instruction for children who have some particular learning handicap, or who are generally retarded and thus developmentally behind their peers. The plight of such children is a serious one. Although they may often aspire to learn with their peers, and although this may in fact be the most desirable option in many instances, this same option too often confronts them with a great deal of frustration, when they discover that they cannot benefit from the existing curriculum. Although from certain perspectives one might view the plight of these students as being different from that of normal students, from the present perspective their plight is almost identical to that which has just been described for normal students on a task like ratio. Essentially the students are confronted with the requirement of learning something that is beyond their current developmental level. In principle, therefore, the educational task is also the same: namely that of changing the type of instruction so that it is appropriate for their current developmental level. As an example, consider the problem of remedial instruction in telling the time.

Phase 1: Specification of the Goal

Time telling is a skill that develops spontaneously in normal children, during the dimensional period. It is also a skill that is of clear cultural relevance. However, it is a skill which retared children have great difficulty in mastering. This is hardly surprising, given the fact that educably retarded children often fail to develop past the unidimensional stage, and that trainably retarded children often fail to develop past the predimensional stage (Rich, 1980). However, since so many everyday situations require this skill for effective functioning, the difficulties that retarded children encounter are a considerable source of frustra-

---

[4]For additional examples, and a more formal specification of the details of the approach, see Case (1978b).

tion, both for them and for their parents and teachers. Thus, time-telling is a skill—like ratio—where the difficulties students experience may well stem from a mismatch between their level of development and that which is required for executing a skill in an adult fashion. Accordingly, Bob Sandieson and I decided to set as a goal the task of teaching retarded students how to tell the time, using a procedure which would be better matched to their current level of development.

Phase 2: Analysis of Adult Control Structure

When adults glance at their watches they note the position of each hand, using the small hand to determine the nearest hour, and the large hand to determine how many minutes separate the present time from this on-the-hour value. The details of the procedure that adults use have been presented elsewhere (Sandieson & Case, 1984). What is important for the present is that executing this strategy requires one to think along two quantitative dimensions simultaneously. Indeed, when the long hand is near the half-past position, one must often oscillate back and forth between each dimension, using the position of the long hand (e.g., 27 past or 28 to the hour), to determine which value on the hour scale one will read off. Although time telling can be treated as an algorithm, therefore, it is an algorithm that requires the ability to oscillate back and forth between two dimensions, both conceptually and computationally. Perhaps not surprisingly, it is rarely mastered completely until the age of 9 or 10 years, and the first reasonable approximations do not normally appear until the age of 7 or 8 years (i.e., grade 2).

Phase 3: Analysis of Developmental Precursors

In the course of their development, normal children appear to go through the following general stages in their acquisition of the time-telling skill. During the preliminary substage of the dimensional period ($3\frac{1}{2}$–5 years) children often learn to recognize a few clock patterns by global inspection, normally ones that show a particular time on the hour, and which are associated with the occurrance of some important event. They also learn to use polar terms for time in an accurate fashion (e.g., a long time, or a short time). During the unidimensional substage (5–7 years), children become capable of coordinating their understanding of number with their understanding of time. They thus become adept at conceptualizing minutes and hours as continuous variables, and at reading off their values from the clock face. However, they still have great difficulty keeping the two dimensions straight, and often use the numbers on the clock face to read both minutes and hours. During the bidimensional substage (7–9 years), they become capable of keeping the two dimensionals distinct. They also become capable of understanding the relationship between the two dimensions, and using a different scale for reading each. Finally, during the last substage of the period (9–11 years), they eliminate their residual difficulties in dealing with times that require a more careful coordination of the two dimensions (e.g., 29 past five versus 29 to six).

Phase 4: Design of the Curriculum

The first object of the curriculum was to bring children as far through the normal developemental sequence as possible, by constructing a carefully graded sequence of tasks that would minimize the EPL that was entailed, and accomplish via massive practice and automization what must normally await naturally occurring increases in STSS to take place. The second objective was to provide the children with an algorithm for reading a clock which would be meaningful to them at their current level, and which would enable them to solve problems that normally require a higher level of functioning to solve. These goals were accomplished by beginning with a highly simplified time-telling task: one whose goals were clear, and which involved a level of thinking of which the children were already capable; then progressively elaborating this task in a context where the initial operations that were required were simple, and where a great deal of coaching and practice could be provided. Details of the initial curriculum are available in Sandieson (1984), and of the revised curriculum in Sandieson & Case (1984).

Phase 5: Implementing the Curriculum[5]

In implementing the curriculum, the number of practice examples children were given was adjusted to the difficulties which they experienced in consolidating a new structure. In addition, any additional difficulties that were made were noted and responded to. This meant that different students received a different amount of assistance in the restructuring that was required, and a different number of practice examples.

After the curriculum had been implemented, it was compared to two existing curricula that had also been carefully developed and researched, but from a different theoretical perspective. All three curricula showed some degree of success. However, the developmentally based curriculum was considerably superior to the others, so much so, in fact, that there was almost no overlap in the distribution of post-test scores. This difference was maintained in a post-test given 1 month after the instruction. With one exception, the child who profitted the least from the developmental curriculum did better than the child who profitted most from the other curricula (Sandieson, 1984). Similar results were obtained in a replication in which a revised developmental curriculum was compared with an "information-processing" curriculum, that is a curriculum which attempted

---

[5] The initial curriculum was developed, implemented, and evaluated by Bob Sandieson as part of his doctoral dissertation (Sandieson, 1984).

to bring children from their initial (novice) strategy to an adult (expert) strategy, in a carefully graded series of logical steps that did not attempt to "recapitulate development."

Although these are the only formal studies we have conducted on the effectiveness of our technology as a remedial tool, quite a number of clinical studies have been conducted, most of them by trained teachers with several years experience. In the area of mathematics the approach has been applied to the missing addend problem, two-digit addition problems, the addition of positive and negative numbers, long division, and the addition of fractions. In the area of language arts, the approach has been applied with students experiencing difficulties in discriminating letters, sounding out words, spelling, and reading for meaning. In the area of social studies, the approach has been applied with students having trouble in learning the concepts of latitude and longitude. In the area of physical education, the approach has been applied to children having problems catching a ball, serving with a forehand stroke in tennis, volleying in volleyball, and catching a football. Finally, in the area of life skills, the approach has been applied with students having trouble in learning to tie their shoes and to make change with money, as well as in learning to tell the time.

On the basis of these case studies, several conclusions may tentatively be suggested. First, the domain of application of the remedial approach is quite broad. It may be applied not only to basic subjects but to complex ones, not only to subjects which are primarily skill-oriented, but to subjects which are primarily concept-oriented. Second, the type of difficulty that special students encounter is rarely different, in general form, from that which is encountered by normal students at a younger age. The reason for the difficulty may be idiosyncratic, and may include emotional problems, lack of prerequisite experience, mental retardation, or some particular perceptual handicap. However, the difficulties themselves are normally quite typical. Finally, it appears that the developmental approach is quite successful, and can enable the students to acquire many of the same concepts and skills as their more advantaged peers, during the same approximate age range (i.e., at a much younger age than they would acquire them normally).

These three conclusions gain further support from a curriculum project that was conducted by Dewsbury in Australia. Dewsbury's approach to curriculum was developed independently of our own. However, it was rooted in a very similar conception of development, and involved the application of a similar instructional technology (Dewsbury 1983; Dewsbury, et al., 1983). The goal of her project was to design new reading and mathematics curricula for children who suffered from severe developmental retardation. The results of the two curricula were quite dramatic, both intellectually and socially. All the children learned to read at least at a grade 1 level—a goal which is almost never achieved with such populations under present conditions. All the children also learned to add single- and double-digit numbers as well as simple fractions, another goal which is far beyond current achievement levels. Finally, all the children found their experience highly rewarding. For many children, the result of the curriculum was that complex meanings could be received from, or transmitted to, members of their own family for the first time. Similar results have since been produced with children having a wide range of disabilities, including deafness, cerebral palsy, and dyslexia. While it is too early to be completely certain, then, it seems quite likely that the results that are obtained when a developmental approach is applied to the design of entire remedial curricula will be even more powerful than when the approach is applied to isolated remedial problems.

SUMMARY

Previous developmental theorists have agreed on the desirability of fostering the development of high-level intellectual operations as part of the educational process. They have also agreed that one must meet children at their current level, and foster some sort of active processing. Where they have disagreed, however, is on how to conceptualize the nature of these underlying operations, and the process by which they develop. As a consequence of this disagreement, they have also disagreed on the sort of general approach to education that is most desirable. The approach with which Piaget's theory has most frequently been associated is a child-centered one, in which children are encouraged to explore as wide a variety of situations as possible on their own, and to reflect on the results of their activity. The approach with which Bruner's theory has been associated is one of cultural empowerment in which children are exposed to the most recent structure of traditional academic disciplines, in an inquiry- or discovery-oriented mode. Finally, the approach with which information-processing theory has been associated is the same one as learning theory was associated before it, namely a skills-instruction approach, in which both basic and high-level operations are taught directly, via a well-planned sequence of instruction.

Because the present theory of development has elements that were derived from each of the above theories, the educational approach with which it is most congruent is one that has elements in common with each of the above approaches as well. At the same time, however, the approach also has a distinctive structure of its own. The basic aim of the approach is to provide children with the sort of high-level problem-solving structures most valued in their own particular culture, and the basic method is to involve them in actual problem-solving—at their own developmental level—from the outset. The major steps that are involved in planning such a curriculum are as follows.

Phase 1. Specify the values, concepts, and skills, which are to be the long-range goals of the educational enterprise.

Phase 2. Analyze the control structures that are employed by adults who embody these values, and possess the relevant concepts or skills.

Phase 3. Analyze the developmental process of acquiring these structures, by examining the problem solving of children at a variety of different developmental levels.

Phase 4. Design a set of educational activities that will be appropriate for children at each level, yet which will also facilitate their ultimate transition to the next. In designing these activities, pay particular attention to the top-level goal that is involved, and make sure that all students understand it from the outset. In addition, make sure that they genuinely understand the rationale for any modifications or elaborations which they must introduce, and that sufficient assistance and practice are available for these changes to be consolidated.

Phase 5. In implementing the curriculum, provide such additional support for teachers as is necessary to insure that they can adapt to individual differences (1) in the children's initial level of development, (2) in children's preference for independent versus socially regulated problem solving, and (3) in the ease with which children can effect the subcomponents of the restructuring process.

In principle, the preceding five-step procedure should be applicable to three different educational tasks: (1) the design of new curricula, in which a concern for cognitive development and for the teaching of basic and high-level skills is combined, (2) the redesign of existing curricula to do a more effective job of fostering the development of difficult cognitive operations, and (3) the design of remedial activities, for individual students who are developmentally retarded, or who have learning disabilities. So far, the latter two tasks are the only ones that have been tackled. However, because the preliminary results have been encouraging, it seems that work on the first task should also be begun.

CHAPTER 19

Retrospect and Prospect:
A View of the Present Theory
in Historical Perspective

INTRODUCTION

The assertion that was advanced at the end of the first section was that by the late 1970s, the field of cognitive development was in a state of disequilibrium. On one hand, research in the Piagetian tradition had made it clear that Piaget's theory had as many weaknesses—rational, empirical, and heuristic—as it did strengths. Moreover, it was clear that many of these weaknesses stemmed from its structuralist approach to human cognition, and that they were to a large degree overcome by the new generation of process theories.

On the other hand, sufficient time had passed that weaknesses were beginning to surface with the new generation of process theories as well. Some of these weaknesses took the form of isolated empirical or theoretical problems (i.e., problems which were unique to one particular theory or another). There were at least two weaknesses, however, which were more general. The first was that none of the post-Piagetian theories offered a solution to the grain-of-analysis problem. The second was that none of the post-Piagetian theories seemed capable of organizing the newly emerging data on children's cognitive, linguistic and social functioning, in a coherent and heuristically powerful fashion.

Ironically, it was precisely these latter two capabilities that had been the hallmark of Piaget's theory. In its prime, one of its greatest strengths had been the overview it provided of children's functioning at different ages and in different content domains. This overview had been as broad as it had been elegant. Moreover, it had led to the discovery of an astonishing range of new phenomena. Finally, it had achieved this power, at least in part, by postulating that there was a natural grain to human cognition (i.e., a natural series of stages or levels through which this cognition tended to progress).

The dilemma with which the field was faced by the end of the 1970s, therefore, was a paradoxical one. By abandoning Piaget's structuralist assumptions, the new generation of process theories had eliminated most of the major weaknesses in his theory. At the same time, however, and by the same token, they had also eliminated certain of its major strengths. This being the case, the challenge with which the field was faced was to develop a new theory, one which would preserve the strengths of both previous sorts of theory, yet eliminate their weaknesses.

The theory that has been outlined in the present volume constitutes one possible response to this challenge. In explicating the theory, I have attempted wherever possible to acknowledge its debt to the theories that have preceded it, and on which it has been based. As yet, however, I have not attempted to outline the solution that it offers to the problems posed by previous theories. Nor have I attempted to specify the new questions and problems which it, in its turn, opens up.

These are my objectives in the present chapter. First, I will summarize the essential aspects of the present theory in postulate form. Next, I will outline the solution that these postulates offer to the problems posed by previous theories. Finally, I will mention several new questions that are opened up by the theory: either in isolation, or in comparison with the other new theories that have been proposed during the same time period.

SUMMARY OF THE THEORY

The basic postulates of the present theory may be divided into three major groups, according to whether they deal with the nature of children's basic intellectual structures, the stages through which these structures develop, or the process of stage transition.

Model of Children's Basic Intellectual Structures

A1. At the most elementary level, children's mental processes may be divided into two categories, (a) those which represent recurrent patterns of stimulation, and (b) those which represent ways in which these patterns can be transformed. The former may be labeled *figurative schemes*, or *state representations*. The latter may be labeled *operative schemes* or *operations*.

A2. From the age of birth, if not earlier, the activation of any scheme or set of schemes is experienced as having a particular affective character: either positive, negative, or neutral.

A3. From the age of 1 month, if not earlier, children are capable of exercising some degrees of voluntary control over their own cognitive and affective experience.

A4. The structures that permit this executive control consist of temporally organized sequences of figurative and operative schemes, which may be parsed into three components: (a) schemes representing some particular state in which children recurrently find themselves, (b) schemes representing some other state that has a higher affective value, and (c) schemes representing the sequence of operations that will take children from one of these states to the other. These three components may be labeled *problem representations*, *objectives*, and *strategies* respectively.

Model of Stages

B1. Although each executive control structure represents a device for dealing with a different specific problem situation—and although many of these problem situations are culturally specific—all executive control structures nevertheless undergo a similar set of transformations with time, and pass through a general and universal sequence of stages, en route to assuming their adult form.

B2. Four major stages of executive development may be identified: the stages of sensorimotor, relational, dimensional, and vectorial operations. What differentiates these stages is the type of mental element which the executive control structures comprise.

B3. Within each major stage a universal sequence of three substages may also be identified, the substages of *unifocal*, *bifocal*, and *elaborated* coordination. What differentiates these substages is the number of elements which they represent, and the way in which these elements are organized.

B4. Under normal rearing conditions, each stage and substage of development is traversed during a characteristic time period, across a broad range of content domains. The particular ages which are associated with each stage and substage are given in Figure 19.1.

Model of Stage Transition

C1. Transition from one stage to the next in any given problem domain is brought about by the *hierarchical integration* of executive structures that were assembled during the previous stage, but whose form and function were considerably different.

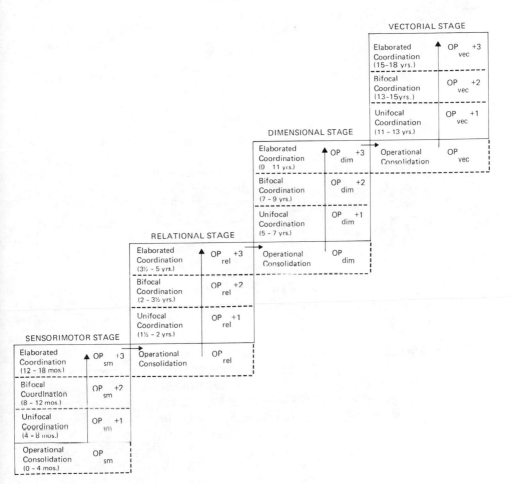

Fig. 19.1. Type of operation and concomitant STSS at each successive stage and substage of development.

C2. Transition from one substage to the next in any domain also occurs by a process of integration. However, this integration need not be hierarchical, and the elements that are involved need not be very different from each other.

C3. Although each new executive structure is assembled independently of each other new structure, four general processes may be identified which regulate the assembly process. These are problem solving, exploration, imitation, and mutual regulation.

C4. An important form of mutual regulation, and one which plays an increasingly significant role in children's development at each successive stage of their development, is *instruction*.

C5. The four general processes mentioned in C3 all involve a common set of subprocesses, including schematic search, evaluation, retagging, and consolidation.

C6. Regardless of the general process by which it is produced, children's capability for hierarchical integration is constrained by the size of their STSS. The amount of STSS available at each stage and substage is also shown in Figure 19.1.

C7. The growth of STSS within each stage is brought about by an increase in operational efficiency.

C8. Increases in operational efficiency are to a considerable extent dependent on maturational factors such as neurological myelinization. However, a certain amount of practice is necessary as well.

Model of Individual Differences

No formal model of individual differences was proposed in the present volume. Nevertheless, the foregoing postulates do have three general implications with regard to the way in which individual children can differ from each other.

D1. Individual children can differ in the rate of their general executive development. These differences can result from (1) differences in the rate of growth of their STSS (Rich, 1980) or (2) differences in the efficiency of their general regulatory processes (Rich, 1982).

D2. Individual children can also differ from each other in the rate of their executive development on one particular set of tasks or another. These differences can result from (1) differences in the efficiency of their domain-specific operations (Case et al., in press), or (2) differences in the efficiency of their regulatory sub-processes.

D3. Both of the preceding types of individual difference can result from either biological or cultural/experiential factors.

PROBLEMS POSED BY PIAGET'S THEORY

The Role of General Logical Structures

As was pointed out in Chapter 3, one of the most serious problems with Piaget's theory was its assertion that general logical structures, or structures of the whole, were the source of the stage-like phenomena that are observed in intellectual development. From a purely rational point of view, the difficulty with this assertion was that general logical structures were difficult to define, to explicate, and to operationalize: particularly in domains whose content was not mathematical or logical in nature. From an empirical point of view, the difficulty was that the assertion led to two predictions which were repeatedly disconfirmed, namely (1) that different forms of the same logical insight should be acquired at the same point in development, and (2) that tests of related logical insights should be highly correlated.

In the revised theory of development that is proposed in the present volume, stage-like phenomena are presumed to result from the combined action of two factors: (1) the construction of domain-specific executive control structures (Postulate A4) and (2) the limiting influence of children's STSS (Postulate C6). As was demonstrated in Chapters 11 through 17, both of these postulates can be explicated with reasonable precision and operationalized with reasonable ease, across a wide variety of content domains. Taken together, the two postulates can also resolve both of the empirical problems mentioned above.

1. The problem of décalage can be resolved by pointing out that different forms of the same logical insight may require executive control structures of differing complexity and may therefore entail a different executive processing load (EPL). As was mentioned in Chapter 11, conservation of number can be acquired by counting each of the two transformed arrays, and making a determination of relative number the means to a determination of relative quantity. This requires a unidimensional control structure, of the sort that entails an EPL of $OP_{dim} + S$. Accordingly, it is acquired at about 5 or 6 years of age. By contrast, conservation of liquid volume cannot be acquired—regardless of the particular justification that is employed—unless the child makes a quantification along two dimensions, and thus realizes that judgments that are made when the beakers have the same diameter are more reliable than those that are made when they do not (Case, 1977a). This insight requires a bidimensional control structure, which in turn entails an EPL of $OP_{dim} + 2S$. Consequently, it is not acquired until 7 or 8 years of age. Although logically equivalent, then, these two forms of conservation are not psychologically equivalent. That they are not acquired at the same point in development thus ceases to be a problem.[1]

2. The problem of low intertask correlations can be resolved by referring to the situation-specificity of children's executive control structures (Postulate A4). Given that the structures in each domain are assembled independently, and given further that children can have either experience or talents that are domain specific as well (Postulates D2 and D3), it follows that one should not expect high intertask correlations—even among tasks which tap executive control structures of the same general form and complexity—unless these sources of individual differences are controlled.

---

[1]For more classical solutions to the décalage problem, see Inhelder *et al.* (1974) and Pinard (1975).

The Role of Equilibration

The second major problem with Piaget's theory was its assertion that stage transition is produced by a slowly acting autoregulative process, equilibration. From a rational point of view, the difficulty with this assertion was that its core construct (i.e., equilibration), was rather globally defined and explicated. As a consequence, it was quite difficult to operationalize. From an empirical point of view, the difficulty was that the assertion led to two incorrect predictions, (1) that training should have a very small effect on children's stage of functioning in any given domain, unless it first induces some sort of cognitive conflict, and (2) that such effects as are achieved by training should be limited to those children who are already at a transitional stage.

In the present theory of development, stage transition is presumed to be under the control of two factors, (1) a set of general regulatory processes which orient children toward structural change, and which effect this change under the appropriate environmental circumstances (Postulate C3), and (2) a gradually occurring change in the size of the children's STSS (Postulate C6). From a rational point of view, the advantage of these changes is that each one of the general regulatory mechanisms can be defined in a reasonably clear fashion, and operationalized without undue difficulty. The same may be said for STSS, and the underlying processes which cause it to change. From an empirical point of view, the advantage of the new formulation is that both problems posed by the training data can also be resolved.

1. The success of training that does not involve conflict can be explained by noting that only one of the four processes, problem-solving, involves conflict or disatisfaction as a necessary component.
2. The success of training with children who are not yet transitional can be explained by noting that—as long as the training does not impose an EPL on children which exceeds their STSS—rapid progress is to be expected, regardless of children's starting point in a particular developmental sequence.

While the present theory does not constitute the only possible solution to the rational and empirical problems posed by Piaget's theory, then, it does constitute at least one such solution. Moreover, the solution is one with considerable heuristic power, as was demonstrated in Chapters 5–17. In an attempt to test the core postulates of the theory, a variety of experiments were conducted, and several new sorts of data brought to light. These included data on preschooler's development in a variety of content domains (Chapter 5), data on social cognition from birth to adulthood (Chapters 6–10), on the growth of span in each stage (Chapter 14), on the relationship between span and learning (Chapter 15), and on the relationship between span and operational efficiency

(Chapter 16). While none of these data were incompatible with Piaget's theory, they could not have been predicted by it, either. That they were successfully predicted by the present theory thus indicates a considerable heuristic advantage.

PROBLEMS POSED BY EARLIER ALTERNATIVES TO PIAGET'S THEORY

Three post-Piagetian theories had already been proposed at the time when work on the present theory was initiated. All of these theories focussed on some aspect of the process of children's development instead of, or in addition to, its structure. Moreover, all three seemed extremely promising, and exerted at least some influence on the shape of the present theory. On the other hand, each of the new theories also posed a set of problems of its own, which the present theory was designed to resolve.

Pascual-Leone's Theory

The difficulties with Pascual-Leone's theory stemmed from its assertion that the transition from one Piagetian stage or substage to the next could be explained by increases in M-power. From a purely rational point of view, this assertion posed two difficulties. The first was that it treated major qualitative shifts, or stage transitions, and minor qualitative shifts, or substage transitions, as essentially equivalent. The second was that it provided insufficient guidance with regard to the grain of analysis which was appropriate for anaylzing cognitive tasks.

From an empirical point of view the theory was plagued by two problems as well. The first of these was that, even when factors such as chunking and field effects had been controlled, certain tests of span appeared to asymptote well before the age specified by the theory, and to reach values that were considerably less than seven. The second problem was that, even when overlearning had taken place, children at different ages appeared to invest different amounts of mental effort in executing basic operations, and to perform them at different speeds. Yet the M-power hypothesis was premised on the assumption that any scheme would take the same amount of attention to activate at any age level.

In the present theory, the above problems have been considerably reduced, if not eliminated completely. Consider first the rational problems. The present theory makes a distinction between the sort of change that occurs at major stage boundaries—and which involves the coordination of two qualitatively different and fully elaborated control structures—and the sort of change that occurs at minor stage boundaries—and which involves the coordination of two qualitatively similar and only partially elaborated control structures (Postulates C1 and C2). Whether or not this distinction will prove useful remains to be seen. However, from a purely rational point of view, it has the advanatage of rendering the relationship between the present theory and Piaget's theory more clear, and of preserving an important developmental distinction, that between stage transition or structural assembly on one hand, and substage transition or structural elaboration on the other.

A similar point can be made with regard to the grain of analysis problem. Because the present theory postulates four qualitatively distinct categories of cognitive operation, it implicitly acknowledges that different quantitative estimates of EPL will be obtained, depending on the grain of analysis that is employed. It also provides a basis for determining what grain of analysis is most appropriate for what task. Having hypothesized (or empirically determined) the strategy that is most prevalent on a task, one should set the grain of analysis equal to the highest level operation which the strategy entails.

What about the empirical problems posed by Pascual-Leone's theory? Since the present theory suggests that each major stage of development has its own attendant form of STSS increase (Postulate C5), the existence of span tests that asymptote at different age levels and that reach terminal values less than seven is no longer problematic. In fact, the present theory predicts the age levels at which different classes of span test should asymptote, and the asymptotic values that should be reached.

The fact that the mental effort required for executing basic operations varies with age is also unproblematic. Because the present theory postulates that changes in STSS are due to changes in operational efficiency (Postulate C6), it cannot only explain this datum, it can make predictions concerning the magnitude and the time course of the age differences that should be observed.

Although the present theory does not constitute the only possible solution to the rational and empirical problems posed by Pascual-Leone's theory, then, it does constitute at least one possible solution. And, once again, it constitutes a solution with considerable heuristic power. Of the new data to whose discovery the present theory has led, only the data on span growth during the dimensional stage, and on the relationship between this growth and structural change, had already been predicted from Pascual-Leone's theory. The data on structural change in infancy and the preschool period, the data on the growth of span during these same periods, and the data on the growth of operational efficiency during each period were predicted as a result of the new postulates that the present theory advanced.

Bruner's Theory

Two empirical problems were mentioned in Chapter 4 in connection with Bruner's theory. The first was that—while there does appear to be a general parallel between linguistic and non-linguistic development—there appears to be a considerable degree of independence as well. The second problem was that—while the form of children's representations does appear to influence the strategies they employ—the mode of their representations does not. Thus, mode of representation does not appear to be a viable construct for differentiating among the major stages of development.

In the present theory, neither of the foregoing problems arises. The relative independence of thought and language is explained by suggesting that each domain poses a set of distinct problems, and is controlled by a distinct set of intellectual structures. That a change in linguistic structure does not automatically bring with it a change in non-verbal structures therefore ceases to be a problem. At the same time, however, it remains possible to explain the general developmental parallel that is observed, by suggesting that development in each domain proceeds through the same general sequence of stages and substages (Postulates B1 and B2), and is controlled by the same general processing factors (Postulate B6). It also remains possible to explain the difficulty that language-deprived populations experience in acquiring certain high-level cognitive skills by suggesting that, while these skills may not be dependent on language per se, they are likely to be dependent on instruction (Postulate C4). And without the benefit of language, instruction in certain abstract concepts or skills can become extremely difficult.

The problems encountered by the mode of representation hypothesis may be handled in a similar fashion. Because mode of representation is no longer taken as the criterion for defining stages, or as the mechanism that is hypothesized to produce them, it becomes possible to imagine enactive, ikonic, and verbal/symbolic development as proceeding relatively independently, yet as progressing through the same general sequence of stages and substages (Postulates B1 and B2). Instances where a change in mode of representation does not lead to a change in development are thus no longer problematic. At the same time, it remains possible to preserve the notion that the general form of a child's representation will determine the form of strategy that he or she employs (Postulate A3), and to specify exactly what elements must be represented on any given task for a particular set of goals to be established, and for a particular strategy to emerge. Finally, it remains possible to preserve the notion that many cognitive structures—regardless of their mode of representation—are cultural inventions, which can function as tools for independent thought once they have been reconstructed by the young child, and which can contribute to the process of stage transition.

Klahr and Wallace's Theory

From an empirical point of view, the difficulty with Klahr and Wallace's theory was that it provided no explanation for cross-domain parallels in cognition (i.e., for horizontal structure). From a rational point of view, the difficulty was similar to that encountered by Pascual-Leone's theory, namely, the absence of any principaled basis for determining the appropriate grain of analysis. Regardless of a child's age or the nature of the task, the mental processes that were postulated were modeled at an extremely fine-grain level of analysis, thus making it difficult to see the woods for the trees. Finally, from a heuristic point of view, the difficulty was that novel predictions could only be generated in domains for which a great deal of prior data was already available, as well as a running computer model.

The present theory overcomes all three of these difficulties. Cross-domain parallels are explained by postulating very general classes of operation (Postulates B2 and B3), which emerge at the same point in human development due to the common EPL which they entail (Postulate C6). The woods-and-the-trees problem is solved by shifting the grain of analysis from stage to stage, and by noting the overall structure of children's thinking as well as its component parts. Finally, the heuristic problem is resolved by the same modifications. Once a mechanism for explaining horizontal structure is proposed, and once children's thinking is modeled at an intermediate grain of analysis, it becomes possible to generate a wide variety of novel predictions, even in domains for which relatively little data is already available, and where computer simulation given the present degree of knowledge would be impossible.

NEW QUESTIONS RAISED BY THE PRESENT THEORY

The most direct way in which a new theory can influence the course of future empirical research is by the answers it provides to previously existing problems. Assuming that these answers also entail a set of novel predictions, the way for further research is clearly paved. There is another way in which a new theory can influence the direction of future work, however, which is equally important. That is by bringing a new set of questions and problems into focus. This being the case, it seems worthwhile to conclude by listing some of the most salient questions that are raised by the present theory, either on its own, or in conjunction with other recent theories that have been proposed.

Questions Posed in Conjunction with Other Developmental Theories

Although the present theory constitutes one possible solution to the theoretical dilemma of the 1970s, it is by no means the only one. At about the same time as work on the present theory was initiated, both Pascual-Leone and Klahr began to refine and expand their own theoretical systems, in order to overcome the problems which their theories posed in their early stages of development (cf., Klahr, 1984; Pascual-Leone, 1984). In addition, two other investigators began work on general systems of their own, which also included both structural and process components (Fischer, 1980; Halford, 1980). Finally, still another group of investigators began work on detailed theoretical models of specific tasks, and then went on to show how these models could be generalized to a broad range of other developmental tasks (cf., Chi & Rees, 1983; Siegler, 1981; Sternberg, 1983). The result is that a whole family of theories and budding theories now exists; each of which is spawning a distinctive research programme of its own. For obvious reasons, a summary of each of these theories (or proto-theories) is beyond the scope of the present volume. However, it does seem possible to mention three issues on which various theories differ, and on which further work is likely to focus.

Horizontal Structure

The first issue concerns the nature and/or the existence of horizontal structure. Although the present theory has construed the nature of horizontal structure somewhat differently from Piaget, it has preserved the Piagetian assumption that such structure exists, and that it indicates the presence of very broad stages in children's development. The same may be said for Pascual-Leone's theory and for Halford's theory. Two of the alternative theories that have been proposed, however, namely Fischer's theory and Klahr's theory, challenge this assumption quite directly. And, at least so far, both Chi (1981) and Keil (1985) seem to be following Klahr's lead in this regard.

Given the data that were presented in Chapter 11, it seems unlikely that future work in the area will deny the existence of horizontal structure entirely. However it does seem likely that a good deal of theoretical and empirical work will be necessary before consensus can be reached on how much structure to postulate, and on how to conceptualize such structure as exists.

Preschool Development

Among those theorists who do postulate the existence of general stages, there is considerable variability in the way in which development in the preschool years is construed. Following Piaget, Fischer postulates that children go through the first two substages of what he calls the representational tier during this period, passing on to the second two substages during the elementary school years. Pascual-Leone does not divide development into a series of major stages and substages. However, he does divide the preschool period into only two M-levels, whereas other periods are divided into three or four. This suggests that his position is also quite close to Piaget's on this score as well.

By contrast, in both Halford's theory and the present theory it is assumed that preschool children have a mode of cognitive functioning which is distinctive. The nature of this mode of functioning is construed somewhat differently in the two theories. However, the general position appears to be the same, that first-order relations or symbols constitute the basis of this thought, whereas second-order relations or symbols (dimensions) form the basis of thought during the elementary school years. Another possible question that future theoretical work will have to address, then, is how best to specify the nature and number of transitions that take place during the preschool years. This problem does not appear to be as fundamental as the one regarding horizontal structure. However, given the importance of the developments that take place during the pre-school years, it seems likely to be the focus of at least some further work and controversy.

STSS Growth

A third issue on which contemporary theorists are divided is the role of STSS in children's cognitive development. In Halford's theory, in Pascual-Leone's theory, and in the present theory STSS growth is assigned a central role. In Fisher's theory the growth is referred to, but assigned a more peripheral role. Finally, in Klahr's theory, it is assigned no role at all. While the data that were presented in Chapters 14 and 15 seem compelling evidence to me that STSS does play a critical role, the history of science forces one to be very circumspect in one's predictions about what will be taken as compelling evidence by the community at large (Lakatos, 1974). Moreover, even if the experiments that were reported were accepted as compelling evidence regarding the notion that STSS growth plays some role in development, it seems likely that further controversy would ensue concerning how best to conceptualize this role.

A similar point can be made with regard to the determinants of STSS growth. Among those who believe that STSS growth plays an important role in cognitive development, Pascual-Leone believes that this growth cannot be attributed to changes in operational efficincy, I myself believe that it can, and Halford appears to be relatively neutral on this point. While the data in Chapter 16 appear to implicate operational efficiency in some fashion, it seems likely that further theoretical controversy will continue concerning the precise way in which the concept of operational efficiency should be explicated, and the precise way in which its impact on the growth process should be conceptualized. In fact, it would appear that this controversy has already begun (see Hulme et al., 1984, versus Howard & Polich, 1985).

Questions Posed in Connection with Other Developmental Data Bases

The above questions are ones that emerge when the present theory is compared with other contemporary general theories. There exists a second group of questions, however, that are raised not by other contemporary theories but by other contemporary data bases, data bases that were previously considered to lie at the outer limits of cognitive-developmental theory, but which appear increasingly to lie squarely within it, and to demand a more detailed explication.

Affective Development

One of the most important of these data bases has to do with children's affective development. Just as thought and feeling are intimately related in one's everyday experience—with each change in thought having the potential to lead to some change in feeling, and each change in feeling having the potential to lead to some change in thought—so thought and feeling are intimately related in the development of the young child. Clinical data on the nature of this relationship have been available for some time, and experimental studies are becoming increasingly frequent (cf. Lewis & Rosenblum, 1978). Thus, the problem of developing an integrated theory of cognitive and affective development is becoming an increasingly pressing one.

Of course, this is not a problem that is unique to the present theory. However, it is one which the present theory makes a good deal more acute. For one thing, the present theory assigns children's goals an important role in determining their intellectual functioning at any stage of development, and implicitly assumes that affective processes play a major role in establishing these goals. For another, the present theory assigns exploration and mutual regulation two processes that both have a strong affective component—an important role in stage transition. In neither case, however, does the theory provide an account of how the affective processes in question actually function.

At the same time as the present theory intensifies the need for an integrated theory of cognition and affect, it provides at least some of the tools for effecting such an integration. One of these is the more detailed account it offers of the substages through which children pass during the first five years of their life: the years during which many of the most important affective developments take place. Another is the more detailed view of stage transition it provides, and the description of its regulatory subprocesses. Elsewhere I have outlined the general form that a model of affective development might take, if it were to be consistent with the present theory (Case, 1985). My general point at the present, however, is not that any particular model is right or wrong, but simply that the present theory brings the problem of affective development into focus, and provides one possible base from which to approach it.

The Development of Other Types of Knowledge

A similar point can be made with regard to the development of other types of knowledge. The present theory focuses on the development of executive control structures; that is, on the sort of procedural knowledge that children acquire about how to reach certain classes of goals in certain classes of situations. A substantial data base exists, however, with regard to the development of other types of knowledge as well. Thus, if a complete picture of children's development is to be attained, the relationship between the sort of knowledge that is described in the present volume and that which has been described elsewhere must be explicated.

The most obvious type of knowledge whose relationship to procedural knowledge must be explicated is declarative knowledge. Over the past few years, a number of investigators have focused on children's declarative knowledge, and pointed out that it can have a great impact on the strategies which children employ, and on the control structures which they assemble (see Anderson, 1982; Chi & Rees, 1983; Siegler & Shrager, 1983). As yet, however, no attempt has been made to suggest any particular influence in the other direction. In the present volume, such an influence has been suggested. For example, it was suggested that acquisition of the declarative knowledge that a balance beam is an object which can move is dependent on the prior acquisition of an executive control structure for scanning moving objects. Similarly, it was suggested that acquisition of the insight that a balance beam is an object which moves at one end when pushed at the other, is dependent on the acquisition of bifocal pushing. A similar relationship was suggested at higher stages and substages.

Given that such a relationship exists, it follows that certain levels of declarative knowledge cannot easily be acquired until certain stages of development, when the relevant procedural structures are available. To make this assertion is not to dismiss the relationship that exists in the opposite direction. Infants would be unlikely to develop a control structure for unifocal pushing on a balance beam, for example, unless they had previously acquired the declarative knowledge that objects with this general appearance can move. Nor would they be likely to develop the control structure for bifocal pushing unless they had previously acquired the unifocal knowledge that a beam will move at the point where it is touched, in response to a push or a pull. Thus, without the presence of some sort of declarative knowledge, there would be no network of associations to guide the infants' movement from the activation of one task feature or goal to the activation of the next, in the sort of zig-zag fashion that was repeatedly assumed in the task analyses. And there would be no development of executive control structures or stage transition as a consequence.

In effect, therefore, the relationship between the two types of knowledge that has been assumed in the present volume is a reciprocal one, with advances in each area being seen as taking off from advances in the other, in a sort of intellectual leapfrog. While this has been the underlying assumption, however, it was never stated explicitly. Nor was it tested. With the advances that have been made in the technology for studying declarative knowledge, however, this now becomes a possibility. One should now be able to build explicit models of children's declarative knowledge networks at different stages, and to test the hypothesized relationship between these networks and their control structures quite directly.

Development at Other Points in the Life Cycle

A third set of data on which the present theory focuses attention is the data on intellectual development at points outside the classic time span, that is, outside the period from 1 month to 18 years of age. In recent years, investigators have begun to examine the sort of intellectual development that takes place from conception to the age of 1 month on the one hand (e.g., Fischer, personal communication, June, 1983), and that which takes place after the age of 18 years on the other (Baltes, 1983; Commons *et al.*, 1984). The challenge that this work raises is how best to integrate these data and the models that have been proposed to explain them, with theory and data that are already available.

Once again, this is not a question that is unique to the present theory. However, it is a question that poses a particular challenge for the present theory, because the present theory places such a heavy emphasis on the similarities and differences that exist across the four stages that have been explored so far. If strong parallels really do exist across the four traditional stages it follows that the same parallels may also exist across earlier and later stages as well. In particular, it follows (1) that any higher-order operations may be shown to be assembled from already identified vectorial operations, via a process of hierarchical integration (2) that any lower-order operations may be shown to constitute components of already identified sensorimotor operations, (3) that a sequence of three substages may be identified during the pre-sensorimotor and post-vectorial stages and (4) that the growth of STSS may play a role in permitting subjects to progress through these substages.

A second general assumption of the present theory is that biology plays a decreasing role in stage transition across the four major stages, while culture plays an increasing role. This being the case, it follows that this trend, too, may be extrapolated. In particular, it follows (1) that biologically regulated increases in operational efficiency may play a more important role in any pre-sensorimotor developments that may be found than in any post-vectorial development, (2) that experientially produced changes in automaticity and chunking may play a more important role in any post-vectorial changes that may be found, and (3) that very early development may be much more rapid and very late development more slow, than that which has been studied so far.

Until the specific nature of pre-sensorimotor and post-vectorial operations is explicated, of course, none of the above predictions can be tested. However, once again, the point is not that the present theory offers a testable solution to the problems that are posed by the newly emerging data, merely that the theory focusses attention on these problems, and provides a possible base from which they can be attacked.

Questions Raised by the Internal Structure
of the Present Theory

In addition to the questions that are raised by other developmental theories or data bases, there exists a final class of questions which are raised by the internal structure of the present theory itself. Three of these seem of particular interest.

Conceptualization of Stage-Specific Operations

The first question has its origin in the theory of stages, and concerns the nature of the underlying operations that are characteristic of each general stage. According to the theory, the operations of any given stage have a general character which transcends any specific content area. In the present volume, these operations were assigned the labels sensorimotor, relational, dimensional, and vectorial. Although a wide variety of examples of each type of operation was presented, however, the operations themselves were never defined. Thus, a question that is raised by the theory in its present form is exactly how to accomplish this task: how to define the operations of each stage in a fashion which is narrow enough to satisfy the rational criteria of clarity and precision, yet broad enough to insure that the domain of applicability of the operations will not be unduly restricted.

An example may help to clarify the nature of the dilemma that the problem of definition entails. The operations that children develop at about the age of 6 years, and which were described in Chapter 5, are quite well characterized by the term dimensional. Whether one is talking about a concept like intelligence, or a concept like weight, it is quite easy to conceptualize the underlying mental entity as one that is rooted in the notion of two polar values (smart–stupid, heavy–light, etc.) and a set of infinite possible points in between. The control structure and operations that lead to the construction of these entities could therefore be defined in a manner that is quite explicit, and which captures this particular property.

The problem with providing such a definition at the moment, however, is that it might overly restrict the domain of tasks to which the theory is applicable. For example, at the same time as children develop a global sense of the way in which physical objects can affect each other in mechanical systems whose relations are spatial, they also develop a global sense of the way in which human beings can effect each other, in social systems whose relations are temporal. One such development is evident in children's story telling, and has been studied by McKeough (1982). At the age of 4 years, children become capable of composing stories that have a global episodic character. The structure of these episodes bears a strong formal resemblance to the structure of children's balance beam performance, and appears at the same stage. There are the same number of elements involved, and the same number of relations among them. This parallel continues at higher ages as well. As children move into the dimensional stage, they coordinate two different sorts of episodes into a plot which has a recognizably literary quality for the first time, and which centers on some thematic dimension. Moreover, the parallel continues throughout the dimensional period, with children embedding a minor plot theme in the major theme at age 8 years, and elaborating on this at age 10 years. The observed progression also bears the same quantitative parallel to our measures of dimensional span as does the progression on the balance beam (McKeough, 1982; Case et al., 1985).

Because the network of relations that are involved in story telling is temporal and not spatial, and because it also involves no element of quantification, it is obviously not dimensional in the strict sense that entities such as weight, distance, or intelligence are. Were the term dimensional to be defined in a strict spatial-quantitative sense, therefore, the definition might be overly restrictive. What is needed is a definition that is sufficiently broad to capture the full range of operations, yet sufficiently specific to differentiate these operations from those of other stages. Either that, or what is needed is a set of precise definitions of operations with a medium scope. (e.g., dimensions, categories, themes), and a more global term that captures the common element in all of them (e.g., third-order relations; see Case et al., 1985).

Conceptualization of the Cycles in STSS Growth

A second question that is raised by the present theory has to do with the model of stage transition. A central postulate of the theory is that STSS grows within each stage, from a value of 1 at the first substage, to 3 at the final substage. In and of itself, this postulate seems reasonably clear. What is not clear, however, is why this should be so. Why should the growth of STSS be cyclic, and why should it reach the same value of OP + 3 at the end of each stage?

At the end of Chapter 17, a tentative answer to this question was proposed. The answer was that the maximum number of operational products that human neurological tissue can store when fully myelinated is on the order of 3 or 4 units. Thus, once a child reaches this critical level of neurological efficiency, further development depends on the emergence of some higher-order system which can coordinate the structures that are represented in the lower-order one. The relationship of the different operational spans according to this view is illustrated in Figure 19.2. As may be seen, basic capacity never exceeds about 4 units. What happens is that successive levels of operation become progressively more efficient, until they reach this asymptotic value. And, as they do so, some higher-level operation begins its development and the entire process recycles. This model might be called the *common-ceiling model*.

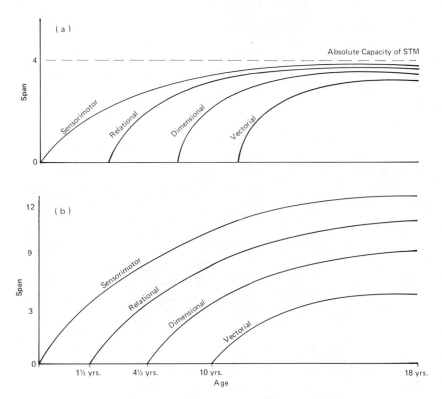

Fig. 19.2. Alternative models to account for the cyclic growth of STSS: (a) "common ceiling" model, (b) "re-scaling" model.

The common-ceiling model is capable of explaining why it is that adults' span on relational measures such as the action-span test does not exceed that of 4-year-olds by more than about 1 unit. It is also capable of explaining why adults' span on dimensional measures such as the counting-span test does not exceed that of 10-year-olds by more than about $\frac{1}{2}$ a unit. Finally, it is capable of explaining why certain neurological dysfunctions or injuries will reduce dimensional span to a very low level, while leaving relational span (e.g., on forward digit span) untouched (Luria, 1973).

On the other hand, however, the common ceiling model is not capable of explaining why forward digit span reaches an asymptotic value that is well in excess of 4 or 5 units. To explain this datum, some supplementary explanation such as chunking or rehearsal must be invoked, and it must be predicted that, if only these factors could be eliminated, span would fall back to its true asymptotic value of about 4 units. The common-ceiling model is also not the simplest or most straightforward one that could be proposed. Figure 19.2 shows a second model that is a good deal simpler, and which explains the same cyclic pattern. According to this second model, the maturational growth of the human nervous system is essentially continuous. Beginning with a value of OP_{basic} at age 1 to 4 months, the capacity of the central system grows in a rapid although gradually decellerating fashion, until it reaches a value of $OP_{basic} + 11$ at age 15 to 18. Every time a reserve capacity of 3 or 4 units is attained, however, the subject is able to assemble a higher-order control structure that has considerable functional significance. It therefore becomes possible to rescale one's analyses of children's mental functioning, and to consider the number of these higher order units which they can coordinate. According to this view, then, no new biological system or capacity emerges with each new stage. Rather, what emerges is a functional capacity. One could just as easily say that the adult human system has a span of 11 or 12 sensorimotor units, or 9 relational units, or 6 dimensional units, as that it has a span of 3 vectorial units. This second model might be called the *rescaling model.*

The rescaling model explains certain of the data on span which are anomalous for the common-ceiling model. For example, it would assert that the digit span which graduate students attain (8–9 units) is in fact a reflection of their true capacity, as is the value of 6 or so units which they attain on some of Pascual-Leone's dimensional measures. What is difficult for the model to explain, however, are the data that are quite easily handled by the former model, namely, (1) the cyclic spurts of myelination in different areas of the brain at different points in development, (2) the reduction of dimensional span in certain neurological dysfunctions to 1 unit, while forward digit span remains untouched at 8 units, and (3) the asymptoting of span at 4 and 10 years on well-controlled relational and dimensional measures of STSS.

On balance, the former of the two models seems to have a slight edge at the present moment. It seems easier to explain away the anomalous performance on digit span as a function of chunking than to explain away the variety of data that are anomalous for the re-scaling model. Once again, however, my point is not that the common-ceiling model is correct. Rather, it is that the present theory focuses attention on what model of STSS growth to choose, and thus that it raises new questions concerning the relationship between cognitive and biological development.

Conceptualization of Regulatory Subprocesses

A final problem that is raised by the present theory is how best to conceptualize the regulatory subprocesses that were mentioned in Chapter 10: subprocesses such as schematic search, evaluation, retagging, and consolidation. At the moment, these words constitute an invitation to develop a set of models, not a set of models in themselves. While the words are sufficiently clear to permit measurement devices to be constructed, and statements about individual differences to be proposed (see Rich, 1982), they cannot substitute for a detailed description of how the various processes actually function, and how they interrelate.

What would need to be accomplished, before such a model could be proposed? As a minimum, it seems to me, one would have to make a fairly detailed set of assumptions about the internal structure of the various types of schemes that were postulated in the present volume, and the way in which the subject's entire repertoire of such schemes might be organized as a function of this structure. Presumably the sort of *schematic-network* model that is currently favored by information theorists would form a good basis for articulating such a set of assumptions. Such a model would undoubtedly have to be enriched, however, with additional assumptions of the sort made by Pascual-Leone (i.e., assumptions about schematic weighting and conflict resolution). It would also be important to include both affect and field factors as possible sources of weighting and conflict, in addition to learning or associating strength, if the full range of developmental phenomena were to be explained (see Pascual-Leone, 1969, 1970).

Given that such a set of assumptions were articulated, it would then be possible to say how a particular scheme would be accessed: that is, how it would be activated in response to a particular situational demand. It would also be possible to say how subjects could judge the adequacy of any scheme as a response to the current situational demand, and how their schemes would have to be reorganized internally, so that they could be accessed without a prolonged search in the future. Finally, it would be possible to say whether some sort of separate process must be postulated, in order to account for the phenomenon of consolidation or whether a continuation of existing processes would suffice.

Such a model does not seem to be very far beyond our reach, given the theoretical tools that are presently available. Its specification, however, remains a task for the future, and not one which can be accomplished in the present volume.

FUTURE DIRECTIONS

What I have attempted to show in this final chapter is that the general theory of development that is proposed—by virtue of the new postulates it introduces—offers at least one possible solution to the problems posed by previous general theories, as well as a heuristic device with considerable potential for the future. One aspect of this potential has already been partially explored, namely the potential for generating a set of novel and testable predictions. There is a second aspect, however, whose utility cannot as yet be assessed. That is the potential to bring a set of new questions and problems into focus, and to suggest a general fashion in which they may be addressed.

Three broad classes of such questions have been considered in the present chapter, those raised by comparing the present theory to other newly emerging theories, those raised by attempting to explicate other newly emerging developmental data bases, and those raised by the internal structure of the theory itself. At the moment, no prediction can be ventured concerning which (if any) of these sets of questions will turn out to be the most important ones. Nor can any prediction be ventured concerning the new postulates that will have to be introduced, or the old postulates that will have to be amended or deleted in order for these questions to be addressed. What can be safely ventured, however, is this: because scientific theories develop as inexorably as the culture and individuals that produce them, this process is virtually certain to continue in the future as it has in the past, and to lead to further advances in developmental theory.

References

Abramovitch, R., Corter, C., & Lando, B. (1979). Sibling interaction in the home. *Child Development, 50,* 997–1003.

Abramovitch, R., Corter, C., & Pepler, D. J. (1980). Observations of mixed-sex sibling dyads. *Child Development, 51,* 1268–1271.

Abramovitch, R., & Grusec, J. E. (1978). Peer imitation in a natural setting. *Child Development, 49,* 60–65.

Ainsworth, M. D. (1964). Patterns of attachment behavior shown by the infant in interaction with his mother. *Merrill-Palmer Quarterly, 10,* 51–58.

Allaire-Dagenais, L. (1977). *Etude transversale et apprentissage des structures de combinatoire et de double reversibilité.* Unpublished doctoral dissertation, University of Montreal.

Als, H. (1979). Social interaction: dynamic matrix for developing behavioral organization. *New Directions For Child Development, 4,* 21–39.

Anderson, R. C., & Faust, G. W. (1973). *Educational psychology: The science of instruction and learning.* New York: Dodd, Mead.

Anderson, L. H. (1977). *Developmental effects in learning hierarchy structure for problems involving proportional reasoning.* Unpublished doctoral dissertation, University of California, Berkeley.

Anderson, J. R. (1982). Acquisition of a cognitive skill. *Psychological Review, 89,* 369–406.

Anglin, J. (1979). *Over and under extension in children's receptive and productive speech.* Paper presented at the biennial meeting of the Society for Research in Child Development, San Francisco.

Antinucci, F., & Parisi, D. (1973). Early language acquisition: A model and some data. In C. A. Ferguson & D. I. Slobin (Eds.), *Studies of child language development* (pp. 607–609). New York: Holt.

Baldwin, J. M. (1894). *The development of the child and of the race.* New York: MacMillan. (Reprinted by Augustus M. Kelley, 1968).

Baltes, P. B. (1983, August) *New perspectives on the development of intelligence.* Invited address, APA, Anaheim.

Bayley, N. (1969). *The Bayley scale of infant development manuals*. New York: The Psychological Corporation.

Bates, E. (1976). *Language and context*. New York: Academic Press.

Beery, K. & Buletinica, N. A. (1967). *Developmental Test of Visual Motor Integration*. Chicago: Folett.

Beilin, H. (1971a). Developmental stages and developmental processes. In D. R. Green, M. P. Ford & G. B. Flamer. *Measurement and Piaget* (pp. 172–196). New York: McGraw-Hill.

Beilin, H. (1971b). The training and acquisition of logical operations. In M. F. Rosskopf, L. P. Steffe, & S. Taback (Eds.), *Piagetian cognitive-developmental research and mathematical education* (pp. 81–124). Washington, DC: National Council of Teachers of Mathematics.

Beilin, H. (1975). *Studies in the cognitive basis of language development*. New York: Academic Press.

Beilin, H. (1983). The new functionalism and Piaget's program. In E. Scholnick (Ed.), *New trends in conceptual representation* (pp. 3–40). Hillsdale, NJ: Erlbaum.

Beilin, H. (1984a). Cognitive series and mathematical cognition: Accounting and space. In B. Gholson & T. G. R. Rosenthal (Eds.), *Applications of cognitive developmental theory* (pp. 49–93). New York: Academic Press.

Beilin, H. (1984b). Functionalist and structuralist research programs in developmental psychology: Incommensurability or synthesis? In H. W. Reese (Ed.), *Advances in child development and behavior* (pp. 245–257). New York: Academic Press.

Belmont, J. M., & Butterfield, E. C. (1971). What the development of short term memory is. *Human Development, 14,* 236–248.

Bell, (1970). The development of a concept of object as related to infant–mother attachment. *Child Development, 41,* 291–311.

Bereiter, C., & Scardamalia, M. (1979). Pascual-Leone's M-construct as a link between psychometric and developmental conceptions of intelligence. *Intelligence, 4,* 22–31.

Bernstein, N. (1967). *The coordination and regulation of movement*. New York: Pergamon Press.

Berzonsky, M. (1971). The role of familiarity in children's explanations of physical causality. *Child Development, 47,* 705–715.

Biemiller, A. J. (1966). *The effect of varying conditions of exposure to a novel object on manipulation by human infants*. Unpublished Master's Thesis, Cornell University.

Biemiller, A. J. (1981, January). *A neo-Piagetian Approach to development during the formal operational period*. Paper presented at the Annual Conference on Piaget and the helping professions, Los Angeles.

Biemiller, A. J., & Bowden, J. (1977, December). *Predicting reading achievement from picture identification times*. Paper presented at the Annual Convention of the Ontario Research Council, Toronto.

Binet, A., & Simon, T. (1916). *The development of intelligence in children*. Baltimore: Williams & Wilton, 1916. (Originally published in 1905).

Black, A. (1976). *Coordination of logical and moral reasoning in adolescence*. Unpublished doctoral dissertation, University of California, Berkeley.

Bödy, B. C. (1977). *Language development and cognitive development: A neo-Piagetian interpretation of 'before' and 'after'*. Unpublished doctoral dissertation, University of California, Berkeley.

Borke, H. (1971). Interpersonal perception of young children: egocentrism or empathy? *Developmental Psychology, 5,* 263–269.

Bower, T. G. R. (1966). The visual world of infants. *Scientific American, 215,* 80–92.

Bower, T. G. R. (1974). *Development in infancy*. San Francisco: Freeman.

Bowlby, J. (1969). *Attachment and loss*. London: Hogarth.

Braine, M. D. S. (1963). On learning the grammatical order of words. *Psychological Review, 70,* 323–348.

Brainerd, C. J. (1973). Neo-Piagetian training experiments revisited: Is there any support for the cognitive developmental stage hypothesis? *Cognition, 2,* 349–370.

Brainerd, C. J. (1976). *Piaget's theory of intelligence.* Englewood Cliffs, NJ: Prentice–Hall.

Brainerd, C. J. (1978). The stage question in cognitive-developmental theory. *The Behavioral and Brain Sciences, 1,* 173–182.

Brazelton, T. B. (1969). *Infants and mothers.* New York: Dell.

Brazelton, T. B., Tronick, E., Adamson, L., Als, H., & Wise, S. (1975). Early mother infant reciprocity. In *Parent–infant interaction,* CIBA Foundation Symposium Number 33. Amsterdam: Associated Scientific Publishers.

Brown, A. L. (1974). The role of strategic behavior in retardate memory. In *International review of research in mental retardation* (pp. 55–111). New York: Academic Press.

Brown, A. L., Bransford, J. D., Ferrara, R. A., & Campione, J. C. (1983). Learning, remembering, and understanding. In J. H. Flavell & E. M. Markham (Eds.), *Carmichael's manual of child psychology* (Vol. 1, pp. 77–166). New York: Wiley.

Brown, R. (1973). *A first language: The early stages.* Cambridge, MA: Harvard University Press.

Brown, R., & Bellugi, U. (1964). Three processes in the child's acquisition of syntax. *Harvard Educational Review, 34,* 133–151.

Brown, R., & Fraser, C. (1963). The acquisition of syntax. In C. N. Cofer & B. S. Musgrave (Eds.), *Verbal behavior and learning: Problems and process* (pp. 158–196). New York: McGraw-Hill.

Bruchkowsky, M. (1984). *The development of empathic understanding in early childhood.* Unpublished M.A. Thesis, University of Toronto (OISE).

Bruner, J. S. (1960). *The process of education.* Cambridge, MA: Harvard University Press.

Bruner, J. S. (1964). The course of cognitive growth. *American Psychologist, 19,* 1–15.

Bruner, J. S. (1965). *Man: A course of study.* Cambridge, MA: Educational Services.

Bruner, J. S. (1966). *The growth of representational processes in children.* Paper presented at the 18th International Congress of Psychology, Moscow. (Reprinted in J. S. Bruner, 1972, *Beyond the information given* [pp. 313–334]. New York: Norton).

Bruner, J. S. (1968). *Processes of cognitive growth. Infancy.* Worcester, MA: Clark University Press.

Bruner, J. S. (1977). Early social interaction and language acquisition. In H. R. Schaffer (Ed.), *Studies in mother–infant interaction* (pp. 271–290). New York: Academic Press.

Bruner, J. S. (1979, June). *The pragmatics of acquisition.* Paper presented at the MPG/NIAS Conference: Beyond Description in Child Language Research. Kasteel Heyendael, Niemegen University, The Netherlands.

Bruner, J. S. (1980a). Afterword. In D. R. Olson (Ed.), *The social foundations of language and thought.* W. H. Norton, 1980.

Bruner, J. S. (1980b). J. S. Bruner. In G. Lindzey (Ed.), *A history of psychology in autobiography* (Vol. VII, pp. 74–151). San Francisco: Freeman.

Bruner, J. S., Goodnow, J. J., & Austin, G. A. (1956). *A study of thinking.* New York: Wiley.

Bruner, J. S., Oliver, R, R., & Greenfield, P. M. (1966). *Studies in cognitive growth.* New York: Wiley.

Bruner, J. S., & Sherwood, V. (1976). Peekaboo and the learning of rule structures. In J. S. Bruner, A. Jolly, & K. Sylva (Eds.), *Play, its role in development and evolution* (pp. 277–285). Harmondsworth, Middlesex: Penguin Books.

Burtis, P. J. (1974). *Two applications of measurement theory in developmental psychology.* Unpublished manuscript, York University.

Burtis, P. J. (1982). The development of short term memory: Capacity increases or chunking? *Journal of Experimental Child Psychology, 34,* 387–413.

Butterworth, G. (1979). *What minds have in common is space: A perceptual mechanism for joint reference in infancy.* Paper delivered to the Developmental Section, British Psychological Society, Southampton.

Butterworth, G., & Jarrett, N. (1979). *The geometry of pre-verbal communication.* Unpublished report, Department of Psychology, University of Southampton.

Carpenter, G. (1975). Mother's face and the newborn. In R. Lewin (Ed.), *Child alive*. London: Temple Smith.

Carpenter, T. P., Moser, J. M., & Romberg, T. A. (1982). *Addition and Subtraction: A Cognitive Perspective*. Hillsdale, N.J.: Erlbaum.

Case, R. (1968). *Analysis of difficulties encountered by disadvantaged children in solving a visually represented problem*. Unpublished M.A. Thesis, University of Toronto.

Case, R. (1970). *Information processing, social class, and instruction: A developmental investigation*. Unpublished doctoral dissertation, University of Toronto.

Case, R. (1972a). Learning and development: A neo-Piagetian interpretation. *Human Development, 15*, 339–358.

Case, R. (1972b). Validation of a neo-Piagetian capacity construct. *Journal of Experimental Child Psychology, 14*, 287–302.

Case, R. (1973). Piaget's theory of child development and its implications. *Phi Delta Kappan, 55*(1), 20–25.

Case, R. (1974). Structures and strictures, some functional limitations on the course of cognitive growth. *Cognitive Psychology, 6*, 544–573.

Case, R. (1976). *Intellectual and linguistic development in the preschool years: A neo-Piagetian Interpretation* (Working paper No. 1). Constructive cognitive group, Berkeley, California.

Case, R. (1977a). Responsiveness to conservation training as a function of induced subjective uncertainty, M-space, and cognitive style. *Canadian Journal of Behavioral Science, 9*, 12–26.

Case, R. (1977b). *The process of stage transition in cognitive development* (Final report, Project No. R01 HD09148-01. NIMHCD).

Case, R. (1978a). Intellectual development from birth to adulthood: A neo-Piagetian interpretation. In R. S. Seigler (Ed.), *Children's thinking: What develops?* (pp. 37–72). Hillsdale, NJ: Erlbaum.

Case, R. (1978b). Piaget and beyond: Toward a developmentally based theory and technology of instruction. In R. Glaser (Ed.), *Advances in instructional psychology* (pp. 167–228). Hillsdale, NJ: Erlbaum.

Case, R. (1978c). A developmentally based theory and technology of instruction. *Review of Educational Research, 48*, 439–469.

Case, R. (1978d). Implications of developmental psychology for the design of instruction. In R. Glaser, A. Lesgold, J. Pellegrino, & J. Fokkema (Eds.), *Cognitive psychology and instruction* (pp. 441–463). New York: Plenum.

Case, R. (1979). *Learning, maturation, and the development of computational strategies in elementary arithmetic*. Paper prepared for the Wisconsin Conference on the initial learning of addition and subtraction skills, Racine, Wisconsin.

Case, R. (1982). The search for horizontal structure in children's development. *Genetic Epistemologist, 11*, 7–15.

Case, R. (1984). A developmentally based approach to the problem of instructional design. In S. S. Chipman, J. W. Segal, & R. Glaser (Eds.), *Thinking and learning skills: Current research and open questions* (Vol. II). Hillsdale, NJ: LEA Associates.

Case, R. (1985). Toward a Neo-Piagetian theory of affective and cognitive growth. Unpublished manuscript, University of Toronto (OISE).

Case, R., & Bruchkowsky, M. (1984). *The block-scale in early childhood: Some new data*. Unpublished manuscript, University of Toronto (OISE).

Case, R. & Globerson, T. (1974). Field independence and mental capacity. *Child Development, 1974, 45*, 772–778.

Case, R., & Hayward, S. (1984). *Understanding causality in the sensorimotor period: The infant balance beam test*. Unpublished manuscript, University of Toronto (OISE).

Case, R., & Khanna, F. (1981). The missing links: Stages in children's progression from sensorimotor to logical thought. In K. W. Fischer (Ed.), *New directions for child development* (Vol. 12, pp. 21–32). San Francisco: Josey Bass.

Case, R., & Kurland, M. (1978). *Construction and validation of a new test of children's M-space*. Unpublished manuscript, University of Toronto (OISE).

Case, R., Kurland, M., & Goldberg, J. (1982). Operational efficiency and the growth of short term memory. *Journal of Experimental Child Psychology, 33*, 386–404.

Case, R., Marini, Z., McKeough, A., Dennis, S., & Goldberg, J. (1985). Horizontal structure in middle childhood: The emergence of dimensional operations. In S. Strauss & I. Levine (Eds.), *State and structure in children's development*. New York: Ablex.

Case, R., & Serlin, R. (1979). A new model for simulating performance on Pascual-Leone's test of M-space. *Cognitive Psychology, 11*, 308–326.

Catell, P. (1940). *The measurement of intelligence in infants and young children*. New York: The Psychological Corporation.

Cellerier, G. (1972). Information processing tendencies in recent experiments in cognitive learning-theoretical implications. In S. Farnham-Diggory (Ed.), *Information processing in children* (pp. 115–123). New York: Academic Press.

Chandler, M. J. (1977). Social cognition: A selective review of current research. In W. F. Overton & J. M. Gallagher (Eds.), *Knowledge and development* (Vol. 1): *Advances in research and theory* (pp. 93–147). New York: Plenum.

Chandler, M. J., Mangione, P., & Moss, P. (1977, June). *Developmental changes in the structure of children's inferences about intelligence in their peers*. Paper presented at the Annual Meeting of the Jean Piaget Society, Philadelphia.

Charbonneau, C., Robert, M., Bourassa, G., & Gladu-Bisonnette, S. (1976). Observational learning of quantity conservation and Piagetian generalization tasks. *Developmental psychology, 12*, 211–217.

Chi, M. T. H. (1975). *The development of short-term memory capacity*. Unpublished doctoral dissertation, Carnegie Mellon University.

Chi, M. T. H. (1976). Short term memory limitations in children: Capacity or processing deficits? *Memory and cognition, 23*, 266–281.

Chi, M. T. H. (1978). Knowledge structures and memory development. In R. S. Siegler (Ed.), *Children's thinking: What develops?* (pp. 73–97). Hillsdale, NJ: Erlbaum.

Chi, M. T. H. (1981). Knowledge development and memory performance. In M. Friedman, J. P. Das, & N. O'Connor (Eds.), *Intelligence and learning*. New York: Plenum.

Chi, M. T. H., & Klahr, D. (1975). Span and rate of apprehension in children and adults. *Journal of Experimental Child Psychology, 19*, 434–439.

Chi, M. T. H., & Rees, E. T. (1983). A learning framework for development. In M. T. H. Chi (Ed.), *Trends in memory development*. New York: Karger.

Chomsky, C. (1969). *The acquisition of syntax in children from 5 to 10*. Cambridge, MA: MIT Press.

Chomsky, N. (1957). *Syntactic structures*. The Hague: Mouton.

Chomsky, N. (1959). A review of B. F. Skinner's verbal behavior. *Language, 35*, pp. 26–58.

Chomsky, N. (1965). *Aspects of the theory of syntax*. Cambridge: MIT Press.

Clark, E. (1973). What's in a word? In T. E. Moore (Ed.), *Cognitive development and the acquisition of language* (pp. 65–110). New York: Academic Press.

Clark, H., & Clark, E. (1977). *Psychology and language*. New York: Harcourt.

Clarke, E. (1972). On the meaning of before and after. *Journal of Verbal Learning and Verbal Behavior, 11*, 750–758.

Cole, M., Gay, J., Glick, J. A., & Sharp, D. D. (1971). *The cultural context of learning and thinking*. New York: Basic Books.

Cole, M., & Scribner, S. (1973). *Culture and thought: A psychological introduction*. New York: Wiley.

Collis, K. F. (1975). *A study of concrete and formal operations in school mathematics: A Piagetian viewpoint*. Hawthorne, Victoria: Australian Council for Educational Research.

Collis, K. F., & Romberg, T. A. (1979). The assessment of children's M-space (Technical report No. 1). University of Wisconsin Graduate School, Research and Development Center.

Commons, M. F., Richards, F. A., & Armon, C. (Eds.). (1984). *Beyond formal operations.* New York: Praeger Scientific.

Condon, W. S. (1975). Speech makes babies move. In R. Lewin (Ed.), *Child alive.* London: Temple Smith.

Damon, W. (1973). *The child's conception of justice as related to logical thought.* Unpublished doctoral dissertation, University of California.

Damon, W. (1979). *The social world of the child.* San Francisco, Josey, Bass.

Daneman, M., & Case, R. (1981). Syntactic form, semantic complexity, and short term memory: Influences on children's acquisition of new linguistic structures. *Developmental Psychology, 17,* 367–378.

Dasen, P. (1972). Cross-cultural Piagetian research: A summary. *Journal of Cross-Cultural Psychology, 3,* 23–39.

Davydov, V. V. (1982). The psychological characteristics of the formation of elementary mathematical operations in children. In T. P. Carpenter, J. M. Moser, & T. A. Romberg (Eds.), *Addition and subtraction: A cognitive perspective* (pp. 224–238). Hillsdale, NJ: Erlbaum.

Day, M. C. (1975). Developmental trends in visual scanning. In H. W. Reese (Ed.), *Advances in Child Development and Behavior, 10,* 154–188. New York: Academic Press.

DeAvila, E. (1974). *Children's transformations of visual information according to nonverbal syntactical rules.* Unpublished doctoral dissertation, York University.

Decairie, T. G. (1974). *Intelligence and affectivity in early childhood.* New York: International Universities Press.

Demerssman, S. L. (1976). *A developmental investigation of children's moral reasoning and behavior in hypothetical and practical situations.* Unpublished doctoral dissertation, University of California, Berkeley.

Dempster, F. N. (1977). *Short term storage space and chunking: A developmental study.* Unpublished doctoral dissertation, University of California, Berkeley.

Dempster, F. N. (1978). Memory span and short term memory: A developmental study. *Journal of Experimental Child Psychology, 26,* 419–431.

Dempster, F. N. (1981). Memory span: Sources of individual and developmental differences. *Psychological Bulletin, 89,* 63–100.

Dennis, S. (1981). *Developmentally based instruction: How low memory demand, contextual meaningfulness, and concrete objects influence the learning of proportionality.* Unpublished M.A. thesis, University of Toronto (OISE).

Dennis, S. (1984, April). Stages in the development of children's drawings. Paper presented at AERA, New Orleans.

DeVries, R. (1969). Constancy of genetic identity in the years three to six. *Monographs of the Society for Research in Child Development, 34*(3, Serial Number 127).

Dewsbury, A. (1983). *Easy math.* Toronto, OISE Press.

Dewsbury, A., Jennings, J., & Botle, D. (1983). *The bridge reading kit.* Toronto, OISE Press.

Diaz, S. (1974). *Cucui scale: Technical Manual Multilingual Assessment Program.* Stockton Unified District, Stockton, California.

Donaldson, M. (1978). *Children's minds.* London: Croom Helm.

Dromi, E. (1985). The one word period as a stage in language development: Quantitative and qualitative accounts. In S. Strauss & I. Levine (Eds.), *Stage and structure in children's development.* New York: Ablex.

Dunker, K. (1945). On problem solving. *Psychological Monographs, 58*(5, Whole No. 270).

Eimas, P. D., Siqueland, E. R., Jusczyk, P., & Vigorito, J. (1971). Speech perception in infants. *Science, 171,* 303–306.

Eisner, W. E. (1974). Applying the five curricular approaches to Man: A course of study. In W. E. Eisner & E. V. Vallance (Eds.), *Conflicting conceptions of curriculum* (pp. 193–200). Berkeley, CA: McKutcheon.

Eisner, E. W., & Vallance, E. (1974). *Conflicting conceptions of curriculum*. Berkeley, CA: McKutcheon.

Ennis, R. H. (1975). Children's ability to handle Piaget's propositional logic: A conceptual critique. *Review of Educational Research, 45*, 1–41.

Erikson, E. H. (1950). *Childhood and society*. New York: Norton.

Fabian, V. (1982). *Language development after 5: A neo-Piagetian investigation of subordinate conjunctions*. Unpublished doctoral dissertation, University of California, Berkeley.

Fabian-Kraus, V., & Ammon, P. (1980). Assessing linguistic competence: When are children hard to understand? *Journal of Child Language, 7*, 401–412.

Fafouti-Milenkovic, M., & Uzgiris, I. C. (1979). The mother–infant communication system. *New Directions for Child Development, 4*, 41–56.

Fenson, L., & Ramsay, D. S. (1981). Effects of modelling action sequences on the play of twelve, fifteen, and nineteen-month-old children. *Child Development, 52*, 1028–1036.

Ferguson, C. A., & Slobin, D. I. (Eds.). (1973). *Studies of child language development*. New York: Holt.

Fillmore, C. (1968). The case for case. In E. Bach & R. Harris (Eds.), *Universals in linguistic theory* (pp. 1–88). New York: Holt.

Fischer, K. W. (1980). A theory of cognitive development: The control and construction of hierarchies of skills. *Psychological Review, 87*, 477–531.

Fischer, K. W., & Bullock, D. (1981). Patterns of data: sequence, synchrony, and constraint in cognitive development. In K. W. Fischer (Ed.), *Cognitive development: New directions for child development* (Vol. 12, pp. 1–20). San Francisco: Josey Bess.

Fischer, K. W., Hand, H. H., Watson, M. W., Van Paris, M., & Tucker, J. (in press). Putting the child into socialization: The development of social categories in the preschool years. In L. Katz (Ed.), *Current topics in early childhood education* (Vol. 6). Norwood, NJ: Ablex.

Flapan, D. (1968). *Children's understanding of social interaction*. New York: Teachers College Press.

Flavell, J. H. (1963). *The developmental psychology of Jean Piaget*. Princeton, NJ: Van Nostrand.

Flavell, J. H. (1971). Stage-related properties of cognitive development. *Cognitive Psychology, 2*, 421–453.

Flavell, J. H. (1980, October). *Structures, sequences, and stages in cognitive development*. Paper presented at the Minnesota Symposium on Child Psychology, Minneapolis, Minnesota.

Flavell, J. H. (1982). On cognitive development. *Child Development, 53*, 1–11.

Flavell, J. H., Beach, D. R., & Chinsky, J. M. (1966). Spontaneous verbal rehearsal in a memory task as a function of age. *Child Development, 37*, 283–299.

Flavell, J. H., Bolkin, P. T., Fry, L. C., Wright, J. W., & Jarvis, P. E. (1968). *The development of role-taking and communication skills in children*. New York: Wiley.

Flavell, J. H., & Ross, L. (Eds.). (1981). *Social cognitive development: Frontiers and possible futures*. New York: Cambridge University Press.

Flavell, J. H., & Wohlwill, J. F. (1969). Formal and functional aspects of cognitive development. In D. Elkind & J. H. Flavell (Eds.), *Studies in cognitive development* (pp. 567–720). London, Oxford University Press.

Fortin-Theriault, A. (1977). *Comparaison de deux methodes d'apprentissage par conflit cognitif*. Unpublished PhD thesis, University of Montreal.

Fowler, W., & Swenson, A. (1979). The influence of early language stimulation on development: Four studies. *Genetic Psychology Monographs, 100*, 73–109.

Freud, S. (1953). *Three essays on sexuality*. London: The Hogarth Press. (First published in 1905).

Furman, I. (1976). What determines the span of immediate memory: A new outlook on an old issue. Unpublished manuscript. University of California, Berkeley.

Furman, I. (1981). *The development of problem solving strategies: A neo-Piagetian analysis of children's performance in a balance task*. Unpublished doctoral dissertation, University of California, Berkeley.

Furth, H. G. (1966). *Thinking without language: Psychological implications of deafness.* New York: Free Press.

Furth, H. G. (1980). *The world of grown-ups: Children's conceptions of society.* New York: Elsevier, North Holland.

Fuson, K. C. (1982). An analysis of the counting-on solution procedure in addition. In T. P. Carpenter, J. M. Moser, & T. A. Romberg (Eds.), *Addition and subtraction, a cognitive perspective* (pp. 67–81). Hillsdale, NJ: Erlbaum.

Gagné, R. M. (1968). Contributions of learning to human development. *Psychological Review, 75,* 177–191.

Gagné, R. M. (1970). *The conditions of learning.* New York: Holt.

Gagné, R. M., & Briggs, L. J. (1979). *Principles of instructional design.* (2nd ed.). New York: Holt.

Gajewski, S. (1980). *An analysis of solution strategies and processing times in ratio and proportion problems.* Unpublished M.A. thesis, McGill University.

Gallagher, J. M. (1978). The future of formal thought research: The study of analogy and metaphor. In B. Z. Presseisen, D. Goldstein, & M. H. Appel (Eds.), *Topics in cognitive development: Language and operational thought* (Vol. 2, pp. 77–98). New York: Plenum.

Gardner, B. T., & Gardner, R. A. (1980). Comparing the early utterances of child and chimpanzee. In A. Pica (Ed.), *Minnesota symposium on child psychology* (Vol. 8, pp. 3–22). Minneapolis: The University Press.

Garvey, C. (1976). Some properties of social play. In J. S. Bruner, A. Jolly, & K. Sylva (Eds.), *Play—Its role in development and evolution* (pp. 570–583). Harmondsworth, Middlesex: Penguin Books.

Gelman, R. (1969). Conservation acquisition: A problem of learning to attend to relevant attributes. *Journal of Experimental Child Psychology, 7,* 167–187.

Gelman, R. (1972). The nature and development of early number concepts. In H. W. Reese (Ed.), *Advances in child development and behavior,* (Vol. 7, pp. 115–168). New York: Academic Press.

Gelman, R. (1978). Counting in the preschooler: What does and what does not develop? In R. S. Siegler (Ed.), *Children's thinking: What develops?* (pp. 213–242). Hillsdale, NJ: Erlbaum.

Gelman, R. (1979). Why we will continue to read Piaget. *The Genetic Epistemologist, 8*(4), 1–3.

Gentner, D. (1975). Evidence for the psychological reality of semantic components: The verbs of possession. In D. A. Norman, D. E. Rumlhart, & The LNR Research Group (Eds.), *Explorations in cognition* (pp. 211–247). San Francisco: Freeman.

Gesell, A., Halverson, H. M., Thompson, H., Ilg, F. L., Castner, B. M., Ames, L. B., & Amatruda, C. S. (1940). *The first five years of life: A guide to the study of the preschool child.* New York: Harper.

Gholson, B. (in press). *The cognitive-developmental basis of human learning: Studies in hypothesis testing.* New York: Academic Press.

Gholson, B., & Beilin, H. (1979). A developmental model of human learning. In H. W. Reese & L. P. Lipsitt (Eds.), *Advances in child development and behavior* (Vol. 13, pp. 47–81). New York: Academic Press.

Ginsburg, H., & Opper, S. (1969). *Piaget's theory of intellectual development.* Englewood Cliffs, NJ: Prentice-Hall.

Ginsburg, H. (1977). *Children's arithmetic: The learning process.* New York: Van Nostrand.

Glaser, R. (1976). Cognitive psychology and instructional design. In D. Klahr (Ed.), *Cognition and instruction* (pp. 303–316). Hillsdale, NJ: Erlbaum.

Gold, A. P. (1978). *Cumulative learning versus cognitive development: A comparison of two different theoretical bases for planning remedial instruction in arithmetic.* Unpublished doctoral dissertation, University of California.

Goldberg, J. (1984). Young girls' understanding of their mothers' role: A developmental investigation. Unpublished doctoral dissertation. University of Toronto (OISE).

Goldin, G. A. (1982). Mathematical language and problem solving. *Visible Language, 16,* 221–238.

Goldman, B. D., & Ross, H. S. (1978). Social skills in action: An analysis of early peer games. In J.

Glick & K. A. Clarke-Stewart (Eds.), *Studies in social and cognitive development: Vol. 1. The development of social understanding* (pp. 177–212). New York: Gardner Press.

Gopnik, A. (1982). Words and plans: Early language and the development of intelligent action. *Journal of Child Language, 9,* 303–319.

Gopnik, A. (1983). The acquisition of goals and the development of the object concept. *Journal of Child Language, 10,* 617–633.

Gopnik, A., & Meltzoff, A. (1984). Semantic and cognitive development in 15–21 month olds. *Journal of Child Language.*

Greenfield, P. M. (1966). On culture and conservation. In J. S. Bruner, R. R. Oliver, & P. M. Greenfield. *Studies in cognitive growth* (pp. 225–256). New York: Wiley.

Greenfield, P. M., & Bruner, J. S. (1966). Culture and cognitive growth. *International Journal of Psychology, 1,* 89–107.

Greenfield, P. M., Nelson, K., & Salzman, E. (1972). The development of rule bound strategies for manipulating seriated cups: A parallel between action and grammar. *Cognitive Psychology, 3,* 291–310.

Greeno, J. G. (1978). A study of problem solving. In R. Glaser (Ed.), *Advances in instructional psychology* (Vol. 1, pp. 13–76). Hillsdale, NJ: Erlbaum.

Griffiths, R. (1954). *The abilities of babies.* London: University of London Press.

Griffiths, R. (1970). *The abilities of young children.* Chard, Somerset: Young and Son.

Groen, G. J. (1978). The theoretical ideas of Piaget and educational practice. In P. Suppes (Ed.), *Impact of research on education: Some case studies* (pp. 267–318). Washington, DC: National Academy of Education.

Gruber, H. E. (1974). *Darwin on Man: A psychological study of creativity.* New York: Dutton.

Haeckel, E. (1866). *Generelle Morphologie der Organism.* Berlin: Georg Reimer.

Halford, G. S. (1980). Toward a redefinition of cognitive developmental stages. In J. Kirby & J. B. Biggs (Eds.), *Cognition, development, and Instruction* (pp. 39–64). New York: Academic Press.

Hall, G. S. (1883). The contents of children's minds. *Princeton Review, 3,* 249–272.

Hall, G. S. (1908). *Adolescence.* New York: Appleton.

Hayes, J. R., & Flower, L. S. (1980). Identifying the organization of the writing process. In L. W. Gregg & E. R. Steinberg (Eds.), *Cognitive processes in writing* (pp. 3–30). Hillsdale, NJ: Erlbaum.

Howard, L., & Polich, J. (1985). Latency and memory span development. *Developmental Psychology, 21.*

Hulme, C., Thomson, N., Muir, C., & Lawrence, A. (1984). Speech rate and the development of short term memory span. *Journal of Experimental Child Psychology, 38,* 241–251.

Humphrey, G. (1955). The importance of the Würzburg work on contemporary psychology. In *Jubilee Album for Professor B. F. Mel.* Pretoria: Van Schaik.

Hunt, E. B. (1974). Quote the raven? Nevermore! In L. W. Gregg (Ed.), *Knowledge and cognition* (pp. 129–157). Hillsdale, NJ: Erlbaum.

Hunt, J. M. (1961). *Intelligence and experience.* New York: Ronald.

Hurst, P. E. (1980). *A comparison of death concept development in emotionally disturbed and non-disturbed children.* Unpublished doctoral dissertation, University of Toronto (OISE).

Huttenlocher, J., & Burke, D. (1976). Why does memory span increase with age? *Cognitive Psychology, 8,* 1–31.

Inhelder, B., & Piaget, J. (1958). *The growth of logical thinking from childhood to adolescence.* New York: Basic Books.

Inhelder, B., & Piaget, J. (1964). *The early growth of logic in the child.* London: Routledge & Kegan Paul.

Inhelder, B., Sinclair, H., & Bouvet, M. (1974). *Learning and the development of cognition.* Cambridge, MA: Harvard University Press.

Jackson, E., Campos, J. J., & Fischer, K. W. (1978). The question of décalage between object and person permanence. *Developmental Psychology, 14,* 1–10.

James, W. (1950). *The principles of psychology.* New York: Dover. (First published in 1890).

Jensen, A. R. (1964). Individual differences in learning: interference factors. Final report, 1964. Office of Education, Cooperative Research Project No. 1897.

Jensen, A. R., & Rohwer, W. D. (1970). An experimental analysis of learning abilities in culturally disadvantaged children. Final report #2404. Office of Economic Opportunity.

Jenson, A. R. (1980). *Bias in mental testing*, New York: The Free Press.

Kamii, C. K., & Radin, N. L. (1967). A framework for a preschool curriculum based upon Piaget's theory. *Journal of Creative Behavior, 1*, 314–324.

Kandel, E. R. (1979). Small systems of neurons. *Scientific American, 241*, 66–88.

Kant, I. (1781). *Critique of pure reason*. New York: Anchor Books, 1966.

Karmiloff-Smith, A. (1979). Language development after five. In P. Fletcher & M. Garman (Eds.), *Language acquisition: Studies in first language development* (pp. 307–323). Cambridge, Cambridge University Press.

Karplus, R. (1964). The science curriculum improvement study. In R. E. Ripple & V. N. Rockcastle (Eds.), *Piaget rediscovered* (pp. 113–118). Ithaca, NY: Cornell School of Education Press.

Karplus, R., & Peterson, R. (1970). Intellectual development beyond elementary school II: Ratio, a survey. *School Science and Mathematics, 70*(9), 813–820.

Kauffman, A. S. (1971). Piaget & Gesell: A psychometric analysis of tests built from their tasks. *Child Development, 42*, 1341–1360.

Keil, F. (1985). *On the structure dependent nature of stages of cognitive development*. In S. Strauss & I. Levine (Eds.), *Stage and structure in children's development*. New York: Albex.

Kellogg, R. (1967). *The psychology of children's art*. San Diego: CRM.

Kendler, T. S. (1963). Development of mediating responses in children. In J. C. Wright & J. Kagan (Eds.), Basic cognitive process in children. *Monographs of the Society for Research in Child Development, 28*(2), 33–48.

Kessel, F. S. (1970). The role of syntax in children's comprehension from ages six to twelve. *Monographs of the Society for Research in Child Development, 35*(c). Serial #139.

Khanna, F. C. (1985). *Horizontal structure in the cognitive development of pre-school children: An information processing hypothesis*. Unpublished doctoral dissertation, University of Toronto (OISE).

Klahr, D. (1973). A production system for counting, subitizing and adding. In W. G. Chase (Ed.), *Visual information processing* (pp. 527–546). New York: Academic Press.

Klahr, D. (1976). *Cognition and Instruction*. Hillsdale, NJ: Erlbaum.

Klahr, D. (1978). Goal formation, planning and learning by pre-school problem solvers or: "My socks are in the dryer." In R. S. Siegler (Ed.), *Children's thinking: What develops?* (pp. 181–212). Hillsdale, NJ: Erlbaum.

Klahr, D. (1984). *Transition processes in quantitative development*. In R. Sternberg (Ed.), *Mechanisms of cognitive development* (pp. 101–140). San Francisco: Freeman.

Klahr, D., & Wallace, J. G. (1976). *Cognitive development: An information-processing view*. Hillsdale, NJ: Erlbaum.

Klein, M. (1957). *Envy and gratitude: A study of unconscious sources*. London: Tavistock.

Kohlberg, L. (1963). The development of children's orientations toward a moral order. *Vita Humana, 6*, 11–33.

Köhler, W. (1921). *The mentality of apes*. Berlin, Springer.

Kohnstamm, G. A. (1967). *Piaget's analysis of class inclusion: Right or wrong?* The Hague, Mouton.

Krasnor, L. R., & Rubin, K. H. (1983). The assessment of social problem-solving skills in young children. In T. Mercuzz, C. Glass, & M. Getvert (Eds.), *Cognitive assessment*. New York: Guilford.

Kuhn, D. (1983). On the dual executive and its significance in the development of developmental psychology. In D. Kuhn & J. A. Meachum (Eds.), *On the development of developmental psychology* (pp. 81–110). New York: Karger.

Kuhn, D., Nash, S. C., & Brucken, L. (1978). Sex role concepts of two and three-year-olds. *Child Development, 49*, 445–451.

Kurland, D. M. (1981). *The effect of massive practice on children's operational efficiency and memory span*. Unpublished doctoral dissertation, University of Toronto (OISE).

Lakatos, I. (1970). Falsification and the methodology of scientific research programmes. In I. Lakatos & A. Musgrave (Eds.), *Criticism and the growth of knowledge* (pp. 91–196). London: Cambridge University Press.

Lakatos, I. M. (1974). The role of crucial experiments in science. *Studies in the History and Philosophy of Science, 4*, 309–325.

Larkin, J. (1983). Working toward a unified theory of how people use mathematics. (1983) Invited address. AERA, Montreal, April.

Laurendeau, M., & Pinard, A. (1970). *Development of the concept of space in the child*. New York: International Universities Press.

Lawson, A. E., & Wollman, W. T. (1977). Developmental level and learning to solve problems of proportionality in the classroom. *School Science and Mathematics, 77*, 69–75.

Lefebvre, M., & Pinard, A. (1972). Apprentisage de la conservation des qualités par une méthode de conflit cognitif. *Canadian Journal of the Behavioral Sciences, 4*(1), 1–12.

Levine, M. (1966). Hypothesis behavior by humans during discrimination learning. *Journal of Experimental Psychology, 71*, 331–338.

Levinson, J. D. (1978). *The seasons of a man's life*. New York: Ballantine Books.

Lewis, M., & Rosenblum, L. A. (1978). *The development of affect*. New York: Plenum.

Link, N. F. (1979). *The effects of arousal on information processing*. Unpublished doctoral dissertation, University of Toronto (OISE).

Lipsett, L. (1969). Learning capacities of the human infant. In R. J. Robinson (Ed.), *Brain and early behavior in the fetus and infant*. New York: Academic Press.

Liu, P. (1981). *An investigation of the relationship between qualitative and quantitative advances in the cognitive development of preschool children*. Unpublished doctoral dissertation, University of Toronto (OISE).

Liu, P., & Case, R. (1981). Quantitative and qualitative changes in preschool development. Paper presented at the annual conference on Piaget and the helping professions, Los Angeles, January, 1981.

Logan, G. D. (1976). Converging evidence for automatic perceptual processing in visual search. *Canadian Journal of Psychology, 30*, 193–200.

Lovell, K. A. (1961). A follow-up study of Inhelder & Piaget's The Growth of Logical Thinking. *British Journal of Psychology, 52*, 143–153.

Lunzer, E. A. (1965). Problems of formal reasoning in test situations. In P. H. Mussen (Ed.), European research in cognitive development. *Monographs of the Society For Research in Child Development, 30* (2, Whole No. 100), 19–46.

Luria, A. R. (1973). *The working brain: An introduction to neuropsychology*. London: Penguin Books.

McCall, R. B. (1979). Quantitative transitions in behavioral development in the first two years of life. In M. H. Bornstein & W. Kessen (Eds.), *Psychological development from infancy: Image to intention* (pp. 183–229). Hillsdale, NJ: Erlbaum.

Maccoby, M., & Modiano, N. (1966). On culture and equivalence: I. In J. S. Bruner, R. R. Oliver, & P. M. Greenfield (Eds.), *Studies in cognitive growth* (pp. 257–269). New York: Wiley.

McKeough, A. (1982). *The development of complexity in children's narratives*. Unpublished M.A. thesis, University of Toronto (OISE).

McLaughlin, G. H. (1963). Psychologic: A possible alternative to Piaget's formulation. *British Journal of Educational Psychology, 33*, 61–67.

McNemar, Q. (1942). *The revision of the Standford-Binet scale, analysis of the standardized data*. Boston: Houghton–Mifflin.

McNeill, D. (1966). Developmental psycholinguistics. In I. Smith & G. A. Miller (Eds.), *The genesis of language: A psycholinguistic approach* (pp. 15–84). Cambridge, MA; MIT Press.

Maier, N. R. F. (1931). Reasoning in humans, II. The solution of a problem and its appearance in consciousness. *Journal of Comparative Psychology, 12,* 181–194.

Mandler, J. M., & Johnson, N. S. (1977). Remembrance of things parsed: Story structure and recall. *Cognitive Psychology, 9,* 111–151.

Maratos, O. (1973, April). *The origin and development of imitation in the first six months of life.* Paper presented at the British Psychologial Society Annual Meeting, Liverpool.

Martarano, S. C. (1977). A developmental analysis of performance on Piaget's formal operation tasks. *Developmental Psychology, 13,* 666–672.

Marini, Z. (1981). *The relationship between social and non-social cognition in elementary school children.* Unpublished Master's Thesis, University of Toronto (OISE).

Marini, Z. (1984). *The development of social and physical cognition in childhood and adolescence.* Unpublished doctoral dissertation, University of Toronto, (OISE).

Maurer, D., & Martello, M. (1980). The discrimination of orientation by young infants. *Vision Research, 20,* 201–204.

Meltzoff, A. N. (1981). Imitation, intermodal coordination and representation in early infancy. In G. Butterworth (Ed.), *Infancy and epistemology* (pp. 85–114). Brighton, England: Harvester Press.

Meltzoff, A. N., & Moore, M. K. (1977). Imitation of facial and manual gestures by human infants. *Science, 198,* 75–78.

Meltzoff, A. N., & Moore, M. K. (1983a, April). *Facial imitation in newborn infants.* Paper presented at the Biennial Meeting of the Society for Research in Child Development, Detroit.

Meltzoff, A. N., & Moore, M. K. (1983b). Newborn infants imitate adult facial gestures. *Child Development, 54,* 702–710.

Menyuk, P. (1977). *Language and maturation.* Cambridge, MA: MIT Press.

Miller, G. A. (1956). The magical number seven plus or minus two: Some limits on our capacity for processing information. *Psychological Review, 63,* 81–97.

Miller, W. R., & Ervin-Tripp, S. M. (1964). The development of grammar in child language. In U. Bellugi & R. Brown (Eds.), The acquisition of language. *Monographs of the Society for Research in Child Development, 29*(1), 9–35.

Mosher, F. A., & Hornsby, J. R. (1966). On asking questions. In J. S. Bruner, R. R. Oliver, & P. M. Greenfield (Eds.), *Studies in cognitive growth* (pp. 86–102). New York: Wiley.

Mounoud, P. (1982). Revolutionary periods in early development. In T. G. Bever (Ed.), *Regressions in mental development: Basic phenomena and theories* (pp. 119–131). Hillsdale, NJ: Erlbaum.

Mueller, E., & Brenner, J. (1977). The origins of social skills and interaction among playgroup toddlers. *Child Development, 48,* 854–861.

Mueller, E., & Lucas, T. A. (1975). Developmental analysis of peer interaction among toddlers. In M. Lewis & L. A. Rosenblum (Eds.), *Friendship and peer relations* (223–258). New York: Wiley.

Mueller, E., & Vandell, D. (1979). Infant–infant interaction: An empirical and conceptual review. In J. D. Osofsky (Ed.), *Handbook of Infant Development* (pp. 591–622). New York: Wiley.

Murdock, Jr., B. B. (1974). *Human memory: Theory and data.* Hillsdale, NJ: Erlbaum.

Murray, F. B. (1972). Acquisition of conservation through social interaction. *Developmental Psychology, 6,* 1–6.

Muter, P. (1979). Response latencies in discrimination of recency. *Journal of Experimental Psychology: Human Learning and Memory 5*(2), 160–169.

Neimark, E. D. (1975). Intellectual development during adolescence. In F. Horowitz (Ed.), *Review of the child development research* (pp. 541–594). Chicago: University of Chicago Press.

Nelson, K. (1973). Structure and strategy in learning to talk. *Monograph of the Society for Research in Child Development, 38* (149).

Nelson, K. (1978). How children represent knowledge of their world in and out of language: A preliminary report. In R. S. Siegler (Ed.), *Children's thinking: What develops?* (pp. 255–274). Hillsdale, NJ: Erlbaum.

Newell, A., Shaw, J. C., & Simon, H. A. (1958). Elements of a theory of human problem solving. *Psychological Review, 65,* 151–166.

Newell, A., & Rosenbloom, P. S. (1981). Mechanisms of skill acquisition and the law of practice. In J. R. Anderson (Ed.), *Cognitive skills and their acquisition.* Hillsdale, NJ: Erlbaum.

Ninio, A., & Bruner, J. S. (1978). The achievement and antecedents of labelling. *Journal of Child Language, 5,* 1–15.

Noelting, G. (1975). Stages and mechanisms in the development of proportionality in the child and adolescent. In G. I. Lubin, J. F. Magery, & M. K. Poulsen (Eds.), *Piagetian theory and the helping professions* (Vol. 5). Los Angeles, USC press.

Noelting, G. (1980). The development of proportional reasoning and the ratio concept. *Educational Studies in Mathematics, 11,* 217–253(I) & 331–363(II).

Noelting, G. (1982). *Le développement cognitif et le mécanisms de l'équilibration.* Chicoutimi Canada: Gaëtan Morin.

Nuffield Foundation: Nuffield Foundation Science Teaching Project. London: Nuffield Foundation, 1964.

Olson, D. R. (1966). On conceptual strategies. In J. S. Bruner, R. R. Oliver, & P. M. Greenfield (Eds.), *Studies in cognitive growth* (pp. 135–153). New York: Wiley.

Olson, D. R. (1977). From utterance to text: The bias of language in speech and writing. *Harvard Educational Review, 47,* 257–281.

Olson, D. R. (1980). (Ed.), *The Social Foundations of Language and Thought.* New York: W. H. Norton.

Olson, D. R., & Hildyard, A. (1981). Assent and compliance in children's comprehension. In P. Dixon (Ed.), *Children's oral communication skills* (pp. 313–336). New York: Academic Press.

Parkinson, G. M. (1976). *The limits of learning.* Unpublished doctoral dissertation, York University.

Papousek, H. (1969). Individual variability in learned responses in human infants. In R. J. Robinson (Ed.), *Brain and early behavior development in the fetus and infant* (pp. 251–262). New York: Academic Press.

Pascual-Leone, J. (1969). *Cognitive development and cognitive style.* Unpublished doctoral dissertation, University of Geneva.

Pascual-Leone, J. (1970). A mathematical model for the transition rule in Piaget's development stages. *Acta Psychologica, 32,* 301–345.

Pascual-Leone, J. (1972, June). *A theory of constructive operators: A neo-Piagetian model of conservation, and the problem of horizontal décalage.* Paper presented at the annual meeting of the Canadian Psychological Association, Montreal.

Pascual-Leone, J. (1974, August). *A neo-Piagetian process-structural model of Witkin's psychological differentiation.* Paper presented at the Second International Conference of the Association for Cross-Cultural Psychology. Kingston, Ontario.

Pascual-Leone, J. (1976). A view of cognition from a formalist's perspective. In K. F. Riegel, & J. Meacham, (Eds.), *The developing individual in a changing world.* (pps. 89–100). The Hague: Mouton.

Pascual-Leone, J. (1978). Compounds, confounds, and models in developmental psychology: A reply to Trabasso and Foellinger. *Journal of Experimental Child Psychology, 26,* 18–40.

Pascual-Leone, J. (1984). Attentional, dialectic, and mental effort. In M. L. Commons, F. A. Richards, & C. Armon (Eds.), *Beyond Formal Operations.* New York: Plenum.

Pascual-Leone, J., & Smith, J. (1969). The encoding and decoding of symbols by children: A new experimental paradigm and a neo-Piagetian model. *Journal of Experimental Child Psychology, 8,* 328–355.

Peel, E. A. (1960). *The pupil's thinking.* London: Oldbourne Press.

Piaget, J. (1926a). *The language and thought of the child.* London: Routledge & Kegan Paul.

Piaget, J. (1926b). *Judgment and reasoning in the child.* New York: Harcourt.

Piaget, J. (1932). *The moral judgment of the child.* New York: Harcourt.

Piaget, J. (1950). *The psychology of intelligence.* London: Routledge & Kegan Paul.

Piaget, J. (1951/1962). *Play, dreams, and imitation in childhood* (La Formation Du Symbole). New York: Norton.

Piaget, J. (1952). *The origins of intelligence in children.* New York: International Universities Press.

Piaget, J. (1954). *The construction of reality in the child.* New York: Basic Books.

Piaget, J. (1964). Development and learning. In R. E. Ripple & V. N. Rockcastle (Eds.), *Piaget rediscovered* (pp. 7–20). Ithaca, NY: Cornell School of Education Press.

Piaget, J. (1970). *Science of education and the psychology of the child.* New York: Orion Press.

Piaget, J. (1972). Intellectual evolution from adolescence to adulthood. *Human Development, 15,* 1–12.

Piaget, J. Montagero, J. & Billetier, J. (1979). *La formation des correlats.* In *L'Abstraction réflechissante.* Paris: Presses Universitares du France, pp. 115–129.

Piaget, J., Grize, J., Szeminska, A., & Bang, V. (1977). *The epistemology and psychology of functions.* Dordrecht: Reidel.

Piaget, J., & Szeminska, A. (1952). *The child's conception of number.* London: Routledge & Kegan Paul.

Pike, R., & Olson, D. R. (1977). A question of 'more' and 'less'. *Child Development, 48,* 579–586.

Pinard, A. (1975). Note sur la compatibilité des notions de stade et de décalage dans la théorie de Piaget. *Canadian Psychological Review, 16,* 255–261.

Pinard, A., & Laurendeau, M. (1969). Stage in Piaget's Cognitive developmental theory: Exegesis of a concept. In D. Elkind & J. H. Flavell (Eds.), *Studies in cognitive development* (pp. 121–170). London: Oxford University Press.

Polya, G. (1945). *How to solve it; a new aspect of mathematical method.* Princeton, NJ: Princeton University Press.

Premack, D. (1983). The codes of man and beast. *The Behavioral and Brain Sciences, 6,* 125–167.

Price-Williams, D., Gordon, W., & Ramirez, M. (1969). Skill and conservation: A study of pottery-making children. *Developmental Psychology, 1,* 769.

Pulos, S. (1979). *Developmental constraints on concept formation and problem solving: A test of a structural learning model.* Unpublished doctoral dissertation, York University.

Raven, J. C. (1958). *Standard progressive matrices.* London: Lewis.

Raven, J. C., Court, J. H., & Raven, J. (1977). *Manual for Raven's progressive matrices and vocabulary scales.* London: Lewis.

Ray (1974). An adaptation of the WISC-R for the deaf. Natchitoches: Northwestern State University of Louisiana.

Resnick, L. B. (1976). Task analysis in structural design: Some cases from mathematics. In D. Klahr (Ed.), *Cognition and instruction* (pp. 51–80). Hillsdale, NJ: Erlbaum.

Rich, S. A. (1980). *The development of information processing, speed and span in normal and retarded children.* Unpublished M.A. thesis, University of Toronto.

Rich, S. A. (1982). *Cognitive restructuring in children: The prediction of intelligence and learning.* Unpublished doctoral dissertation, University of Toronto (OISE), 1982.

Robinson, E., Goelman, H., & Olson, D. R. (1983). Children's understanding of the relationship between expressions (what was said) and intentions (what was meant). *British Journal of Developmental Psychology, 1,* 75–81.

Rohwer, Jr., W. E. (1970). Mental elaboration and proficient learning. In J. P. Hill (Ed.), *Minnesota symposium on child psychology* (Vol. 4, pp. 220–260). Minneapolis: University of Minnesota Press.

Rosenzweig, M. R., & Bennett, E. L. (Eds.). (1976). *Neural Mechanisms of Learning and Memory.* Cambridge, MA: MIT Press.

Ross, H. S. (1982). The establishment of social games among toddlers. *Developmental Psychology, 18,* 509–518.

Rubin, K. H. (1973). Egocentrism in childhood: A unitary construct? *Child Development, 44,* 102–110.

Rubin, K. H., & Everett, B. P. (1982). Social perspective-taking in young children. In S. Moore & C. Cooper (Eds.), *The Young Child.*

Sander, L. W. (1969). Regulation and organization in the early infant–caretaker system. In R. J. Robinson (Ed.), *Brain and early behavior, development in the fetus and infant* (pp. 311–331). London: Academic Press.

Sandieson, R. (1985). *The developmental theory of instruction: A method for teaching difficult academic skills to the trainable mentally retarded.* Unpublished doctoral dissertation, University of Toronto, OISE.

Sandieson, R., & Case, R. *Life skill training programmes for the mentally handicapped: A developmental approach.* Interim Report, OISE, 1984.

Saxe, G. B. (1979). A comparative analysis of the acquisition of numeration: Studies from Papua, New Guinea. *The Quarterly Newsletter of the Laboratory of Comparative Human Cognition, 1,* 37–43.

Scaife, M., & Bruner, J. S. (1975). The capacity for joint visual attention in the infant. *Nature, 253*(5489), 265–266.

Scardamalia, M. (1974). Some performance aspects of two formal operational tasks. In G. I. Lubin, J. F. Magery, & M. K. Poulsen (Eds.), *Piagetian theory in the helping professions.* Proceedings of the Fourth Interdisciplinary Seminar, University of Southern California.

Scardamalia, M. (1977). Information processing capacity and the problem of horizontal décalage: A demonstration using combinatorial reasoning tasks. *Child Development, 48,* 28–37.

Scardamalia, M., & Bereiter, C. (1984). Development of strategies in text processing. In H. Mandel, N. L. Stein, & T. Trabasso (Eds.), *Learning and comprehension of text* (pp. 379–406). Hillsdale, NJ: Erlbaum.

Scardamalia, M., & Bereiter, C. (in press). Written composition. In M. Wittrock (Ed.), *Handbook of research on teaching* (3rd ed.).

Schaffer, H. R. (1971). *The growth of sociability.* Harmondsworth: Penguin.

Schaffer, H. R. (1977). Early interactive development. In H. R. Schaffer (Ed.), *Studies in mother–infant interaction* (pp. 3–16). New York: Academic Press.

Schlessinger, I. M. (1974). Relational concepts underlying language. In R. L. Schiefelbusch & L. L. Lloyd (Eds.), *Language perspectives: Acquisition, retardation, and intervention* (pp. 129–151). Baltimore: University Park Press.

Scribner, S., & Cole, M. (1973). Cognitive consequences of formal and informal education. *Science, 182,* 553–559.

Scribner, S., & Cole, M. (1980). *Consequences of literacy.* Cambridge: Harvard University Press.

Selman, R. L. (1980). *The growth of interpersonal understanding: Developmental and clinical analyses.* New York: Academic Press.

Seraficia, F. C. (1982). *Social-cognitive development in context.* New York: Guilford Press.

Sharp, D., Cole, M., & Lave, C. (1979). Education and cognitive development: The evidence from experimental research. *Monographs of the Society for Research in Child Development, 44* (Serial No. 178).

Shatz, M., & Gelman, R. (1973). The development of communication skills: Modifications in the speech of young children as a function of listener. *Monographs of the Society for Research in Child Development, 38*(5, Serial No. 152).

Shantz, C. V. (1975). The development of social cognition. In E. M. Hetherington (Ed.), *Review of child development research* (Vol. 5, pp. 257–324). Chicago: University of Chicago Press.

Siegel, I. E. (1969). The Piagetian system and the word of education. In D. Elkind & J. H. Flavell (Eds.), *Studies in cognitive development* (pp. 465–489). New York: Oxford University Press.

Siegler, R. S. (1976). Three aspects of cognitive development. *Cognitive Psychology, 4*, 481–520.

Siegler, R. S. (1977). Cognition, instruction, development, and individual differences. In A. M. Lesgold, J. W. Pellegrino, S. D. Fokkema, & R. Glaser (Eds.), *Cognitive Psychology and Instruction*. New York: Plenum Press.

Siegler, R. S. (1978). The origins of scientific reasoning. In R. S. Siegler (Ed.), *Children's thinking: What develops?* (pp. 109–150). Hillsdale, NJ: Erlbaum.

Siegler, R. S. (1981). Developmental sequences within and between concepts. *Monographs of the Society for Research in Child Development, 81* (Serial No. 189).

Siegler, R. S. (1982). The development of numerical understandings. In H. Reese & L. P. Lippsett (Eds.), *Advances in child development and behavior* Vol. 16, pp. 241–312). New York: Academic Press.

Siegler, R. S. (1983). Information processing approaches to development. In P. H. Mussen, *Handbook of Child Psychology, 4*, 129–211.

Siegler, R. S., Robinson, M. Liebert, D. E., & Liebert, R. M. (1973). Inhelder and Piaget's pendulum problem: Teaching preadolescents to act as scientists. *Developmental Psychology, 9*, 97–101.

Siegler, R. S., & Richards, D. D. (1979). Development of time, speed and distance concepts. *Developmental Psychology, 15*, 288–298.

Siegler, R. S., & Shrager, J. (1983, May). Strategy choices in addition: How do children know what to do? Paper presented at the Carnegie Symposium on Cognition, Pittsburgh.

Simon, D. P., & Simon, H. A. (1978). Individual differences in solving physics problems. In R. S. Siegler (Ed.), *Children's thinking: What develops?* (pp. 325–348). Hillsdale, NJ: Erlbaum.

Simon, H. A. (1972). On the development of the processor in S. Farnham Diggory (Ed.), *Information processing in young children* (pp. 3–22). New York: Academic Press.

Simon, H. A. (1962). An information processing theory of intellectual development. *Monographs of the Society for Research in Child Development, 27*(2, Serial No. 82).

Simon, H. A. (1974). How big is a chunk? *Science, 183*, 482–488.

Simon, H. A. (1980). *How applicable is cognitive theory to educational practice?* Invited address, AERA, Boston.

Sinclair, H. (1969). Developmental psycholinguistics. In D. Elkind & J. H. Flavell (Eds.), *Studies in cognitive development* (pp. 315–336). New York: Oxford University Press.

Sinclair, H. (1971). Sensorimotor action patterns as a condition for the acquisition of syntax. In R. Huxley & E. Ingram (Eds.), *Language acquisition: Models and methods* (pp. 121–135). New York: Academic Press.

Siqueland, E. R., & Lippsett, L. P. (1966). Conditioned head turning in human newborns. *Journal of Experimental Child Psychology, 3*, 356–376.

Slobin, D. I., & Welsh, C. A. (1973). Elicited imitation as a research tool in developmental psycholinguistics. In C. A. Ferguson & D. I. Slobin (Eds.), *Studies of child language development* (pp. 485–496). Holt.

Slobin, D. I. (1973). Cognitive prerequisites for the development of grammar. In C. A. Ferguson & D. I. Slobin (Eds.), *Studies of child language development* (pp. 175–276). New York: Holt.

Snow, C. E. (1977). The development of conversation between mothers and babies. *Journal of Child Language, 4*, 1–22.

Snow, C. E., Arlman-Russ, A., Hasting, Y., Jobse, J., Juotsten, J., & Vorsten, J. (1970). Mothers' speech in three social classes. *Journal of Psycholinguistic Research, 5*, 1–20.

Sparling, J., & Lewis, I. (1979). *Learning games for the first three years.* New York: Berkeley Books.

Spelke, E. (1982). Perceptual knowledge of objects in infancy. In J. Mehler, E. C. T. Walker, & M. Garrett (Eds.), *Perspectives on mental representation* (pp. 409–430). Hillsdale, NJ: Erlbaum.

Spitz, R. A. (1950). Anxiety in infancy: A study of its manifestations in the first year of life. *International Journal of Psychoanalysis, 31*, 138–143.

Spitz, R. A., & Wolf, K. M. (1946). The smiling response: A contribution to the ontogenesis of social relations. *Genetic Psychology Monographs, 34*, 57–125.

Stein, N. L., & Glenn, C. G. (1979). An analysis of story comprehension in elementary school children. In R. Friedle (Ed.), *Discourse processing: Multidisciplinary perspectives* (pp. 53–120). Norwood, NJ: Ablex.

Stern, D. N. (1974). Mother and infant at play: The dyadic interaction involving facial, vocal, and gaze behaviors. In M. Lewis & L. Rosenblum (Eds.), *The effect of the infant on his caregiver* (pp. 187–214). New York: Wiley.

Stern, D. N. (1983). The early development of schemes of self, of other, and of various experiences of self with other. In S. Kaplan & J. D. Liehtenberg (Eds.), *Reflections on self psychology.* New York: International Universities Press.

Sternberg, R. J. (1977). *Intelligence, information processing, and analogical reasoning: The componential analysis of human abilities.* Hillsdale, NJ: Erlbaum.

Sternberg, R. J. (1984). *Mechanisms of cognitive development.* San Francisco: Freeman.

Sternberg, R. J. (1984). Mechanisms of cognitive development: A componential approach. In R. J. Sternberg (Ed.), *Mechanisms of cognitive development.* (pp. 163–186). San Francisco: Freeman.

Sternberg, R. J., & Rifkin, B. (1979). The development of analogical reasoning processes. *Journal of Experimental Child Psychology, 27*, 195–232.

Stone, C. A. (1976). *Logical and psychological processing accounts of the transition from concrete to formal operations.* Unpublished doctoral dissertation, University of Chicago.

Stone, C. A., & Day, M. C. (1978). Levels of availability of a formal operational strategy. *Child Development, 49*, 1054–1065.

Strauss, S. (1972). Inducing cognitive development and learning: A review of short-term training experiments. *Cognition, 1*, 329–357.

Strauss, S., & Langer, J. (1970). Operational thought inducement. *Child Development, 41*, 163–175.

Sullivan, E. V. (1967). Acquisition of conservation of substance through film modelling techniques. In D. W. Brison & E. V. Sullivan (Eds.), *Recent research on the acquisition of conservation of substance* (pp. 53–72). Toronto: OISE. (Educational Research Series No. 2).

Tanner, J. M. (1970). Physical growth. In P. H. Mussen (Ed.), *Carmichael's Manual of Child Psychology* (Vol. 1, pp. 77–156, 3rd ed.). New York: Wiley.

Tasaki, I. (1953). *Nervous transmission.* Springfield, IL: Thomas.

Terman, L. M., & Merrill, M. A. (1960). *Stanford-Binet intelligence scale.* Boston: Houghton–Mifflin.

Todor, J. (1979). Developmental differences in motor task integration: A test of Pascual-Leone's theory of constructive operations. *Journal of Experimental Child Psychology, 28*, 314–322.

Tolman, E. C. (1932). *Purposive behavior in animals and men.* New York: Century.

Toussaint, N. A. (1974). An analysis of synchrony between concrete-operational tasks in terms of structural and performance demands. *Child Development, 45*, 992–1001.

Trabasso, T., & Foellinger, D. B. (1978). Information processing capacity in children: A test of Pascual-Leone's model. *Journal of Experimental Child Psychology, 25*, 1–17.

Trehub, S. E. (1973). Infants' sensitivity to vowel and tonal contrasts. *Developmental Psychology, 9*, 91–96.

Trevarthan, C. (1974). Conversations with a two-month old. *New Scientist, 62*, 230–235.

Trevarthen, C. (1977). Descriptive analyses of early infant communicative behavior. In H. R. Schaffer (Ed.), *Studies in mother–infant interaction* (pp. 227–270). London, Cambridge University Press.

Trevarthen, C. (1980). The foundations of intersubjectivity: Development of interpersonal and cooperative understanding in infants. In D. R. Olson (Ed.), *The social foundations of language and thought* (pp. 316–342), New York: W. H. Norton.

Trevarthen, C. (1982, June). Paper presented to the Toronto semiotic circle. University of Toronto.

Trevarthen, C., & Hubley, P. (1979). Sharing a task in infancy. *New Directions in Child Development*, *4*, 57–75.

Turiel, E. (1969). Developmental processes in the child's moral thinking. In P. H. Mussen, J. Langer, & M. Covington (Eds.), *Trends and issues in developmental psychology* (pp. 92–133). New York: Holt. pp. 7–37.

Turiel, E. (1975). The development of social concepts. In D. DePalma & J. Foley (Eds.), *Moral Development*. Hillsdale, NJ: Erlbaum.

Uzgiris, I. C. (1976). Organization of sensorimotor intelligence. In M. Lewis (Ed.), *Origins of intelligence: Infancy and early childhood* (pp. 123–163). New York: Plenum.

Uzgiris, I. C., & Hunt, J. M. (1975). *Toward ordinal scales of psychological development in infancy*. Champaign, IL: University of Illinois Press.

Vygotsky, L. S. (1962). *Thought and language*. Cambridge, MA: MIT Press. (First published in Russian in 1934.)

Wagner, W. J. (1981). *Reasoning by analogy in the young child*. Unpublished Ed.D. thesis, University of Toronto (OISE).

Watson, J. S. (1966). The development and generalization of "contingency awareness" in early infancy: Some hypotheses. *Merill-Palmer Quarterly*, *12*, 123–135.

Watson, M. W., & Fischer, K. W. (1977). A developmental sequence of agent use in late infancy. *Child Development*, *48*, 828–836.

Wechsler, D. (1958). *The measurement and appraisal of adult intelligence* (4th ed.). Baltimore: Williams & Wilkins.

Wechsler, D. (1967). *Wechsler preschool and primary scale of intelligence manual*. New York: Psychological Corporation.

Weir, R. H. (1962). *Language in the crib*. The Hague: Mouton.

Werner, H. (1948). *Comparative psychology of mental development*. Chicago: Follett. (3rd ed.).

White, B. (1975). *The first three years*. New York: Englewood Cliffs, NJ: Prentice Hall.

White, R. (1959). Motivation reconsidered: The concept of competence. *Psychological Review*, *66*, 297–333.

White, S. H. (1970). Some general outlines of the matrix of developmental changes between five and seven years. *Bulletin of the Orton Society*, *20*, 41–57.

Wilkening, F., & Anderson, N. H. (1980). *Comparison of two rule assessment methodologies for studying cognitive development* (Technical Report # 94). Centre for Human Information Processing, University of California, La Jolla, California.

Witkin, H. A., Dyk, R. B., Faterson, H. F., Goodenough, D. R. & Karp, S. A. (1962). *Psychological differentiation*. New York: Wiley.

Wohlwil, J. (1970). The place of structural experience in early cognitive development. *Interchange*, (2), 13–27.

Yakovlev, P. I., & Lecours, A. R. (1967). The myelenogenetic cycles of regional maturation of the brain. In A. Minkowski (Ed.), *Regional development of the brain in early life*. Oxford, Blackwell.

Zimmerman, B. J., & Rosenthal, T. L. (1974). Observation learning of rule governed behavior by children. *Psychological Bulletin*, *81*, 29–42.

Author Index

Subject Index

DEVELOPMENTAL PSYCHOLOGY SERIES

Continued from page ii